Presented to:

Mrs. Mary Mawhinney

by:

Hyde Park Presbyterian Church

in appreciation of her dedicated

service as a

Sunday School Teacher.

June 1994

THE BIBLE USER'S MANUAL

THE BIBLE USER'S MANUAL

THE COMPLETE
DO-IT-YOURSELF GUIDE

Consulting editors:
John F. Balchin
David H. Field
Tremper Longman III

Inter-Varsity Press
Scripture Union

INTER-VARSITY PRESS
38 De Montfort Street, Leicester LE1 7GP, England

SCRIPTURE UNION
130 City Road, London EC1V 2NJ, England

First published 1991

British Library Cataloguing in Publication Data
The Bible user's manual.
1. Bible. Interpretation
I. Balchin, John F. II. Field, David H. III. Longman, Tremper
220.6

IVP ISBN 0-85110-642-0
SU ISBN 0-86201-734-3

Set in 10/11pt Souvenir

Design, artwork and typesetting by
Swanston Graphics Limited, Derby, England

Printed by Tien Wah Press (Pte) Ltd, Singapore

Inter-Varsity Press is the book-publishing division of the Universities and Colleges Christian Fellowship (formerly the Inter-Varsity Fellowship).

Photographs

The photographs in this book are reproduced by permission of the following persons or agencies:

British Musuem pages 37, 53

Cephas Picture Library pages 60, 71, 83, 99, 103, 243, 272

Chester Beatty Library page 69

FEBA Radio page 216

Image Bank pages 113, 127, 155, 167, 223, 287

March for Jesus page 248

Pictor International Limited page 148

Rex Features Limited pages 51, 79

Scripture Union/Gordon Gray pages 21, 42, 161, 191, 200, 234, 238, 268, 328, 355

Universities and Colleges Christian Fellowship page 218

D. J. Wiseman page 271

ZEFA Picture Library (UK) Limited pages 130, 146, 157, 171, 174, 193, 194, 203, 255, 263, 265, 281, 289, 293, 304, 307, 309, 313, 314, 331, 338

Contributors

The Revd Dr John F. Balchin, formerly Lecturer at London Bible College, now Bible teacher and Minister of Purley Baptist Church, Surrey, England.

CONSULTING EDITOR: UNPACKING THE NEW TESTAMENT: INTERPRETING THE BIBLE: KEY TO PROGRESS.

The Revd David H. Field, Vice-Principal of Oak Hill College, London, Dean of Part-time Training and Tutor in Christian Ethics at the College.

CONSULTING EDITOR: GOD'S WORD FOR TODAY'S CHOICES.

Professor Tremper Longman III, Associate Professor of Old Testament at Westminster Theological Seminary, Philadelphia, U.S.A.

CONSULTING EDITOR: POETRY, PSALMS AND WISDOM.

The Revd Dr Paul Beasley-Murray, formerly Pastor of Altrincham Baptist Church, Cheshire, now Principal of Spurgeon's College, London.

GUIDELINES FOR CHRISTIAN LIVING (THE NEW TESTAMENT LETTERS).

The Revd Donald Bridge, formerly Chaplain of the Garden Tomb, Jerusalem, now a staff member of The Evangelisation Society.

DEFINING THE ESSENTIAL MESSAGE.

Mary J. Evans, Lecturer in Old Testament Studies at London Bible College.

THE PROPHETS.

The Revd Dr Peter Hicks, part-time Lecturer at London Bible College and Minister of Bushey Baptist Church, Hertfordshire, England.

A VERY SPECIAL BOOK (AUTHORITY AND INSPIRATION OF THE BIBLE).

Susan K. Rebis, freelance editor.

INDEXES.

Dr Deborah Reed, Civil Servant working in Exeter, England.

THE PROMISED LAND.

The Revd Dr David Stone, Curate-in-charge of St Jude's Church, South Kensington, London.

THE LIFE OF CHRIST AND THE ORIGINS OF THE CHURCH.

Geoffrey Treasure, Headteacher of Christ Church School, Barnet, London.

IN THE BEGINNING (THE BOOKS OF THE LAW).

Professor John H. Walton, Associate Professor of Old Testament at Moody Bible Institute, Chicago, U.S.A.

UNPACKING THE OLD TESTAMENT.

The Revd Michael J. Wilcock, formerly Director of Pastoral Studies at Trinity College, Bristol, now Vicar of St Nicholas Church, Durham, England.

A VISION OF JUDGMENT (REVELATION).

The Revd Derek L. Williams, freelance writer, text editor for *Handbook of life in Bible times* and *New Concise Bible Dictionary*.

TEXT EDITOR FOR PART THREE, SUMMARY AND APPLICATION OF THE BIBLE.

Derek R. W. Wood, Senior Editor, Inter-Varsity Press.

ORGANIZING EDITOR: INTRODUCTORY MATERIAL: PICTURE RESEARCH.

CONTENTS
AT A GLANCE

The best access points into the Manual are marked ▶

PART FOUR: PUTTING IT ALL TOGETHER 233

Investigating the Bible's claim to guide our way of life; defining the Bible's message and how to make moral choices:

PART FIVE: KEY TO PROGRESS 319

The nuts and bolts of Bible study; how to get on with it:

PART SIX: INDEXES 369

Where to find all you need:

Explanation

The references in the margin point to another part of the book where you will find more information on the same topic.

The symbols are included and coloured for ease of reference.

One arrow indicates the nearer column; two arrows the further column, for example:

110-112

37

The judges

The government of the judges period was intended to be a theocracy ('God is king') administered by the leadership of the individual tribes. The history of the period (narrated in Judges 2-16) shows the continual failure of the people to be loyal to the Lord. When the Lord punished them by political oppression, the people would cry out for deliverance. Graciously, the Lord would provide a deliverer in the person of a 'judge' (*i.e.*, one bringing justice, deliverance, often by military action) who would receive support from a num-

23). With God's planned punishment of the Canaanites unaccomplished, the Israelites suffered the consequences and were constantly exposed to the influences of Canaanite religions.

The 400 years of the judges period ought to be divided in half when viewed against the backdrop of the ancient Near East. Until about 1200 BC, the international scene featured several major powers (especially Egypt and the Hittites, people from the central part of modern day Turkey) battling for control

PART 1

WELCOME!

This book has been designed to make you feel at home. It has six sections, each distinguished by colour coding and a symbol. Start where you like; the best entry points are arrowed in the contents list.

This short section gives you three approaches to the Bible. Why not work through one or all of them? Don't hurry though. It's a very rich menu.

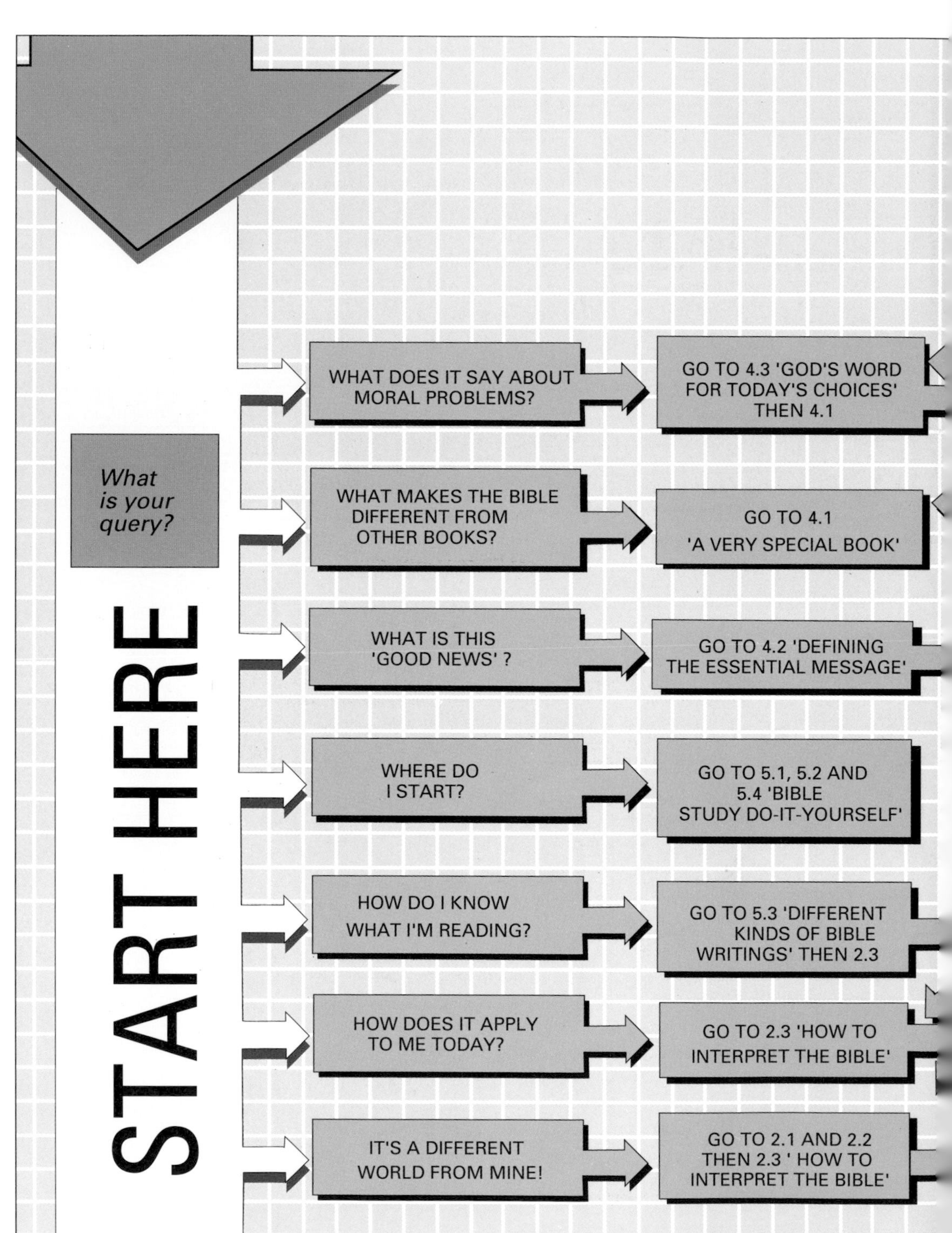
START HERE
What is your query?
WHAT DOES IT SAY ABOUT MORAL PROBLEMS?
GO TO 4.3 'GOD'S WORD FOR TODAY'S CHOICES' THEN 4.1
WHAT MAKES THE BIBLE DIFFERENT FROM OTHER BOOKS?
GO TO 4.1 'A VERY SPECIAL BOOK'
WHAT IS THIS 'GOOD NEWS' ?
GO TO 4.2 'DEFINING THE ESSENTIAL MESSAGE'
WHERE DO I START?
GO TO 5.1, 5.2 AND 5.4 'BIBLE STUDY DO-IT-YOURSELF'
HOW DO I KNOW WHAT I'M READING?
GO TO 5.3 'DIFFERENT KINDS OF BIBLE WRITINGS' THEN 2.3
HOW DOES IT APPLY TO ME TODAY?
GO TO 2.3 'HOW TO INTERPRET THE BIBLE'
IT'S A DIFFERENT WORLD FROM MINE!
GO TO 2.1 AND 2.2 THEN 2.3 ' HOW TO INTERPRET THE BIBLE'

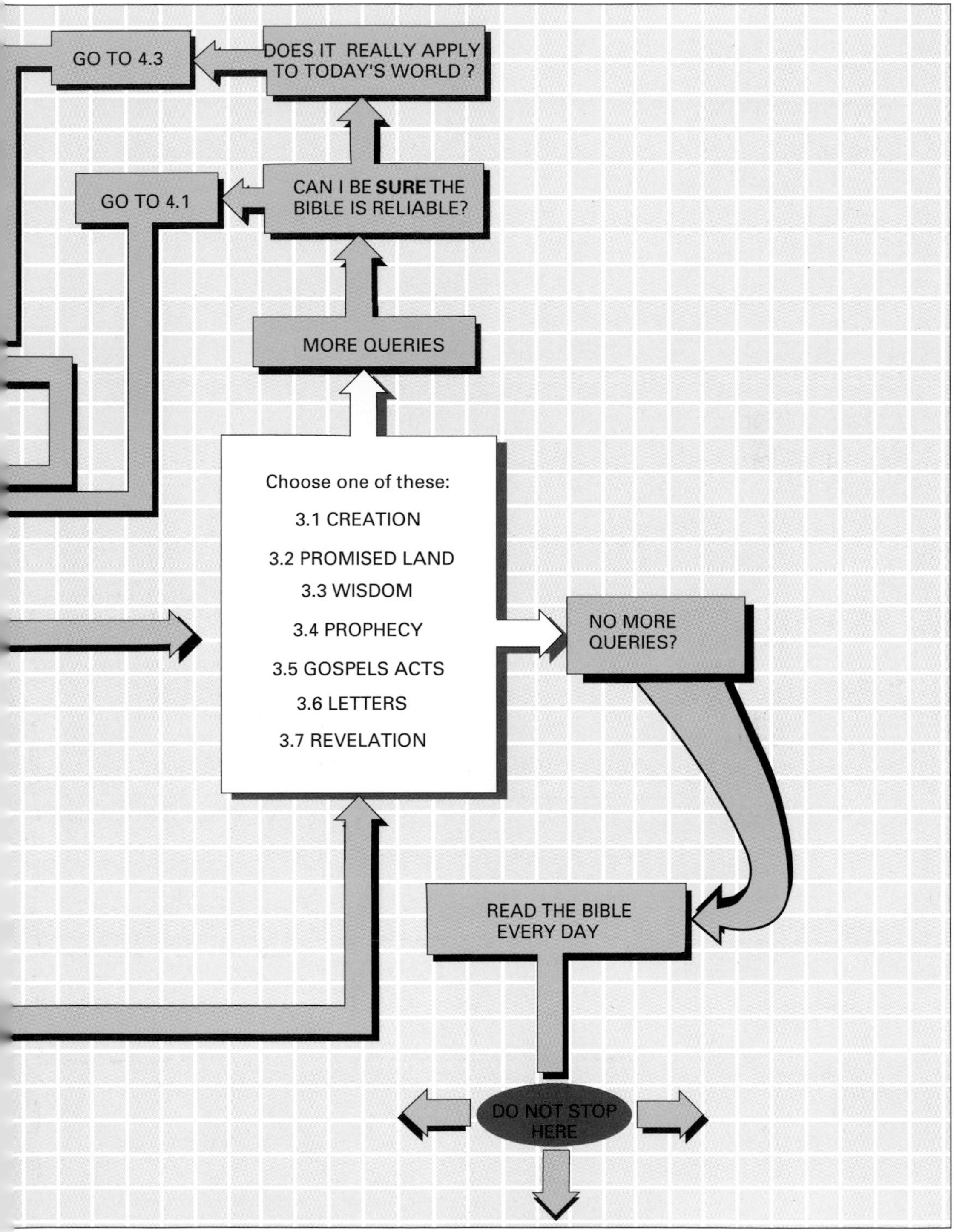

DOES IT REALLY APPLY TO TODAY'S WORLD ?
GO TO 4.3
CAN I BE **SURE** THE BIBLE IS RELIABLE?
GO TO 4.1
MORE QUERIES
Choose one of these:
3.1 CREATION
3.2 PROMISED LAND
3.3 WISDOM
3.4 PROPHECY
3.5 GOSPELS ACTS
3.6 LETTERS
3.7 REVELATION
NO MORE QUERIES?
READ THE BIBLE EVERY DAY
DO NOT STOP HERE

Where can I find it?

The Garden of Eden	Genesis 2:8-3:24
The flood	Genesis 6:9-8:22
The Exodus	Exodus 12
The Ten Commandments	Exodus 20:1-17
The crossing of the Jordan	Joshua 3
The fall of Jericho	Joshua 5:13-6:27
The covenants with: Noah : Abraham : Moses : David	Genesis 9:8-17 Genesis 17 Exodus 24 2 Samuel 7
The life of David	1 Samuel 16-1 Kings 2:12
The building of the temple: Solomon's : Ezekiel's vision : Ezra's : Herod's	1 Kings 5-8 Ezekiel 40-43 Ezra 3-6 Matthew 12:4-8; Luke 19:41-46*
Exile of Israel	2 Kings 17:1-6
Exile of Judah, fall of Jerusalem	2 Kings 25; 2 Chronicles 36:11-21
John the Baptist	John 1:6-35; Luke 7:18-35; Mark 6:14-29; Matthew 17:10-13
Jesus' birth	Matthew 1:18-2:23; Luke 2
Jesus' transfiguration	Matthew 17:1-13*
Jesus' trials	Matthew 26:57-68; 27:11-26*
Jesus' crucifixion	Matthew 27:27-56*
Jesus' burial and resurrection	Matthew 27:57-28:15*
Jesus' ascension	Luke 24:50-53; Acts 1:6-11
Pentecost	Acts 2:1-11
Conversion of Saul (Paul)	Acts 9:1-19
Paul's missionary journeys	Acts 13-20
Paul's arrest and journey to Rome	Acts 21-28
John's letters to the young churches	Revelation 1-3

* and parallel passages in other gospels

Some well-known chapters

Isaiah 53	The Saviour expected
Psalm 23	Comfort
Psalm 51	Repentance
1 Corinthians 13	Love
1 Corinthians 15	Resurrection
Romans 8	Victory

When I have problems......

Accidents and bad news	Luke 13:1-5; 1 Peter 5:6-7
Bereavement	1 Corinthians 15:50-58
Confusion	2 Corinthians 12:9-10
Depression	Matthew 6:25-34; Romans 8:28-39
Doubt	Mark 9:17-24
Facing death	Psalm 23; 1 Thessalonians 4:13-18
Fear	Psalm 34:1-10; Matthew 10:26-31
Forgiveness	Matthew 6:5-15; Acts 13:38; Ephesians 1:7-8
Guidance	John 16:12-15; James 1:5
Guilt	Psalm 51; 1John 1:5-10
How to pray	Luke 11:1-13
Pain	James 5:13-16 but see 2 Corinthians 12:7-9
Purposelessness	1 Peter 1:3-9
Temptation	1 Corinthians 10:11-13

... or take as long as you like. This bird's-eye view of the Bible will give you a solid base on which to build your Bible knowledge.

The Bible in three weeks

When you want to build something new, it's best to start with the overall plan. This will give you a picture of the finished article, how it works and how the pieces relate to one another.

We can do a similar thing with the Bible. To get full value from this plan, set aside some time every day for three weeks and let the whole picture come into focus. It will be an enriching experience.

Let's begin at the beginning:

Read Genesis, chapters 1-2.

When God made the world it was perfect, and that included the people living in it. But things went wrong:

Read Genesis, chapter 3.

From then on the road was downhill. Sinners and sinfulness multiplied with each generation. Then God stepped in:

Read Genesis, chapter 12, verses 1-7.

God's promise to Abraham was to work out through his son, Isaac, and his grandson, Jacob, who was also called 'Israel'. Jacob's sons headed up the tribes which were to be known as 'the Children of Israel'. But hard things were to happen to them before they inherited the land of Canaan. They were enslaved in Egypt for many years, and then:

Read Exodus, chapter 3.

God brought them out of Egypt and made a special agreement with them which we know as 'the Old Covenant' or 'Testament'. He had liberated them. He promised to be their God, but they must keep his commandments:

Read Exodus, chapter 20, verses 1-17.

In spite of this, they rebelled against the Lord and, as a punishment, wandered in the Sinai desert for forty years. Then, after Moses died, they finally began to take possession of their own land:

Read Joshua, chapter 1.

After they had conquered Canaan, there was an unsettled period when they repeatedly forgot God and suffered the consequences in terms of invasion by foreigners. He sent them a series of leaders, the judges, to rescue them. Finally he gave them their first king, Saul, who turned out to be a disappointment. His replacement,

David, in spite of his mistakes, reigned well and established peace:

Read 2 Samuel, chapter 7.

He was succeeded by Solomon, who built the temple in Jerusalem. During his reign the nation rose to heights of prosperity, though only with a great deal of oppression and spiritual backsliding before Solomon's death:

Read 1 Kings, chapter 12.

The kingdom divided into Israel in the north – a state which was rocked by successive rebellions, and ruled generally by weak kings – and Judah in the south, more firmly based but with some equally corrupt rulers. Israel was judged first, being taken into exile by the Assyrians, and Judah later by the Babylonians:

Read Isaiah, chapter 1.

It was while the Old Covenant was finally falling to pieces, that God gave his people the promise of a renewal of the old arrangement:

Read Jeremiah, chapter 31, verses 31-34.

He also promised that, one day, he would give them an ideal ruler who would bring forgiveness and justice:

Read Isaiah, chapter 11.

During the exile, some Jews, like Daniel, rose to high office, but many longed and prayed for the day when they would return as God had promised. A small group were allowed to return only to find Jerusalem destroyed, and the neighbouring people hostile. Under great difficulties, they rebuilt the temple:

Read Nehemiah, chapters 1-2.

Under Nehemiah and Ezra the people held together, but life was hard, and the Old Testament ends on a sad note, though with the hope that God would one day fulfil his promises of restoration. During the silence between Old and New Testaments, empires rose and fell. First came the Greeks, who were in turn replaced by the Romans. They ruled Palestine through the corrupt leaders the people had inherited:

Read Luke, chapter 2, verses 1-7, and Matthew, chapter 2, verses 1-12.

In this way God sent his Son into the world. He went about healing and teaching, most people little guessing who he was. Because his actions and his claims embarrassed the authorities, they connived his death:

Read Matthew, chapter 26, verses 36-68; chapter 27, verses 11-54.

Just before his death, however, Jesus had foretold that what was about to happen would bring the New Covenant into being:

Read Matthew, chapter 26, verses 17-29.

And his death was not the end:

Read John, chapter 20.

It was because of who Jesus was and what he did that his followers could offer God's promise of forgiveness and new life to all who would accept it:

Read John, chapter 1, verses 1-18.

In order to do this, God equipped them by sending the Holy Spirit:

Read Acts, chapter 2.

Not only did many Jews believe in Jesus, the message spread out into the non-Jewish world through people like the apostle Paul. Churches were established all over the known world. To further explain what God had done for them, the apostles wrote letters:

Read Ephesians, chapter 1.

However, Christian living was not easy. They not only had to cope with the very immoral society of the day, but also with great opposition. This came, first of all, from the Jews, and then from the secular authorities. But there's always a note of triumph in their writings. One day the Lord would come back to judge and to reign:

Read Philippians, chapter 2, verses 5-11.

After that God would remake all things as he originally intended them to be:

Read Revelation, chapters 21-22.

Now go back to the contents page and take one of the other entry points into the Manual.

PART 2 STUDYING THE PLANS

Opening up the background to the Bible and how we can set about making sense of it.

Weights and measures

Old Testament

Dry measures (volume)

Bible term	Bible equivalent	Approximate modern equivalents	
Homer		220 litres	48.5 gallons
Cor	Equal to homer	220 litres	48.5 gallons
Ephah	1/10 homer	22 litres	38.5 gallons
Seah		7.3 litres	13 pints
Omer	1/10 ephah	2 litres	3.5 pints
Cab	1/4 seah	2 litres	3.5 pints

Liquid measures

Bible term	Bible equivalent	Approximate modern equivalents	
Bath	Ephah (dry measure)	22 litres	38.5 pints
Hin	1/6 bath	3.6 litres	6 pints
Log		0.3 litre	0.5 pint

Measurement of length

Bible term	Bible equivalent	Approximate modern equivalents	
Cubit		44.45 cm	17.5in
Span	1/2 cubit	23 cm	9in
Palm		7.37 cm	3in
Digit	1/4 palm	1.85cm	0.75in
Gomed	2/3 cubit	29.6 cm	11.75in
Reed	6 cubits	266.7 cm	8ft 9in
Hellenistic times			
Schoinos		184.9 cm	196.5yd
Stadion		6.1 km	3.75miles

Weights

Bible term	Bible equivalent	Approximate modern equivalents	
Talent (light)	3,000 shekels	30kg	66lb
Mina	1/60 talent 50 shekels	0.5kg	1.6lb
Shekel (royal)		13g	0.5oz
Shekel (common)		11.5g	0.4oz
Shekel (temple)	1/2 or 1/3 shekel	5g	0.2oz
Pim		7.5g	0.25oz
Beka	1/2 shekel	6g	0.25oz
Gerah	1/20 shekel	0.5g	0.02oz

New Testament

Dry measures (volume)

Bible term	Bible equivalent	Approximate modern equivalents	
Koros		525 litres	114 gallons
Saton *(sata)*		12.3 litres	21 pints
Bushel *(modios)*	8 quarts	8.5 litres	15 pints
Quart *(choinix)*		1litre	1.7 pints

Liquid measures

Bible term	Bible equivalent	Approximate modern equivalents	
Measure *(batos)*		39.5 litres	9 gallons
Firkin *(metretes)*		39.5 litres	9 gallons
Pot *(xestes)*		500 cc	1 pint

Measurement of length

Bible term	Bible equivalent	Approximate modern equivalents	
Cubit		44.4/ 52.5cm	17.5in/21in
Fathom *(orgyia)*		1.8m	6ft
Furlong *(stadium)*		185m	202yd
Mile *(milion)*		1,478m	1,618yd

Weights

Bible term	Bible equivalent	Approximate modern equivalents	
Pound *(litra)*	(Latin *libra*)	327g	7.5lb
Talent	125 libra	40kg	88lb

2.1 UNPACKING THE OLD TESTAMENT

by John H. Walton

The Old Testament is the story of how God created the world and made an agreement ('covenant' or 'testament') with the Israelite people. He was their God; they were to follow him and be prepared for the coming 'new deal', the coming of the Messiah, the God-sent deliverer. The Old Testament was compiled over more than a thousand years.

This section majors on the lands of the Bible, the story of its people, how they lived and how they saw their world from Genesis (the 'beginning') through to Roman times.

Page

Back in time

As we try to think what it was like in the days when the Bible was written, we are faced with a problem which is both hard and easy. It is hard in that most of us are locked into our own way of living and thinking. It takes a great deal of imagination to step into another time and another culture. It is easy – or certainly easier than it ever has been – in that, when it comes to finding out what it was like in those far-off days, we are better off than any generation which has gone before us. Over the years, all kinds of people have spent time and energy doing the hard work for us. We have the results of their efforts readily available in a host of Bible reference books (see section 5.4).

63

Where do we start when we want to form a picture of what it was like when people like Abraham, Moses, Peter and Paul were around? We will need to begin with the Bible lands themselves, as the places *where* they lived largely determined *how* they lived. It is, of course, a great privilege – and one which has become more readily available than ever before – actually to visit the Holy Land, or Greece and Turkey, to see for ourselves the places where the Bible stories were acted out. A journey like that throws a flood of light on our understanding of Scripture. In one sense, you can never read the Bible in quite the same way again because, when you do, in your mind you can see the hills and the valleys, you can feel the climate, and you can re-experience the whole shape of the country where the biblical events took place.

21-23

● Landscape

Even if we have never been able to make that sort of trip, there are plenty who have spent years in the Bible lands and who have taken time to describe them. Some of their findings come to us in the form of the maps in Bible atlases, and often in the back of our Bibles. These give us an idea of how hilly the country is, and of the directions and distances involved, and other details which help us to imagine what the country is like. How else, if we have not been there, would we have any idea of what it must have meant for Jesus and his friends to walk from Galilee in the north to Jerusalem in the south? Similarly those same atlases give us an idea of where the towns were located, and where the land was fertile – as well as those places where the farmers must have had a very hard time of it.

The Holy Land contains arid deserts and almost tropical jungle within a short distance of each other.

● Climate

Then there have been those who have written about the climate with its quite wide extremes at different times of the year in different places. It can snow in Jerusalem, while at the same time it can be hot in Jericho, less than fifteen miles away, because one is so much lower than the other. What does the Bible mean by the early and the latter rains? This is important, in that, in an otherwise dry area, the whole of the agricultural programme depended on them. As they were an agricultural community right through Bible times, the whole of life must have been influenced by them in a way that we generally cannot know.

● Plants, animals, outboard motors and nylon nets

Others have spent years studying the plant and animal life of the Holy Land, giving us an insight into Bible references to creatures we do not have in our own country, and flowers which, even in these days of garden centres, are strange to us.

All these things are still there today to be seen and recorded, even though in many other respects life has moved into the twentieth century. Buses now run regular schedules on routes where Jesus and his disciples walked, and although there are still fishermen in Galilee, they use outboard motors and nylon nets.

The land of Israel

The area known today as the Middle East has long been referred to as the fertile crescent. Beginning in the south-east at the Persian Gulf, this huge crescent follows the basin of the Tigris and Euphrates rivers toward the north-west. Reaching the mountains of south-eastern Turkey, it curves southward along the coast of the Mediterranean until it reaches the Nile valley in Egypt. The region is well watered by a number of large rivers. In contrast the area within the crescent is barren wilderness.

In Old Testament times, Palestine, the Holy Land, was a narrow section of this crescent. Scarcely seventy-five miles wide, it is pinched between the desert and the Mediterranean. Passing through the land from west to east, the traveller would find four different landscapes arranged as thin strips running north and south. By the sea is the coastal plain. Though there are no natural harbours, several small rivers and an adequate rainfall make this region quite rich. This was the area most stubbornly protected by the Canaanites when the Israelites

Modern Israel. Stainless steel sculpture at the Shrine of the Book, Jerusalem.

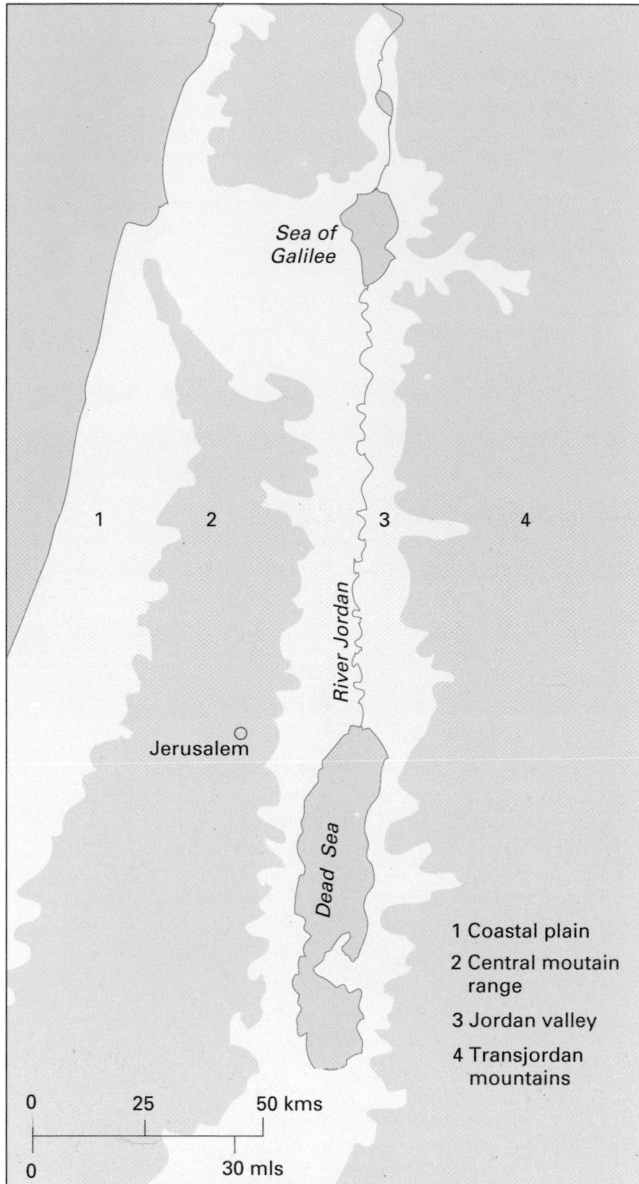

The Holy Land showing the four different types of landscape described on this page.

first came into the land, and the southern plains were later the territory of the Philistines. The major overland trade route between Egypt and Syria passed through Palestine mainly through this coastal plain.

Moving to the next strip east, the traveller would encounter much more difficult hiking in the central mountain range. This was the core of ancient Israel and featured cities such as Hebron, Jerusalem, Shechem and Samaria. The land here was much less inviting to farmers, though some of the valleys were more hospitable. The hills are interrupted by the broad valley of Jezreel (Esdraelon) that joins the coastal plain to the Jordan river valley. It was here that the trade route crossed the land of Palestine before moving north into Syria.

The third region was the lush, narrow valley of the Jordan river that wound from the northern mountains, through the Sea of Galilee and down to the Dead Sea. Though only sixty-five miles separate the Sea of Galilee from the Dead Sea, the Jordan's course covered some 135 miles. The river averaged about one hundred feet in width and three to ten feet in depth in ancient times, though modern irrigation has diverted the river at various points, reducing its size. The Dead Sea, the lowest point on earth, is over 1,300 feet below sea level. Through most of its course the Jordan was lined with undergrowth. Marshes in the north, oases and near-jungles to the south, all faded to desert in the Dead Sea region. Here there was little that could survive the arid desolation.

The fourth strip was made up of mountains on the eastern side of the valley referred to as Transjordan (modern day Jordan). Though the ascent was steep coming out of the Jordan valley, the mountains levelled out quite gradually into the eastern desert. The composition of the soil was volcanic and the greater amount of rainfall combined to make this a fertile area, especially in

the north. A second major trade route, the King's Highway, passed through this region.

Palestine was not rich in soil or in natural resources. Though it was described as a land 'flowing with milk and honey' (Exodus 3:8), these are not products of farmers, but of herdsmen and food gatherers. It was the trade routes more than anything else that gave Palestine its importance in ancient times. Great empires constantly interfered in Palestine over the centuries to secure these routes for use by merchants as well as armies.

The overall climate in Palestine is generally tolerable if not always pleasant. There are two seasons which can be predicted fairly accurately. The rainy season lasts from October through to April, while it is rare to have any rain from June to September. Summer days tend to be dry and cloudless with daytime temperatures ranging in the nineties, but cooling into the sixties in the evening. In the south the humidity is very low, so this is not uncomfortable though dehydration can come easily. As a result, water sources were very important for the land as well as for the people. Further north the humidity is higher. Much of the moisture for the growing season relies on the ground holding the rains and the dew from those cool summer evenings. The rainy season brings cooler temperatures, frequent rain and occasionally a little snow. The amount of rain received and the length of the rainy season greatly affect the farmers' yield in the following summer. Whether water came from the clouds, from the dew, from the mountain snows, or from natural springs, it was the most precious commodity to those ancient farmers.

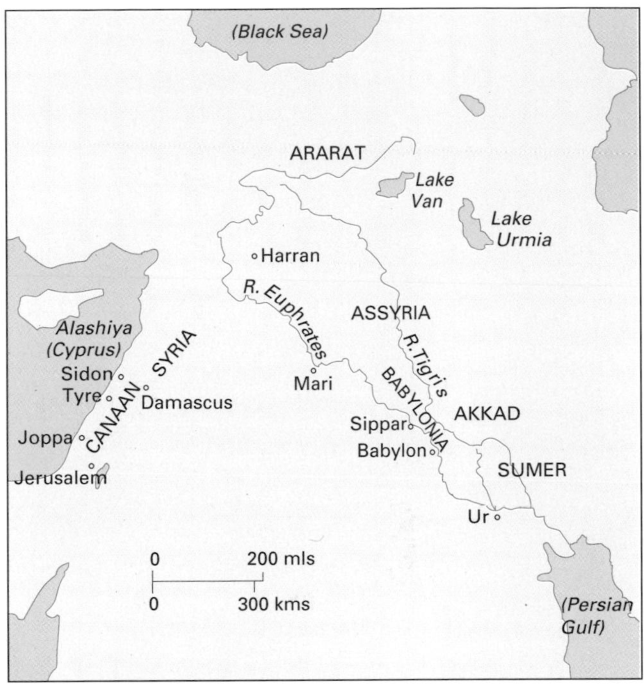

The ancient Near East showing the 'fertile crescent'.

'The promised land'

For the Israelite people it was neither the natural resources nor the strategic location of the land that mattered. This was the land that their God had promised to them (Genesis 15:18-21). Then, over 400 years later, he had honoured his promise. The covenant promises the Lord made with the people of Israel became the centre-piece of their understanding of themselves as the people of God. The land was at the core of the covenant. Therefore it did not matter whether the land of Palestine was strategically located or fertile. Israel's possession of this strip of land was proof of the fact that the Lord had singled them out to be his people. In this sense, it was a token. But each family's little plot of soil, however rocky or marshy it might be, was their claim to being part of God's chosen people. It is therefore quite appropriate that Palestine be referred to as 'the promised land'.

34

29

Events recorded in the Bible	Parallel headlines from general history
2000 BC Abraham and the patriarchs	1792-1750 BC Hammurabi king of Mesopotamia
1700 BC Entry into Egypt 1550 BC Slavery in Egypt	1710-1570 BC Hyksos kings rule Egypt 1361-1345 BC Akhenaten king of Egypt or 1376-1360 BC
1260 BC Exodus 1220 BC Crossing the Jordan	End of the 'Bronze Age'
1200-1050 BC The Judges	The 'Iron Age' begins The 'Sea Peoples' invade
1050-930 BC United Monarchy Saul/David/Solomon	945-924 BC Sheshonq I (Shishak) king of Egypt
930 BC The kingdom divided Israel in the N: Judah in the S	
724 BC Israel exiled to Assyria	722-705 BC Sargon king of Assyria
597 BC Judah exiled to Babylon	605-562 BC Nebuchadnezzar II king of Babylon
538 BC Jews return to Jerusalem. Temple rebuilt. Persian rule.	486-465 BC Xerxes I king of Persia (Ahasuerus)
Israel between the two testaments	
331-320 BC Macedonian rule	332-323 BC Alexander the Great emperor
310-198 BC Egyptian rule. The Ptolemies.	Egypt declining
198-63 BC Syrian rule. Revolt of the Maccabees.	223-187 BC Antiochus the Great Seleucid king of Syria
63 BC Roman rule 40 BC Herod the Great king of Judea	102-44 BC Julius Caesar 55 BC Caesar invades Britain 29 BC-AD 14 Augustus Caesar Roman emperor

Time chart: Old Testament. Many dates are approximate.

The history of the Old Testament period

● The patriarchs (Abraham, Isaac and Jacob)

The history of Israel begins in earnest with Abraham. At least that is the view of the Old Testament, for its special interest is in the history of the covenant (agreement) between the Lord and the Israelites that was started with Abraham. In this covenant the Lord promised Abraham a land for his family and many descendants, and promised to make them a blessing to the whole world.

The earliest chapters of Genesis, while preserving a historical record of earlier events, focus on God's plan of working through a chosen people.

Abraham came from Mesopotamia, the area surrounding the Tigris and Euphrates rivers chiefly modern day

93

Iraq. The civilization of Mesopotamia had been founded by the Sumerians from a little before 4000 BC until about 2000 BC. The Sumerians are thought to have invented writing, as well as making advances in fields such as mathematics, architecture, literature, education, law and medicine. Mesopotamia, in turn, through the influence of its native Babylonians and Assyrians, left its cultural mark on the whole ancient world.

Abraham's roots

By the time of Abraham, the region of Mesopotamia was largely controlled by Semitic peoples (said to be the descendants of Shem, son of Noah, Genesis 10:21-31). This control had surfaced first in the empire of Sargon the Great (about 2350-2200 BC) and had been continued by kings ruling from the town of Ur (about 2100-2000 BC). Archaeology has uncovered the city of Ur from this period and many beautiful objects were found in this sophisticated political centre. While some have suggested that these excavations provide a good picture of where Abraham grew up, such may not be the case. First of all, while Abraham may have lived at that time, many would place him in a later period. Secondly, some have located Abraham's Ur of the Chaldees as a smaller town far north near the modern Syrian–Turkish border. Thirdly, even if Abraham did live at this time in the famous, southern city of Ur, he may well have been a herdsman in the countryside rather than a refined city-dweller.

● First interlude: captivity in Egypt

Abraham's family was in Palestine for only two generations when famine led them to migrate to Egypt at the time of Joseph. During part of the 400 years that they lived there, Egypt was ruled by a people known as the Hyksos. When Egypt became strong again the Hyksos were driven out, and it was probably at this time, in the mid-sixteenth century BC, that the Israelites were enslaved by the fiercely nationalistic Egyptians of the eighteenth dynasty (Exodus 1). The Israelites were forced to provide slave labour for the construction of Pharaoh's cities in the northern delta region of Egypt, but they never forgot about the land that God had promised them. After more than four centuries in Egypt, the Lord provided a deliverer in the person of Moses, an Israelite who had been raised and educated in the household of the Pharaoh.

The Egyptians did not want to free the Israelites to pursue their God-appointed destiny. Their stubbornness provided the Lord with an opportunity to display great power on behalf of his people. God revealed his sovereignty through the mighty plagues and the parting of the sea and finally revealed to his people the Law, including the Ten Commandments, at Mount Sinai (Exodus 20). Despite seeing God at work so dramatically, the faith of that generation of Israelites faltered. They did not have the courage to enter a promised land that was filled with threatening enemies. Thus they were doomed to remain in the wilderness and it was left to the next generation to inherit the hope of the covenant promise which was their own land.

95-97

● The conquest and the judges period

Through the skill and dedication of Moses' successor, Joshua, the Lord gave the land to the Israelites as he

The judges

The government of the judges period was intended to be a theocracy ('God is king') administered by the leadership of the individual tribes. The history of the period (narrated in Judges 2-16) shows the continual failure of the people to be loyal to the Lord. When the Lord punished them by political oppression, the people would cry out for deliverance. Graciously, the Lord would provide a deliverer in the person of a 'judge' (*i.e.*, one bringing justice, deliverance, often by military action) who would receive support from a number of the tribes and restore freedom. These judges were God's instrument for exercising his kingship over Israel.

The theme of this period is the constant failure of the Israelites to remain loyal to the Lord and the merciful willingness of the Lord to give them another chance. Though their failure is inexcusable, we can well understand it. The Law (including worship of the Lord only) that had been given at Sinai was supposed to be passed on primarily within the structure of the family. Yet just one generation later they found themselves spread out over a land still inhabited by Canaanite peoples who were worshipping many pagan gods. The result was that the ideas included in the Law never got a chance to take root.

had promised. The historical account of the conquest of the land in the book of Joshua gives very little information on the military encounters except to show how the Lord acted on behalf of Israel. Furthermore, though God made the entire land available to Israel, the Israelites failed to control it all because they did not drive out all of the native inhabitants as they had been commanded to do (Joshua 23). With God's planned punishment of the Canaanites unaccomplished, the Israelites suffered the consequences and were constantly exposed to the influences of Canaanite religions.

The 400 years of the judges period ought to be divided in half when viewed against the backdrop of the ancient Near East. Until about 1200 BC, the international scene featured several major powers (especially Egypt and the Hittites, people from the central part of modern day Turkey) battling for control of the trade routes and sea ports. This situation changed sharply in the decades surrounding 1200 BC. A group known as the Sea Peoples, which included the well-known Philistines, invaded the region and so upset the political balance of power. As a result, the last half of the judges period saw a near vacuum in international politics. This situation lasted into the period of the Israelite monarchy and set the scene for the emergence of the Israelite empire during the days of David and Solomon.

● Second interlude: Samuel and the monarchy

It was Samuel, prophet, priest and judge, who presided over the period between the judges and the monarchy. When the ark of the covenant was taken by the Philistines in battle, it was clear that the Lord had abandoned Israel (Psalm 78:54-64). The period while the Lord turned away did not end until David brought the ark into the new capital city, Jerusalem (2 Samuel 6), though it could never be said that the Lord was totally absent.

In response to the demands made by the people, Samuel appointed Saul to be the first king of Israel. The

119

Lord made it clear to Samuel that 'it is not you they have rejected as their king, but me' (1 Samuel 8:7). In other words the people had not rejected the judges, but they had rejected God's rule over them. They thought that a king could fight their battles for them better than the Lord could.

Saul managed to contain the Philistines, but continued to struggle with them throughout his reign. Though Saul had been appointed by God as a king, he was chosen in accordance with the people's idea of what a king should be; and he was never approved to head a dynasty of kings under God's covenant agreement. As a result, he served more as a judge, who provided deliverance during his lifetime. As with many of the judges, Saul had faults. Some of them led to his undoing. The result was that David was chosen to be Saul's successor, and it was with David's line that a new covenant was made (2 Samuel 7), for David was a king chosen to represent God's idea of kingship (1 Samuel 13:14) in which the Lord fought their battles for them.

● The period of the monarchy

After he gained control over all of Israel and captured Jerusalem for a capital city, David succeeded in subduing the Philistines. He extended Israel's political control over most of the territory from the Euphrates river in the north-east to the Sinai peninsula in the south. This was Israel's golden age. Though, like Saul, David had his faults, his reputation for godliness established him as the model for kingship in Israel. And when Solomon, his son, had gained a firm grip on the kingdom, the violence in the royal family abated.

Solomon's wisdom was a gift from the Lord. It enabled him to build what appeared to be a model kingdom. Peace and prosperity abounded. Glorious building projects were undertaken. Profitable foreign trade was expanded beyond what anyone would have dreamed, bringing a constant flow of the finest imported products. All the nations of the Middle East sought political relations with him. His large *harem* is evidence of this, as many of his wives came to him as part of political alliances.

Yet all was not well. Wisdom helps one to know the right decisions to make, but does not always provide the will to carry them through. Solomon's spiritual resolve was weak in that he not only provided places of worship for his foreign wives, but joined them in their worship himself (1 Kings 11). Further-

116-117

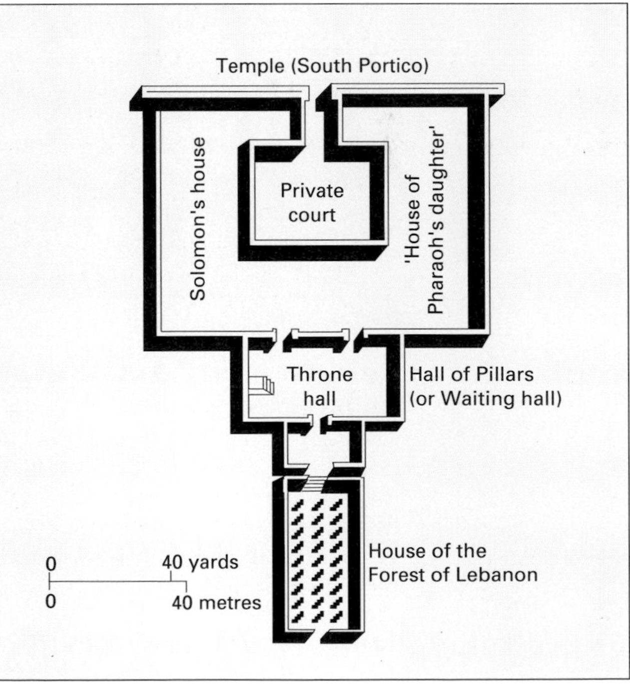

Plan of Solomon's palace.

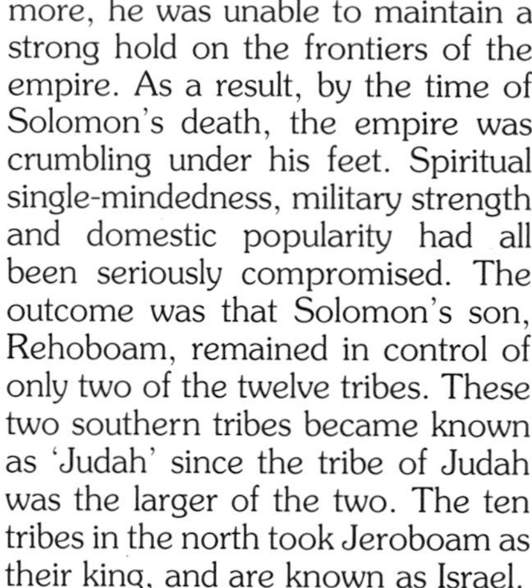

more, he was unable to maintain a strong hold on the frontiers of the empire. As a result, by the time of Solomon's death, the empire was crumbling under his feet. Spiritual single-mindedness, military strength and domestic popularity had all been seriously compromised. The outcome was that Solomon's son, Rehoboam, remained in control of only two of the twelve tribes. These two southern tribes became known as 'Judah' since the tribe of Judah was the larger of the two. The ten tribes in the north took Jeroboam as their king, and are known as Israel.

120

● The Bible and parallel history

37

So far little has been unearthed by archaeology to offer explicit confirmation of the biblical details up to the tenth century BC. On the other hand, much information has come to light that allows the broad historical and cultural background to be filled in. The exodus is not mentioned in historical records of Egypt, but many of them are intended for propaganda purposes. An account of the humiliation of the Egyptians would not have been recorded. The absence of any mention of David or Solomon is likewise understandable given that archaeology has recovered very little from that period from any nation that would have had contact with Israel. Others who are prominent in the biblical record such as Abraham or Jacob would have been too obscure to warrant mention in contemporary historical documents. As a result, though it would be helpful to have archaeology's independent witness to the accuracy of the biblical record on some of these matters, it is not odd that no trace has yet been found. Once we get to the ninth century BC, however, that will change.

The early years of the divided monarchy brought constant warfare between Judah and Israel. But as the ninth century BC opens, the emergence as a political power of the Aramaeans in the region of Syria to the north of Israel brought them together. This happened during the reign of Omri's son, the infamous Ahab. Under the influence of his notorious wife, Jezebel (a princess from the city of Tyre), he attempted to lead Israel to the worship of the Canaaite god, Baal. Unfortunately, the friendly relations developed between Ahab and Jehoshaphat (king of Judah), allowed this pagan influence to penetrate into the southern kingdom as well. It took several decades for Israel and Judah to recover from the effect of this lapse.

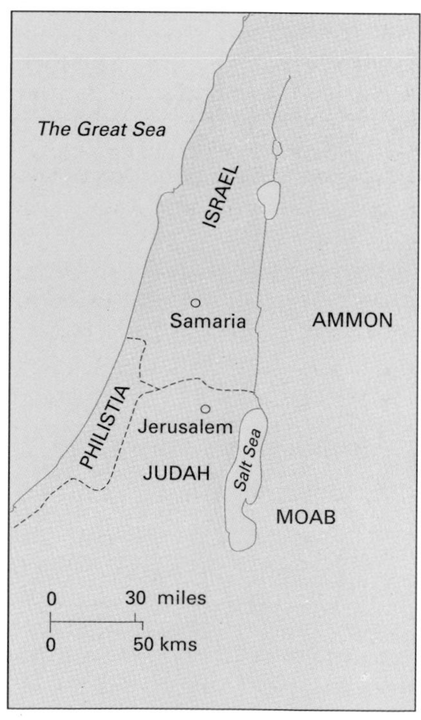

The divided kingdom.

The Assyrians

By the mid-ninth century BC a power from the north Tigris valley became a threat to Israel: the Assyrians. In 841 BC King Jehu of Israel agreed to be a servant of Assyria. Shalmaneser III, king of Assyria had pictures carved in stone to show Jehu bowing before him, the earliest picture of an individual known from the Bible.

Assyrian power weakened but returned in new strength in the next century, to such an extent that Shalmaneser V in 724 BC annihilated the northern kingdom of Israel and deported a large proportion of the survivors.

The Babylonians

Then a new instrument of God's judgment came onto the world scene: the Babylonians. Babylon had made itself independent of Assyria by 626 BC and their King Nebuchadnezzar began to conquer the Old Assyrian empire. The Babylonians however did not stop at Israel but invaded the southern kingdom of Judah as well. Jerusalem was destroyed and many of the inhabitants of Judah, including Ezekiel the prophet, were exiled to Babylon in 597 BC and 586 BC.

> **The land**
>
> Because of the covenant, the land was of great importance to the Israelites. The Babylonian exile meant that God had taken the land away from them. The prophets made it clear that this did not mean that the covenant was therefore null and void, only that they were being punished for their rebellion and disobedience. God intended to bring them back some day.

● Third interlude: the exile in Babylon

It was this period of exile that finally convinced the Israelites of the folly of worshipping other gods. When they eventually came back to the promised land, they were strongly committed to one God. They nevertheless continued to struggle with their self-identity. What did it mean to be God's people? This identity crisis continued into the period after their return.

37

Race, religion and land have always been aspects of 'Jewishness'.

Meanwhile, the Babylonian empire barely outlived the great King Nebuchadnezzar. Within a few years of his death, Cyrus the Persian began to gain in political strength. He conquered the Medes in the middle of the sixth century BC and thus founded the Medo-Persian empire. In 539 BC the Babylonians, tired of their irresponsible and incompetent kings, opened the gates of Babylon and welcomed Cyrus as deliverer, ending the Babylonian domination.

126

Cyrus chose to rule benevolently. Though the majority of the exiled Israelites had not really been prisoners in Babylon, they, along with other conquered people, were now encouraged to return to their homelands and rebuild their temples (with government assistance). Contented people are much less likely to be rebellious and troublesome. And so, after they had suffered several decades in exile, God brought his people back to the land of the covenant, and in 515 BC the rebuilt temple was completed. The monarchy, however, was not restored. The Israelites were still subjects of the Medo-Persian empire awaiting the fulfilment of God's promises of restoration.

● After the exile: under the Persian empire

Israel's identity crisis that had begun during the exile deepened after it was over. The temple had been rebuilt and sacrifices were again being offered, but were they still the Lord's chosen people? Was it practicable to remain racially separate in the cosmopolitan world of the Medo-Persian empire? Was the kingdom of God something spiritual only or should they still expect that they would again have a king like David ruling an independent and politically strong Israel? The prophets Daniel, Haggai, Zechariah and Malachi were deeply concerned about these problems and individuals such as Ezra and Nehemiah provided leadership and guidance. But the Persian empire remained in power as decade followed decade and century followed century.

126-128

Early on, however, it became clear that the Persians were not invincible. They attempted to extend their control into Greece during the reigns of Darius, Xerxes and Artaxerxes but the Greeks triumphed in major battles at Marathon, Salamis, Mykale, Eurymedon and numerous other skirmishes, driving the Persians from Europe. All of these took place in the first half of the fifth century BC, yet it was not until the latter part of the fourth century BC that the Greeks gained enough confidence to move against the Persians. This seemingly impossible task was undertaken by Alexander the Great who saw the mighty Persian empire crumble at his feet in 331 BC. The Old Testament period has by now come to a close, with the Jews awaiting the next step of the plan of God.

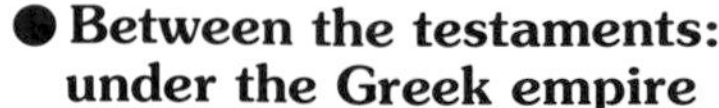

● Between the testaments: under the Greek empire

Alexander the Great's early death shattered the Greek empire; it was divided between four of his generals. The Middle East was primarily divided between Ptolemy, who controlled Egypt, and Seleucus, who over the next two decades gained power over the rest of the region from Persia to the Mediterranean. Palestine was again in the middle. For the first hundred years, Palestine was controlled by the Ptolemies. This changed toward the end of the third century BC on the accession of Antiochus III to the Seleucid throne. He campaigned tirelessly throughout the empire and won back the control that his party had lost. The Egyptian army was soundly defeated in 198 BC, allowing Antiochus to incorporate Palestine and Phoenicia into the Seleucid empire. The Jews had supported the Seleucids and were treated very well by Antiochus.

Just as the Persians 300 years earlier had had great success in the Middle East, but failed miserably when they tried to extend their control too far to the west, so even during the time of Antiochus III, the Seleucids had tried to do too much. Advancing into Greece, they found themselves facing the Romans. Antiochus' army was soundly defeated by the Romans. This was the beginning of Seleucid decline, and led the Seleucid kings to worsening relations with their subject peoples, including the Jews.

The pleasant living conditions for the Jews came to an abrupt halt during the reign of Antiochus IV Epiphanes (the second son of Antiochus III to succeed him to the throne). Just as the Jews had strug-

gled throughout their history to maintain their racial identity, they were now struggling against being totally absorbed into the Greek culture of the day. Some refused to accept Greek culture and this created tensions within Jewish society. It also made the Jews specific targets of Antiochus IV's policy of enforcing Greek culture. The post of high priest became a political appointment that was awarded to whoever could offer the most money and cooperation to Antiochus. The tensions at times boiled over into outright rebellion against Antiochus, and on one such occasion Jerusalem was occupied by the Seleucid army and many of its citizens slaughtered. Control of the temple was seized and it was made a centre for the worship of Zeus. The practice of Judaism was prohibited.

By the middle of the second century BC, such outrageous actions and the persecution of Jews who resisted the adoption of Greek culture had stirred up Jewish nationalism again. Problems in other parts of the empire kept Antiochus busy while a small, determined group of Jews under the leadership of Judas Maccabeus mounted a successful revolt. They defeated the Seleucid army in battle after battle and finally reoccupied Jerusalem and cleansed the temple.

As the Seleucids struggled to maintain control of their rapidly deteriorating empire, this upstart Jewish state survived and eventually gained the support of the Romans. The Jewish rulers who gained power by the Maccabean revolt came to be known as the Hasmonean dynasty, which lasted for a century. But disputes continued to weaken their control. Finally the Romans had to intervene, and in 63 BC, general Pompey entered the city of Jerusalem, and Roman rule was established in Palestine.

53

Cultural changes

Very little is known about cultural changes in Israel during the 'Greek' period, but the Judaism at the end of the Old Testament and the Judaism that emerged by the New Testament can be compared. Just as the Canaanites and the Babylonians had had their influences on the Israelites, Greek culture had a profound effect on Judaism. This is particularly evident in the Jewish writings from the intertestamental period, often called the Apocrypha. Beliefs concerning after-life and spiritual beings, for instance, seem to have been stimulated by Greek ideas. It was also during this period that the development of the synagogue took place, and groups such as the Pharisees (known from the New Testament) came into being.

43-44

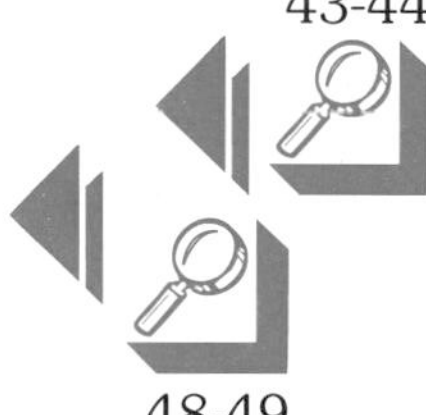

48-49

History as 'God's story'

The way in which history has been presented above would seem quite foreign to the biblical authors. The simple recital of facts and events would be meaningless to them unless the information was put to some use. The biblical authors used history as a tool for theology. They did not write history for the simple purpose of conveying what happened. Rather it was the evidence that God has a plan and was carrying it out. History was the witness to God's sovereignty.

245

Israel shared with her neighbours the view that God was the basic cause of every historical event. They tried to describe what made God act

Many Israelites lived in houses like this one; a few rooms grouped round a courtyard and a flat roof strong enough to work or rest on.

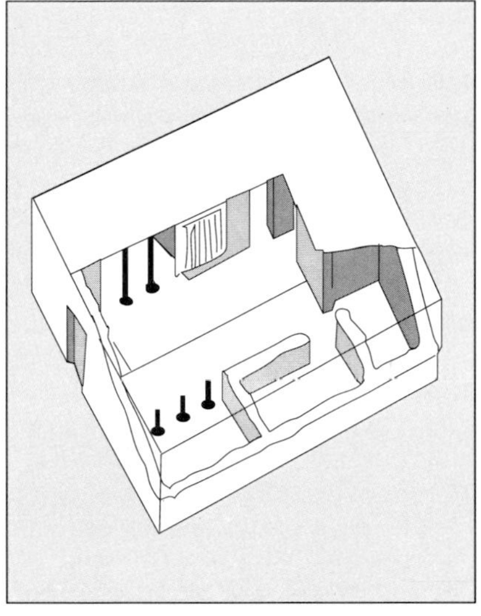

in history in the way that he had. Certainly people could be seen to do things but the human role was secondary and, in the end, didn't matter. If God's actions were not accounted for, the understanding of history would be impossible. This is in stark contrast to our modern view of history. Our history is concerned only with human cause and effect. It leaves out the role of God, except in the most unusual situations (such as the impact of earthquakes, volcanoes and so on).

The biblical writers were using history to report about God. His role was highlighted, his purposes were explained. History was viewed as God in action. That is why the miraculous at times was given such a high profile. It was first-hand evidence of God's role.

167

So the Old Testament is a history of Israel because they are the people through whom God had chosen to reveal himself and his plan. The covenant with Israel was at the core of God's plan for humanity. More properly then, rather than being viewed as a history of Israel, the Old Testament, after being God's story, is a history of the covenant. The significance of history is in what it tells us about God and about his plan for us.

Israelite society

● Social classes in ancient Israel

When the Israelites first came out of Egypt they were a semi-nomadic people, keeping animals and doing some basic farming. Their society was tribal, not urban. As they became settled in the land, the weight of society gradually shifted to farming, though herding continued to be quite common.

With the coming of the monarchy, an administrative class was formed, and the increase of international trade saw the development of a merchant class and more town-dwelling. By the first half of the eighth century BC, political expansion and prosperity had created a very structured society featuring an elite of wealthy individuals comprising the urban/merchant class. Meanwhile the farmers and herdsmen, dependent on the fickle climate, became increasingly burdened by debt, taxation, inflation and, in general, became the victims of the system. It is in this context that the prophets denounce the injustice of the upper classes.

● Society as God's people: the Law

Israelite society was governed by a set of laws, as are all other societies. But Israel's law was different. In many societies law is made up of the conventions that contribute to its smooth operation. Society itself is the source of its own laws. Not so in Israel. In Israel the source of law was

God. It was derived from the character of God and it was absolute. Law was not simply the conventions of society, it was God's revelation of what conduct would please him or displease him. Rather than emphasizing order within society, it emphasized right behaviour in the eyes of God. What pleased him is for someone to be like him ('Be holy, because I, the LORD your God, am holy', Leviticus 19:2).

It may come as a surprise that the Israelites expressed nothing but the deepest delight in the Law (see Psalm 119 for example). It was not an immense burden to them. The explanation for this is simple. God's revelation of the Law was an act of grace that affirmed Israel as his chosen people. It was part of their covenant heritage. The neighbours of Israel had very little clue concerning what would please their gods and what would offend. Since their gods were far from moral or just, it certainly would not do to imitate them. One of the greatest insecurities of ancient times was this inability to predict how the gods might act. In contrast, when the Lord gave the Law to Israel, he proclaimed his consistency and innate goodness. This willingness of the Lord so to define himself through the Law was recognized by Israel as an unmistakable act of mercy.

Israelite faith

The Old Testament is not intended to be a systematic account of Israel's beliefs, so it is difficult to reconstruct them. It is rather intended to show how God revealed himself to Israel. So we can at least describe some of the more central aspects of Israel's faith, particularly what they believed about God.

● One God

One of the greatest distinctives of the faith of Israel was that it required the worship of only one God. In contrast, the religions of Israel's neighbours were quite open-ended, that is, there was no limit to the number of gods who might be acknowledged. Abraham had lived among such a religion and was called out of it. Though God nowhere demanded that Abraham worship only him, and there is no record of Abraham putting away idol worship, the picture given of Abraham in Genesis is that of a loyal worshipper. Though Israel apparently fell back into worshipping many gods during their stay in Egypt (Joshua 24:14), when the ten commandments were given at Sinai, the first one on the list required that Israel should acknowledge no other God.

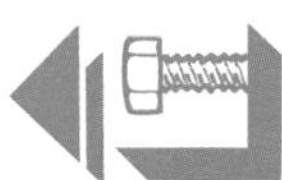
254-255

The chequered history of the judges period and the monarchy show clearly that Israel found it difficult to keep to this ideal. The prophets denounced Israel's faithlessness and condemned her for worship of other gods. It was normal procedure in the ancient Near East to believe in a structured system of gods and goddesses. National gods helped the king and priesthood to bring prosperity to the nation. Cities likewise had patron gods who guarded the interests of the town. But most intimately connected with the everyday activities of the common folk were their family gods. These were lower-level deities who had, usually for unknown reasons, shown favour in the past to particular families and were in turn revered by them. The Israelites had no difficulty in viewing Yahweh as their national God, but

97

35

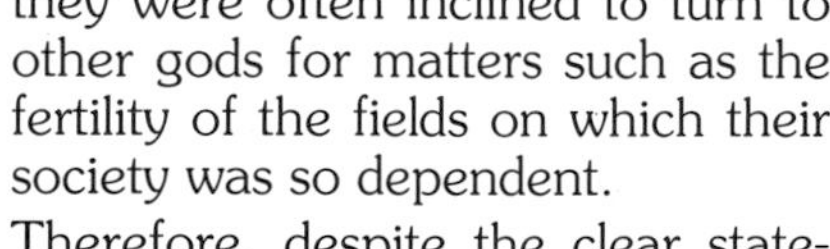

they were often inclined to turn to other gods for matters such as the fertility of the fields on which their society was so dependent.

43

Therefore, despite the clear statements of the Law, it is not really until the Babylonian exile that Israel fully grasped that there was one God in practice, and from that point on they held to that belief passionately. In all, it had taken nearly a thousand years for this transformation to take place. World-views change slowly.

● The covenant

23

God expressed himself to his people in the Old Testament chiefly through the 'covenant' that he made with Abraham, Israel and David. We could speak of three separate covenants, but it is important to see the unity that binds these together. God promised Abraham that he would give him a *land*, multiply his descendants to become a *nation*, and make them a *blessing* to the rest of the nations.

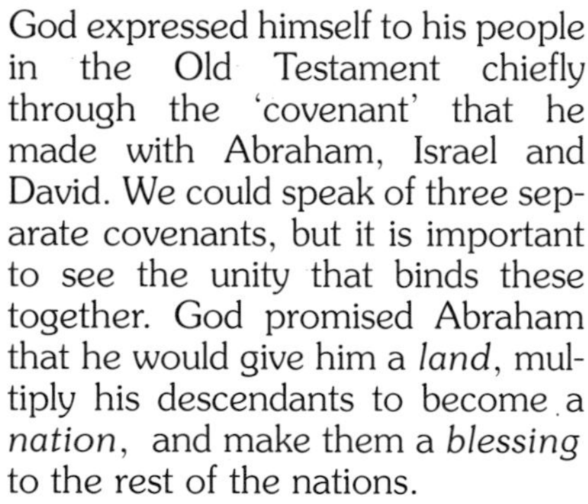

When God brought Israel out of Egypt and gave them the Law on Mount Sinai, he was not only fulfilling some of his promises to Abraham, but he was adopting the people of Israel as his own chosen people (Exodus 6:7). This covenant then became the core of Israel's belief and self-identity. They became the people of God because God would reveal himself to the world through them. As his people they became a blessing to the world, for God revealed himself through the Law, through the history of Israel, through the Scriptures and through Christ.

117

The covenant with David gave Israel a king and officially made her a nation. These had been included in the promises to Abraham. The covenant at Sinai had expanded the covenant idea by adding the concept of Israel as God's chosen people. The covenant with David added the idea of his dynasty as the chosen kings for Israel. Just as God's concept of law entered the covenant at Sinai, so God's concept of kingship became a part of the covenant with David. Thus God continued to reveal himself through the covenants. In the former, the Law revealed God's character. In the latter, God's position as king was revealed. Old Testament history is primarily the story of the covenant rather than a history of Israel. The prophets also spoke of Israel's breaking the covenant and how God intended to punish them.

Covenants old and new

The covenant, then, is the major theme of the Old Testament, and the central feature of Israelite faith. God reveals himself by means of it and Israel understands its relationship to God through it. The covenant represents God's plan for history, for humanity and for Israel. The covenant is also the point of transition from the Old Testament to the New, for the coming of Christ, from his birth to the redemption that he provides, represents a new development in the covenant. It offers fulfilment of promises as well as new horizons just as the previous covenants had done. In Christ the revelation of God and plan of God both reach their climax.

● Ritual: its place and function

What does God want from us? This is a very natural question that most peoples try to answer. For many of Israel's neighbours, the answer would have been: 'The gods want us to take care of them.' They saw sac-

rifice as providing the gods with food. The temples were the dwelling-places of the gods, and must be neat and clean, even luxuriously furnished and decorated. The statues of the gods must be treated well and properly honoured. These rituals were thought to provide the needs of the gods. In return, of course, it was expected that if the gods were treated well they would repay the hospitality with generous blessings.

The difficulty in Israel was that the Israelites might think about their God in the same way. The Lord had to insist that he did not need to be fed, clothed or housed (Psalm 50:7-15). He could not be manipulated or bribed. What did the Lord want from Israel? 'And now, O Israel, what does the LORD your God ask of you but to fear the LORD your God, to walk in all his ways, to love him, to serve the LORD your God... with all your soul, and to observe the LORD's commands and decrees that I am giving you today for your own good?' (Deuteronomy10:12-13).

The prophets such as Amos and Micah picked up this theme by making it clear that God expected justice and righteousness from the people, not simply ritual responses. Ritual by itself was considered worthless. The Lord was not to be treated as one of the pagan gods. The rituals were only intended to provide a symbolic action to represent the thinking or attitude of the individual performing it. The ritual is not an end in itself and ought not take place at all if nothing has taken place in the life of the worshipper. Continuing social injustice was evidence that the rituals the Israelites were performing could not be considered true worship.

From a general reading of the Old

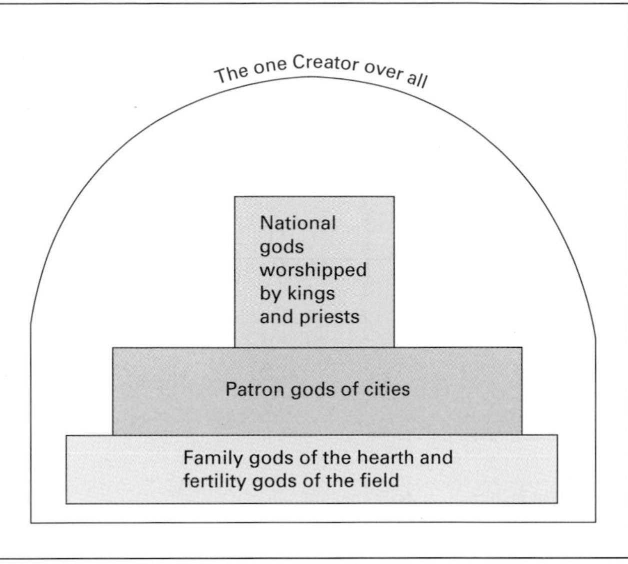

The Canaanites worshipped gods of varying importance but never recognized one Creator over all.

Testament one might think that the biggest problem the Israelites had to overcome was worshipping idols. But idols were only one symptom of a much bigger problem. If we could combine all the gods that the Canaanites worshipped, and if we did not allow them to use idols to worship them, we would still be very far away from the way that the Lord wanted Israel to treat him and think about him. Israel was to have an unrestricted view of God. There was nothing that he could not do. No event happened that was beyond his control. Everything was created by him. There was no power above him and no limit to his jurisdiction. This is a far different picture from that painted of the gods of the Canaanites. In their religion, the gods simply did not possess this kind of power and unrestricted kingship. The difference is that the Canaanites had made the gods in their own image. The Israelites were inclined, as we all are, to do the

same. That is why the Lord had to remind them time and again, 'I am not like a man' or 'My ways are not your ways' (Isaiah 55:8-9). Idolatry and the use of ritual to try to influence God were the most obvious symptoms of the dis-ease that threatened their existence: a pagan view of God that imposed severe limitations on him.

Israel's view of the world

● Creation

92

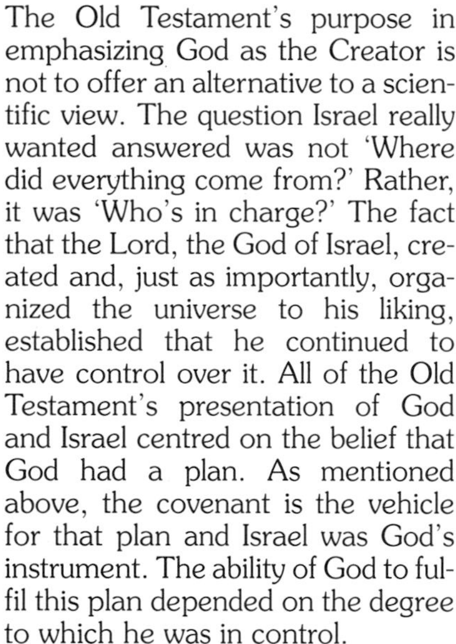

The Old Testament's purpose in emphasizing God as the Creator is not to offer an alternative to a scientific view. The question Israel really wanted answered was not 'Where did everything come from?' Rather, it was 'Who's in charge?' The fact that the Lord, the God of Israel, created and, just as importantly, organized the universe to his liking, established that he continued to have control over it. All of the Old Testament's presentation of God and Israel centred on the belief that God had a plan. As mentioned above, the covenant is the vehicle for that plan and Israel was God's instrument. The ability of God to fulfil this plan depended on the degree to which he was in control.

In the beginning, then, God created. His plan was built into the very fabric of the created world and was in motion from day one. There may be numerous ways that believers could view the claims of modern science, but any view that discounts the role of God as Creator cannot claim to be biblical. If God did not create, then one could question whether a plan exists, and even the claims of Christ (as central to the plan) lose their meaning.

72

255

● Mankind

From the very beginning this world was designed by God to have people on it. This understanding is basic to the biblical view, though it is in sharp contrast to the general view today as well as to the general ancient view. In the modern scientific view, mankind is a product of chemical chance, but in the ancient view, people were an afterthought of the gods. (The mythology of the ancient Near East maintained that people were created to do slave labour when the gods tired of taking care of themselves.) The Old Testament will tolerate neither of these. When God created, everything was so designed and arranged that it would be just right for the people that God intended to create. Once all was prepared, the first man and woman were lovingly crafted in the very image of God. All seemed to be lost when this high state was forfeited by disobedience, but God immediately put into effect his plan of reclamation. This view is the source of all human dignity. We find hope and purpose as we adopt the Israelite view of ourselves as heirs of God's programme of recovering mankind gone astray. It would be presumptuous and arrogant of us to think of ourselves in this way had not the Old Testament told us that it was true.

Unified structure

It is the Israelite view of creation, then, that is the beginning of the story of the covenant. The view of the world and of humanity that the Old Testament offers is a single, integrated one that merges together creation, covenant, God, people, Israel, law, prophecy and history into a unified structure of reality and existence.

Pagan beliefs

As we have seen, the pagan religions of the Canaanites and Babylonians were open-ended. By this we mean that they were always willing to acknowledge the power of new gods previously unknown to them. They would worship any god who had given evidence of his power. Unlike the God of Israel, the pagan gods did not reveal themselves to their worshippers. Worshippers could determine that a god was upset when they experienced trouble or suffering. They would then seek the advice of priests regarding what rituals or incantations needed to be performed so that the angry god would be appeased. This could be a long and futile process. The gods did not act in logical or consistent ways, so people came to view themselves as at the mercy of a massive divine bureaucracy.

It seems clear that the religion of the ordinary people was often self-centred. The gods they worshipped were nature gods who were believed to have sufficient power to affect the daily life of the individual. Fertility gods were particularly important to them, since they were so dependent on agriculture. The rituals directed towards the fertility gods were often sexual in nature and the prophets continually warned the Israelites against their perversions.

The most direct general attack against pagan deities is launched by the prophet Isaiah (chapters 40-48), who builds his case on the claim that these gods are incapable of making a plan and carrying it out. That is, they cannot rise above time and history. Their 'gods', local or national, were constructed by the people and were of no use at all.

Since the gods were viewed in very human terms, it is natural that people treated their gods in much the same way that they would treat people who were in positions of power. Flattery, bribes and favours were considered essential. So ritual prayers were repeated, sacrifices were offered and temples were provided and maintained. If worshippers could meet the needs of the gods, then perhaps the gods would treat them kindly. This is why ritual plays such a major role in religious practice. The name of the god and the idol of the god figured very prominently in these rituals. These means of manipulation were the only recourse of a people in the desperate state of being without guidance from the true God. The fact that Israel's God had revealed himself to them should have made all of this unnecessary for them.

Philosophy

Several books of the Old Testament are concerned with wisdom, reflecting the importance of wisdom in the Israelite approach to living. God is seen as all-wise and the source of human wisdom. Though wisdom covered many aspects of life, one of the chief effects of wisdom was the ability to make good decisions. Decisions about how to act, how to respond to situations, how to relate to people and how to set priorities all required wisdom and, in the Israelite view, could not be made properly without the 'fear of the Lord'. Neither knowledge nor intelligence were sufficient to make one wise. Neither wealth nor fame would substitute for wisdom. Only an appropriate view of God and

132-148

a proper relationship with God could serve as foundation for true wisdom.

354-358

Wisdom is the practical side of intelligence and knowledge. As raw materials, intelligence and knowledge can be misused for either selfish or evil purposes. Wisdom represents the proper use of them. When the Old Testament talks about God, it does not bother much with his intelligence or his knowledge (what our theologians call 'omniscience'). Rather it is concerned to describe his wisdom. It is not much good to know everything if one does not put it to good and proper use. That is the Israelite view of both God and man.

Since God is understood to be all-wise, it is reasonable to assume that people will not always be able to understand why God acts in certain ways in certain situations; for instance, the suffering of the innocent. Human wisdom fell short of understanding how a wise and just God who was in control of everything could allow good people to suffer; especially when obviously wicked people seemed to suffer no ill-effects for their wretched conduct.

282-284

The Israelites firmly believed in what can be called the 'retribution principle'. The first part of this principle maintains that the righteous will prosper and the wicked will suffer. The second part follows from a strict belief in the first: if a person is prospering, he/she must be righteous and if a person if suffering, he/she must be wicked. It is this last part that explains why Job is treated by his friends as though he has committed some great wickedness. To them, his suffering is the evidence.

132-136

Much of the wisdom literature of the Old Testament is out to show that the first part of the principle is true only so far as it reflects God's ultimate intentions and his general treatment of people. That is, it needs to be understood as a proverb. In English we say that 'Crime doesn't pay'. While we affirm the truth of that, we all know of exceptions to the rule. In the same way, since the first part of the retribution principle is subject to exceptions, the second part of the rule does not follow. We cannot infer that someone is righteous or wicked because of their prosperity or lack of it. The Israelites saw this much but it did not necessarily resolve the tension over why the retribution principle would not be true in a world ruled by a wise and just God.

● Judgment

Though we still struggle with the same issues today, for the Israelites this was a much more poignant problem, because God had revealed little to them concerning the after-life. As a result the Israelites had no knowledge of a judgment to take place after death. In their understanding whatever reward or punishment God intended to dole out would come about during this lifetime. The suffering of a righteous person was therefore difficult for them to accept, and this is why the book of Job is so significant. As that book develops its message, the philosophy of Israel takes shape. In the end God's just reputation is maintained simply on the basis of his infinite wisdom. God knows what is ultimately good for all his creatures, and he is Creator and controller of all.

2.2 UNPACKING THE NEW TESTAMENT

by John F. Balchin

The New Testament sets out the 'new deal' (testament) offered to the world by the birth, life, death and rising again of Jesus Christ. That theme is examined in Section 4.2 of this book.

Here we focus on the land that Jesus lived in, dominated by the Romans and, to some degree, by the Jewish religious leaders.

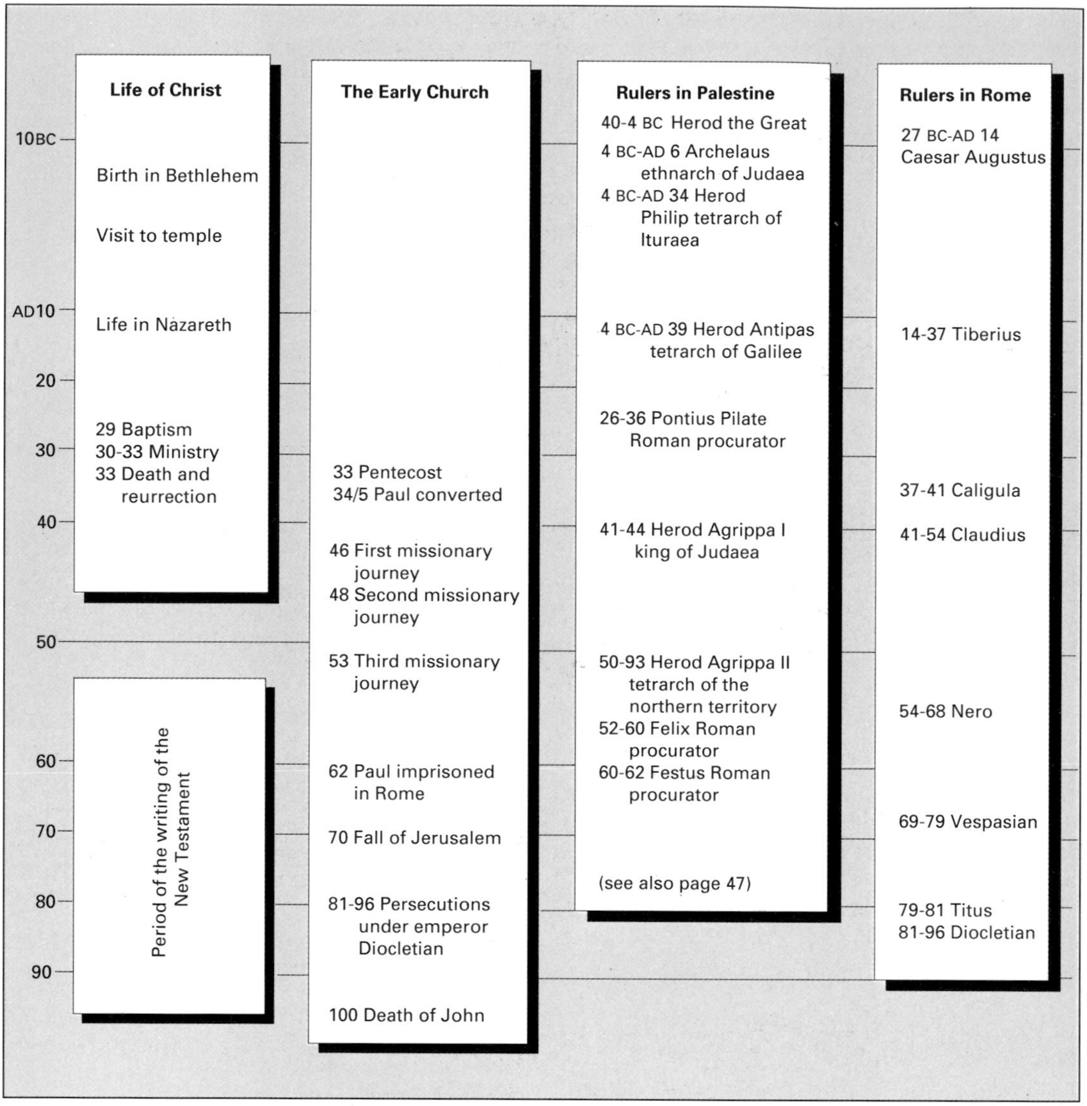

	Life of Christ	The Early Church	Rulers in Palestine	Rulers in Rome
10BC	Birth in Bethlehem Visit to temple		40-4 BC Herod the Great 4 BC-AD 6 Archelaus ethnarch of Judaea 4 BC-AD 34 Herod Philip tetrarch of Ituraea	27 BC-AD 14 Caesar Augustus
AD10	Life in Nazareth		4 BC-AD 39 Herod Antipas tetrarch of Galilee	14-37 Tiberius
20	29 Baptism 30-33 Ministry 33 Death and reurrection		26-36 Pontius Pilate Roman procurator	
30		33 Pentecost 34/5 Paul converted		37-41 Caligula
40		46 First missionary journey 48 Second missionary journey	41-44 Herod Agrippa I king of Judaea	41-54 Claudius
50	Period of the writing of the New Testament	53 Third missionary journey	50-93 Herod Agrippa II tetrarch of the northern territory 52-60 Felix Roman procurator 60-62 Festus Roman procurator	54-68 Nero
60		62 Paul imprisoned in Rome		69-79 Vespasian
70		70 Fall of Jerusalem	(see also page 47)	
80		81-96 Persecutions under emperor Diocletian		79-81 Titus 81-96 Diocletian
90		100 Death of John		

Time chart: New Testament. Many dates are approximate.

The Jewish people

●Towns and villages

As always, in Jesus' day your quality of life depended on where you lived and where you were in society.

The towns, and particularly a city like Jerusalem, tended to attract the wealthy who lived fairly sumptuously. They dressed and ate well, lived in fine houses, and generally had little time or thought for the poor (Luke 16:19-21). They were well served by family retainers, who might manage their country estates for them (Luke 16:1-9), and by slaves. Slavery was a fact of life in the Roman empire, the whole Roman economy being based on

302

slave labour. A man or woman, sold into slavery as a punishment, or because of debt (Matthew 18:25), was no longer regarded as a person. They were seen as merely possessions or tools. Although the Jews had humane laws governing their treatment of slaves, they could still own and use them. The lot of some slaves was cruel in the extreme, although many rose to influential positions in their masters' service. For example, if you were a Roman, your doctor or those who entertained you might well be slaves.

Living in a town or city in Palestine, you would be more likely to be influenced by Greek culture, particularly if you belonged to the upper classes. Even in Jerusalem, dominated by the temple, there were all the trappings of the Greek way of life, with the theatre, the hippodrome (for horse races), and the amphitheatre (for gladiators). You would also find the gymnasium, not just a place for physical work-outs, but rather the school whose curriculum was aimed at producing the ideal Greek gentleman. The pupils not only developed their bodies by exercise, but also read the Greek classics and studied subjects like philosophy and drama. Then there was always the intrigue of local politics or money-making to keep the rich man occupied between banquets. When you realize the gulf between rich and poor in those days, you begin to understand what has been called Jesus' 'bias to the poor'.

For there were plenty of poor people at the bottom of the heap. Many worked as day-labourers whose employment – and income – was far from certain. Illness or some other misfortune could very easily push a family into starvation, slavery or beggary, and there were plenty of beggars in Palestine in Jesus' day.

The various trades were family affairs and, whereas the Greeks had despised manual work, orthodox Jews always taught their sons their own trade. Jesus was taught to be a carpenter by Joseph. In a place like Jerusalem you would find all the shoe-makers or potters or weavers or carpenters in the same area of the city, so that competition must have been brisk.

Whereas the houses of the rich were grand affairs with their mosaic floors and painted walls, the dwellings of the poor were very basic. They were one- or two-room structures, sometimes having an upper storey which could be rented out (Luke 22:7-12) or used by married children. Water had to be drawn from wells or, in the hills, from cisterns cut in the rock where rain water had been stored. There was no plumbing or sewage system.

218

Many people lived much nearer to nature in the country villages. In some places, particularly in the Judean hills, life must have been quite hard. Except in the valley floors, the soil tends to be thin, and over the years the hillsides have had to be terraced in order to grow any sort of crop. Elsewhere, in the plain of Jezreel, or in Galilee, for instance, the ground is fertile, and although the peasant farmer might have had to work from dawn to dusk, six days a week, he would normally have had a crop to show for it. If instead he was a fisherman on the Sea of Galilee, he would know that the lake teemed with fish.

294-300

The villager might work for himself, in his own trade, or on his own or rented land, or he might work as a day-labourer for a wealthy estate owner or for one of his better-off fellows. On the land, his life was regulated by the seasons and the weather. If the weather was bad – in particular, if the rains failed – he could face ruin. Even what he did make was heavily taxed, in that he was liable to both the Roman taxes and to the Jewish temple tax.

Village houses were also one-room structures lit by oil lamps and accommodated both the family and their animals, the family living on a raised platform. A pleasant feature was the flat roof reached by steps or a ladder outside. Here the family might relax, or sleep on hot nights. This, like the walls, was made of dried mud, and was fairly easy to dig through (Mark 2:4). It was always surrounded by a low wall for safety.

There were still some in Palestine, like the Bedouin today, who had never settled down either in towns or villages. They lived in skin tents usually in the open country just as Abraham had done. They were continually on the move, driving their livestock from one patch of grass to the next. We have no direct reference to them in the New Testament.

29

Israeli agriculture, showing a terraced hillside in the ancient style.

Generally free from the politics of the city, village affairs would be run by the elders and centre on the synagogue. There would be a strong sense of community belonging, and many of the families would be interrelated by marriage.

●Away from home

It may come as something of a surprise to learn that by the time we get to the New Testament there were far more Jews living outside Palestine than in the country itself (which is also the situation today). For a wide variety of reasons Jews had left their homeland and were scattered across the known world, so that we find one Roman history writer complaining that he found them everywhere.

For some, of course, it was nothing to do with them that they were no longer living in their ancient land. They had been carried away, either by mass deportation or as prisoners of war. Others had fled the country looking for peace and security in times of trouble and conflict. Many had gone seeking their fortunes as traders or craftsmen. It's very difficult to estimate population figures but it has been reckoned that, at the time of Jesus' birth, there were probably four times as many Jews living elsewhere in the Roman empire as in Palestine itself.

Two main settlements had much greater influence than others, particularly on the way in which the Jewish faith developed at this time. In Mesopotamia (modern Iraq and Iran), and particularly in Babylon, the majority of the Jews who had been exiled there did not go home when they had the chance to return. They settled down and many did very well for themselves. It was a similar story in Egypt which had

long been a refuge for Jews escaping trouble at home (which is why Joseph took Jesus and his mother there). By New Testament times there were many Jews settled and prospering in Egypt.

Sometimes Jews living in this dispersion (or *Diaspora* as it is called) faced a great deal of opposition. Being Jews they kept to themselves, intermarried, practised their own customs and worshipped their own God. They often refused to join in the activities and pastimes of pagan society. Because they would not march on the sabbath day (for them that was work), they were exempt from military service. Neither were they required to offer the official sacrifices. So they appeared to be oddities to the easy-going pagans among whom they lived. This led to the unfortunate situation that at those times when the populace or the officials wanted someone to blame for something, the Jews found themselves suffering.

Another reason for this dislike was simple jealousy, in that when the Jews were left alone, they worked hard, became prosperous and sometimes rose to high positions. Officially they were legally accepted by the Roman authorities. This is why the early Christians were not persecuted at first by the Romans who saw them as merely another Jewish sect. The earliest persecution of Christians came from the Jews themselves.

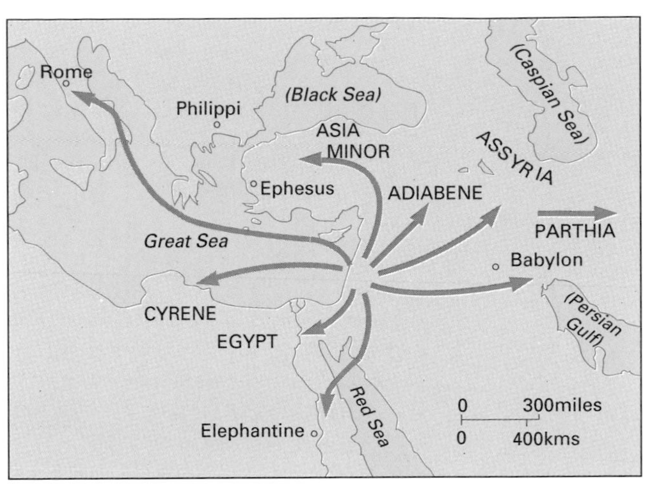

By the first century AD *Jews had settled in many parts of the world.*

● The synagogue

It was not easy, as many immigrants have discovered since, to hang on to their religion and culture in strange lands. The pressures to conform from outside the family were often great and frequently very subtle. Undoubtedly some Jews did adopt pagan ways, some renouncing their faith altogether. Others found non-Jewish ways of thinking very attractive. They began to read the Old Testament in the light of the great philosophies which had started in Greece, years before, and which were taken for granted among most educated people in the ancient world. It is not surprising that their ideas were influenced in this way. It is more remarkable that they held together as closely and as successfully as they did, and one of the most powerful reasons for this was the synagogue.

We do not know exactly when the first synagogue was set up. Most think it must have been during the exile, when thousands of Jews were transported across the Babylonian empire. That was surely one of the hardest punishments for them to bear. God had given them their land as part of their inheritance, and now he had taken it away. They had lost everything, their homes, their towns, their freedom and, perhaps saddest of all, the temple, which meant no more feasts nor sacrifices

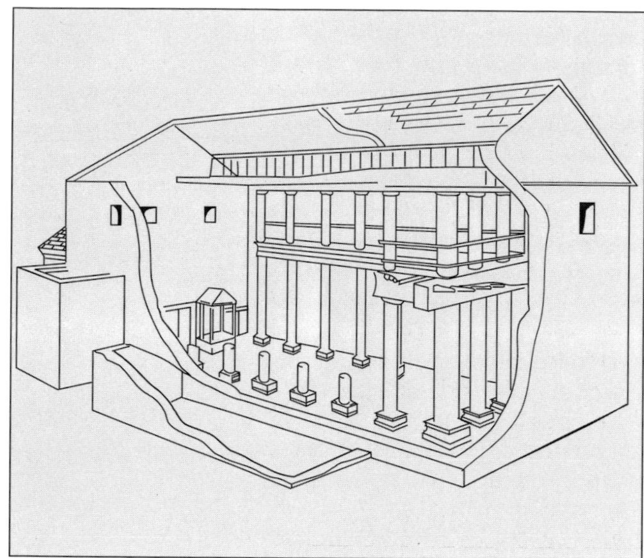

Artist's impression of a synagogue, showing the Ark of the Law.

in Jerusalem. What could they do?

They began gathering ('synagogue' means 'a gathering') for prayer and for the reading and study of the Old Testament. They reckoned that they only needed ten adult Jewish males (the ladies did not count) to set up a synagogue. If there were fewer than that, or if they had no building in which to meet, they would gather at a 'place of prayer' such as the one where Paul preached at Philippi (Acts 16:13). These were often by rivers so that they could wash before worship.

As they became established, they put up buildings, and although some were very ornate, they were usually built on a simple plan. It centred around the scrolls of the Old Testament kept in a box (or 'ark') which stood against the wall facing the door. These were read from a platform at the front. Seating arrangements differed, but the chief seats for the leaders were also usually at the front, facing the people. The readings, prayers and preaching were not the job of any one person, but the responsibility of the whole congregation (except the women who were kept segregated from the men). This was how Jesus was asked to read from the Scriptures in his home town synagogue at Nazareth (Luke 4:16-21), and why Paul was so frequently asked to preach in synagogues on his missionary journeys.

The synagogue became so popular with the Jews that they brought the idea back with them when they were allowed to return to Palestine. Even in Jerusalem, dominated as it was by the temple, there were many synagogues in the time of Christ. As in the *Diaspora*, they served a very useful purpose, for the function of the synagogue was not just as a place of worship. It became the centre of the local Jewish community. It was through the synagogue that gifts for the poor were passed on to those in need. The Jewish boys were educated there, taking part in the services when they were old enough. The elders of the synagogue also exercised discipline. If any Jew stepped out of line, he might be beaten as Paul was more than once (2 Corinthians 11:24). The severest punishment was to expel the offender, something which frequently happened in the early days when Jews believed in Christ (John 9:22).

●Keeping in touch

It was in ways like these that Jewish communities throughout the empire stuck together, and what was more important, held on to their faith in situations where otherwise they would doubtless have lost their identity altogether. As it was, the Jews of the *Diaspora* continued to worship the Lord and to maintain their own

traditions. The fact that they also had strong links with the homeland helped. Apart from family ties with those who had returned, Jews travelled to Jerusalem on pilgrimage to the great feasts, which is why there were Jews from all over the world present at Pentecost (Acts 2:5-11). Boys like the young Paul were sometimes sent back for an education (Acts 22:3). Possibly his nephew followed his example, unless his married sister was living there (Acts 23:16). Older Jews also went back to the Holy City to die so that they could be buried there in order to greet the Messiah at the resurrection.

The homeland also reached out to the Jews scattered around the world. All Jews had to pay the half shekel temple tax, and officials travelled from Jerusalem to the outlying communities. In ways like these, even though separated by long distances, Jews still saw themselves as part of the same nation, and also felt that Palestine was home, even though many had never been there.

●A new translation of the Bible

One of the very important spin-offs of this scattering of Jews was that many forgot how to speak their native language. By the time of Jesus, Hebrew was a dead language confined to the synagogue and theological debates. Even Aramaic, the mother tongue of the Holy Land (and the language Jesus spoke at home), was foreign to them. Like many thousands of others in the Roman empire they spoke, not Latin, which was the official language of the empire, but Greek, a left-over from Alexander's conquests.

This meant, among other things, that they were not really at home with the Hebrew of the synagogue services. In order to help them, the readings from the Bible (our Old Testament of course) were either accompanied with an explanation in Greek (or in Palestine in Aramaic) or turned into a full blown translation. The most popular Greek version was known as the Septuagint, which was used by many of the New Testament authors.

An interesting side-effect of all this was that their Greek-speaking neighbours could now, if they wanted to, read the Old Testament for themselves. When they did, some were attracted to the Jewish way of life. Compared with their own paganism, it seemed to have a good deal to offer with its high moral standards and worship of one God. Some went all the way and became Jewish converts (or 'proselytes'); others attended the synagogues, where they were welcomed as 'godfearers' or 'worshippers of God'. We find this group mentioned often in the New Testament, as many found the Christian message even more attractive than the Jewish faith.

The other by-product of Jews speaking Greek was that they, in turn, could read and be influenced by the many Greek writings which were in circulation at that time. It was in this way that a cross-fertilization between Greek (or 'Hellenistic') and Jewish ideas took place, of which we find plenty of traces in the New Testament.

●Life in Palestine

Back in the homeland the Jews had also come under the influence of the Greek way of life, having had Greek overlords for about 300 years. Their story had been rather different from

30-31

31

Feasts and seasons

The Jewish year does not correspond to our generally used Roman calendar with its 365 days. It is made up of twelve 28-day months, each beginning when the new moon becomes visible, which meant that, every now and then, they had to add an extra month to catch up. This is why Easter, which is linked with the Feast of the Passover, occurs on a different date each year.

96

Passover commemorated God's great deliverance under Moses of his people from the slavery of Egypt. It was the beginning of the Jewish religious year, although in Palestine the civil new year (the Feast of the Trumpets) was the first of the seventh month, Tishri, in September or October. This was followed on the 10th of the month with Yom Kippur, the day of Atonement, when Israel solemnly mourned her sins. This was the occasion when the high priest entered the Holy of Holies in the temple at Jerusalem with the blood of sacrifice.

130

This sad time was relieved by one of the most popular feasts of the year, Booths or Tabernacles, when for seven days the people lived outside in makeshift structures to remind them of the time they lived in tents in the wilderness. It is just about the last time they could live outside as in the following month the early rains began to fall and the grain was planted out. Tabernacles was one of the three feasts (along with Passover and Pentecost) when the people came into Jerusalem from the countryside (John 7:1-4).

On 25th Kislev (November to December), they celebrated an event which happened between the Testaments. Hanukkah (short for 'the Cleansing of the House') or Dedication (John 10:22), reminded them of the dark days when their Syrian overlord, Antiochus Epiphanes, had attempted to force paganism on them. He had desecrated the temple, and martyred many of the faithful when a revolt led by Judas Maccabeus had turned the tide in their favour. Jerusalem was captured, and the temple rededicated. The weather can be very cold at this time of the year with even snow in the hill country (which is why kings like Herod had winter palaces at Jericho or by the Dead Sea, low enough to enjoy a pleasant climate in winter).

December to January is the rainy season in Palestine, although the latter rains in February to March are vital for a good crop (as this will be the last rain until late autumn). It is then, in the twelfth month (13th-14th Adar) that another great deliverance, this time from the Persian Haman, is commemorated with the Feast of Purim (Esther 9:26-28).

The barley harvest takes place the following month, Nisan, which is why the Feast of the Passover (Matthew 26:2), eaten on the 14th day, is followed a week later by the offering of the firstfruits. The general harvest takes place after this, so that seven weeks after Easter we remember Pentecost which, as Feast of Weeks and connected with the giving of the Law, was also a harvest festival (Acts 2:1). From then on the weather gets hotter and hotter, ripening first the grapes and then the olives, although the actual timing of these and the other harvests depends on how high or low the crop is growing. Crops growing in the Jordan valley ripen earlier than those growing in the hills.

that of the *Diaspora* settlers however, what with their fight for religious freedom, and even a brief period of political independence before the Romans took over.

As far as the Roman empire was

concerned, Palestine was not a very important place. The centre of the world was now Rome, and the way there from Egypt (which supplied it with huge amounts of grain) was by sea. At the same time the ancient trade routes through Palestine and around into the east (through the 'fertile crescent') had been disturbed in the north by the fierce Parthian raiders. The Romans led several campaigns against them, and well-protected caravans bringing things like silks and spices from China and India could still get through (although some preferred to cross the desert to the Nabataean city of Petra in southern Jordan). In practical political terms, Palestine had become something of a dead-end.

Jewish patriotism

It is hard to separate religious from political patriotism at this period. Their faith, their land and their unity as a people were closely interwoven.

●Herod the Great

In parts of the empire like Palestine, the Roman authorities usually felt safe enough to appoint a local ruler (or 'ethnarch', literally 'ruler of a people') to do their work for them. This is how the Jews came to be ruled by a person known as Herod the Great. Although only a half-Jew himself (his family having come from Idumea, that is ancient Edom), he had been granted authority over them and the title 'king'. Because of this and his high-handed behaviour, they bitterly resented him and hated both him and his family, even though his friendship with the Romans won them many concessions.

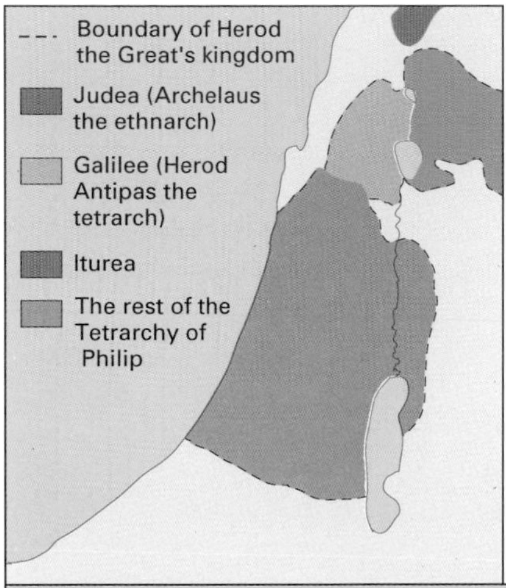

- - - Boundary of Herod the Great's kingdom
Judea (Archelaus the ethnarch)
Galilee (Herod Antipas the tetrarch)
Iturea
The rest of the Tetrarchy of Philip

23

The Herods. Left: the territories they ruled and below: a simplified family tree. *See also page 40.*

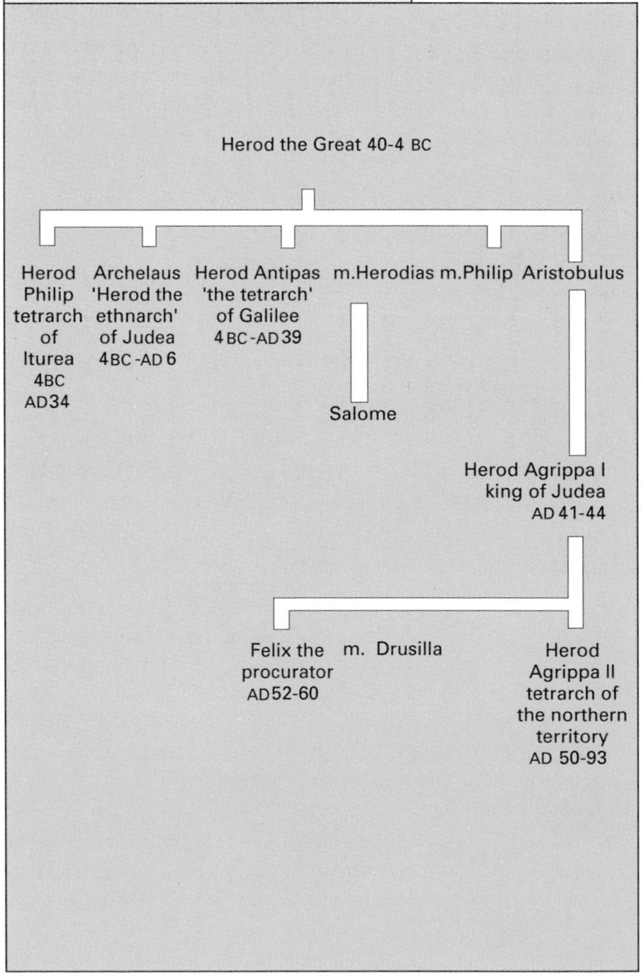

Herod the Great 40-4 BC

- Herod Philip tetrarch of Iturea 4BC AD34
- Archelaus 'Herod the ethnarch' of Judea 4BC-AD 6
- Herod Antipas 'the tetrarch' of Galilee 4BC-AD39 m.Herodias
- m.Philip
  - Salome
- Aristobulus
  - Herod Agrippa I king of Judea AD 41-44
    - Drusilla m. Felix the procurator AD52-60
    - Herod Agrippa II tetrarch of the northern territory AD 50-93

During his reign, he did his best to leave his mark on the country. He built for himself several palaces and fortresses. He rebuilt Samaria, and he constructed a whole new seaport city, naming it Caesarea after his patron. It became the centre for the civil administration of the country rather than Jerusalem. In the capital itself he spent many years rebuilding the temple and its courts. He spared no expense in creating the magnificent building which was known to Jesus and his disciples (Mark 13:1). He also built a race track, a sports arena and a theatre, the sort of thing you would find in most Greek-type cities in those days. For those who were attracted to Greek culture these were a good thing; to the orthodox Jews they represented a sell-out to worldly ways.

Towards the end of his life, he became a bitter and murderous old man, condemning several of his immediate family to death because he thought that they were plotting his overthrow. Although the massacre at Jesus' birth is not recorded elsewhere in history (Matthew 2:16), it is quite in character with what we know of the old tyrant.

● Herod's successors

When he died in 4 BC, he left his kingdom to three of his surviving sons. To Archelaus he bequeathed Judea, Samaria and Idumea, as 'king' (Matthew 2:22 – although the Romans disallowed this calling him 'ethnarch'). To Antipas went Galilee and Perea, east across the Jordan and the title 'tetrarch' (literally 'ruler of quarter of a nation': Luke 3:1), and to Philip he gave the north-eastern area of his domain. Archelaus did not last, proving to be as brutal but not as clever as his father, and he was replaced by a series of Roman governors (or 'procurators').

As Palestine was a political backwater, this job did not attract the best men. In fact, they went from bad to worse until eventually Pontius Pilate was appointed, and he governed from AD 26-36. He ruled absolutely, even controlling the temple funds and the priests' official clothing (without which they could not perform their duties). He had very little time for the Jews, and backed up his demands, frequently for cash, with the army. He alone had the authority to pass the death sentence, which is why Jesus was tried before him.

The Jews had a brief rest from Roman governors when Herod's grandson, Agrippa I, was allowed to rule over them. Although he had been educated in Rome and was on good terms with the Romans, he also behaved like a devout Jew and so got the support of the people. It was in order to please them that he persecuted the young church (Acts 12:1-3). He was succeeded by his son, Agrippa II, although the Romans also restored governors such as Felix and Festus whom we meet in the story of Paul (Acts 24). This Agrippa was also well versed in Jewish law, but did not keep it himself, and therefore the Jews had little time for him. It was before him that Paul defended himself (Acts 25:13–26:32).

● Scribes and Pharisees

The Jewish faith in Jesus' day was a very denominational affair. There was a variety of groups and parties believing different things, some concerned as much with political influence as with their religion.

As far as we can see, most of the parties we read about in the gospels

and Acts had their roots back in the time between the Testaments. During the time between the Old and New Testaments, those who copied out the Scriptures (the scribes) also became very influential as teachers of the Law. In Jesus' day there were many of these theologians who spent a good deal of time discussing ways of keeping the Law (they were often addressed as 'Rabbi' which originally meant 'great one' or 'Sir').

The Pharisees were the natural heirs to those faithful Jews who had hung on to their faith, and eventually fought for it, in the days when pressure on them to turn pagan had been intense. Their sincere concern had originally been to please God by keeping his laws. Unfortunately the way they did this was by adding a whole range of rules and regulations of their own (in the end they had over 600!). It was this tradition which the scribes and rabbis were continually discussing. There were two main schools of thought: some followed the great rabbi Shammai, who had been very strict, while

30-31

Marriage and family life

In New Testament times, youngsters had little say in whom they married. Marriages were arranged by their parents, usually when the young people were in their late teens. As the girl was seen as belonging to her father, this included paying him a bride price. Once a couple was betrothed, although they lived separately, they were regarded legally as husband and wife. Any children conceived during that period were accepted as legitimate. Should the groom die, his fiancée was regarded as a widow.

On the wedding day itself, the groom and his friends went to collect the bride – dressed in her finery and jewels – from her house, taking her and her attendants back to a feast at his own home (Matthew 25:1-13). The guests wore festive clothes (Matthew 22:11-12), and were well supplied with food and drink (John 2:1-11). The party might go on for some days.

Marriage was generally seen as permanent and lifelong, although one of the areas of debate in Jesus' day had to do with grounds for divorce (Matthew 19:3). The more liberal argued that a man might divorce his wife for almost any reason, while others felt that adultery was the only legitimate ground (only men had the right to divorce their spouses). Divorce dissolved the original partnership and allowed the partners to remarry. Infidelity was no longer punished by death (John 8:1-6) but an adulterous woman was ostracized by the rest of the community (as was the Samaritan woman drawing water at midday (John 4:4-7).

One of the wife's greatest achievements was seen as bearing children, especially sons who would carry on the family name. Childlessness was therefore a great sadness, just as childbirth was a great joy (Luke 1:57-58). A baby boy would be circumcised on the eighth day (Luke 2:21), and from his 13th birthday he would be regarded as a man, able to take his part in synagogue worship.

Children were very much under the authority of their parents. The father taught the whole household, and was seen as head of the family, expecting obedience and respect from his children. He would teach his son his trade, just as his wife would instruct her daughters in household duties.

others preferred the views of Hillel, who had been much more lenient in his interpretation of the Law.

Either way, the Pharisees frequently clashed with Jesus. Whereas they quoted the opinions of great rabbis like these, Jesus spoke with an authority all his own, and frequently contradicted their teaching. And yet although, as he pointed out, many of the Pharisees had become self-righteous hypocrites, not all of them were insincere. Some were on his side, and two, Nicodemus and Joseph of Arimathea, became his followers.

It took a great deal of effort to be a Pharisee, although any Jew could become one. Because of this, they were often respected as people who took their faith seriously. They were not always 'pharisaical'.

●Freedom fighters

Although their forbears had been prepared to fight for religious freedom, the Pharisees were quite content when they had it. They did not hanker after political independence like the Zealots (sometimes called 'Canaaneans', or 'Sicarii' – 'daggermen' because of the way they operated). These were the freedom fighters of the day, continually taking on the Romans in terrorist attacks and murders, and every now and then trying to stir up a general revolution. One of Jesus' followers, Simon, was a Zealot (Matthew 10:4).

Although they were not an officially recognized religious or political party they had a great deal of popular support because the Romans were so unpopular. Even before Jesus' day, there had been popular uprisings (Acts 5:36-37), and in AD 70 Jewish unrest would boil over into general rebellion. It isn't difficult to see that the Jewish authorities feared that Jesus and his followers might have had this in mind.

308

The sabbath

Once a week, from Friday sundown until the same time on Saturday, the pace of life changed dramatically for most Jews. For this was the sabbath, the traditional day of rest commanded by God in the Law, and in Jesus' day well observed by anyone who wanted to be known as a Jew. Sabbath-breakers were disowned by their neighbours who would never have thought of engaging in any kind of work on that day.

By Friday afternoon, the men completed their work and the women prepared food for the evening and the next day. They were summoned to the synagogue by three blasts on a ram's horn, as the stars came out, and after the service went home to a festive meal. It was synagogue once more on Saturday morning, and the day officially ended in the evening.

The Pharisees had the ritual worked out elaborately. They would tell you just what might or might not be done on the sabbath, including things like how far you might walk, and even what you might do to help others. It was in this area that Jesus clashed with them on several occasions, in that he healed people on the sabbath day, something which they considered to be work. Jesus not only argued that it was legitimate to do good on the sabbath (Mark 3:4), but that the sabbath had been given for man's benefit and should not be a burden. More, he claimed to be Lord of the sabbath, thereby putting himself above the Law, something for which they never forgave him (Mark 2:27-28).

Priests and Levites

Of all the tribes of Israel the tribe of Levi had been chosen to help administer the worship of Israel, and within this tribe the family of Aaron was chosen to provide the actual priests. Although the high priest was originally appointed for life, in Jesus' day it was as much a political as a religious position. This meant that high priests, who also served as leaders of the Sanhedrin, might be deposed and replaced (John 18:13).

Under the high priest were the chief priests, and below these were the ordinary priests. Between them they were responsible for leading the worship and offering the sacrifices in the Jerusalem temple. Although some of them lived in the city, most would come in from their homes in the country to serve their turn, when their names came up on a roster (Luke 1:8), along with the Levites whose jobs included every other aspect of running and regulating daily life in the temple. This included doorkeeping, singing, and looking after the offerings as well as serving as musicians and guards.

Although the old rule about not having land of their own seems to have been changed by New Testament times (Acts 4:36-37), priests and Levites generally lived on money donated as temple taxes. They were also allowed a share of the sacrifices, including the skins which could be sold for leather.

● Saddducees and the Sanhedrin

The people who did wield a great deal of influence in Jerusalem were the Sadducees. They comprised a core of high-priestly families, rich merchants, government officials and land owners. As far as their faith was concerned, they claimed to be conservative, accepting only the five books of Moses (Genesis to Deuteronomy). Because of this they differed on a whole number of issues from the Pharisees, and on one occasion, Paul cleverly exploited those differences (Acts 23:6-10). In practice they worked closely with the Roman authorities as they had most to lose by any disturbance of the peace.

As it was, the Romans were happy to give the Jews a measure of liberty in running their own affairs. This they did through a council (a 71-member body known by its Greek name as the 'Sanhedrin'). In Jesus' day, this was largely controlled by the high priest and the Sadducees, although the Pharisees were also well represented. This council had the delicate and difficult task of keeping what power and privileges they had under the Romans. They knew just how unstable some of the people were, and were quite prepared to sacrifice one man rather than risk trouble (John 11:45-50).

●Out in the desert

There were some who turned their backs on this political wrangling altogether. They do not appear in our New Testament, although John the Baptist might have had some links with them. These were the Essenes who set up a sort of monastery out in the wilderness by the shores of the Dead Sea. There they lived as a community, studying the Scriptures and writing their own religious books, many of which have been discovered (the 'Dead Sea Scrolls'). They believed that it would not be long before the Messiah came, and they wanted to be ready for him. Their writings are very important in the study of the New Testament because, although there is no direct connection, they show us how diverse Jewish thinking was.

69

●The people of the land

Meanwhile the ordinary people of the land, the peasant farmers, fishermen and craftsmen, had to get on and earn a living as best they could. They bitterly resented the Romans, who taxed them heavily. Even more, they hated those of their own race who collaborated with the occupying army and did their work for them. We often read about tax collectors in the gospels, and the fact that they were condemned as outcasts. Matthew was one before he became a follower of Jesus.

The average Jew, while not aspiring to the religious heights of the Pharisees, would do his best to keep God's law, attending the synagogue each week and ordering his work and family life accordingly. He would feel himself to be part of the chosen race in spite of the fact that the Promised Land was being run by pagans who had little respect for his rights or his religion.

●The Samaritans

If the Jew hated the Romans, he had even less time for the Samaritans. Samaria, sandwiched between Judea in the south and Galilee in the north, was populated by a mixed race dating back to the time when the Jews had been taken into exile. Even though they had adopted the Jewish faith, they had not been allowed to share in the rebuilding of the temple, and so had built their own on Mount Gerizim. Although this had been destroyed, in Jesus' day they were still regarded as heretics. Jews travelling from Galilee to Judea would cross over to the east bank of the Jordan rather than go through their territory. Jesus' dealings with Samaritans (John 4:1-42), like his accepting repentant tax collectors (Luke 19:1-10), must have seemed very shocking.

●Longing for freedom

In the circumstances, it's not surprising that the Jews' great hope and longing was that one day they might be free. What is more, they believed that, because God was on their side, it would happen. He would send them his own chosen leader and king, the Messiah, who would overthrow the Romans and set up the kingdom of God (although there were other ideas about the Messiah, this seems to have been the popular view).

It was into this scene that Jesus stepped, preaching with authority, working the sort of miracles they expected the Messiah to perform, even riding into Jerusalem in royal style (in those days, a good donkey was regarded a bit like a Rolls Royce). No wonder the crowds, not to say Jesus' own disciples, thought that freedom was in sight. And no wonder the Jewish authorities felt

that they had to do something with this man who seemed to be a dangerous agitator.

But although they thought that they had got rid of Jesus, they could not secure a lasting peace. Because of Roman mismanagement, there was continual unrest in the country, and the Zealots finally brought about an uprising in AD 66. They took over the whole country, starting in Galilee and actually occupying Jerusalem. But it was only a matter of time before the Roman backlash came. With frightful loss of life, the Roman troops overran the land. When they eventually got to Jerusalem, they besieged the freedom fighters in the temple area and, in fulfilment of Jesus' predictions, that wonderful building was destroyed (in AD 70). After that it was just a matter of mopping up, although it took three more years before they broke into the last stronghold, Masada, on the shores of the Dead Sea, one of Herod's fortress-palaces. The defenders there committed suicide along with their families, rather than become Roman slaves.

It was not to be the last time the Jews rose against the Romans. In AD 132 Bar Kochba claimed to be the Messiah and led a rebellion. This was brutally crushed three years later, and this time Jerusalem itself was destroyed and remodelled as an entirely pagan city.

The Romans

What sort of world was it in which the apostles first preached the Good News? From their point of view it was one with great advantages and disadvantages.

● The Roman peace

The Roman empire, of which Galilee to Judea was just part of a province, stretched from Britain down through Europe, into North Africa and Egypt, and the Middle East. It was efficiently run by a people with extremely tidy minds. One of the Roman strengths was administrative ability. They had won, and they meant to hold on to, their empire. It was a hard rule and the rights of ordinary people were, in practice, minimal. To be a Roman citizen like Paul was a great privilege. But there was peace – the *Pax Romana*, the Roman Peace they called it – and with peace trade flourished.

50

The Romans also brought fashions which offended strict Jews. See also 1 Peter 3:3.

The Romans were also great engineers, and we can still see the remains of well-constructed forts, public buildings, theatres, aqueducts and the like even today. They were magnificent road builders, and travel through the empire was easier than it had ever been. The seas were cleared of pirates and there were well-used trade routes round the coasts, although skippers preferred not to sail in winter (Acts 27:9; 28:11). It is interesting to see how frequently Paul took to the water although, as he himself tells us, travel was not without its risks (2 Corinthians 11:25-26).

Herod's temple

The temple in Jerusalem which Jesus and his disciples knew was the largest of a number of huge building works undertaken there by King Herod. He not only built himself a lavish palace, several towers and the Antonia fortress (named for Mark Anthony); in order to win over the Jews he set out to create what must have been one of the most splendid structures in the Near East.

Using 10,000 labourers, and 1,000 priests specially trained as carpenters and masons, he had the temple mound levelled and extended with massive supporting blocks until it covered about thirty acres. This vast area was surrounded by colonnades and included the meeting hall for the Jewish Sanhedrin. Within this space, known as the Court of the Gentiles, were three courts surrounded by rooms and colonnades and entered through elaborate gateways. The first was the Court of Women, marked out by a low wall with notices (one of which has survived) which forbade any Gentile from going further on pain of death (Acts 21:28). Inside this were the Court of Israel (normal limits for Jewish men) and the Court of the Priests where the altar was situated. Inside this was the temple proper, its inner sanctum, the Holy of Holies separated from the outer Holy Place by a curtain and, in Jesus' day, entirely empty (Matthew 27:51). The wooden Ark containing the Ten Commandments written on stone tablets had perished long ago when the first temple was destroyed.

51

Quite apart from the sacrifices offered by the priests, there was always a great deal going on in the temple courts. Teachers would meet there with their disciples. There would always be worshippers and visitors, and at the time of the great feasts the place would be packed with pilgrims from all over the world (Acts 2:9-11). As the temple tax was calculated in shekels, and the nearest currency to that was the Tyrian shekel, Roman money had to be changed into these at the money-changers' tables. Add the animals and birds waiting to be bought for sacrifice, and you will see that it could be a very busy and noisy place. No wonder Jesus reacted to it as he did by driving them out (Mark 11:15-17).

Herod spared no expense in the construction, using gold and marble to produce a startling sight for the visitor as he came over the Mount of Olives. 'Viewed from without', wrote Josephus, 'the Sanctuary had everything that could amaze either mind or eyes. Overlaid all round with stout plates of gold, in the first rays of the sun it reflected so fierce a blaze of fire that those who endeavoured to look at it were forced to turn away... to strangers as they approached it seemed in the distance like a mountain covered with snow; for any part not covered with gold was dazzling white.'

The building began in 19BC, and was not complete until AD64 (John 2:20). It was just six years later that, as Jesus had predicted (Mark 13:1-2), it was totally destroyed by the Romans. Only the huge blocks of stone which made up the base remain in place today.

Pagan belief and thought

All these things were generally in the favour of those first missionaries, but there were also difficulties, for there were already plenty of religions and cults competing for people's allegiance.

● Competing claims

The old national religions were in decline by New Testament times. Belief in the gods and goddesses of Greek and Roman mythology was no longer as popular as it had been, except in places where there was some major temple or shrine. This was the case at Ephesus where the city's life and economy were bound up with the great temple of Diana, in its time one of the wonders of the world. Looking at the massive remains of places like that today reminds us what that obscure band of Jews took on when they went out preaching the Good News about an executed Galilean peasant, and also of the amazing fact that Christianity eventually took over.

Not that there weren't other contenders for people's hearts and minds. The spiritual vacuum left by the decline of the older faiths was filled with a growing interest in astrology, magic and the occult. The ordinary person felt trapped in the world, his life under the control of impersonal fate. He was for ever looking for a way out.

What we know as the mystery religions claimed to be that way out. Sweeping the empire from Egypt and the East, they variously offered freedom, communion with the divine or secret knowledge. To receive these things, the worshipper had to go through many weird and wonderful initiation rites. Although some of these religions were frowned upon by the authorities because of their excesses, they had wide appeal and support.

Later on all kinds of myths and theories were to cluster around these ideas in a movement called Gnosticism. Some versions would take over some elements of the Christian message, and the church had to deal with it very strongly. But the roots are all there in the philosophic mish-mash of Greek and Oriental thinking.

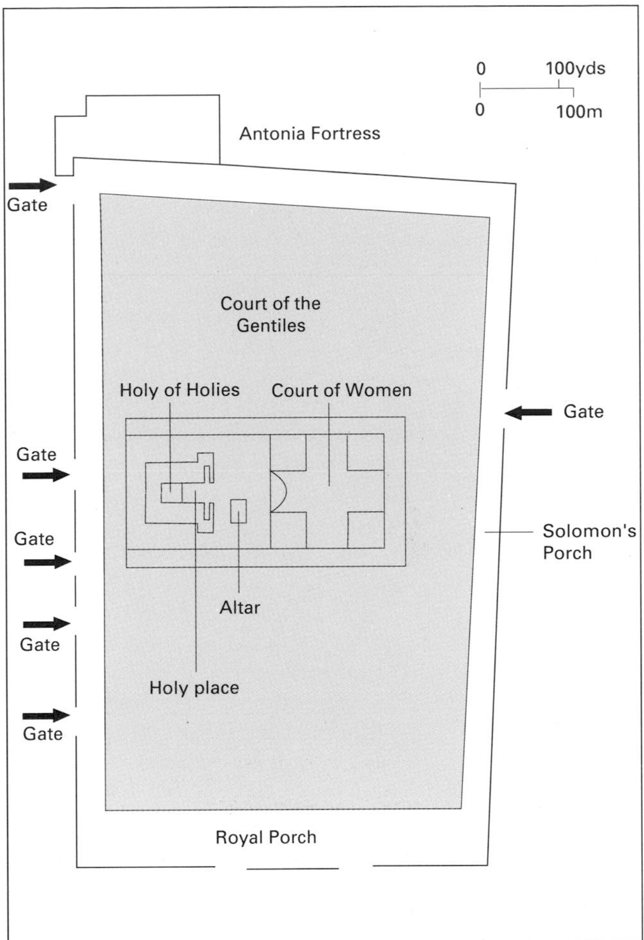

Plan of Herod's temple, Jerusalem (see facing page).

213

● Caesar is lord

Those in power had a different problem, and they came up with a solution which was to hurt Christians a great deal. They ruled over a vast and varied population which had very little to hold it together except Roman standing armies. Hence they invented a new religion for everyone, the worship of the emperor. This was not an original idea, as it had been practised in Egypt and the Middle East for many years, and it was somewhat artificial. It became, however, a sign and test of allegiance.

For the average pagan, this was not difficult (another god more or less did not really matter), but for Christians it became a frightful trial. How could they confess their faith in one God and one Lord and offer worship to a mere man? And yet if they refused to do so, their actions would be interpreted as a form of treason. If they refused, they were liable to be executed. During the first 300 years of the church's story, depending on who the emperor was or how the local magistrates enforced the law, Christians were to suffer fearfully in this way. Many would deny their faith and offer sacrifice (and receive a certificate to say that they had) rather than face the alternative. And if anyone had a grudge against a Christian, it was a good way to get even. If Christians were denounced, the authorities had to do something about it, even though normally they might be somewhat lax when it came to enforcement.

202-203

It seems from the book of Revelation that this had already begun to happen in New Testament times. Certainly as more and more Gentiles – and fewer Jews – became Christians, it became obvious to everyone that Christianity was not just another Jewish denomination. When that happened it lost its legal protection. In the early days people like Paul could appeal to the Roman magistrates for help against the Jews (Acts 18:12-17). Later, Christianity came to the notice of the state as a new faith, and Christians suffered as a result.

228-232

It seems strange to those of us living today in the West that there was no religious liberty in those days, especially when we learn just how free and easy everyday life had become. Although there were laws and social rules, behaviour in the Roman empire was what we would call 'permissive'. Personal morality, particularly in matters of sex, was very much your own affair, and although some reacted into extreme self-denial, the majority were content.

● Getting it wrong

So when the first Christian missionaries went out preaching about Jesus, there was plenty of spiritual hunger in the world, but also a welter of popular ideas which were anything but Christian. It was very easy to mix up the truth with error, and to import paganism into the church. But that's how we got our New Testament. Many of the letters, for example, were put together in order to help some group of Christians which was being influenced by some sort of error or false teacher. Elsewhere the apostles had to deal with pagan permissiveness which had crept into the church. And so they wrote to instruct, to correct, to encourage, and to warn in a generation which needed all of those things. It is as we become aware of the sort of problems their first readers faced that we will understand better what these writings can say to us today.

2.3 HOW TO INTERPRET THE BIBLE

by John F. Balchin

This section is all about how we get the message of the Bible off the printed page and into our lives, how to make *sense* of it all.

'How can I understand the Bible for myself?' you might ask. 'It's all right for those who have had a theological training or who have learned Hebrew and Greek, but what about those of us who haven't? How can I, with very little help, know what God is saying to me through his Word? Or do I really have to leave it to the experts?'

The answer to that one is both 'Yes' and 'No'; 'Yes' in the sense that there are some things in the Bible which are very hard to understand, and which even the experts can't agree on, and 'No' in that there is nothing to stop the ordinary person understanding a great deal on their own. But if that person is going to be you, you must be prepared to put a bit of work into it.

Asking the right questions

75

80

Interpreting the Bible is all about asking questions, which is the way we generally get information. We have been doing it from childhood when we first started asking 'Why?' or 'How?', and sorely tried our parents' patience in the process. The difference with direct Bible study, however, is that it's not merely a matter of asking someone we know about what this or that passage in the Bible means; we have to start asking the Bible itself or, if you like, the people who first wrote the Bible.

Of course, as with all interrogation, we will only get the right answers if we ask the right questions. It would be unfair to ask the Bible to answer questions it was never intended to answer. So if we are to understand the Bible at all, we must begin by going to it as it is, with an open mind, and asking that fundamental question, 'What did it say?', or put another way, 'What did the writer intend his readers to understand?

So when I open my Bible to read it for myself, I must first use both my mind and my imagination to put myself back in time to when those who wrote the Bible actually put the words together. The sort of thing I must be asking is, 'What did the apostle Paul mean when he composed this or that passage in his letters?' or 'Why did Jeremiah dictate those particular words in that order to his secretary?' Another way of putting it would be, 'If I were sitting with the first group to have this letter or prophecy read to them, what would I have understood by it?' Unless we begin here, we shall be guilty of doing what many have done throughout the history of the church, and that is to read things into the Bible which simply are not there. Generally they had decided already what they wanted to believe, before going to the Bible to hunt for passages or verses which propped up those beliefs. In this way they replaced, 'What did it say?' with, 'What do I want it to say?' something which is still a temptation today. For example, 'Use a little wine because of your stomach (1 Timothy 5:23), does not mean that drinking alcohol is always good for everybody!

● Taking it all literally?

When the Reformers came on the scene, about 400 years ago, they found the whole science of understanding the Bible in a considerable mess. Because that first, basic question had been neglected, there seemed to be no end to what different people had made of the Bible stories and Bible teaching. In fact, it was seen to be especially 'spiritual' if you could find hidden meanings in the most straightforward of Bible passages.

How not to do it

We have plenty of examples from the history of the church of how we should not deal with the plain, straightforward teaching of the Bible. Perhaps the biggest mistake that Christians ever made was to try to see secret 'spiritual' meanings beneath the surface. In this way they turned many of the Bible stories into what we call 'allegories'.

Take, for example, what the influential North African bishop, Augustine, did with the story of the Garden of Eden. The four rivers mentioned became the four cardinal virtues, the fig leaves represented hypocrisy, and the skins with which Adam and Eve were eventually clothed were supposed to indicate their mortality. All of which is nothing more than the product of a lively imagination. It has nothing to do with the plain statements of Genesis.

Or take his treatment of that beautiful praise passage, Psalm 104. For him, mention of the sun 'going down' must speak of Christ's death, references to beasts are understood as persecutors, while lying down to sleep indicates Jesus' death and resurrection (verses 19-22).

Much later, the well-known medieval theologian, Thomas Aquinas, was still playing the same game. For him, John the Baptist must represent Christ (after all, 'John' means 'gift of God'), while the fact that he ate locusts and wild honey must refer to his preaching. It was sweet like honey, but swift in flight like locusts. That's not all. His camel-hair dress represents the non-Jewish Christians! It meant that, with the right sort of manipulation, you could find support for anything you wanted in the Bible. In fact, one theologian said, 'Learn first what you should believe, and then go to the Bible to find it there'. No wonder that the Reformers insisted that we take seriously what the Bible actually says, and then build our beliefs on that, and Bible scholars today all agree that they were right.

This is why one of the ways in which they reformed the situation was to insist that we should begin with what they called 'the plain and literal sense' of Scripture. This is not the same as 'taking everything in the Bible literally'. After all, there are some things in Scripture which it would be wrong to take 'literally'. There is a great deal of poetry which has to be understood as poetry, and there is fiction too – for example, Jesus' parables were fiction.

Ordinary metaphors cannot be taken literally. Jesus said, 'I am the bread of life.' Surely the last thing he intended was that we should worship a loaf. If we are going to understand what the original authors intended their first readers to understand, we will have to recognize that the Bible is not just words; it is *literature*. It is the skilled use of words to create certain effects. In order to get over the truth they had to share in ways that would grip their readers, and lodge in their memories, they used words in particular ways. Look at English literature, from thrillers to Shakespeare, and you will see the way in which the authors use the English language. It isn't all one sort of writing. Some paint pictures using words like brush strokes; others get your pulse racing with short terse sentences. Some make their statements bald and factual. Some take off into poetry.

Just as later writers have used all kinds of methods for getting across what they wanted to say, so the authors of the Bible books used a variety of styles. Some may seem strange to modern eyes and ears. For example, Hebrew poetry is not much like our traditional idea of

poetry. It does not rhyme and it follows different rules. Or take the dramatic picture language of a book like Revelation. It seems odd to us today, but it obviously meant a great deal to the people for whom it was first written.

228-232

What the Reformers re-established was the principle that, when we come to the Bible, we should try first and foremost to understand what the Bible authors actually meant by the words they used. Take Jesus' parables, for example. When we read them, we do not assume that all the characters actually existed or that the events took place (although some were clearly based on things that had happened). We look for the lesson which is wrapped up in the story. But when we turn to the Old Testament and read some of the great accounts of Israel's history, we take them as they are – as the story of God's people – and not as some gigantic *Pilgrim's Progress* where every character or event has some hidden spiritual meaning.

344-348

The Reformers were right. Common sense tells us that nowadays. It's not being clever or spiritually-minded to make the Bible say what it doesn't. It stands to reason that if we want to understand what someone has written, we must take what they say seriously and not read some meaning of our own into their words. That would be unfair and untrue, just as it would be unfair to read all kinds of hidden motives and meanings into a letter from a friend. If we did that we would be simply misleading ourselves, and the results would tell us more about ourselves than about our friend's intentions.

So then our first job, when it comes to understanding the Bible, will be to try to get into the shoes of those who first wrote and read it. And that will take hard work and imagination, because it was all written a long time ago, when the world was a very different place.

Back in time

If we are to grasp what the Bible is saying we need not only proper principles of interpretation but also *imagination*. What was it like in those days? Fortunately it is not just guesswork. We can call on the archaeologists, who make it their task to dig back into time. Patient archaeological work has done much to reconstruct what it was like in Bible times. Archaeologists have taken literally years to excavate dozens of sites in the Near East. They have found everything from the remains of huge buildings to tiny ornaments. They have dug up kings' palaces as well as the remains of the houses of ordinary people. They have sifted through ancient rubbish heaps and painstakingly taken apart ancient graves.

For most of us, the whole operation might breathe mystery and treasure hunting. However, some of their most valuable finds have been pieces of pottery which have helped them to fix the date of what they have been excavating. Some of their most exciting have been scrolls of the Bible and other ancient books, thousands of years old.

As a result of all this, they have been able to fill out the picture of how things were in Bible times – things like the sort of houses people lived in, their customs and the way in which they behaved from day to day, what they cooked and ate, how they dressed, how their society was ordered, how they conducted their business, how they organized home and family life. They have reconstructed the campaigns that their kings fought, and their periods of settled occupation. Details like these are important if we are going to step into that world in our imagination in order to get the full impact of the words of the Bible books when they were first written.

Of course, to learn everything that has been discovered in these ways would take most of us more time than we have. Even if you went to a theological college and took a

What archaeologists do

When a place was lived in, those who lived there left behind all kinds of evidence for later researchers. They threw things away, like broken jars or bones (very useful for telling us what they ate). Sometimes they lost articles like coins or ornaments. Every now and then small hoards of valuables turn up, which might have been either a cache of stolen goods, or something buried for safety's sake (in the days before secure banks this was quite common, especially in times of war).

Frequently archaeologists come across graves with bones and other articles buried in them. They then become forensic scientists, working out the age and sex of those who died, and sometimes the cause of death. Sometimes, as a result of some disaster like an earthquake or a fire, all manner of things were buried just waiting to be dug up later. A layer of ash is often the tell-tale indicator that some such tragedy has occurred. In recent years, underwater archaeology, which involves the locating of the remains of ancient ships and their cargoes, has made great strides.

There is also written evidence from the past. There are the official inscriptions, with which every administration likes to decorate its buildings in order to perpetuate its name. There are the records which come down to us from before the invention of paper. Digging in the Near East has produced literally thousands of clay tablets, many of which are still undeciphered. Papyrus, the ancient equivalent to paper, made in Egypt, has only survived in places where it is extremely hot and dry, but vellum, animal skins prepared for writing, is much more common. Sometimes archaeologists come across part of, or even complete, manuscripts, either of Bible books or of other writings.

But their job does not end there. Having collected and recorded all this evidence, they then have to reconstruct the world of those who used these things. They can tell some things easily. For example, well constructed buildings or advanced writing tell them that the people of those days were both skilled and sophisticated. Articles which come from different places found at the same location tell them much about trade in those days, while the remains of ancient field and irrigation systems show them just how advanced their agriculture was.

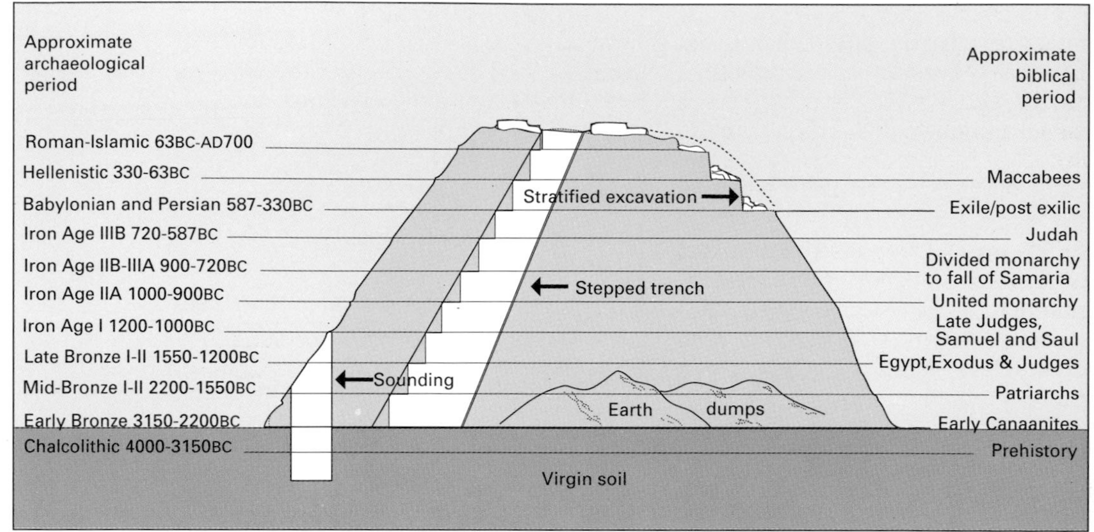

Ruin mounds (tells) are made up of one layer of history above another, the most recent at the top. This simple diagram shows how archaeologists uncover the past.

degree in biblical studies, you would only receive a broad introduction to the whole subject, while being told where you could find out more. But we do not need to go to college for much of this – if we read English, that is.

364-368

Many of these findings have been collected in works like Bible dictionaries, which deal with Bible subjects and words in order, and in Bible commentaries, which go through each Bible book explaining the background to statements as they go along. Some of these are written for people like students and ministers who have already had a theological training, but there are others which bring this information to the ordinary reader without too many technical terms.

● Getting the dates right

When did the events of the Bible take place? The only way we can be anything like sure is to check them against dates that we know in the outside world. This means comparing something referred to in the Bible with dated inscriptions or written accounts of the same event elsewhere. For example, we know from documents outside the Bible that Herod the Great died in 4 BC, which means that the birth of Jesus must have taken place before that time (strange though that may seem). We know, from an inscription, that when Gallio was proconsul in Corinth, it was around AD 51, and so we know when Paul visited the city, as he was accused before Gallio. We can say similar things about the dating of the reigns of the kings in the Old Testament, comparing the Bible accounts with the records of Egypt, Assyria and Babylon.

Cross-references like this give us fairly accurate dates, but archaeologists have other ways of telling when a thing took place. When a succession of people lived in one place, they tended to build their houses and town walls on top of the remains of those who had lived

there before. In this way, over the years, a mound, or *tell*, builds up. By cutting a trench into the mound, rather like cutting into a layered cake, archaeologists will be able to see the different stages in the development and occupation of that place.

Quite apart from inscriptions and other written finds, they have a number of clues when it comes to putting dates to the different layers. One of the most common is the pottery remains. Although earthenware pots break, the bits are almost indestructible. If they find a particular style of pot in a particular layer, the chances are that they can roughly date those remains. In this way, they can trace the history of the place through a succession of bits of broken pot!

At the other end of the range they have the sophisticated radio-active dating methods which need a well-equipped laboratory. Because of the way living things take in radiation, and then lose it over a number of years, articles like pieces of wood or cloth can tell us within certain limits when they were growing.

Taken all together, methods like these can give us a broad idea of when the sites of biblical towns were occupied, and this in turn can be fitted in with the happenings recorded in the Bible. Some are more exact than others, but many are approximate at the best. One of the reasons for this is that, although the writers do sometimes give us a hint of a date, generally they were not as interested in dates as we are. They were much more concerned with what happened and why.

A related problem – for us, not for them – is when the books of the Bible were written themselves. Although we can get a fairly clear idea about some of them, like some of the Old Testament prophecies or some of the New Testament letters, we simply do not know when most of the Bible books came together.

Over the language barrier

Other scholars have been working hard to solve another of our difficulties, for the simple fact is that the Bible was not written in English. The Old Testament is mostly in Hebrew with a little Aramaic (which is like Hebrew), and the New Testament is in Greek. Some find that hard to take. 'If only I could read the Bible in its original languages', they will tell you, 'I would be able to understand it'. In fact, some spend a great deal of time and effort trying to master New Testament Greek on their own or in evening classes in that belief. There is a sense in which they are both right and wrong.

They are right, of course, in that unless we get an accurate translation of the original words, so that we know exactly what the authors were trying to say, we will never really understand the message of the Bible for ourselves. And there was a time in Europe when ordinary people were denied just that. Such Bibles as existed were in Latin, which no-one except priests and scholars could understand. If you have a particular interest in foreign languages there are both correspondence and evening class courses available in Hebrew and, more commonly, Greek nowadays. They involve a great deal of work, but can be very rewarding, if you are able to stay the course. But let's not forget that to

73-77

get a thorough-going grasp of biblical languages is a life-time's work, work which others have already done for us.

There are scholars whose one aim in life is to understand the actual wording of the Bible in its original languages. It's a job that will never end because every now and then discoveries are made which throw a flood of light on what the Bible authors actually wrote. These have to be examined and weighed, and the results built into the on-going work of Bible translation.

239

The other reason why their work is never finished is that English itself, being a living language, is slowly and subtly changing all the time. We have only to compare the way in which ordinary people speak today with the way they spoke even a hundred years ago. Read some of the novels written then, and you will see how strange and stilted the way they spoke seems to us. What is more, it's a process of change which is speeding up all the time, especially because of the mass media. Words and expressions are coined or borrowed, and then pass into ordinary, everyday usage very quickly indeed.

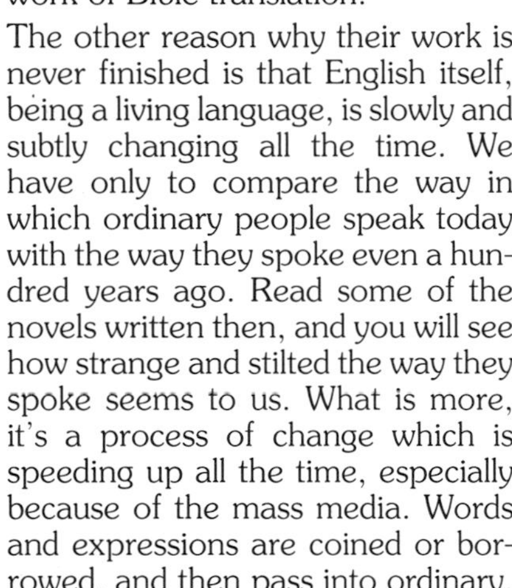

368

●Bible versions

Because of all this, the average person would do well to get hold of a good translation. What we want is one which is as near to the original text as possible. After all, our first aim is to find out what the Bible actually meant when it was first written. Versions like the *New International* or the *Revised Standard* not only stick fairly closely to the Hebrew and Greek, they take into account the large amount of work done on the biblical manuscripts in recent years. Other versions may seem easier to read, and sometimes their racy, up-to-date English helps us to understand things better, but they are not always as accurate as translations. A good approach, of course, is to get hold of several different versions (say the *Good News Bible*, the *New International Version* and the *Revised Standard Version*) and to compare them with one another.

We have already said that Bible dictionaries are useful for understanding the background to the Bible; they are also good for understanding the exact meaning of words and how they were used. Words alter in meaning when they are used in different ways. For example, when Paul talked about 'faith', he usually meant nothing less than wholehearted commitment to Jesus as Lord (see Romans 1:5) . When James used the same word, he was talking about a head knowledge of the facts, which did not affect a person's behaviour (James 2:14-19). On the surface, it may seem that they were contradicting one anoth-

Personal encounter

The Bible and the truths it teaches are not an end in themselves. They are a means to an end. Perhaps the most curious and the most wonderful feature of it all is that the Holy Spirit uses an ancient book to introduce us to a living Person. It is through Scripture that we not only learn about Christ, we come to know him. This is more than rediscovering some interesting character from the past by reading their biography. This is coming into a person-to-person encounter with the risen Christ who is as alive today as when he first rose from the dead. The One you discover, the One you hear speaking to you from the pages as you read the Bible is no less than the Son of God himself.

er, but if we examine what they say more closely, we see that they were simply using the same word in two different ways.

●Some golden rules

All this reinforces a basic lesson when it comes to understanding what the Bible is saying: try to understand a word or a statement in its original setting. We call it 'putting the text in its context'. Politicians, film-stars and other people in the public eye often complain about journalists who, they say, misquote them. What the reporters are frequently doing, of course, is to isolate something they said from the rest of the interview, which might have been harmless enough when taken along with everything else, but which on its own is scandal or political dynamite.

In the same way, Bible words and statements have to be read against the background of the whole book in which they are found, and that means taking the trouble to read more widely than just the chapter you happen to be studying. By picking and choosing from this verse and that, however, you could prove almost anything you like from the Bible, and there are some cults and sects that operate that way. It might be clever; it's not good Bible study.

This leads us to another golden rule. If I am dealing with a passage which I find particularly difficult, I often find it helps to look up what it says in easier passages on the same subject in other parts of the Bible. If I am finding it hard, for example, to understand something Jesus said, I will first of all hunt around the rest of his teaching to see if he dealt with that subject elsewhere in a way which might throw light on it. In this way, I am comparing a harder passage of Scripture with an easier one. But I need not stop there. Because it was the same Holy Spirit who prompted and controlled all the writers of the Bible books, I can extend my search more widely. I may find the answer in something which Peter or Paul wrote, or I may find the clue I need to understanding Jesus' words in the Old Testament.

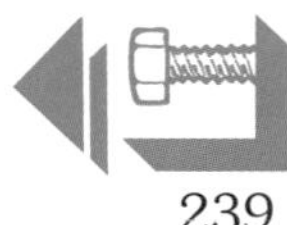

239

The Old Testament is especially important in this way when it comes to understanding the New Testament. It seems that nearly all those who wrote the books of the New Testament were brought up as Jews. This means that they had been taught the Old Testament from childhood. What is more, they accepted and respected it as the Word of God. It carried the stamp of his own authority. For Jews, what *it* said *he* was saying. It's no surprise, therefore, that we find many, many references to Old Testament themes and incidents in the New Testament. In fact, we will not really understand

86

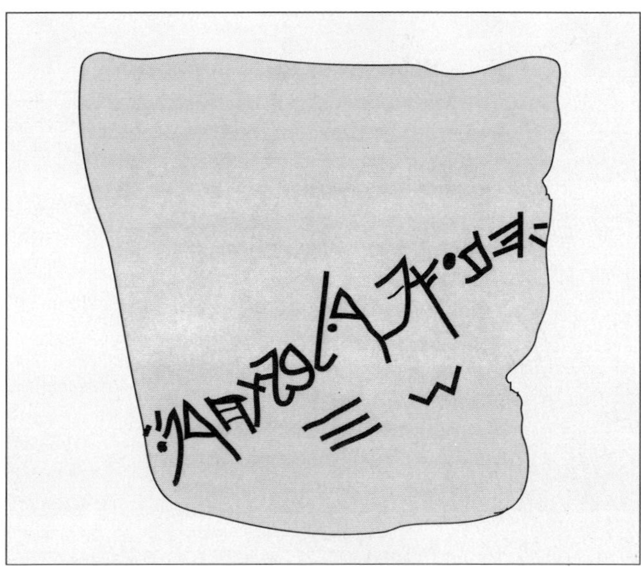

Ancient Hebrew writing (8th century BC). This inscription reads, 'gold of Ophir for Beth Horon, 30 shekels'.

the New Testament if we neglect the Old. Many of the actual words which the New Testament writers used come from the Old Testament, and have to be understood against their Old Testament background. It's just another case of remembering to read the words of the Bible in their setting. In this case, we acknowledge that the proper setting for the whole of the New Testament is the Old Testament.

●Bible languages

The Bible was written in three languages, Hebrew, Aramaic and Greek.

68-69

The Old Testament is mostly Hebrew, the language spoken in Israel during those times. It looks totally unlike written English. It is read from right to left (so that a modern version of the Hebrew Scriptures begins 'at the back', as far as we are concerned). It was originally written without vowels, that is, if we wrote the last statement that way it would appear like this:

'T WS 'RGNLL' WRTTN WTHT VWLS

This might seem an impossible way of writing. In theory, a word like BBL could read Babel or Bible. In practice, however, it is not so. The way the words are pronounced depends on where they come in the sentence, and there are rules for working out how they should sound. There are some places in the Hebrew Old Testament where the exact meaning of a word is unclear, but these are rare and, in such instances, the Jews had traditional ways of pronouncing them. Eventually they wrote the vowel sounds in, under and over the letters.

Aramaic was written in the same script as Hebrew; in fact Hebrew was a dialect of Aramaic, which was a language spoken widely throughout the Middle East in Old Testament times. There is very little Aramaic in the Old Testament (chiefly Ezra 4:8-6:18 and Daniel 2:4-7:28, together with a number of words and phrases). By Jesus' day, Hebrew had become a dead language, in that no-one spoke it any more. But all Jewish boys learned it in synagogue school so that they could publicly read from the Scriptures on the sabbath day.

The mother tongue which Jesus and his friends spoke, and the language in which he taught, was Aramaic, and we have several Aramaic words preserved for us in the gospels. For example, Jesus' awful cry from the cross, 'Eloi, Eloi, lama sabachthani?' is Aramaic for 'My God, my God, why have you forsaken me?' (Mark 15:34). One of the earliest administrative problems facing the early church was a dispute between Aramaic-speaking Christians, who were native to Palestine, and Greek-speaking Christians, who were immigrants (Acts 6 :1-6).

WYCLIFF	about 1380
TYNDALE (NT only)	1526
COVERDALE ('GREAT BIBLE')	1539
GENEVA BIBLE	1560
AUTHORIZED (AV or 'KING JAMES ')	1611
REVISED (RV)	1885
AMERICAN STANDARD (ASV)	1901
REVISED STANDARD (RSV)	1952
NEW AMERICAN STANDARD (NASB)	1963
JERUSALEM BIBLE (JB)	1966
NEW ENGLISH BIBLE	1970
LIVING BIBLE (LB)	1971
GOOD NEWS BIBLE (GNB)	1976
NEW INTERNATIONAL VERSION (NIV)	1978
REVISED ENGLISH BIBLE (REB)	1989

Checklist: major English translations.

53-54

The New Testament, however, is not written in Aramaic, but in Greek. This is not the 'Classical Greek' which, along with Latin, used to take up much of the syllabus in schools in the old days. It was a simpler, more widely used version of the language which was spoken all over the Roman empire, but especially in the East where Alexander the Great had made his conquests. This is because, although the official language of the day was Latin, the Romans took over much of the culture of the Greeks whom they in turn had conquered.

Our English Bible

The first successful attempt to put the Bible into language that every English-speaking person could read was by John Wycliff back in the 15th century. He translated the Latin which was used in churches, and his travelling preachers, the Lollards, took the message all over England. They suffered a great deal for their efforts, and although Wycliff himself was spared during his lifetime, his work was suppressed by the church authorities after his death.

In 1526 William Tyndale produced a translation of the New Testament from the origninal Greek. Outlawed in England, he had to live and work on the Continent. There he had it printed, and it was smuggled into the British Isles. He was eventually betrayed and captured, paying for his efforts with his life. In 1539, however, Miles Coverdale produced a complete translation, and within years, King Henry VIII was persuaded to order Bibles to be placed in every parish church in the land. There were a number of versions current at this time, and it was not until 1611 that these were 'standardized' with what we know as the *Authorized Version* (AV), or *King James Version.*

An excellent translation for its time, it left an indelible mark on English language and literature. Even a revision from earlier manuscripts in the 19th century (the *Revised Version*, 1881-1885) did nothing to replace it in popularity. Since then there have been many other attempts to put the Bible into modern English, some by individual translators like Weymouth, Moffatt or Phillips, and some by committees of scholars like the *American Standard Version* (1901), the *Revised Standard Version* (1952), the *Jerusalem Bible* (1966), the *New English Bible* (1970), the *Good News Bible* (1976), the *New International Version* (1978) and the *Revised English Bible* (1989). And there have been others. For example, the *Living Bible* was one man's attempt to bring the Bible right up to date, for family reading, while the *New King James Version* tries to retain the power of the old *Authorized Version* with modern terms and phrases.

The main reason why there are so many translations is that it is always very difficult to know just how far to go when putting the Bible into modern language. Languages work with different rules, and have different forms of expression, particularly what we call 'idioms'. English is full of them. That's why people from overseas are often confused when we talk about things like 'leg pulling' or 'turning tables' and the like. And American idioms are often very different from British! An exact and literal understanding of phrases like that would read like nonsense. However every language, including Hebrew and Greek, has them and that is why a word for word Bible translation would sound very strange.

This meant that, if you spoke Greek, you could be understood wherever you went, even though normally people might speak in their own local languages. Paul and Barnabas had difficulty over this when they went to Lystra (Acts 14:8-11). Most of the people of Palestine, including Jesus and his friends, would probably have been able to speak both Aramaic and Greek. This arrangement had great advantages. Trade was very easy, and the earliest Christian missionaries did not have to learn another language when it came to preaching the gospel.

There was another advantage in that the Old Testament had been translated into Greek some time before the birth of Christ, and this version was widely available. This meant that young Christians could read the Bible, as it was in those days, in a language with which they were familiar. It was also natural for the early Christian leaders, when they wanted to communicate with the churches, to write in Greek, and in this way our New Testament began to take shape.

● The wonderful world of manuscripts

242-243

Can we be sure that the Bible, as we have it, is really what was originally written? When the books of the Bible were first put together printing had not been invented. This meant that they all had to be hand-written on materials like papyrus, an ancient form of paper made from reeds, or on parchment or vellum, which was made from the skins of animals. They then had to be copied many times over if they were to circulate as books.

We do not have any part of the Bible as it was originally written down. The original pieces of writing material, whether they contained Moses' laws or Paul's letters have long since perished. What we have are thousands of copies of copies.

Copying a hand-written document is not very easy. Although the ancient secretaries were trained to do it – and in fact did it very well – you can see how easily mistakes could creep in. Letters or even words could be missed out, only to be copied by the next generation of scribes, or worse, to be 'corrected' into something which sounded more reasonable, but which by this time was quite different from the original.

This means that, over the years, all kinds of minor differences crept into the copies, all of which has left a fascinating detective job for Bible scholars. The people who specialize in this sort of work painstakingly attempt to reconstruct what was the original writing. For this they not only have a mass of manuscripts, they also have very early quotations from the Bible, sometimes older than the manuscripts, in the Christian writings of the first two or three hundred years of church history. As well as these there are a number of old translations, into languages like Latin or old Egyptian, which were made from very early copies of Bible books. Even some of the very late copies can be very useful, especially if they go back to a high-quality earlier copy.

By comparing the different manuscripts, and by applying rules which have been carefully worked out and tested over the years, the experts try to come up with what was most likely to be the original. It is from this that our modern translations are made.

It sounds a somewhat chancy busi-

ness. Can we really be sure that we do have what the Bible authors wrote? In terms of complete detail, the answer to that one must be 'No'. Having said this we need to remember that the differences are so small that no major teaching of the Christian faith is affected by them. Moreover, fresh discoveries of ancient manuscripts come to light every few years, and these are continually increasing our knowledge in this area.

For example, when the famous Dead Sea Scrolls were discovered in Palestine in the 'fifties, along with them were copies of the Hebrew Old Testament which were about a thousand years earlier than any version we had had previously. It's a tribute to the ancient scribes that, in spite of being copied many times in the intervening years, the main texts were very close to the ones which scholars had been using.

So, although we have to say technically 'No', we do not have *exactly* what the original authors wrote, we can follow that with a resounding 'Yes!' we do have all that they meant to tell us, or, even more importantly, all that God intends to tell us through them. In the light of that truth some of the dots and commas don't matter too much.

Greek text of the New Testament: a fragment of John (10:31 – 11:10). 3rd century AD.

Into another world

It's obvious even from a surface reading of the Bible that people like Abraham, or David or Peter had a very different lifestyle from ours. Whether it was cooking, farming, dressing or any other ordinary, everyday exercise, our customs and modern technological know-how put us in a different world. Not the least, of course, was the fact that their machines were very simple. They had wheels, pullies, ropes and levers, but when it came to energy, they were largely restricted to the muscle power of man or beast, in contrast to all the sophisticated resources that we tap in our homes, on our streets, in our factories and on our farms today.

Because technology has made such strides which have affected all of us, we might be tempted to think of our predecessors as primitive and uninformed. There was so much that they did not know, and so much that they could not do that we might write them off as not having any-

72

thing to teach us. Before we do that let's remember that people were just as intelligent then as they are now. Most original human thinking comes from the ancient world. They did not have the know-how we possess but many of the things that they did were very ingenious. In fact, we have lost many of the skills that they possessed.

●The God-dimension

Something which is harder to understand is the fact that they not only lived differently from us, they also thought differently from us. This is not to say that they did not think logically, it's just that the whole framework of their thinking was different from ours. One of the big draw-backs of the Hollywood productions of Bible stories is that, in spite of the pains they take to get the background right – deserts or cities and the like – they generally assume that the characters speak, think and respond like western Anglo-Saxon protestants! Actually what we call their 'world-view', that is, the way they saw and thought about reality, was different from ours today. It is this which frequently makes it hard for us to read the Bible as it was first written.

72,75

One of the biggest differences between Bible times and ours is the way that they accepted that there was a supernatural dimension to things. Whether it was God, gods, demons or magic, everyone took it for granted. Everyone believed that spiritual beings not only existed, they exerted an enormous influence on the everyday lives of ordinary people. They had to be taken into consideration at every turn. And this was as true for those who did not believe in the God of the Bible as for those who did.

If you have had experience of a non-western culture, you should be able to appreciate this more easily, because in many places in the world today, particularly in the Third World, many people have this same approach to life. It may express itself in a variety of ways from rank superstition to a deep faith in God, but it's something which is part and parcel of their everday lives.

Most who read this book, however, will have been reared in what we call a secular world, that is a world where all belief in the supernatural is deemed to be unnecessary. We have been educated and conditioned into thinking this way. We have been told from childhood that you can understand everything in purely natural terms, and that the idea of supernatural powers is not only unnecessary, it's rather ignorant. We have been told, and many believe, that the world itself came into existence by natural chance, something which also sums up the events of our everyday lives.

Many say that they believe in God and sometimes pray to him but think of him only as a vague creator figure. He would never step into the stream of human life and history to change or guide the course of events. It simply would not happen that way, or so we have been taught to assume. And so the modern, western, secular person lives from day to day, theoretically at least, without any thought for God. What is more, if questioned about it, they would no doubt reply that they had no need for God either. Some would even tell you that the very idea of God is nothing more than the product of our own psychological insecurity. Man lives and dies as an animal, or as a thing. His life has no spiritual dimensions or significance.

This causes real problems for many who, having accepted these ideas with their minds, find that in the business of living, we need more than this. That apart, it also causes problems when it comes to understanding the message of the Bible. We are so conditioned that we simply assume that the way we are used to thinking about the world must be normal, and that every other way of thinking about it must be 'primitive', 'unsophisticated', 'ignorant' or 'misguided'. But this means that what was acceptable faith in Bible times must be really nothing more than superstition.

What about miracles?

In the past, far too many have come to the Bible – and even written about it – with this sort of 'we know better' attitude, and with devastating results. After all, you cannot go far into the Bible without falling over the supernatural – no further than the first words, in fact! But if the supernatural does not really exist, then it has to be explained away, and this is frequently what has happened. How do you cope with the many miracles in the Bible, not to mention Jesus' own life and ministry, if you do not believe in supernatural happenings? You have to conclude that the people who recorded these things would believe anything, or that they were the biggest liars out, or that they were simply mistaken. If supernatural events cannot happen, there must be a natural explanation somewhere.

So, for example, even though the gospel says it happened, Jesus could not have walked on water. After all, if you tried it, you would fall in! So it must have been shallow there, and the disciples were mistaken in thinking that he did. Nor could he have turned water into wine at the wedding feast. Perhaps the guests were too drunk by that time to notice the difference. And what about the resurrection? When people are dead, although there might be the chance of resuscitating them straight away (if you know the modern techniques, that is), they are dead for good. So resurrection is impossible, and there must have been some other explanation of Jesus' appearances to his disciples after he had been buried. Either he wasn't really dead when they laid him in the tomb, or they had some kind of mass illusion, or it was just wishful thinking.

So we could go on, and many do, but we only need to if we take it for granted, as an article of faith, that our modern, western way of looking at things is the only right and normal way. It never seems to occur to many that we might be wrong with our very starting point, and that, by leaving out the supernatural altogether, the very way in which we *think* is actually deficient and unreal.

For the committed Christian it means a good deal of unlearning and relearning. The fact, not only that God really exists, but that he chose to reveal himself to the world as he did in the Bible, should make us pause and consider. In a real sense, we are not passing judgment on the Bible and its teachings; they are passing judgment on us and on our ways of thinking. Which is more reliable; our thinking or theirs?

All this means that if we are going to read the Bible as it was first written we must come with truly open minds. It may mean discarding or suspending some of our ways of thinking which we have always regarded as 'normal', or even 'modern', 'scientific' or 'enlightened'. We must be prepared to admit that we might have got it wrong and that the world of the Bible authors might be more truly normal than our own. If we are not prepared to do this, if we insist that they must have been wrong or misguided every time their way of thinking comes into conflict with ours, we are not really giving the Bible a chance to speak to us.

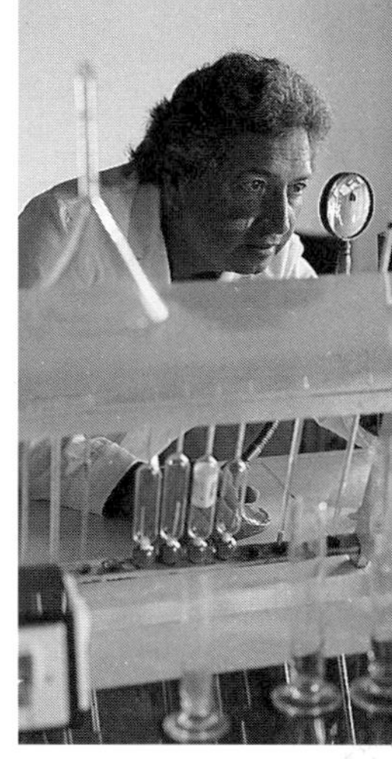

181

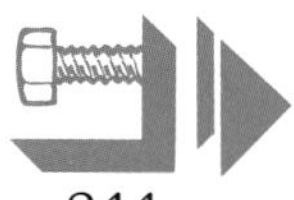

244

● Science versus faith?

We are frequently told that to believe in the Bible – or in God, even – is 'unscientific', and that is why we have discarded these beliefs in this modern, scientific age. But this is really a misuse of the word 'scientific'.

Science is, and always has been, the study of the world in which we live. It asks how things work, and how they relate to other things. Scientific method, which we have become used to, involves carefully examining all the facts available and then attempting to describe the processes involved and discovering 'laws' (what usually happens).

The scientist is enabled to do this – or hampered in his research – by the sort of instruments he has at his disposal. If he cannot learn all the significant facts about something his theories will be necessarily flawed.

In ancient times, when those who described the world had little to help them other than their own five senses, it is understandable that what they said was very limited. But they are not necessarily untrue, for the writers were true to what they saw, felt and smelt and so on. In that sense their conclusions were no less 'scientific' than modern descriptions of the world. Where they differ from modern science is that they are often mixed up with expressions of faith in the God who made it all.

Modern scientists, however, confine themselves to describing the material and physical world. No-one has yet invented instruments which can give them access into the spiritual world, the world of value and meaning. They can tell you all that they have discovered about some physical process, but they cannot tell you, as scientists, whether it is good or bad (although they might frequently be called upon to do so). At that point they stop being scientists and become individuals who measure the morality of what they are doing by their own personal values.

It's the same when it comes to God. The fact that there are, and always have been, many scientists who can faithfully do their work and believe in God should make us see that the one does not necessarily cancel out the other. Science has to do with describing the world around us as we find it. Faith goes beyond that, to say how it all came into existence, what it's all for and where it's all going.

Modern and ancient world-views.

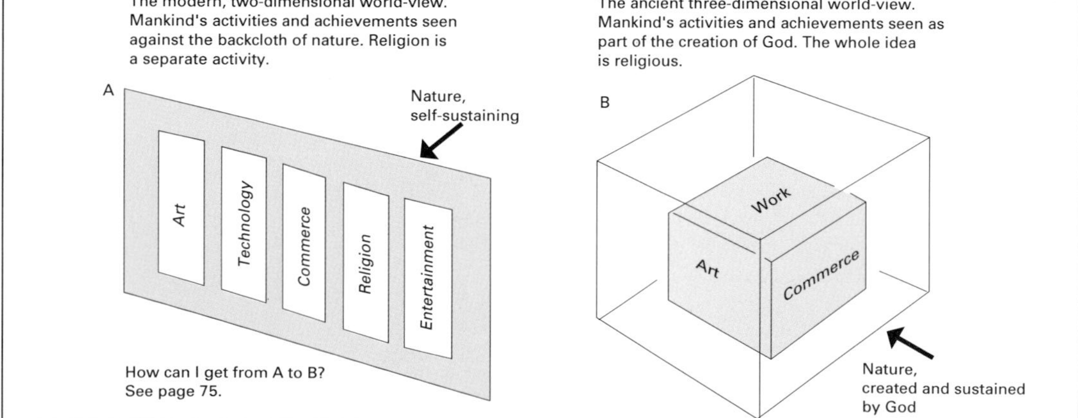

The book that speaks to me

If we stay with our first question and ask only what the Bible meant when it was first written, we will be only half way to interpreting the Bible for ourselves. It would be all very well for those people who are keen on history and geography, but it would not be much use to anyone else. It would be like walking round a museum and examining the exhibits, or looking in on one of those historical dramas on television. If we stop with what the Bible was saying in ancient times, we will have missed out on the very reason that the Bible was written in the first place.

It's quite clear from the Bible itself that God is not concerned merely with our knowing about his people, or even, about him. In fact, we might go so far as to say that the Bible writers were not interested in knowledge for the sake of knowledge (an idea which sometimes comes through to us in certain modern approaches to education); they were much more concerned about living.

We know from sad experience that knowing is not the same as doing. We can have highly educated individuals who know a great deal, but who have made a moral mess of their lives. In the same way, it is possible for someone to amass a great deal of knowledge about the Bible, its contents and its background, without ever translating what they have learned into practical, everyday living. On the other hand, you may have someone who knows very little, but who is prepared to put into practice what they do know. The aim of this book is both to help people understand the Bible better, and also to let it affect their daily lives more. For the fact is that the Bible was written to be lived, not just studied.

64

We can see this in the way Scripture speaks about 'wisdom', which is about as near as we will get to 'philosophy', or love of knowledge, in the Bible. For us, words like these might conjure up things like going to university, taking a course and gaining qualifications. As far as the Bible writers were concerned, however, it was more than just knowledge for its own sake. It was a God-given insight into what he wanted, if you like, into the very way in which God himself thinks, to the end that they might live lives which pleased him. It still took a good deal of hard work, of praying and thinking through the issues, but the result was in terms of practical everyday living. Read the book of Proverbs for examples of the Bible writers' concern, not with what their readers knew, but with how they used it to live from day to day.

354-357

141-144

● Power to make changes

We can see the same principle at work in some of those great passages of the Bible which were certainly not written to be just taken apart word by word. They were written to move their readers to do something. We find them, for example, in the writings of the Old Testament prophets. The truths they have to tell about God are very simple: the fact that he is creator, sovereign, holy, Israel's God. In fact, the prophets were not really teaching people anything about God that they did not know already. They were only reminding them of things which were part of God's original agreement with them.

But the power of what they said had to do with the way in which they said it. They used pictures and images, arguments and charges, promises and predictions, all to get their hearers to *do* something. It's not enough to look in on the truth like spectators at a football match. You have to be part of the game. It has to affect you. One of the masterly things about Jesus' parables was that they caught up the listeners and involved them in the stories, so that whether they accepted or rejected the message, they had to do something about it.

77

235-252

We will be looking at the good reasons why the Bible is different in this respect from any other book or collection of books ever written. It's enough at this point to say that Christians through the ages have found it to be an intensely practical source of instruction, correction, encouragement and challenge. Many who have picked it up and read it, without knowing that it was in any way special, have felt its power to change their lives.

This is because, although it was written to particular situations years ago, God intended that it should have something to say for all time and to every generation. If this is so, the laws God gave through Moses on Mount Sinai were not just for the people of Israel; they have something to say to us today, too. And the parables with which Jesus captivated the crowds were not merely something for that time and place; they have importance for us too. And the letters which Peter wrote to his friends in Turkey are, in a way, addressed to us too. In fact, the Bible is not just an ancient collection of books. In what it has to say to men and women, it is as contemporary and up-to-date as today's newspaper.

So if the first question we have to ask is, 'What *did* it say?', the second must be 'What *is* it saying?' to us, that is, today.

●The Bible answers back

If the Bible were just an ordinary book, written and collected many years ago, 'What is it saying to me?' would be a bit of a non-question. Although it might give us an interesting insight into the way in which people thought and lived in the past, we would not expect it to say anything to us today. But then, it is not an ordinary book, for one of the uncanny things about the Bible which has been recognized ever since it was written is that, when we ask it questions, it answers back!

Although we must use all the tools at our disposal to try to study it as we would study any piece of writing, that is, to discover what the authors had in mind when they wrote it, we find that it can't stop there. If we really come to the Bible with an open mind we find that it begins to speak to us. In this sense, it is what the communists might call a 'dialectical' book. It is not simply a book which informs its readers; it starts debating and arguing with them.

●Enter the spiral

In this way it is possible to enter into a sort of discussion with Scripture and, although we might not realize it at first, with God the Holy Spirit who stood behind its writing in the first place. The whole process has been described as a circle, or better, a spiral. We enter that spiral when we come to the Bible from our own background, with our own way of thinking, asking our own questions, and looking for certain answers.

Getting from A to B (see page 72); the Bible-route from the flat world of today to three-dimensional reality.

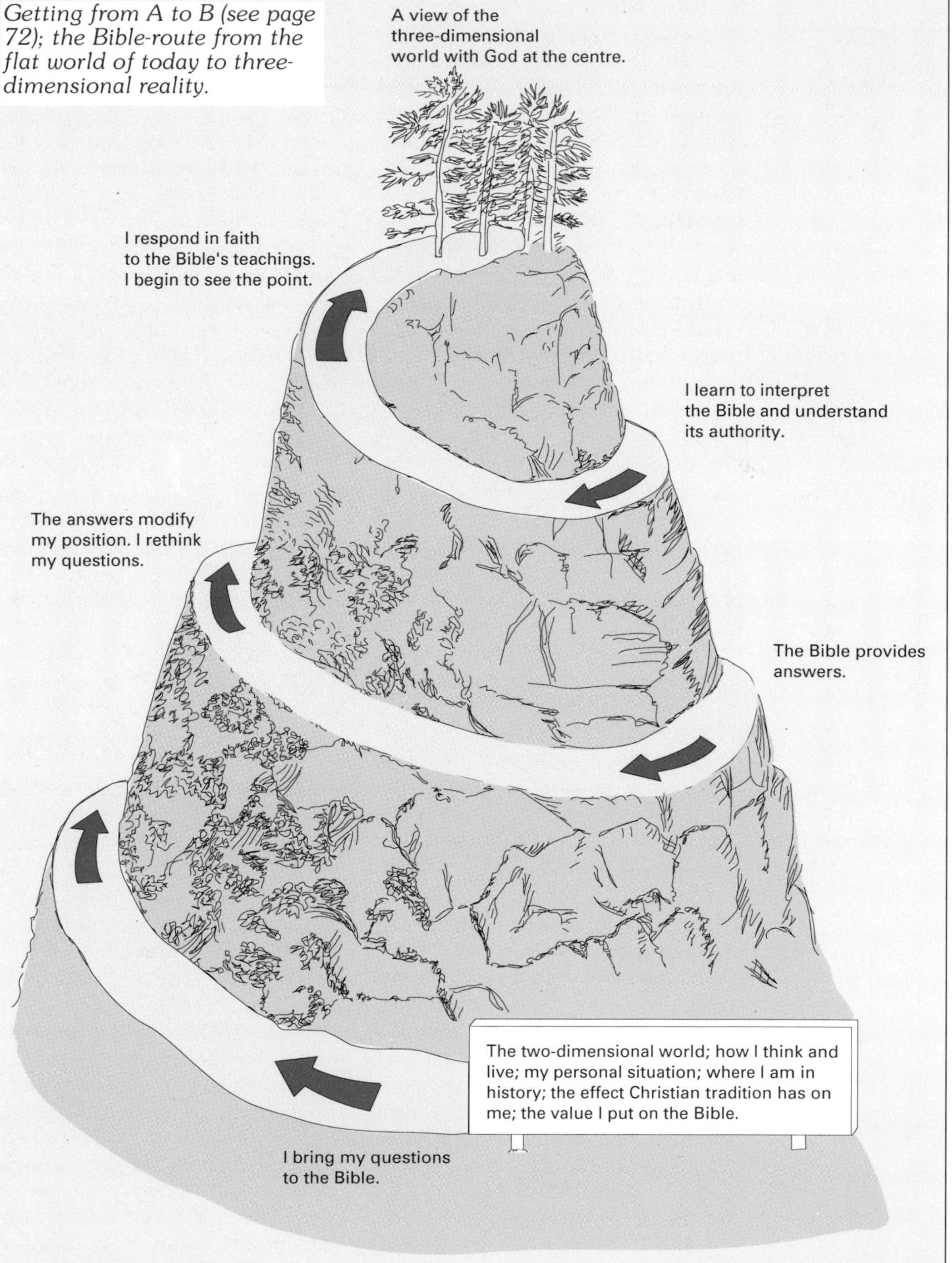

239-245

It might not occur to us, at first, to ask what the Bible might be saying to us. Our only interest in it might be that we enjoy history or literature or the study of religions. But we find a strange quality about this book which refuses to let us hold it at arm's length to examine it. Before we know where we are, we're caught up and drawn in, and what seemed so important when we began no longer holds the same interest. Instead we find ourselves asking a different set of questions – not just things like who wrote what and when, but questions about life and death, the here and the hereafter, what life is all about and the difference that Jesus can make.

In this way many a person has begun to read the Bible with only a passing or even an academic interest, only to find themselves caught up into another world, and face to face with God's reality. If you are already a Christian believer, there is a sense in which you are already 'on the inside' of the process. That's why some who possess very little background knowledge of the Bible books can sometimes live closer to the heart of its message than many who appear to be much better equipped to understand the Bible.

● The role of the Holy Spirit

This is because the Holy Spirit, who is at work in their lives as believers, has already made them sympathetic to what God is saying through the Bible. They probably stepped into Christian experience by taking some promise from the Bible at its face value and by faith. When they did that, the miracle of new birth took place in their lives, and they discovered thereafter that people like Isaiah, Paul and John were talking about the same sort of experience. This is because the One who stands behind the writing of Scripture is the same Holy Spirit who now indwells their lives.

It's a case of like understanding like. If you have lost your job, or if you have been bereaved, you can understand what someone is going through as they face unemployment or bereavement. You have the experience in common. So when the Bible speaks about spiritual experience, you begin to understand what it is saying because, by the same Holy Spirit, you have already come that way yourself.

This does not mean that we can do away with the hard work of researching the background of the books of the Bible, but it does mean that we have an enormous advantage when it comes to appreciating its message. We find ourselves to be on the same side as the authors. Something in our hearts responds to something in their words, and we know it to be truth even though it cuts clean across the ideas, attitudes, values and outlooks of our generation. We are in a position, not just to know what the Bible said when it was first written, but to hear what it is saying to us now, today, in our situation.

If this is the case, it will inevitably begin to affect the way that we live. If we are prepared to open our minds to the message of Scripture, we discover that it begins to shape our ways of thinking. We see the world, we see ourselves and our relationships with others, and so much more, in an entirely different light. If, as we will maintain and as the Bible itself claims, this book is not merely a human production, but that God gave the authors both thought and word, as we study it we will come into touch with the very

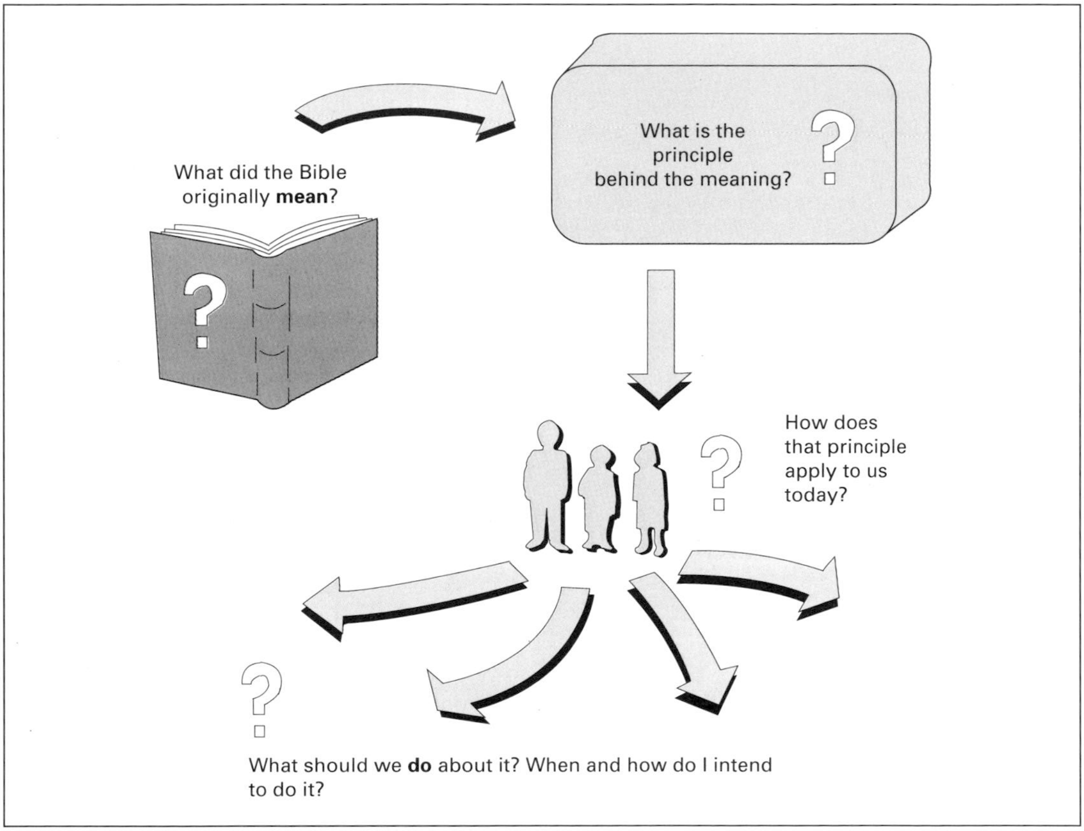

What did the Bible originally **mean**?

What is the principle behind the meaning?

How does that principle apply to us today?

What should we **do** about it? When and how do I intend to do it?

How to interpret the Bible today.

mind of God himself. It will even be possible to think God's thoughts after him, and to see things from his perspective.

This is why we do not merely come searching, but asking that we might find. That's why prayer and genuine Bible study always go hand in hand. Whether it is a matter of hearing Scripture explained and expounded from a pulpit, or reading it on our own for our own personal benefit, we will get the most out of the occasion if we come praying, 'Lord, what do you want to say to me?'

●Appointment with God

There is another curious factor which comes into operation at this point, for not only did God stand behind the writing of this book giving it its strange, gripping quality, he is also absolute master of the affairs of men and women. Hence we may come having 'chosen' to read some passage only to find that God is speaking to our current situation or need through it. We may wander into a church quite casually only to be confronted with a message which fits us in all respects, sometimes through the lips of a complete stranger. For God wants to speak to us through Scripture, and as we listen to it or read it for ourselves, we frequently discover that we have unwittingly made an appointment to meet with God.

330

So real Bible study can never be just a hobby or an academic interest. It's a risky business. It will change your life. It will upset your ideas. It will put you in the dock and pass sentence. It will bring glorious reassurance. It will challenge you to obedience and faith. It will comfort you in life's bitterest hour. It will become your food and drink, your way of life, conditioning the very way you think.

● The Bible and culture

God is able to use the Bible and its teachings, not just to transform the individual's life, but also to change whole cultures. This has certainly been the case historically. Cultures which have been practically non- or even anti-biblical in their standards and values have been turned around to reflect those of Scripture.

As the preaching of the biblical message gathers momentum in a society, what begins with individual response grows to influence a wider circle. Where the gospel is accepted by large numbers there can be dramatic shifts in attitudes and standards which, in a close-knit community, in turn affect public morality and even legislation. Even where true Christians are in a minority, their influence on public attitudes can be disproportionate to their numbers. This is because they not only represent God's idea of what is right and just, they also act as society's conscience in those areas where God's law is disregarded.

In times and places of spiritual awakening, this process can be extremely rapid, especially in smaller, enclosed communities. At other times, the impact of biblical teaching may take years to permeate society, challenging its practices and laws. In time the whole culture is touched and moulded by biblical thinking. This has been the case in western protestant nations, where historically the Bible has had a powerful impact on our whole way of life. Even though some of those nations must now be classified as 'post-Christian', biblical standards and attitudes still persist alongside secular ideals.

These values find expression not only in terms of the arts, public morality and legal codes, it could even be said that western democracy has its roots in the biblical estimate of a person's individual worth and rights. This can be seen in the often sharp contrast in the quality of life in those nations which have had the privilege of years of biblical preaching and teaching, and those which have not.

Many countries where communism has publicly eradicated biblical values have recognized the bankruptcy of atheism. It devalues people. It is probably significant that the churches have been prominent in the overthrow of communism in eastern Europe.

In colonial days, it was extremely tempting for western Christians to export, not just the gospel, but also western culture to developing nations. In some parts of the world this has led to a rejection of both the white man's culture and his religion. The fact is that all cultures, and that includes western protestant culture, come under the judgment of Scripture. What is more, those raised in different cultures can better appreciate different aspects of biblical truth. It is a situation where, within the world church, Christians need to learn from one another, seeking to cultivate a truly Christian culture wherever God may have put them.

Next page: Berlin Wall, 1989.

250

The truth does not come to us undistorted.

● The way we (always) do it!
Apart from the popular philosophies of our generation, one of the most powerful influences on the way we come to the Bible is Christian tradition. This can be an influence for good or evil. Depending on what sort of traditions we are heir to, it can either help us to understand Scripture, or blind us to its meaning.

The powerful influence of tradition can be seen within the Roman Catholic Church before the Reformation. Traditional beliefs had grown up so strongly over the years that the resulting faith and practice of the church was actually contradicting the teachings of Scripture. The Reformers wanted to reform the church's faith by bringing it into line with what the Bible taught. Because tradition had such a hold on the minds of those in authority (and because of the vested interests which would suffer if such a reformation were ever allowed), the Reformers had to become religious revolutionaries. It was in this way that protestant Christianity came into existence.

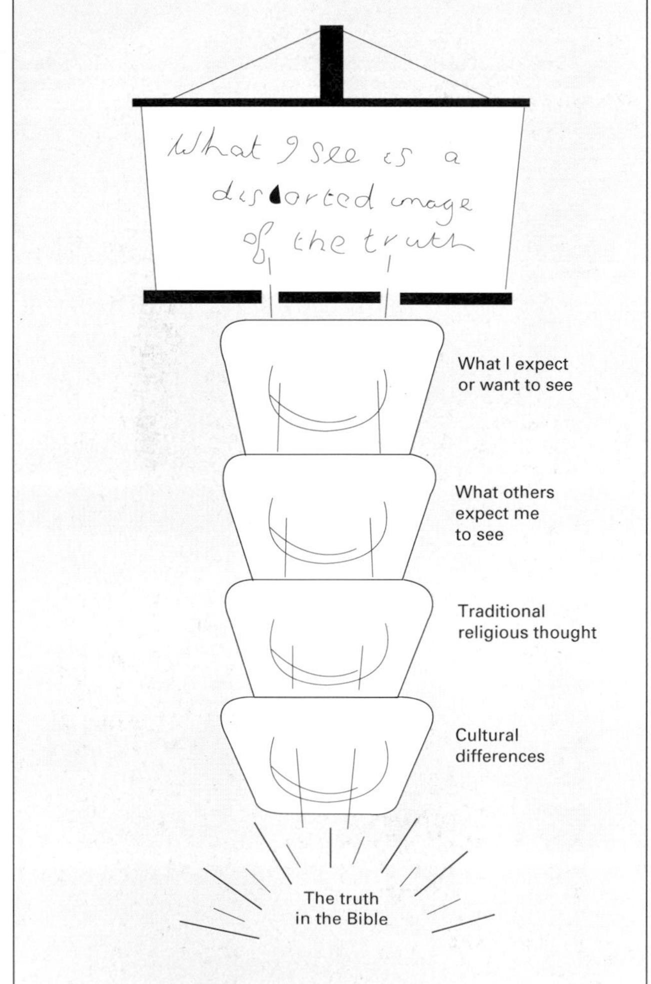

But protestants are not free from tradition either. Even that wing of the protestant church which has sought to maintain the reformed position is still subject to its influence. The fact is that, whether we like it or not, we all depend on tradition to some degree or another. The problem is that most of us are unaware of the fact.

Whoever we are, whether we have been reared in the atmosphere of a Christian home, or have come into Christian experience in later life, we all learn a particular approach to the Bible which affects our understanding of it. It may be the healthy tradition of letting the Bible speak for itself, if necessary passing judgment on the way in which we do things. It may, however, be a background which prejudges statements from the Bible, and prevents it from speaking to us.

We learn our own particular approach to the Bible from ministers, from teachers, from books, and from the sort of Christian community in which we find ourselves. It then becomes part of our mindset when we open the Bible or when we listen to it being preached. Its subtle-

ty is that we are largely unaware of it. As it has become part of what we believe, we tend to dismiss those whose traditions are different from our own. This means that we cut ourselves off from those who might have insights which could correct ours.

This is why we have to ask ourselves why we come to the Bible as we do, why we ask the questions we ask, and what sort of answers we have grown to expect. This is all very necessary if we are not to be actually blinded to what the Bible is saying to us by our very approach.

Perhaps the most sobering warning in this respect is the story of the Pharisees. As far as we can see, they began as sincere people who were ready to die if need be for their faith in Scripture. But over the years they evolved their own traditional way of understanding the Old Testament until Jesus had to accuse them of actually contradicting God's Word by their traditions.

From their world to mine

How can the Bible, written so long ago to different situations from my own, be up-to-date and practical for me? After all, when I start reading at random, I find all sorts of things which have nothing to do with my life or the society I live in. For example, I've never been tempted to eat meat offered to idols, but the apostle Paul goes on about it in his letters. Or how can those ancient laws about removing my neighbour's boundary stones, or building a parapet around my roof, have anything to do with the way I live in the late 20th century?

This is where interpretation really matters, unless, that is, you want to cut out long sections of the Bible and discard them as irrelevant. If God overruled the writing of the Bible, he must have some reason for leaving us with what we read there.

● 'Progressive revelation'

Something that has long been recognized is that, when God wanted to teach human beings about himself, he did not do it all in one go. God's self-revelation as it is called, was a progressive affair, rather like the sunrise. In the beginning, God took people who had very little understanding of him and his ways, and slowly but surely taught them the basic lessons.

48-49

34

The most important way in which God did this was by establishing his covenant with Israel. Along with this sacred agreement between God and man went a whole system of rules and regulations which were designed to teach them that God was holy and that they were special. Some were moral laws, reflecting God's character, and because of that they are just as binding today. Others were ceremonial in nature, and these taught them in very graphic ways what it meant to be God's people. As such they were not meant to be permanent. They pointed forward to what was going to come in the future.

That is why we find Jesus claiming that the Old Testament was fulfilled in him and by his coming into the world (Matthew 5:17-20), and that's why his followers were able to dispense with the Jewish laws like those about the food they were allowed to eat, or the sacrifices they were supposed to offer. What these things teach us, is the deep-laid nature of God's plan prior to his

86

351-354

sending his Son into the world. That's why we can still learn a great deal from the old covenant educational syllabus, even though we too have discarded Old Testament ritual.

When it comes to understanding the Bible for ourselves, although we will encounter problems, there are passages which hardly need any interpretation at all. They are quite straightforward, and hit us right between the eyes. Take, for example, Jesus' command to his disciples, 'Love one another as I have loved you' (John 13:34). Because Jesus was talking to his disciples, it's reasonable to assume that he meant all his followers to live like this. In other words, if you are a Christian believer, this is for you.

326

More than that; it's a statement which interprets itself. We might have difficulty with that word 'love', because as it is used today it can mean one of a number of things from lust through friendship to complete devotion. But Jesus does not just use the word: he gives us the example, 'as I have loved you'. Many a person has learned all over again what real love is all about when they have come to realize what Christ did for them when he died on the cross for them. As he hung there, he was selflessly putting others – who didn't deserve his love – first. So, when he tells his disciples – and all who profess to be Christians could be described like that – to love one another, I have a fairly good idea of what he meant. At this point I do not need commentaries or Bible dictionaries. What he was saying is obvious, even if it's another thing actually to put it into practice.

Sometimes what seems to be a straightforward statement or command might need to be filled out from the other things the Bible says on the subject. Take the commandment (in some versions), 'You shall not kill' (Exodus 20:13). It seems fairly obvious. We must not take another person's life, but it would be wrong to go on and add 'under any circumstances'. In the Old Testament itself they went to war and they had capital punishment, and in each case, on occasion, God told them to. Again those who accidently killed someone were treated differently from those who committed cold-blooded, premeditated murder. So it might be better to translate the commandment (as in the *New International Version*) in that way, 'You shall not murder'. Once we have established this principle, we can then turn to modern situations which we do not have directly spelt out for us in biblical law, like abortion or euthanasia.

But it does not end there. We have not only the Old Testament command; we have a New Testament commentary on it from Jesus' own lips (Matthew 5:21-22). He went behind the action to the motives which prompted it. He was saying that, if you hate someone, it is as though you had already committed murder 'in your heart', even though outwardly you might be living an upright, respectable life. So Jesus' own interpretation is far more radical than anything we could say.

● Timeless principles

This introduces us to something which allows us to apply the Bible to a very wide range of modern situations. We do not live in Old Testament or New Testament times but there are principles underlying what we read in the Bible which are always true.

Take idolatry for example. If we live in 20th century western society, we seldom come across it. We would if we were living in the Third World, and then the straight teaching of the Bible, forbidding all kinds of idolatry, would apply directly. However, the principle underlying the laws against idolatry is that nothing must ever take God's place. Though we do not make literal idols of wood and stone we have all been guilty of demoting God in favour of pleasures, things, people or achievements. If we live from day to day for the things of time and sense, we are worshipping the work of our own hands as surely as the heathen in the Bible did.

Or take that business of eating meat offered to idols which Paul spends so much time over (1 Corinthians 8-10). For them it was a live issue. To eat at a sacrificial meal in a pagan temple, or to eat part of the sacrifice later in the home of an idolater, was seriously to compromise your faith. And even if it did not affect you personally, in that you knew that idols counted for nothing, the example you set to others might well lead them astray.

Idols for many of us may be things of the past, or from foreign lands, but compromising our stand as Christians by getting involved in non-Christian activities, or causing other Christians to fall by our bad example, are both red-hot issues for today.

This gives us a clue about how to handle present situations which we never find in the Bible. For example, should a Christian join a trade union? What should our attitude be to birth control? How should I vote in the next election? What about heart-transplants? There are a whole host of modern problems, some brought about by advanced technology, some simply because we are living in very different circumstances from the Bible writers, which they never had anything to say about.

The answer lies in finding biblical principles which apply to our situation. Honesty, integrity, justice, responsibility, fair play, selflessness, love – these are the sort of principles which come over loud and clear both in the events and the teaching of Scripture. It is our job to rediscover them, and then to apply them

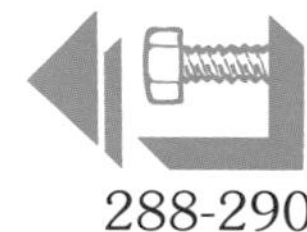

288-290

Advanced technology may itself become a 20th century idol.

to the situations in which we find ourselves.

● Responsible interpretation

You may discover that sometimes one principle modifies another. For example, it may appear to be loving to give money to the tramp who calls at your door, but is it responsible to do so if you know that he will go straight to the nearest bar to spend it on the alcohol which has brought him down in the first place? So you have to ask yourself how you can love him in a responsible way.

300

It is certainly biblical, as we have seen, not to take life but is keeping someone on a life-support machine, long after their brains have ceased to function, merciful to the person concerned or to their relatives? Is it the best use of resources when others' pain could be relieved or others' condition improved by redirecting the time, energy and money involved (it's the sort of question that both Christian and non-Christian doctors are having to ask all the time)?

You will find situations where committed, intelligent and spiritually-minded Christians use the same principles and come to different conclusions. That's why we can have Christians to both the right and the left of the political spectrum, or why we can have Christian pacifists and Christians who are content to serve in the armed forces. And whatever each side may say, it is possible to argue convincingly from the Bible for these opposites and for a good number of others too.

So what do we do? To the best of our ability, we check people's statements by what we know of God's truth in the Bible, and we prayerfully come to our own conclusion. It should make us realize that it's all too easy to become dogmatic about some things which are really open questions. It should make us much more humble in holding our own views.

● We can never know all the answers

For the Bible does not set out to solve all our problems. There are many, many areas – especially when it comes to describing God and his ways – that are utterly beyond us. There are complicated moral situations where it is almost impossible to know what to do for the best. It is not defeat to admit that we honestly do not know all the answers when faced with some issue which is out of our reach. Instead, it should remind us of just how limited is our human understanding, even when aided by Scripture and enlightened by the Holy Spirit. Whereas there are many things of which we can be absolutely sure, there are also a good number of issues which we have to leave open – for the time being, at least – we simply have to trust God.

Sometimes we come across the answer for ourselves at a later date. As a result of our cumulative Bible study, we begin to see the truth that we failed to see before. Sometimes it means changing our minds, confessing that we got it wrong before. Again, that is not necessarily defeat. It's merely a sign that our understanding of what God wants to say to us through his Word is growing and maturing.

There is a good deal, however, which we will never understand in the here and now. When Paul said, 'now I know in part' (1 Corinthians 13:12), he never said a truer word. But he did go on to speak about a time when we shall know complete-

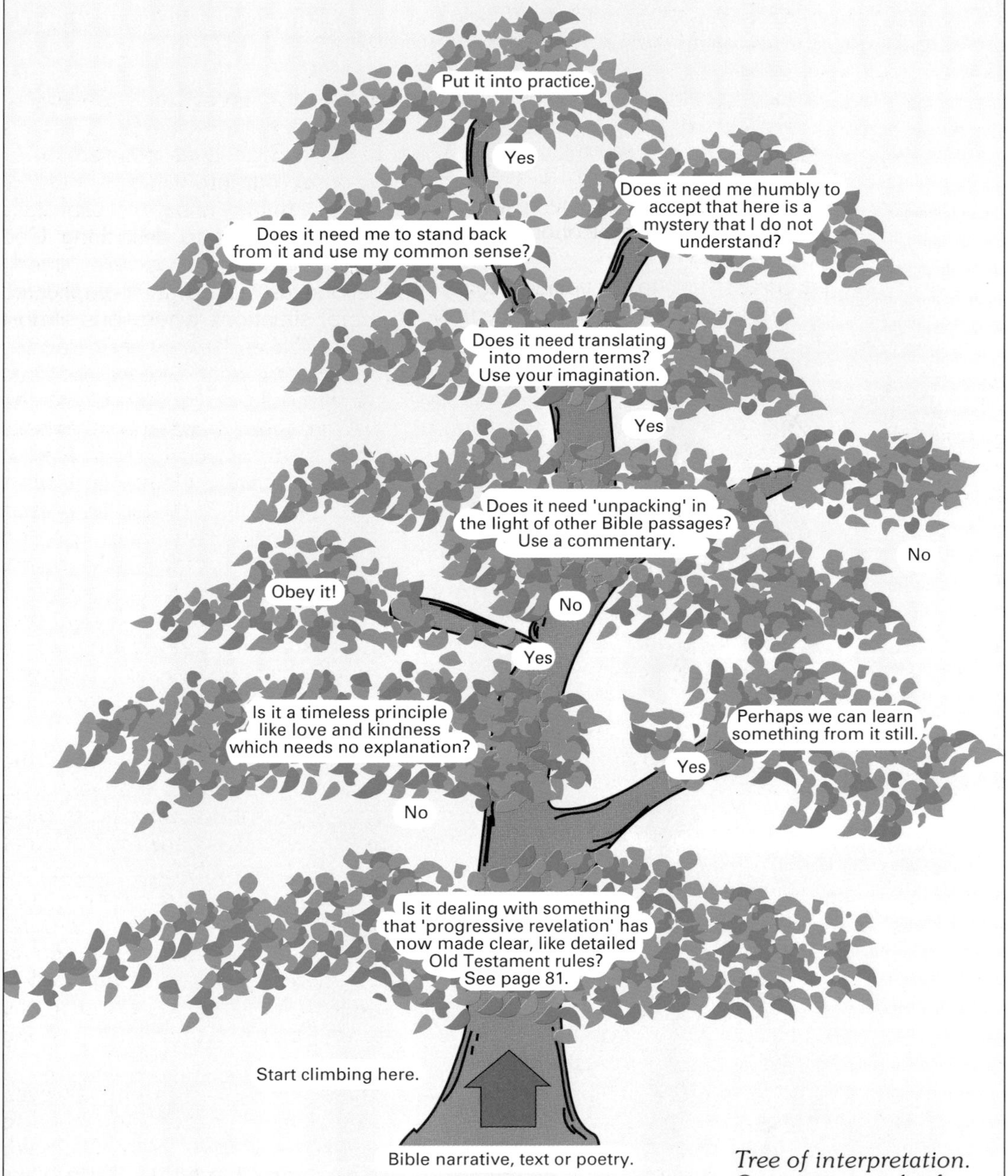

Tree of interpretation. Questions to ask of Bible narrative.

ly, 'even as I am fully known'. The problems of earth will be the happy discoveries of heaven.

To some people this may all seem inadequate. 'If God wanted us to live in a certain way, why didn't he lay it all out in his book in the first place?' People like that are forgetting that times and situations do change and that, as the Bible amply illustrates, sound advice for one generation has to be reinterpreted (though not contradicted) in another. They are also forgetting that God deals with us kindly. He expects us only to live up to whatever light we may have received through his Word. This is reassuring, in that it's easy to look back to previous generations, and to see where they went wrong, and yet to be blind to our own faults. It's also somewhat frightening, for whoever fully lived out what he knew of God's will, except Jesus?

The Old Testament in the New

The New Testament authors were Jews who read their Old Testament in Greek, and also heard it read in the synagogue every sabbath in Hebrew. Because of this, it's not surprising that their writings have an Old Testament ring about them. There is a distinctly Old Testament 'feel' to the language of the New Testament, just as English-speaking people often unconsciously use expressions and phrases from the Authorized Version of the Bible (like 'an eye for an eye' or 'a good Samaritan').

66-69

However, for them the Old Testament was not just a good book; it was God's Word and therefore carried God's authority. So when they wanted to make a point, they frequently supported it with a reference to an Old Testament event or text. They frequently quote from the Septuagint version, a popular Greek translation, and also from others as well as from the Hebrew. Sometimes they quote exactly, sometimes more roughly from memory. There are times when they deliberately alter the text, which was quite incredible behaviour for Jews, unless they believed that they were being directly guided by the same Holy Spirit who had prompted the Old Testament authors to write as they did.

248-252

They often used what we know as 'proof texts', that is, Old Testament texts which either directly refer to the subject in hand, or which they believed found fulfilment in the events surrounding the life and ministry of Christ and its aftermath. Matthew's Gospel is a good example of this. There are times when, like other Jews of their day, they string together verses with a common theme – or even a common word – to produce a cumulative effect on their readers.

Sometimes they concentrate on the exact wording of the Old Testament; sometimes they use general themes as in their references to Old Testament events like Sodom and Gomorrah or the flood.

The most important thing to note is that, following the example of Jesus himself, they believed that the message they had to share was in direct continuity with that of the Old Testament. More than that, they believed that New Testament events and their meaning, the gospel of Christ himself, no less, was the fulfilment of Old Testament promise.

183

●Detecting error

The Jews at Berea during Paul's visit set us an excellent example. They found Paul's preaching interesting, but in order to make sure that it was correct they 'examined the Scriptures every day to see if what Paul said was true' (Acts 17:11). This was because, being Jews, they believed that God was a God of truth and he would not contradict himself. That principle holds good today.

There are plenty of errors and distortions of the Christian faith around, some held quite sincerely, others being an attempt to con people into supporting a particular sect or cult. There are many who will come to you with Bible in hand, maintaining that all they profess is 'scriptural', but who in reality are far from biblical truth. The question therefore arises, 'How do we know when we are being taken in?' 'How can we test for truth?' The answer is exactly the same as in New Testament times. God does not change. If he has made himself and his will known, we may test all claims to truth by what we know to be the truth, by his Word.

The most direct confrontation, of course, is on the part of those who simply deny the authority of the Bible while still professing to be Christians. To profess to accept the authority of Jesus Christ while refusing to take what he said about Scripture (or what is said about him in Scripture) seriously is a contradiction in terms. To accept his lordship means to submit to him at every level, including that of our thinking. If popular ways of thinking run counter to the teaching of Jesus, we are faced with a choice. Which is more reliable? Popular teaching or the words of Jesus? To make the message of Jesus conform to the spirit of the times in which we live is an act of rebellion, however sophisticated and intellectual that rebellion may be.

Sometimes this takes the form of picking and choosing where the Bible is concerned. People will accept those parts of Scripture that are palatable to them, or which chime in with their particular views, while rejecting those parts which do not appeal. But this is inconsistent. Either Jesus is the Son of God, and therefore what he says, including his attitude to Scripture, comes with God's authority, or he isn't. So the Bible either is God's Word or it is not. We cannot consistently occupy a position somewhere in the middle.

There are, of course, differences between Christians in matters of detail (obviously everyone will see the truth from a unique angle) but the point at issue here is whether we believe that God is revealing himself in the Bible or not.

●Paradox and balance

Then there are those who mishandle Scripture by over emphasizing some half-truth. This is easy to do if our knowledge of the Bible is limited. It is easy to make a verse say all that there is to say about something if we are unaware of the other things that the Bible teaches on the subject. There is a balance in Scripture which we need to maintain if we are going to be true to its teaching. For example, the New Testament gives up plenty of evidence that Jesus was fully human, but if we stopped there we would be far from the whole truth. There is an equal stress on Jesus' being the Son of God and all that this involves.

This is only one of a number of instances where the whole truth lies in a paradox, that is, something that

248-252

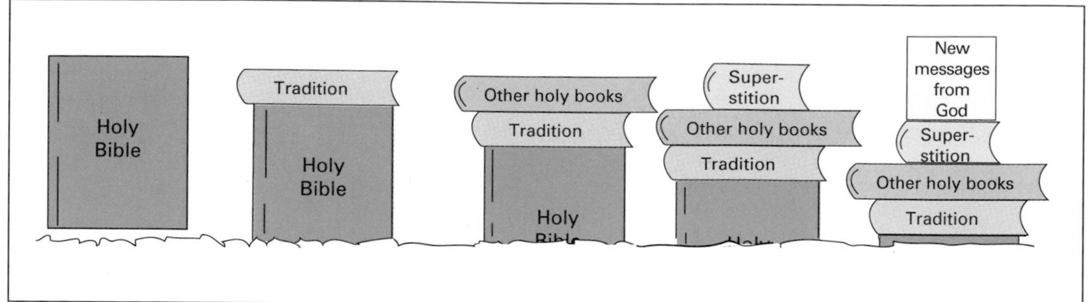

80

seems contradictory to our limited, human minds, but which is clearly taught in the Bible. We are tempted to simplify the situation by placing the stress on one side or the other. In the case of Jesus, there have been many who have reduced him to a mere man, albeit a good one. At the same time, there have been others who have made him so divine that his humanity has been unreal.

Sometimes our distorting of the message arises from the fact that we tend to discover the truth a bit at a time. We come across some aspect of Bible teaching which seems so wonderful that it fills our horizon and obscures everything else. In the normal course of events, we then move on to other tremendous discoveries, and what we have come to know earlier eventually falls into its proper place. At that particular time, however, we are very vulnerable to the temptation to become unbalanced.

If you take a half-truth and believe it to be a whole truth you will end up with an error, however true the half-truth was to start with. That is why some heresies are so difficult to refute. Those who hold them can quote Scripture texts to support their views. The best antidote to error of course is thorough all-round understanding of what the Bible has to say.

● 'The Bible and ...'

The other way of creating a distortion of the truth is to take the Bible and something else as your authority. It might be the hoary traditions of the church, or it might be a claim to supplementary revelation like the Book of Mormon. The fact is that we do not need any more than the Scripture for our salvation. Moreover, when you start adding to the Word of God, you generally end up contradicting it. John's sombre words for those who add to or take away from his prophecy (Revelation 22:18-19) are a warning not to try to reduce or improve on what God has taken such pains to give us.

When the Reformers rediscovered the authority of Scripture and set about testing every other claim to truth by it – the 'touchstone of truth' they called it – they were aware that there were plenty of other views and convictions about. Similarly today we are conscious that there are other voices and other claims to truth which would claim to be Christian views (sometimes the only true Christian view!). But if we have come to know Christ by proving God's Word for ourselves, however strongly and however sincerely these other positions may be maintained we will prefer, like the Reformers, the Word of God in its wholeness as the foundation on which we build our faith.

PART 3 CUTTING OUT THE SECTIONS

A run-down of what each of the sixty-six books of the Bible is about; where they came from, why they were written, how to deal with some of the problems in them and how to apply them to the world of today.

CUTTING OUT THE SECTIONS

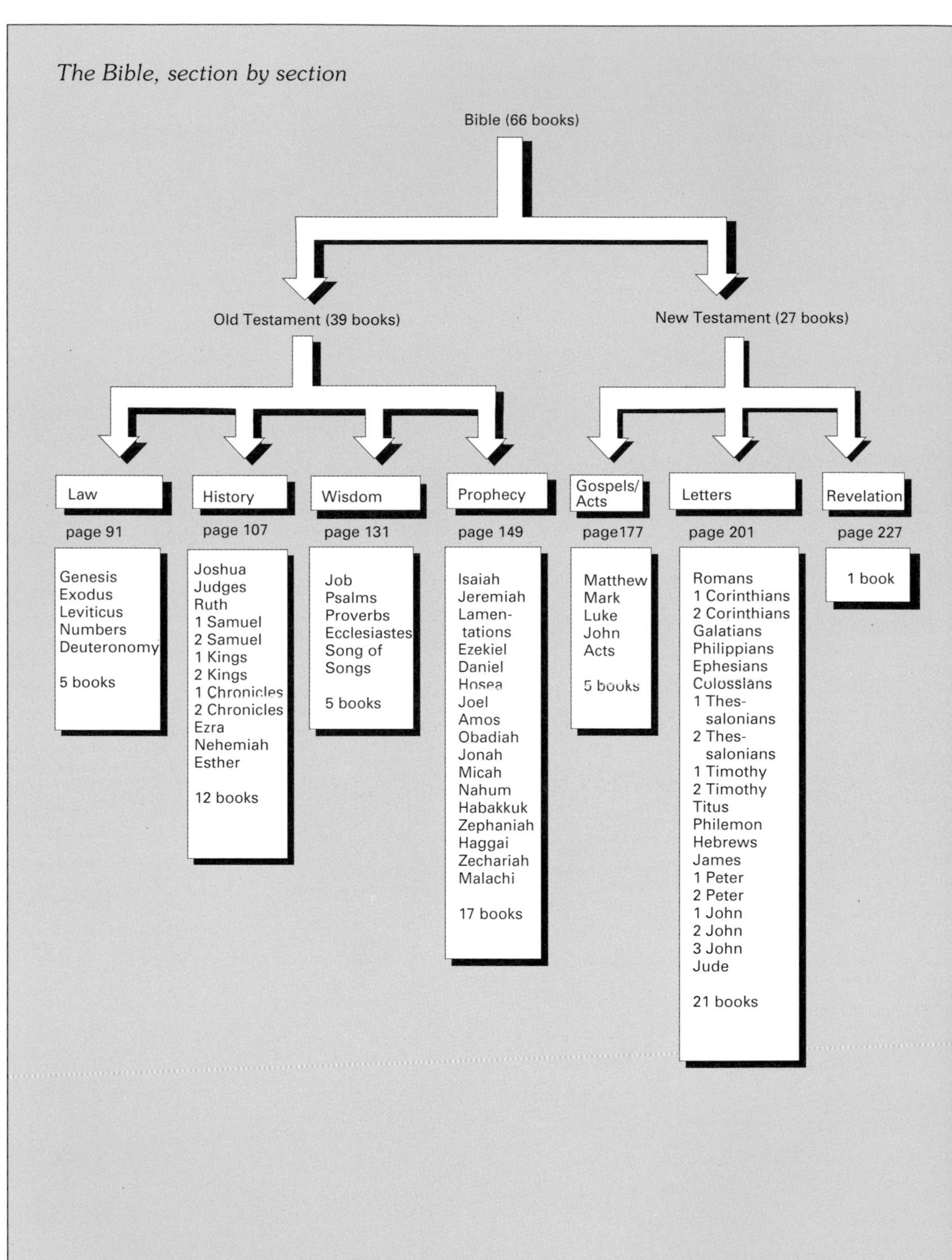

3.1

IN THE BEGINNING
Creation, history and law: Genesis to Deuteronomy

by Geoffrey Treasure

The first five books of the Bible build the foundation on which all the rest is built. Without some knowledge of these books the rest of the Bible would be very difficult to understand.

Genesis begins with God and the creation, the fall of mankind and the flood, and continues with the calling of Abraham, founder of the Israelite people. The young nation's stay in Egypt and return under Moses take up the remaining four books which major on the exodus, the receiving of the law at Sinai and the desert wanderings of the people.

The book of Genesis

36

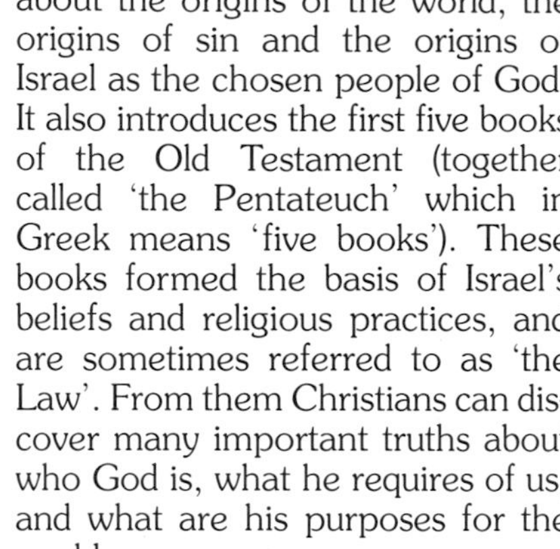

Genesis means 'origins'. It tells us about the origins of the world, the origins of sin and the origins of Israel as the chosen people of God. It also introduces the first five books of the Old Testament (together called 'the Pentateuch' which in Greek means 'five books'). These books formed the basis of Israel's beliefs and religious practices, and are sometimes referred to as 'the Law'. From them Christians can discover many important truths about who God is, what he requires of us, and what are his purposes for the world.

352-353

Summary of Genesis

1 Setting the scene (1:1 - 11:26)
2 The God of Abraham (11:27 - 23:20)
3 The God of Isaac (24:1 - 26:35)
4 The God of Jacob (27:1 - 36:43)
5 The God of Joseph (37:1 - 50:26)

● Setting the scene (section 1)

72

To some people the stories in the opening chapters of Genesis appear to be in direct conflict with what we know today. However, the simple narratives contain timeless truths. Note that:

Genesis does not claim to tell everything about, say, creation. The message of the book must be seen in the context of the rest of Scripture.

Genesis is basically a book of theology. It is about God, not about science.

The author is primarily concerned about why the world is like it is, rather than about how it came to be.

Genesis 1 sketches a magnificent portrait of God which is coloured in by other Bible writers. It forms the basis for Christian worship. God is shown to be supreme; everything owes its origin to him. He works methodically (the 'days'); nothing happens by chance. And everything he does is perfectly good.

Few people would dispute that the world today is in a mess. Both the physical universe and the peoples who inhabit it bear the scars of hatred, violence, greed and immorality.

Chapters 1-5 of Genesis interpret the chaos and confusion which have affected the planet and human society for centuries. They point us to the quality of God's original creation (1:1-2:4), to the nature of mankind's relationship to God and to creation (2:5-25), our abuse of free will and our direct rebellion against God (3:1-13). The consequences of that rebellion – physical suffering and society falling apart – are briefly described (3:14-24).

The story of 'the fall' sets the scene for the Bible's drama: God's rescue plan for mankind. Having been created to live in harmony with God and each other, we fail both ways. Only God can repair

Genesis: data

Author: Jews and Christians have regarded Moses as the author, or compiler, of the book of Genesis. Educated in the Egyptian court, Moses would have possessed the skills of reading, writing, editing and translation required for such a huge task. Furthermore, as Israel's first leader, he had an interest in providing an account of the nation's origins. Copyists may have added explanations at a later date (*e.g.* 12:6; 13:7).

Purpose: to introduce the founding fathers of the nation of Israel.

the damage. Until he does, even our best attempts at social reform and personal morality can never match his requirements.

The biblical story of the flood (chapters 6-9) shows God's attitude towards mankind's disobedience and wilful rebellion. It is different from the similar stories found in other cultures because unlike them it stresses that human sin is a moral offence against a holy God. It reveals two aspects of God's character – his grace and his judgment – showing how God can condemn sin and yet forgive the sinner. (See 6:5,13; 7:23;. Hebrews 11:7.)

These twin themes of grace and judgment were taken up by Jesus. He used the story of Noah's obedience and readiness to encourage his followers to be alert and ready for his own return (Matthew 24:36-41).

● The God of Abraham (section 2)

At the centre of God's plan to rescue mankind from the chaos of his rebellion was Abraham. His obedience to God's call to leave his home land with his family and trek towards the unknown land God had chosen for him showed a quality of faith which never left him (12:1-9; Hebrews 11:8-12,17-19).

God promised the childless Abraham that he would be the founder of God's own special nation. But famine (12:10-20), family feuds (chapter 13), and the advancing years which made parenthood less and less likely, all tested his faith.

Eventually, in God's time, Isaac was born (21:1-7); God was faithful! And even when faced with the perplexing challenge to kill Isaac (22:1-14), Abraham continued to trust that God could even raise the dead

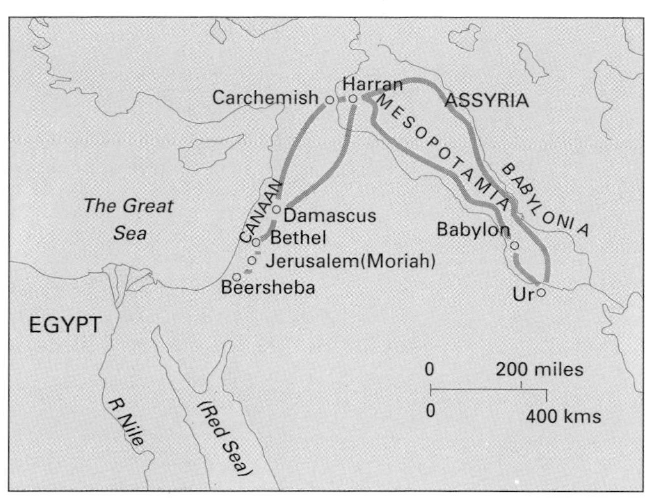

Abraham's journey from Ur to Canaan; possible routes.

to fulfil his plans (Hebrews 11:17-19). The faith was not misplaced. Isaac became the next link in the chain of promise and salvation.

The New Testament letter to the Hebrews includes a commentary on Abraham's life of faith (11:8-12,17-19). It commends the lasting example of a man who preferred to trust God's word rather than his human reason. The real point is that God did not let Abraham down, because he never breaks his promises.

34

24-25

Abraham – the fallible man

The Bible writers never idolize their heroes. Abraham's failings are not hidden behind his successes. He lied about his relationship with Sarah out of pure fear (12:10-13).

Then, when God seemed to have forgotten his promise and Sarah was beyond childbearing age, he took the law into his own hands and had a child through his maidservant (chapter 16). His faith was not perfect, which makes God's faithfulness to him even more encouraging to people who try to live by faith today.

●The God of Isaac (section 3)

Isaac's name means 'laughter'. It suggests that the circumstances of his birth reduced both Abraham (17:17) and his wife, Sarah (18: 12-15) to a laughter which expressed a combination of incredulity, faith and joy.

The joy continued as Isaac grew through adolescence into manhood and married life (chapter 24). But he and his wife Rebekah had no children, a problem which drove them to their knees (25:21). Once again God displayed his power, and the home resounded with the laughter of twins, Jacob and Esau, through whom God would continue to fulfil his promise.

The story of how God led Isaac to his wife Rebekah (chapter 24) is a classic example of God's guidance which has helped generations of Christians. It involved faith, specific prayer, and God leading two strangers to meet at precisely the right moment.

●The God of Jacob (section 4)

Jacob was born with his hand grasping his brother Esau's heel (25:26), which led to him being given the name Jacob ('he clutches'). His attempt to overtake his brother at birth set the pattern of his life.

As the youngest member of the family Jacob was at a definite disadvantage. Social and religious responsibilities, not to mention a double share of inheritance, were the right of the elder brother. But what Jacob lost by birth he tried to restore by guile.

He tricked Esau out of both his father's blessing (25:29-34) and the inheritance (27:1-40). It earned him the hatred of his brother and the life of a refugee (27:41 - 28:9). God had not abandoned him, however (28:10-17). Despite his guile Jacob was to be part of God's plan. Jacob's change of name to Israel was a lasting memorial to God's goodness and faithfulness shown to someone whom other people despise (32:22-32).

Even someone as cunning and devious as Jacob can become a strategic part of God's plan when he turns from self-serving and seeks God. Jacob's story encourages personal humility and a recognition of God's sovereignty and grace in human affairs (1 Corinthians 1:25-31; Romans 9:1-33).

●The God of Joseph (section 5)

Joseph, one of the sons of Jacob, is at the centre of the remaining chapters of Genesis. His exciting story demonstrates God's providence in the most bewildering circumstances of life. Joseph was his father's favourite son. But his own naivety and his brothers' hatred resulted in him being sold as a slave in a strange country (Egypt). With no human friends he remained aware of God's constant presence with him (37:1-28; 39:1).

Abraham and his descendants (simplified).

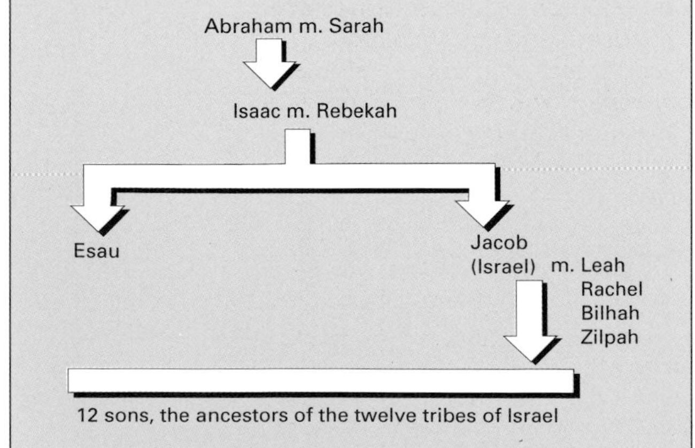

He became an unimportant servant of an army captain (39:1), but God's presence and Joseph's own integrity brought him respect and responsibility (39:2-6). It also brought him a woman's hatred and then imprisonment (39:7-20). He gained more responsibility in prison (39:20-23). After he interpreted the dreams of two fellow-prisoners (chapter 40), Joseph was promoted to the court of Pharaoh (king), first as an interpreter of dreams and then as a government minister with authority throughout Egypt (chapter 41). A famine in Canaan and a surplus of food in Egypt brought Joseph's brothers into his presence, although they did not recognize him (41:50 - 43:15). A series of ploys to bring the whole family to Egypt led to a joyful reunion (chapters 44-45). The dreams which had divided the family (37:5-11) had been fulfilled (42:6-7) and became the means of uniting them.

Joseph's story is an example of how God works for good even in adverse circumstances (Romans 8:28). It challenges Christians to remain faithful to God even when their world seems to be caving in.

The book of Exodus

'Exodus' means 'a journey out'.The book begins with the death of Joseph, and describes the increasing hardship of his descendants before their escape from Egypt and the start of their journey to Canaan.

But the exodus was more than a journey through a geographical area. It was a journey into life. Today Jews across the world still focus on the exodus as they celebrate the birth of their nation. And Christians see in God's freeing of the Israelites from Egypt a picture of their own freeing from sin by Jesus (see 1 Peter 1:18-20, which draws on the image of the Passover meal eaten before the Israelites' hasty departure).

After the initial triumph of an oppressed people, their story becomes one of ingratitude, rebellion, disappointment and failure, despite God's continuous provision of food, water and protection. It illustrates God's patience and long-term purpose for both individuals and nations. This is not history as merely a chronicle of human endeavour, success and failure. It points the reader to a sovereign God who works out his purposes through human affairs.

Exodus: data

Author: both Jews and Christians have accepted the internal impression of Exodus that Moses compiled it.

Date: about the thirteenth century BC. There is some doubt as to the precise date and route of the exodus journey.

Purpose: to record Israel's departure from Egypt.

The triumph of the Israelites over injustice and oppression has encouraged many similarly oppressed groups. It shows how God hates injustice and so challenges people of all generations to live justly.

Summary of Exodus

1 The journey begins (chapters 1-18)

2 Laws and responsibilities (chapters 19-24)

3 Preparing for worship (chapters 25-40)

25

26

●The journey begins (section 1)
Almost 300 years had passed since the death of Joseph. The Egyptians' hospitality had given way to mistrust and suspicion. They tried to destroy the apparent Israelite threat to national security (1:7-22). One family refused to comply with national policy and this led to the survival and royal education of their son Moses, the future leader of Israel (2:1-25).

Moses: the making of a leader
The familiar story of the baby in the bulrushes begins the life-story of one of the Bible's most important personalities. Through the determination of his parents and the intervention of an Egyptian princess, Moses was educated in the courts of the Pharaoh who had originally sentenced all Hebrew children to death (1:1 - 2:10). As a young man he was forced to exchange the life of a courtier for that of a murderer on the run (2:11-25).

While exiled in Midian Moses was called by God to return to Egypt. He was to be God's chosen agent to free the Israelites from the power of Pharaoh (3:1-12). Moses, by then getting old, and a retiring, shy person by nature, was reluctant to respond. So God appointed his brother Aaron to be his mouthpiece (4:14-17). In the years that followed, Moses executed, mostly with honour, the hugely difficult task of leading a mass of people into a new era. *Moses' story illustrates how God sometimes prepares a person for Christian work. And Moses' reluctance will be echoed in many people's experience. God's patient dealing with Moses shows that when he calls someone to service he equips them and controls their circumstances. Neither age nor human limitation is a barrier to God.*

Despite Moses' initial reluctance (3:1 - 4:17), he obeyed God's call and went to the king (or Pharaoh) to request freedom for the Hebrews to worship (5:1-5). The request locked Moses and his brother Aaron into a prolonged battle of wits with Pharaoh (5:6-21). God inflicted a series of natural disasters on Egypt but Pharaoh refused to let the Israelites go. After the death of his eldest son, Pharaoh relented; the Hebrews could go free (5:22 - 12:36). They obeyed God's detailed commands in the first Passover feast (chapter 12), and so escaped both the angel of death and the bondage of Egypt.

The account of Pharaoh's stubbornness is used by Paul to explain the relationship between God's sovereignty and our responsibility (Romans 9:14-18). Pharaoh had no desire to obey God, so God used his hardness to demonstrate his own power and mercy. It is a warning against prolonged opposition to God.

The exodus: possible routes.

The taste of freedom was still fresh in their mouths when the Hebrew people found themselves in the first of a number of life-threatening situations where absolute trust in God was required (14:1-18). With supernatural timing God provided a path of safety through the waters of the Red Sea. But a pattern of praise followed by complaint set in (15:1-25), and was repeated during the coming years of travel. Lack of water (15:22-25), shortage of food (chapter 16) and physical hostility (17:8-16) all revealed Israel's lack of faith in a God who faithfully met their needs, though under such pressure few of us would do better.

The wisdom of his father-in-law enabled Moses to learn the secret of delegating responsibility (chapter 18). This principle of sharing the load of spiritual work and ministry lies behind the New Testament image of the church as a body. All God's people have a part to play in his purposes.

●Laws and responsibilities (section 2)

The Israelites camped at Mount Sinai (19:2). To Moses, it was a visible reminder that God can be trusted to keep his word – it was where he had first met with God (3:12). It was therefore a very suitable place for God to enter into an agreement or covenant with the Israelite people (19:4-6). God promised that Israel would have a special relationship with him, demanding in return Israel's obedience and holiness (19:8). The covenant was later confirmed by a sacrifice (24:1-8), the usual accompaniment to a business agreement in those days.

In chapters 20-24 Moses gave the people firstly the Ten Commandments, which outline God's unchanging principles for human conduct (chapter 20), and secondly the law code for Israel to apply them to the circumstances of the time. The ten basic laws of God are emphasized throughout the Bible and are never cancelled. Jesus stressed that he came to uphold the principles of the commands, and to free people from unhelpful and slavish traditions surrounding them (Matthew 5:17-20). And Paul made it clear that trying to reach God by keeping the law was a futile exercise (Romans 3:20); Christ alone can bring us to God and achieve what the Law was powerless to do (Galatians 3:1-14).

351-359

It is never easy to hold the balance between extreme legalism and extreme licence. An important guideline to remember is that matters of truth in the Ten Commandments are never open to debate; it is always wrong to steal. But matters of application may vary from place to place and time to time. For instance our precise use of Sunday depends to an extent on our needs for worship and recreation and opportunities for service (see Mark 2:23 - 3:6).

●Preparing for worship (section 3)

From Genesis and Exodus so far we have learned that people do not need buildings to worship God. Moses met with God in the desert, on a beach and on a mountain.

But God also wishes his people to offer him worship together as well as individually (Hebrews 10:25). So in chapters 25-27 God instructs Moses to build the tabernacle or meeting tent. Although the detail of these chapters is not applicable today, it does highlight important principles for worship.

Worship demands the very best

which we can bring to God (25:1-9). Notice how God endows people with craft skills to beautify the place of worship (31:1-11).

Furnishings can aid our worship

The ark (25:10-16), the atonement cover (mercy seat) (25:17-19), the table (25:23-30), the veil (26:31) and the altar (27:1-8) were all more than useful tools. They were also visual aids illustrating some truth about God. The atonement cover represented his presence, the veil his formidable holiness, for example.

There is no God-given pattern for church buildings today. Worship is primarily something which comes from the heart (John 4:21-24) and is reflected in daily life (Romans 12:1-2). The variety of church buildings represents human attempts to emphasize particular truths about Christ, his character and his work. When we visit churches, it is helpful to ask, 'What important truth is reflected in this place?' rather than to criticize it because it is different from ours!

The remaining chapters of Exodus deal with further principles of worship. Some of the instructions and teaching are taken up in the book of Hebrews. Its writer looks back to these verses as a shadow of the reality which Jesus Christ brought (see Hebrews 9).

In the middle of the instructions comes a stark reminder that even the people of God can stray far from worship which honours him (chapter 32). Israel turned away from God to worship its own creation. *People do not have to sculpt idols to be guilty of the same sin.*

The challenge of the Ten Commandments (Exodus 20)

1 Is pleasing God my main priority? (verse 3)
2 Do I accept God as he is, or do I cut him down to my size? (4-6)
3 Am I willing to honour him in my daily life? (7)
4 Am I prepared to put his worship and service before my material gain? (8-11)
5 Do I acknowledge my responsibility to my parents and family? (12)
6 Do I truly respect all human life? (13)
7 Am I faithful in thought, word and deed to my marriage partner?(14)
8 Do I treat other people's property with the care I would give my own? (15)
9 Am I truthful in all I say about others? (16)
10 Am I always wishing that I had more than I've got, or am I content with my possessions? (17).

The book of Leviticus

The book of Exodus closed with an account of the 'glory of the LORD filling the tabernacle' (Exodus 40:34-35). It confirmed to the people that God lived amongst them. The book of Leviticus follows this with instructions about how the Israelites were to worship the God who was with them. It gives rules for ritual, worship and conduct which were to be administered by the Levitical priests (descendants of Levi, one of Jacob's sons). This explains the name.

At first, Leviticus seems to take us into a strange world of sacrifice, bloodshed and slaughter which has little relevance to the twentieth century.

However, there is an overall unity of purpose in the Bible, and some New Testament writers build on the ideas contained in Leviticus. For example, the writer to the Hebrews regards the sacrifices of Leviticus as shadows of what was to come. They point to the death of Jesus (Hebrews 10:1-18).

Above all, Leviticus portrays a holy God who must be approached with care and reverence. 'Holiness' is a quality of God which implies absolute perfection and an abhorrence of sin. The rituals of Leviticus demonstrate that only people 'with clean hands and a pure heart' (Psalm 24:4) may approach God.

Summary of Leviticus

1 Rules about offerings (chapters 1-7)
2 Rules about services (chapters 8-10)
3 Rules about daily living (chapters 11-15)
4 Rules for the Day of Atonement (chapter 16)
5 Rules, promises and warnings (chapters 17-27)

220

292-294

Leviticus: data

Author: no-one is named as the compiler, but the phrase 'the Lord said to Moses' occurs some thirty times, and twenty of the twenty-seven chapters begin with it. Therefore it is likely that Moses wrote down the instructions, or supervised the recording of them. Some scholars suggest that later editors rearranged the instructions.

Date: the original instructions are attributed to the period Israel spent in the desert, *i.e.* during the thirteenth century BC.

Purpose: to provide a framework for the services and rituals centred on the tabernacle.

Our worship is a response to God's 'worthship' or worthiness. That is why many church services begin with confession of sin. While Christians are assured of God's complete forgiveness through Christ's death, we are still to approach him with awe and wonder. Your relationship with God will probably be helped if, whenever you pray, you first

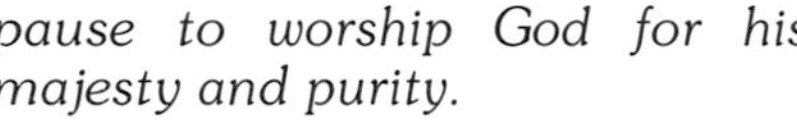

pause to worship God for his majesty and purity.

● Rules about offerings (section 1)

The priests and the people were given instructions about five different kinds of offering which they were to bring to God. Each contains important spiritual principles which remain true today.

The burnt offering (1:1-17; 6:8-13)

This is one of the oldest forms of sacrifice known in the Bible (Genesis 8:20). It became a major Israelite ritual. It was primarily to make atonement for the worshipper's personal sins (1:4), although later it was used for thanksgiving purposes as well. *Behind it lies the principle that God is never content with half-measures. True discipleship is offering our whole self to God.*

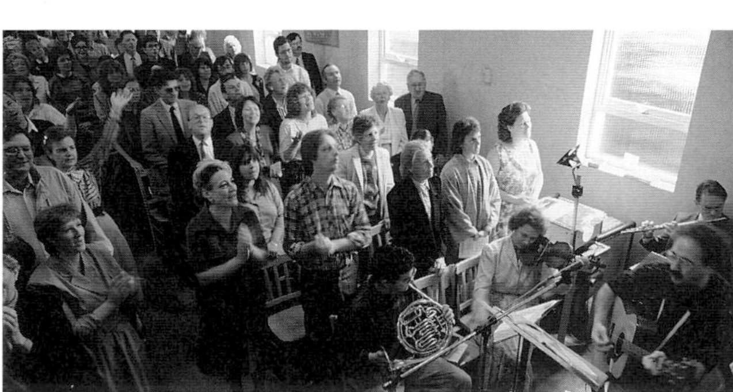

The cereal or meal offering (2:1-16; 6:14-18)

The cereal offering was seen as a gift, a response to God's kindness. It also had an element of atonement for sin. The bulk of this offering went into the priests' foodstore (2:3); they were paid in kind. *'Man does not live on bread alone' (Deuteronomy 8:3) – but we still need it! In thanking God for his provision for us, we have a responsibility to give to those who lack it, and to support Christian ministers.*

The fellowship or peace offering (3:1-17; 7:11-36)

Part of this was eaten by the priests, too – but not the fatty parts. Perhaps this was for health reasons (tapeworm may infest the fat), but also because the fat was seen as a choice offering. God got the best part. *That suggests an important principle in Christian stewardship: God deserves the first choice, not the left-overs, of our time, talent and wealth.* This offering was both a means of restoring the worshipper's relationship with God and an expression of gratitude for its restoration. In Ephesians 2 Jesus is described as a peace offering, drawing together not only God and sinners, but also people estranged from each other by their differences.

Why all the blood?

The stress on bloodshedding in the Levitical offerings strikes many people as barbaric. But when the book is read alongside the New Testament, a reason for the sacrifices emerges.

Leviticus 17:11 uses blood as a symbol of life being given up in death. And death – both in its physical sense and in the spiritual sense of eternal separation from the living God – is the consequence of human sin (Genesis 2:17; Romans 6:23). Therefore, if sin is to be forgiven, life must be given up – which puts the sinner in a no-win situation.

So from the law of Moses, God began to teach Israel through the offerings that sin can be forgiven through someone or something being substituted for the sinner. The substitute takes away the guilt and punishment on our behalf.

At first, the substitutes were animals. But they could never really mend the relationship between God and mankind (Hebrews 10:3-4). Only a perfect human being could do that. Jesus was that person (Hebrews 9:13-14). This aspect of his ministry is central to the New Testament teaching about his death (see Romans 3:21-26; 1 Peter 2:22-24; 3:18-20).

Christianity is based on faith or trust in Jesus' substitutionary act of atonement for our sins. Our good deeds could never accomplish what he did; but our gratitude should be expressed in a God-honouring life (Ephesians 2:8-10).

The sin offering (4:1 - 5:13; 6:24-30)

This offering was made for the forgiveness of sins committed in ignorance or by error, many of which were infringements of the ceremonial law rather than the moral law. *God's concern over such detail reminds us that carelessness over small matters ('no-one will notice') can hinder our relationship with him.*

The guilt offering (5:14 - 6:7; 7:1-10)

This was concerned with unintentional sins against people, and with deception. It was a means of demonstrating acceptance of responsibility and personal sorrow.

What is most likely to help relationships in the church: covering up our failures, or openly confessing them and repairing the damage?

●Rules about service (section 2)

Chapters 8-10 introduce the priests, the 'men in the middle' who mediated between a holy God and his sinful people. The priests were ritually cleansed and specially clothed for their duties. They offered the sacrifices on behalf of the people. Anyone who tried to take their role was punished (10:1-2).

The priesthood of Jesus is shown in the New Testament to be superior to that of any human minister; he is the final mediator between God and man (1 Timothy 2:5; Hebrews 9:15). As a result all Christians have direct access to God through Christ (1 Peter 2:9-10).

Although we do not need mediators to plead with God on our behalf, we do need leaders to direct the church and teach God's truth. The scrupulous concern for correctness and purity in the Levitical priesthood stands as a model of carefulness for all who exercise responsibility in God's name.

●Rules about daily living (section 3)

God's demand for holiness was directed to all his people and not merely to the priests. This section provides laws about physical and moral purity. They show God's interest in healthy diets (chapter 11) and healthy bodies (chapters 12-15) within healthy communities .

These chapters have two important applications for modern readers. They underline the importance of being properly prepared in all aspects of life for the worship of God; it is to be taken seriously, not casually. They also reveal that how we live physically may demonstrate or affect what we are spiritually. Paul said, 'your body is a temple of the Holy Spirit' (1 Corinthians 6:19).

205-206

●Rules for the Day of Atonement (section 4)

Once a year (on the tenth day of the seventh month) the Day of Atonement was celebrated. In a series of solemn rites, Aaron obtained forgiveness for his own sin then entered the innermost part of the tabernacle and made an offering for the nation's sins (chapter 16). An unusual and highly significant ritual was the confession of sin over a live goat (verses 20-22) which was then sent into the desert to die. It represented the complete removal of sin from the camp by God's appointed substitute.

●Rules, promises and warnings (section 5)

Chapters 17-20 contain regulations which cover details of sacrifice (chapter 17) and further moral laws (chapters 19-20). Marriage is prohibited between close relatives, and adultery, child sacrifice, homosexuality and bestiality are outlawed (chapter 18). These laws made the Israelites distinct from their neighbours among whom such practices were common.

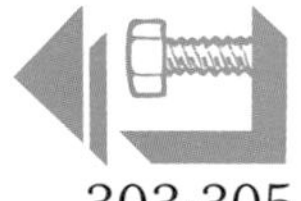

303-305

God's great gift of sex is always celebrated in the Bible within the context of a faithful relationship between a man and a woman. The laws are intended to liberate sex from all that spoils it.

The theme of chapters 19-20 is holiness (19:2). This is expressed by respect for the family, property, truth and justice; by love for the alien, the poor and the great; and by reverence for both the sabbath and the sanctuary. The death penalty for breaches of these laws may seem harsh, but God's concern was that his people's behaviour should reflect his distinctive holiness (20:26). He wanted them to learn that he could not turn a blind eye to any breach of his standards.

Rules for the priests and sacrificial offerings (chapters 21-22) are followed by a list of feasts appointed by God to be observed by the Israelites: the sabbath, Passover. Firstfruits, Feast of Weeks, Feast of Trumpets, the Day of Atonement and the Feast of Tabernacles (chapter 23). The land is to lie fallow every seven years, and every fiftieth year land that has been sold is to revert to its original owner (chapter 25).

These regulations show social as well as spiritual concern. As you read Leviticus, hold its social principles up against the practices of your society, and note where we fall short.

Obedience to God's law will enable the Israelites to 'walk with heads held high' (26:13). Disobedience will bring a range of disasters (26:14-39). If Israel repents, then God will remember his covenant and respond with mercy (26:40-45).

The book of Numbers

Numbers (the title comes from two censuses it contains) is the second volume of the story which began in Exodus. Much of the book describes the experiences of the Israelites during their thirty-eight years of wandering in the desert before their entry into Canaan.

Numbers: data

Author: the main substance of both the narratives and the legislation goes back to Moses, and he is generally regarded as the author. Later changes to the situation in Canaan may have brought some slight modification to the original laws.

Date: the bulk of the book as we now have it would have been committed to writing by the time of the early kings of Israel (950 BC).

Purpose: to show God's concern and provision for the wandering Israelites.

Summary of the book of Numbers

1 Preparing to leave Sinai (1:1 - 10:10)
2 From Sinai to the plains of Moab (10:11 - 21:35)
3 In the plains of Moab (chapters 22-36).

God had already told Moses that he wished to be known as 'I Am'. The choice of name was not simply a declaration of existence. It also affirmed that God displayed his character by his active presence amongst his people.

So as Numbers recounts Israel's experience as a nation whose God is at work, it also reveals God's character. The New Testament sometimes draws a parallel between the church and Israel (1 Peter 2:9). Israel's liberation from Egypt is seen as a picture of the Christian's being freed from sin (1 Peter 1:18-19). Israel's regular disobedience, despite her many privileges, is presented as

a warning (1 Corinthians 10:1-13). *Numbers will therefore be of value to us if we ask of the text, 'First, what does it teach about God? And secondly, 'What does it teach about ourselves as God's people?'*

●Preparing to leave Sinai (section 1)

Preparation for the next stage of Israel's journey included taking a census of the people (1:1-43), allocating responsibilities for the tabernacle (1:44-53), arranging the tribal camps around the tent of meeting (2:1-33) and setting out rules for the care and movement of the tabernacle (3:1 - 4:49). God then reminded them that he was not a disinterested bystander but was active in their affairs and makes demands on them. These include requirements for both physical (5:1-4) and moral (5:5-31) purity for the wellbeing of marriage and family life.

> **The vow of abstention**
>
> The vow of the Nazirite (6:1-21) provided people who were not priests with an opportunity for a distinctive, although usually temporary, separation from others for God's service. Among well-known Old Testament people who took the vow was the colourful strong man, Samson (Judges 13:5). Some scholars suggest that John the Baptist was a Nazirite (Matthew 3:4-6; Luke 1:14-15); Paul took a Nazirite or similar vow (Acts 18:18).
>
> *A temporary act of abstention (such as during Lent) has been traditional among Christians. Rightly used, it can help to focus attention more sharply on God and away from our self-centredness.*

The dedication of the altar (chapter 7) and the consecration of the

Levites (8:5-26) preceded the celebration of the Passover (9:1-14).

This section reminds the reader that God, whose order and perfection is evident within his creation, also requires order in the lives of his people. God's concern for order in Christian worship (1 Corinthians 14:33,40) is stressed in the New Testament also.

206

In today's climate of spontaneity and individualism, disorder in worship can easily displease God. 'Free' worship still needs discipline; and disciplined worship needs flexibility to respond to God's Spirit among us.

●From Sinai to the plains of Moab (section 2)

Now the narrative section begins. At God's command the Israelites left Sinai (10:13) where they had received the Ten Commandments. Their journey was to last thirty-eight years. God led them by a visible cloud (9:15-23).

Life in the wilderness also showed the Israelites their human weakness and God's provision. To meet their physical needs God provided both quails (chapter 11) and later water (20:1-19) in ways which reminded them that God the Creator is also God the sustainer.

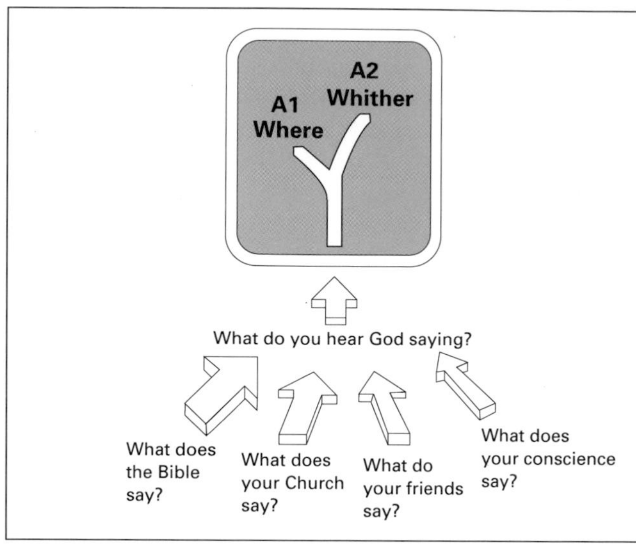

Listen to God carefully before making a major decision.

Further legislation follows regarding the duties of, and sources of income for, the Levites and priests (chapters 18-19). The death of Miriam is recorded (20:1). And then Moses took the hasty action which was to deny him entry into the promised land.

In a fit of frustration at the people's complaints, he hit a water-bearing rock with his staff instead of simply speaking to it as God had commanded. In so doing, he drew attention to himself and away from God (20:1-13). *It was a small thing, but God's reaction underlines the requirement for his people to be scrupulously obedient if they wish to enjoy all his promises.*

● In the plains of Moab (section 3)

The advance of the Israelites struck fear into the heart of Balak, the king of Moab. His decision to call in a diviner, Balaam, to put a curse on the invaders provided him with the unwanted experience of hearing God confirm his word and seeing his power to fulfil it (chapters 22-24).

This story, which has a tinge of humour to it, provides future generations with a warning. We should not seek God's blessing on a course of action which we have already decided to follow. Nor should we simply seek confirmation of our decisions from people we already know will agree. The message here is 'Listen to God carefully before making a major decision.'

With the life of Moses almost over, his successor was chosen by God. Joshua had been a great support to Moses (Exodus 17:9-13; 24:13) and was one of the two faithful spies who believed God's promises (Numbers 14:6-9). He was commissioned by Moses as instructed by God (27:12-23).

The book ends with rules for public worship (chapters 28-30), a description of the allocation of the land on the east side of Jordan (chapter 32) and laws which looked forward to the time when the Israelites would settle in the land of Canaan.

The book of Deuteronomy

The fifth and final book of the 'Pentateuch' takes its name from a mistranslation of 17:18. The verse refers to a copy of the laws found also in Exodus 20-23; the Greek translators rendered it 'The Second Law' – Deuteronomy.

The Jewish title, 'The Words', is more appropriate since the whole book consists of Moses' last words to the Israelites prior to their entry

Deuteronomy: data

Author: internal evidence suggests that the book is based on the work of Moses (31:9-13) who ordered it to be placed beside the ark of the covenant (31:24-26). It is also possible that the first eleven and the last three chapters were recorded and added later by a contemporary of Moses who witnessed the events described.

Date: the form of Deuteronomy is very like the forms of treaties or law codes issued by kings of other nations in the second millennium BC. This further confirms the likelihood that it was complied between 1400 and 1200 BC.

Purpose: to record the detailed teachings of Moses about religious and social conduct.

into Canaan.

Readers of Deuteronomy join the huge crowd being addressed by Moses on the plains of Moab. They are about to experience a major change in their lives. Soon, they will cease to be nomads, with no fixed abode. Ahead lies the unknown land in which they will make a permanent home. *The three basic commands to 'fear the LORD your God... love the LORD your God... and serve him' (6:2,5,13) provide a foundation for Christian living in every generation as change shifts the circumstances and scenery of our lives.*

Summary of Deuteronomy

1 Looking to the past (1:1 - 4:49)
2 Looking at the present (chapters 5-11)
3 Looking to the future (chapters 12-26)
4 Looking at the consequences (chapters 27-30)
5 Moses' blessing and death (chapters 31-34)

● Looking to the past (section 1)

Moses' motive was not nostalgia. He was convinced that yesterday's lessons were essential for tomorrow's living. God's faithfulness to his past promises inspired confidence for the future possession of Canaan (1:6-8). God could equally be trusted for future leadership and organizational needs (1:9-18). And should there be times when the people of Israel could not understand God's purposes, referring to past experiences showed that trust in his wisdom was not misplaced (3:1-3,21-22). To respond in the future on the level of human wisdom and understanding rather than by faith in God, could lead to rebellion and disaster just as it had in the past. *Some people have such long memories that the past always seems better than the present, and they long to turn the clock back. Moses – and the rest of Scripture – does not support them. Nor does he support the people with short memories who abandon the lessons of the past. Look back thankfully at what God has done – then expect him to do great but different things again, is the message.*

● Looking at the present (section 2)

The covenant at Sinai was a past event (4:40) but the obligations resulting from it remain in the present (chapter 5). Moses reminded his listeners of God's Ten Commandments (5:6-33). They were to be the basis for daily living, a constant reminder of God's holiness and of his deliverance from Egypt (6:20-25). At the same time the idolatry of neighbouring nations (chapter 7) and Israel's past experiences of failure and disobedience (chapters 8-9) were factors which

97-98

296-297

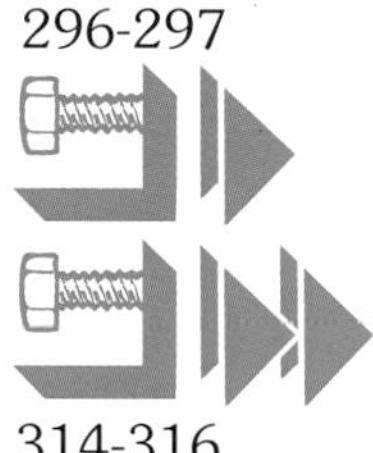

314-316

should throw Israel back on God in love and obedience (10:12 - 11:32).

Deuteronomy introduces more strongly than other books of the Pentateuch the concept of a loving God to whom the appropriate response is one of loving obedience. Look especially at the links between divine love and human obedience in 7:7-16 and 8:1-5.

●Looking to the future (section 3)

Moses reminded the people that holiness involved all aspects of life – religious, family,social and commercial. The person who obeyed God's laws would care for those unable to care for themselves (14:28-29). Offenders would be treated with justice which reflected a balance of strictness and fairness. (19:4-7,11-13; 20:10-12). Women would not be regarded as instruments of men's selfish gratification (20:10-14; 22:22-29). Sensitivity and compassion towards vulnerable people would replace a selfish desire to use them to one's own advantage (23:15-16; 24:10-13).

This section challenges our social relationships. It suggests that people matter more than profit.

●Looking at the consequences (section 4)

Following a list of curses which will result from disobedience and blessings which would follow obedience, Moses made a final appeal to the people he had led. He commanded obedience (27:1-8), promised blessings (28:1-14) and threatened disasters (28:15-68). He then encouraged them to enter a covenant with God (chapters 29-30). They had been chosen by God and were about to receive his inheritance. Their response was to be one of commitment to God.

Why the drastic penalties?

The drastic penalties, including execution, in Deuteronomy may seem to imply that God is capricious, spoiled or selfish. In view of Deuteronomy's stress on God's love, that cannot be the case.

The law code is stressing the serious nature of sin in God's sight, and also its utterly disruptive effect on society. At this stage of its history, Israel needed to learn that lesson graphically; soft application of the law since those times has if anything blinded us to how bad even small crimes or sins can be. Romans 1:18-32 confirms that rejection of God brings natural – and bad – consequences in many areas of daily life, the falling apart of society.

Like the Israelites in the land of Canaan, so the Christian is a stranger in his world (1 Peter 2:11) where popular lifestyles and underlying philosophies are in marked contrast to the way of life demanded by God. The Israelites had to put to death enemies and offenders (7:1-2). The Christian is called to another drastic remedy: to 'die' to our old way of life, in order to enjoy the benefits of new life in Christ (Colossians 2:20 - 3:10).

● Moses' blessing and death (section 5)

Forbidden to enter the promised land himself (32:48-52) Moses' final address was to those who would experience the joy denied to him.

He warned them of the danger of reacting to signs and wonders with amazement but without any understanding of their true significance (30:1-10). He challenged them to go forward with courage, confident that God would lead them faithfully (31:1-8).

3.2 THE PROMISED LAND

History: Joshua to Esther

by Deborah Reed

The land, conveniently called Palestine in recent years, was promised to God's people as they escaped from Egypt. The conquest of the Canaanite tribes who lived in the Promised Land was a very tough assignment, however, and was never really finished.

This section of the Bible describes the conquest, the settlement of the tribes of Israel, their desire for a king and the great reigns of Saul, David and Solomon. We then read of the breakup of the nation between Judah and Israel, the downfall of both and the exile of the cream of the people to Babylon and Assyria.

The history spans about 1000 years from roughly 1400 BC.

93

29

The book of Joshua

Moses had led the Israelites out of Egypt and into the desert but had died before they reached Canaan, the 'promised land'. Joshua had become Moses' second-in-command and was ultimately chosen as his successor (1:1-5).

The book of Joshua is the account of Israel's conquest of Canaan, under Joshua's leadership.

Joshua the leader

Joshua, born in captivity in Egypt, was one of the two adults to survive the desert crossing and enter the promised land (Numbers 14:30). He was one of the twelve spies who explored the land (Numbers 13) and was filled with God's Spirit (Deuteronomy 34:9). He became a first-rate administrator and general.

His story can be read as a model for Christian discipleship. His faith,obedience to God's commands, humility, decisiveness and sense of responsibility are themes to look out for.

Perhaps the greatest dilemma facing modern readers of Joshua is that God commands the destruction of the peoples defeated (6:21; 8:1-2, 24-26 etc.).

How then can he be the same God who commands us to love our enemies? This question is discussed on page 315.

260

Joshua the book: data

Compiled probably during the life of the prophet Samuel, before King David's capture of Jerusalem (15:63). Author: unknown. Purpose: to describe the conquest of Canaan by God's people. The date of the conquest is debatable, either about 1410 BC or about 1220 BC.

●Possession of the land

The call to find a new land for the nation came first to Abraham in Genesis 12. It was a call to drive out those who had occupied it and live under God's rule in freedom and prosperity.

The 'title deeds' to the land were held by God. His people were stewards of his gift. They must look after the unfortunate and the landless (Deuteronomy 14:29) and care for the environment by obeying God's commands (Deuteronomy 11:13-21).

This principle, that all we 'possess' belongs primarily to God who gave it and is ours to use only with love and care, lies at the root of Christian living and of all our concern for 'ecology'. God has entrusted us to be wise stewards of his world, its inhabitants and all our possessions.

The book of Joshua forms a bridge between the books of Moses (Genesis to Deuteronomy) in which the Israelites are wanderers and receive the Law, and the establishment of the monarchy. The theme of possessing the land is central to it.

The New Testament offers believers not a land to live in but the kingdom of God, the rule of Christ over his people. Joshua can be seen as a picture of the Christian's mission to win modern life for God, in obedience to him.

Summary of the book of Joshua

1 Moving in (1-5)
2 A stronghold falls – Jericho (6-8)
3 Battling on (9-12)
4 Staking claims (13-22)
5 Vows redeemed (23-24)

●Moving in (section 1)

For Joshua spiritual and military preparations went hand in hand (chapter 1). Spies were sent to reconnoitre Jericho (chapter 2) which was strategically vital because it commanded the river Jordan and the route to Jerusalem (see map). But the crossing of the river itself was accomplished more by God's intervention than human planning (chapter 3).

This section illustrates the proper balance between spiritual and physical preparation for any project. The Christian will pray and be willing to obey God, but will also make careful arrangements. The two are not mutually exclusive.

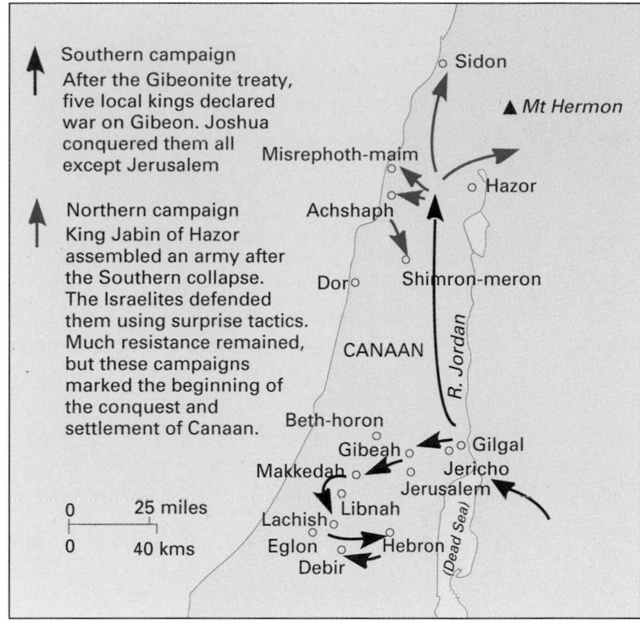

The conquest of Canaan under Joshua.

●A stronghold falls – Jericho (section 2)

Joshua planned to split the land into two. The fortified city of Jericho was in the way. Victory over it would assist his strategy and give the people confidence in a God of miracles. At God's command the people encircled the city and the walls fell 'without a shot being fired'. A violent earth-tremor may well have been the immediate cause of the collapse but God's miraculous intervention was perfectly timed (see Hebrews 11:30).

The 'devotion' of all the inhabitants and objects to God (which means utter destruction, except for Rahab and her family; see chapter 2) may seem harsh to modern readers. But it clearly reveals God's judgment against evil and his displeasure at compromise. God will not tolerate anyone disobeying his ruling and even destroys one of the Israelites, Achan, and his family, for their disobedience. Nevertheless this command has to be balanced against other biblical pictures of the majesty and mercy of God; quite how they relate remains a mystery for human minds.

The principles we see here are faith (the people had to wait for God to demolish the walls), obedience and confession (rooting out disobedience and asking God's forgiveness). Throughout Scripture, God's people are seen to be involved in his battle against all that is evil (see Ephesians 6:10-18).

●Battling on (section 3)

Fear of the Israelites became widespread, as their successes multiplied. 'Surely the LORD was fighting for Israel' (10:14). For the 'long day' recorded in chapter 10, so that the Amorites could be defeated, see page 181.

●Staking claims (section 4)

Not all the land had yet been conquered, however, largely because of disobedience. This section consists of lists of the land they did have. God's promise to Abraham was being fulfilled.

297

The detail of these lists reminds the reader of God's generous provision for his people; no-one is left out when he distributes his gifts (compare 1 Corinthians 12:7).

●Vows redeemed (section 5)

Joshua's farewell speech challenged the leaders of the people to serve God faithfully (chapter 23). They then renewed the covenant with God in a solemn ceremony (chapter 24). This Sinai covenant (see Exodus 23) was a promise of the land and a command to obedience. It was not a bargain with God but a promise from him.

That made it very different from the bargains other nations tried to strike with their gods. It remains a temptation even for Christians to try to manipulate God into doing our will, instead of submitting humbly to his will.

The book of Judges

Joshua had guided the people through a period of great change. After his death the far more mundane task of settling down began. The scattered tribes had been nomadic for several generations. Now they had to learn about settled life and agriculture.

37

They also had to come to terms with competition from the pagan religions of their neighbours. The Canaanites worshipped Baal and Astarte. These were male and female deities thought to own the land and control its fertility. Baal worship proved to be more of a threat than the Canaanite armies, because it cut at the root of the Israelites' existence as the people of the one true God.

With no single strong leader to hold them together the tribes struggled to adapt. When they let their common faith bind them, they were a strong nation. More often they lapsed into worship of the Canaanite gods and suffered weakness and misery.

The book of Judges: data

Date: the book may not have appeared in its present form until the sixth century BC but the substance of it clearly dates from the time of King David. It was written before David captured Jerusalem in about 1003 BC but cannot be earlier than the destruction of the sanctuary at Shiloh, in the days of the prophet Samuel, in the mid-eleventh century BC (1:2; 18:31).

Author: unknown; but he had a high opinion of the monarchy as he attributes many of Israel's problems to its absence.

Purpose: to record the history of a transitional time between the conquest and the monarchy. It celebrates the faith and courage of individuals and warns against falling short of the high standards of the God of Israel. The moral failings of the leaders are not glossed over, but the theme of God's patience in restoring the fortunes of his people is a strong one.

The judges

The book of Judges draws together the stories of twelve of the local leaders of the time. Their names are listed in the summary below. Although they are known as judges,

they were much more than legal administrators. They were heroes, adventurers, advisors, leaders and deliverers, and part-time rulers of the people.

Internal dating in Judges
Reading Judges can be frustrating for those of us who bring a western conception of historical dating to the book. The author simply does not have our interest in a precise timescale. For instance, if all the figures given are added together this period appears to have lasted 390 years. We know from other sources that it was about half that time.

One probable explanation is that the lives of the judges overlapped. There is an example of this in 10:7 where historians know that the Ammonite and Philistine attacks happened simultaneously. Sometimes phrases such as 'forty years', meaning a generation rather than a specific period, are used.

This does not cast doubt on the author's accuracy. He simply approaches things differently from us.

Summary of the book of Judges

1 An unfinished task (1:1-2:5)
2 Some unlikely heroes (2:5-16:31)
  Othniel (3:7-11)
  Ehud (3:12-30)
  Shamgar (3:31)
  Deborah (4:1-5:31)
  Gideon (6:1-8:35)
  Abimelech (9:1-57)
  Tola and Jair (10:1-5)
  Jephthah (10:6-12:7)
  Ibzan, Elon and Abdon (12:8-15)
  Samson (13:1-16:31)
3 Cautionary tales (17:1-21:25)
  Two stories which illustrate the darkness of the times.

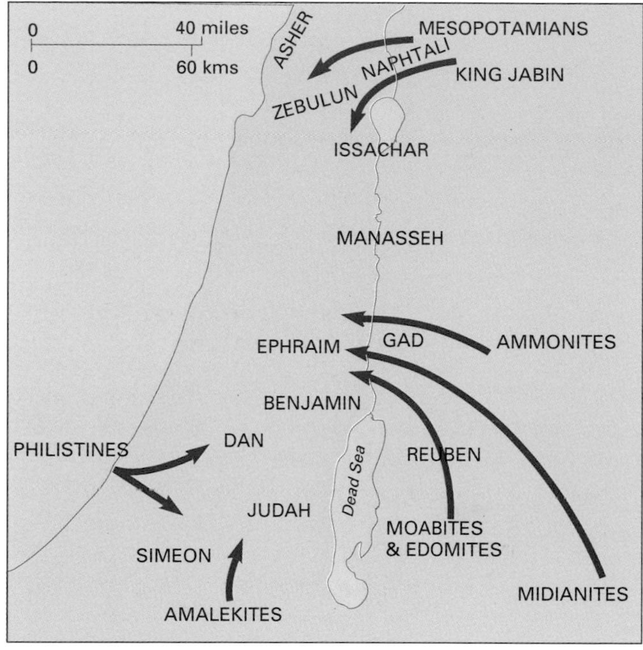

Israel's enemies.

● An unfinished task (section 1)
The Israelites were under constant threat from neighbouring tribes and conquered ones within the promised land. These threats did not really subside until near the end of King David's reign. Israel's persistent disobedience meant they did not have the strength to drive out these enemies.

It is easy to identify with the Israelites. The promise of the land was so enthralling, the beginning of their conquest was so exciting. But the daily reality was so frustrating and disappointing. They must have asked, 'Why doesn't God remove all our problems?' (What equivalent 'neighbouring hostile tribes' do you encounter?) 'Why does God let us drift back to our old ways?' As you read Judges, think about what it may be saying about human responsibility – and what warnings it contains for God's people today.

● Some unlikely heroes (section 2)

Judges 2:6-3:6 describes a repetitive cycle of failures that typified this time. The people deserted God and turned to local gods. God was angry and allowed their enemies to oppress them. Their misery then brought them to repentance and God showed his forgiveness by raising up a judge to deliver them. Unfortunately when each judge died the nation fell back into its old ways and angered God again.

No judge could be described as typical, but three stand out:

Deborah, the prophetess, seems to have been the most gifted. She assumed responsibility when her general, Barak, was hesitant (chapter 4). Her prominence shows that leadership in Old Testament times was not exclusively male.

Gideon grew in faith after hesitant beginnings (chapter 6). He defeated the Midianites after sending most of his soldiers home (chapter 7). Even this evidence of God's power did not prevent him from permitting idol-worship later.

Samson the strong man seems to have lived entirely selfishly and at the mercy of his physical appetites. Yet when the Spirit of God came upon him he performed heroic deeds (chapters 13-16).

The judges were people of their own times. They did not have the benefit of the full revelation of God through Jesus Christ, so it would be unfair to assess them as if they were twentieth-century Christians. But if God could use them – the bold Deborah, the timid Gideon, the outrageous Samson – surely he could work through us, too?

The author is anxious to show that faithfulness to God leads to military success and political stability. Falling back into idolatry and disobedience spells failure in these areas as well as moral and spiritual ones. In other words, religious faith is not simply a private matter of individual conscience, but affects all our activities.

● Cautionary tales (section 3)

These stories of theft, murder, pillage and rape might seem more suited to the sensational newspapers than to the Bible. But 'all human life is here'. The Bible never pretends that life is rosier than it is.

The book of Ruth

The book of Ruth: data

Author: unknown. Date: the story is set at some point in the time of the judges. It was carefully and charmingly written, perhaps during the reign of Solomon. Purpose: to illustrate that, even in times of upheaval, ordinary families experienced God's help. There is an important historical link in that Ruth was to be the great-grandmother of David the king.

Three actors in the drama stand out:

Naomi. Having emigrated to avoid a famine, Naomi had already seen her share of troubles. But then in a foreign land her husband and sons died. She returned home hardened, but came to realize that God had been with her throughout.

Ruth. Although born a Moabite she committed herself to her Israelite husband's faith. She chose to accompany Naomi to Israel. The Israelites were constantly warned not to adopt foreign gods but this

Summary of the book of Ruth

1 Love first (1:1-22)
Ruth will not desert her mother-in-law Naomi.

2 Earning a living (2:1-4:12)
Ruth works for Naomi's relation and asks for marriage obligations to be honoured.

3 A new life (4:13-22)
Boaz honours Jewish law and marries Ruth.

did not mean that foreigners were forbidden to worship Israel's God. Ruth's faith and care for Naomi became part of God's global plan of salvation, for Ruth was an ancestor of King David, and of the family from which Jesus Christ was born.

Boaz. He is the ideal fair-minded, chivalrous and law-abiding man. He was willing to consider the needs of others to the point of sacrificing his reputation by marrying a foreigner. He is described as a 'kinsman-redeemer'; a relative who according to the customs of the time was responsible for providing a home for a widow who had no other means of support. His action has sometimes been seen as a picture of what Christ has done.

This fascinating story gives a glimpse of the everyday life of ordinary people – the people who lived behind the political headlines and horror stories of the book of Judges. God's care is available for the individual even while he works out his wider purposes for the state, whether that individual is a refugee or a politician.

Most people can identify with at least one of the characters – Ruth in her helplessness, Naomi in her bitterness and Boaz in his responsibility. Their story illustrates how God ultimately works out his purposes through difficult or mysterious circumstances.

115

The books of Samuel

Israel longed for national strength and stability. Apart from occasional success the judges had failed to provide it for lengthy periods of time. The Israelites looked at the neighbouring tribes and decided that the missing ingredient was a king. So they demanded one, in a rebellious and resentful manner (1 Samuel 8). Samuel explained all the disadvantages a royal family might bring, including conscription and taxation. But the people insisted, and God acceded to their demands as a loving parent might give in to a sulky child. But God was weaving their petty, short-sighted ambitions into a wider plan.

There are two important themes to look out for. Human weakness used by God results in strength (the obedient child Samuel becomes a great priest/prophet;

26-27

103

Samuel the books: data

Author: unknown (not Samuel, whose death occurs at 1 Samuel 25:1). Date of writing: perhaps soon after the death of Solomon. By the sixth century BC Joshua-Judges-Samuel-Kings formed a complete history of the people of Israel from the conquest to the exile.

Purpose: 1 and 2 Samuel were originally one book and the story is continuous. It describes the change from 'theocracy' – the direct rule of God – to monarchy, the rule of kings. It records the reigns of Saul and David, Israel's first two kings.

the young shepherd-boy David kills Goliath and becomes king; the nation rises from corruption to power). Human strength tends to be corrupted and to become weak (Eli's and Samuel's sons corrupt the true faith; Saul degenerates into madness and suicide).

The principle holds good for all time. True greatness consists in a humble reliance on the strength of God.

Summary of 1 Samuel

1 Samuel's early years (1:1-7:1)
- Samuel's birth (1:1-2:11)
- Corrupt priesthood (2:12-3:21)
- The Philistines capture the 'ark' (4:1-7:1)

2 Samuel the prophet: Saul the king (7:2-16:13)
- The people demand a king (7:2-8:22)
- The choice of Saul (9:1-11:15)
- Saul's decline (12:1-16:13)

3 Saul and David (16:14-31:13)
- The young David (16:14-18:16)
- Saul's jealousy (18:17-28:25)
- David defeats the Philistines (29:1-30:31)
- Saul defeated (31:1-13)

150-153

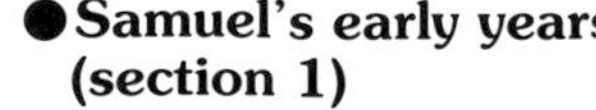

● Samuel's early years (section 1)

In the Old Testament period when God chose a person for a special purpose there was occasionally something remarkable about his birth. In this case Hannah, like several other mothers in the Bible, experienced years of childlessness. When Samuel was born she dedicated him under a Nazirite vow (see Numbers 6), setting him aside for God's special service.

Samuel grew up when religious life was at a low ebb. The priest Eli and his sons stole from the temple offerings (1 Samuel 2:29) and introduced Canaanite practices into Jewish worship (2:22-24). The Israelites even tried to use the ark of the covenant as a magic talisman and lost it in battle to the Philistines. Samuel responded to God's call and his leadership brought about a revival of true worship.

Again we see the pattern of God's plan. He led the Israelites into repentance and they removed the statues of the Canaanite gods. The revival of faith resulted in the Philistine oppression being lifted. The Philistines did not invade Israelite territory again during

Samuel the leader

Samuel may be seen as the last and most godly of the judges. He settled disputes and gave advice but unlike his predecessors he was not a military leader (1 Samuel 7:15-17). The difference emerges clearly during the Israelite victory over the Philistines (1 Samuel 7). Under Samuel the triumph is based less on military prowess and more on godly sacrifice and obedience. From this time onwards it was the prophets who were to play a leading role in Israel's religious life.

Samuel's life.

For the problem of the seventy men whom 'God struck down' (1 Samuel 6:19) see the note on Uzzah (2 Samuel 6:7).

The real sin of Eli's time was that the Israelites allowed the world around them to set their agenda. They were afraid to be different, especially when current practices offered simpler and more sensual solutions to the deep mysteries of faith.

●Samuel the prophet: Saul the king (section 2)

When the Israelites first settled in the land they looked at other tribes and were tempted to bring idol worship into their religion. Now they demanded another feature of their neighbours' way of life; a king. Yet this attempt to make Israel more secure threatened to undermine the very features of its life which made it distinctive.

They were bound together by their covenant with God. Their request for a king showed a lack of trust in the God who promised to be with them and rule them.

God instructed Samuel to anoint Saul as the man to save them from the Canaanites. He seemed to be everything a king should be – a natural leader, tall and strong (though he had not apparently even heard of Samuel before he met him – 1 Samuel 9:1-14). Under God's direction Saul raised an army which assembled at Michmash (1 Samuel 13), but he failed to obey God fully. He offered a sacrifice which Samuel alone had the right to do. He disobeyed God again in not destroying the Amalekites completely or killing their king, Agag (1 Samuel 15:13-33).

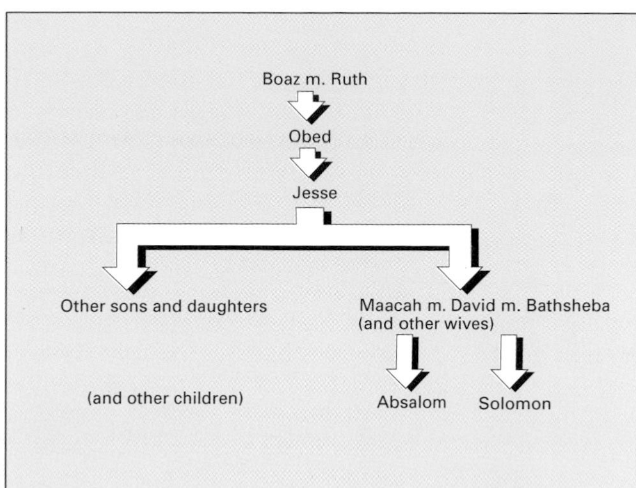

King David's family (simplified).

Saul was prepared to go only part of the way with God. He made good beginnings but impatience and wilfulness replaced obedience. In today's fast-moving world, where even the very existence of God is disputed, thorough and patient obedience to God is very difficult. Saul shows the need to wait for God's clearly defined purpose and not to rush into solutions which seem right to us on the spur of the moment.

●Saul and David (section 3)

Saul was the kind of man people expected to become king. David was not. God directed Samuel to an outlying insignificant farm and then chose the family's youngest son. But David grew into a man after God's own heart. He was not perfect by any means, and he too made decisions out of fear and greed. But he was motivated by desire to see God glorified more than by anything else.

David joined Saul at court but Saul did not obediently accept God's choice. As God rejected his kingship, Saul became more and more prey to his own unstable nature. Out

27

of jealousy he tried to kill David and forced him into hiding. On two occasions (1 Samuel 24:8-10; 26:22-24) David had the chance to kill Saul, but he refused. He was prepared to wait for God's timing no matter how uncomfortable it was.

Two problems in this section may trouble modern readers. Saul's hideous dowry demand in 1 Samuel 18:24-25 has to be seen against the background of the barbaric times in which he lived. It also ensured that the victims were Gentiles.

More difficult is the thrice repeated statement that Saul's evil spirit came 'from the LORD' (1 Samuel 16:14; 18:10; 19:9). For the Old Testament Jew, God was the source of all power so that logically even evil spirits must come from him. The realization that Satan was responsible came later (see Matthew 12:24-28).

133-134

Summary of 2 Samuel

1 Uniting the nation (1-4)
2 Establishing the kingdom (5-10)
3 A king's folly (Bathsheba) (11-12)
4 A father's grief (Absalom) (13-20)
5 Appendix of records (21-24)

●A new beginning

Under Saul the northern tribes had been isolated. They had probably never fully constituted part of his kingdom. David's first task was to unite the nation and command the respect of all the tribal leaders.

136-141

●Uniting the nation (section 1)

The book begins with a problem: Who killed Saul? 1 Samuel 31:4-5 states clearly that he committed suicide. Now (2 Samuel 1:1-10) the Amalekite claims to have killed him. He could well have been lying, hoping to gain David's favour, and certainly not expecting the fate which swiftly overtook him (verses 15-16).

David's lament for Saul and Jonathan (2 Samuel 1:17-27) seems totally sincere, even though their deaths left him on the throne.

His proclamation as king in Judah led to division between his followers in the south and the followers of Ish-Bosheth, Saul's son, and Abner, Saul's army commander, in the north.

After two years of fighting and murder on both sides, David won – but he remained magnanimous, fair-minded and honourable. To the surprise of his supporters, he disgraced the assassins of his enemy and saw Ish-Bosheth buried with honours (2 Samuel 3-4).

David was a generous man. When his enemies fell he mourned for them! Even in Christian fellowships there is often quiet (or not so quiet) satisfaction over the downfall of other people – it makes us feel bigger by comparison. To give way to the feeling in fact belittles us.

David, the hero-king

David was revered as one of Israel's greatest heroes. His military and political expertise was outstanding. Even when Saul was still king, it was David whom the crowds hailed (1 Samuel 18:7). He was a skilled musician and is the traditional composer of many of the Psalms. David was capable of gentleness and graciousness as well as brutality; of devotion to God and shocking behaviour; of humility as well as high-handedness. He was the shepherd-boy ancestor of Jesus Christ who called himself 'Son of David'.

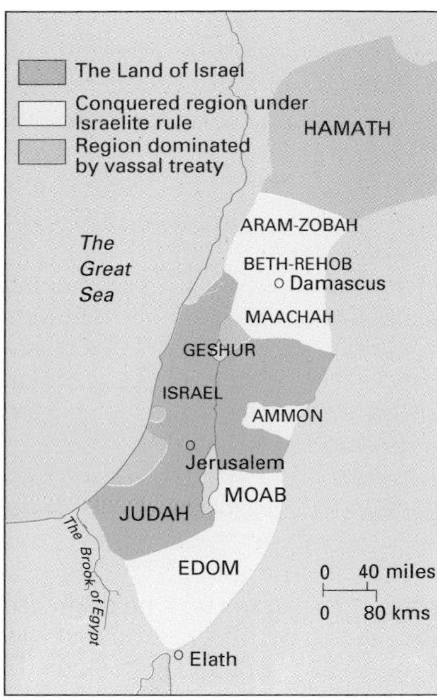

David's kingdom.

2 Samuel: style

This book, especially chapters 9-20, is so vivid and detailed that it could well have been written by a contemporary at the court. It is from these passages that we learn about the king's weaknesses and family troubles. The same episodes are recorded in 1 and 2 Chronicles by a later author intent on showing David as a man of strength. The accounts in Samuel and Kings are more of a personal diary.

●Establishing the kingdom (section 2)

A new capital

The whole nation now recognized David's claim to the throne. His choice of Jerusalem as his capital was masterly. It occupied a powerful strategic position and, as it was held by the Jebusites, was 'neutral' as regards the north/south divide. David's conquest of Jerusalem was seen as a symbolic victory. It became 'the fortress of Zion, the City of David' (2 Samuel 5:7).

A new promise

The Philistines had abandoned the ark of the covenant at Kiriath Jearim. There it lay until David brought it to Jerusalem. He wanted it to stand in pride of place at the heart of the nation symbolizing God's presence with them.

Uzzah's death (2 Samuel 6:6-7) is a puzzle (see also the death of the seventy curious men of Beth Shemesh, 1 Samuel 6:19). The meaning for all time seems to be that God is infinitely holy and in a sense dangerous (C.S. Lewis's God-figure Aslan is 'not a tame lion') and that his actions are not ultimately predictable (the Spirit, like the wind, is not bound by human convention, John 3:8). God's ways to some extent are mysterious to us (Isaiah 55:8-9).

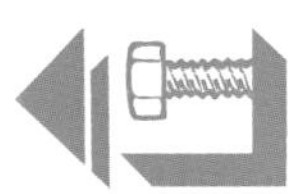

292-294

David had plans to house the ark in a permanent building. As first he received general approval from the prophet Nathan, but God intervened to show him a greater plan (2 Samuel 7).

34

David's reaction was, 'It's entirely up to you, Lord' (2 Samuel 7:18-29). He recognized that his progress thus far was all God's work, and he had no intention of becoming power-hungry and status-seeking. Sadly, human nature often insists on going one step further than God intends; David provides a magnificent exception.

The kings were so arrogant that on many occasions God's promise to David (2 Samuel 7:16) seemed to be in danger of being unfulfilled , but it never failed. For the next 350 years there was a king in Israel until

Jerusalem was destroyed and the people exiled. It was then that they looked to God for the Messiah, his anointed one, through David's line. Hundreds of years later still came the fulfilment of that promise in Jesus.

185

●A king's folly (section 3)

Some ancient Egyptian leaders thought of themselves as being sons of god. They declared themselves to be above the laws which bound their subjects. But David knew that he had a specially close relationship with God under the covenant. This gave him privileges, but it also made him accountable in a way that neighbouring rulers were not.

It was not unusual for ancient rulers to take any woman they desired, but David knew that this was against God's standards.

His taking of Bathsheba and effectively murdering her husband, Uriah (2 Samuel 11) show how even the strongest of men can collapse when confronted with powerful temptation. His repentance (2 Samuel 12 and see Psalm 51) suggests that God will forgive even the worst of misdemeanours – a sign of hope for mankind.

●A father's grief (section 4)

David may have been a powerful king but he was certainly not the strongest of fathers. His lack of action goaded Absalom into taking the law into his own hands and murdering his brother.

134

Absalom then challenged David's right to declare Solomon his heir and the nation teetered on the brink of a new civil war. When Absalom was killed David's grief made him irrational and he was fortunate that his nephew Joab was on hand to provide the needed command.

God does not want us to live in a paralysed regret over what might have been. He asks for repentance, gives us forgivenesss and promises a new start. David had to learn this lesson at least twice.

●Appendix of records (section 5)

In these concluding chapters the writer collects together some information which belongs to a variety of times during David's reign. This includes David's 'song of praise' which celebrates early victories and is similar to Psalm 18. His last poem in 2 Samuel 23 give his thoughts on what makes a good leader – one who is a man after God's own heart.

●The census

Chapter 24 raises questions for the modern reader. Why was a census wrong? (Perhaps because it implied arrogance and the tightening up on extortionate taxation and forced labour). But then why should *God* incite David into such a sin? (verse 1), and why was he angry with his people anyway?

The people's sin was perhaps their rebellion against David, the Lord's anointed. But in seeing God's hand behind David's error the writer is once again recognizing how God overrules in all history. By the time Chronicles came to tell the same story (1 Chronicles 21:1) it had become clear that Satan was the culprit. But even Satan is not a free agent. In his wisdom God must have overseen the whole affair. This is what the writer of Samuel reflects.

God is never taken by surprise. Even when people make wrong or mistaken decisions, we can confidently expect God to work in and through them in ways which will ultimately be for his glory and our benefit.

1 and 2 Kings

Summary of 1 Kings

1 United under Solomon (1-11)
  Solomon secures his position (1-2)
  Solomon's wisdom (3-4)
  The building of the temple (5-8)
  Solomon's disobedience and decline (9-11)

2 The north/south divide (12-16)
  Rehoboam of Judah (12:1-24)
  Jeroboam of Israel (12:25-33)
  Prophetic warnings (13-14)
  Kings of Israel and Judah to Ahab (15-16)

3 Elijah, 'God's troublemaker' (17-22)
  Elijah, a lone voice (17-19)
  Ahab and Jezebel of Israel (20-22)

●United under Solomon (section 1)

The decline and death of David and the sordid business of his successor, Solomon, disposing of his enemies in order to make his throne safe occupy the first two chapters.

Solomon inherited a powerful, united empire. Unlike his father he had no desires to expand it. The international situation was stable and he was able to concentrate on turning Israel into a trading nation.

The name of Solomon speaks of both great wealth and great wisdom. His needs were so lavish that he instituted a network of tax districts to support the massive requirements of his court. One use of his wealth was to build the temple which his father David had planned.

Unfortunately he also deserted many of the old ways. He was more authoritarian than David and not as widely loved by his subjects. He spent more effort in defending his own position than in caring for his people's welfare and nurturing their faith.

As he grew old Solomon began to worship idols and the writer sees this as the reason for his son Rehoboam losing most of the kingdom. The peace which had lasted for most of Solomon's reign was disturbed as God raised enemies against him. It was only because of God's promise to David that there was anything for Rehoboam to inherit at all.

Solomon the wise – and unwise

The mention of the name of Solomon conjures up many varied images of the man. He is known for his wisdom, his building of the temple, his many wives, his great wealth and his administrative genius. There are many sides to his character. His reign began promisingly. God himself reminded Solomon of the warnings and promises which would lead to blessing (1 Kings 3:14). But later he slipped away from God by allowing other issues to become a priority. His devotion to many wives extended to devotion to their gods (1 Kings 11:1-13).

27

127

Not a few men and women with apparently secure faith have slipped sideways into unbelief and bad ways. Behind the example of Solomon is an unspoken warning. A regular check-up is advisable; 'Am I slipping too?' Open-eyed disobedience (in whatever is our own equivalent of worshipping foreign gods or marrying those whose faith will corrupt our own) will lead to personal disaster however attractive it appears on the surface.

1 and 2 Kings: data

Author (or rather editor) and date: unknown but probably in exile in Babylon about 550 BC. The two books were written as one. Source material included court records (see 1 Kings 11:41; 14:19; 15:7) and the writings of prophets.

Theme: Israel is the chosen people of God and the kings are his representatives. Israel's disobedience to God leads inevitably to defeat and exile. Since the kings generally fail, God's will is conveyed through the prophets, notably Elijah and Elisha.

Period covered: from the death of David to the death of Zedekiah; *i.e.* from about 970 to 586 BC, or 384 years.

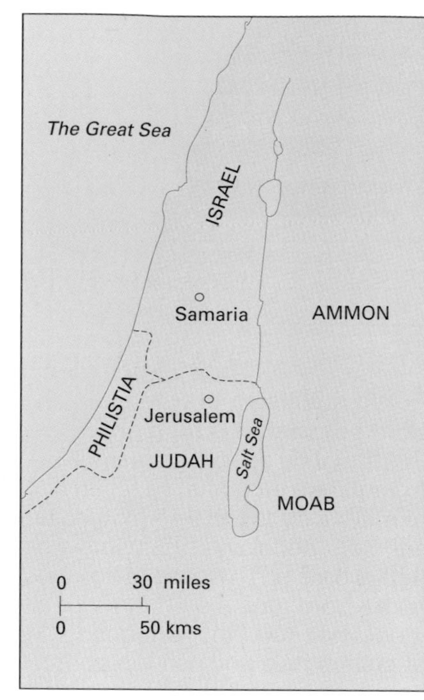

Israel and Judah divided, from 930 BC.

●The north/south divide (section 2)

The prophetic origin of Jeroboam's rebellion is described in 1 Kings 11:26-40. The ten northern tribes had lost confidence in Solomon, not least because he taxed his own tribe of Judah less heavily than the others. Jeroboam fled to Egypt and awaited Solomon's death.

28

At that point the kingdom divided in two (about 931 BC). Jeroboam attempted to reconcile the tribes (1 Kings 12:3-17) but Rehoboam, Solomon's son, refused to grant concessions and Jeroboam was proclaimed 'king of Israel', leaving Rehoboam the southern area of Judah around Jerusalem.

37

Jeroboam quickly set up pagan shrines and in general the northern tribes turned away from the God of David. The south fared a little better but the slide into pagan ways was scarcely halted by Hezekiah and Josiah, the 'good kings'.

Chapters 13 and 14 of 1 Kings contain writings from the prophets rather than court records and shed light on what life was like at grass-roots. The story of the 'man of God' and the old prophet is told to underline once again the need for unswerving obedience to God's commands. Ahijah's prophecy against Jeroboam is another warning of disaster for the disobedient.

One can hardly help feeling sorry for the prophet who was deceived (1 Kings 13). The story contains two warnings for people who want to follow God. First, it reminds us of the need to fulfil God's requirements completely; whatever their apparent importance, our obedience is being tested. And secondly it shows that not everyone who claims to speak in God's name actually does so (see also Matthew 7:21-23); we need discernment too.

●Elijah, 'God's troublemaker' (section 3)

The kings of Israel were described as bad because they did not encourage worship of God. The writer does not try to assess their political, economic or military successes. Some of them were actually worse than others and at these especially low points the prophets were most active.

Prophets were messengers sent from God. The authority for their words lay not in their learning or official appointment but in direct commands they received from God. They were primarily concerned with the present time, calling for a change in the king's planned course of action. Elijah was one of the greatest of all the prophets. And Ahab was one of Israel's really bad kings. He allowed himself to be dominated by his Phoenician wife Jezebel who was trying to remove the worship of God from Israel. Little wonder that Ahab and Jezebel saw Elijah as a troublemaker.

To Elijah it seemed that any hope of true worship in Israel had disappeared. He complained that he was the only faithful believer left (1 Kings 18:22). Yet he confronted the Baal worshippers on Mount Carmel with a faith that appeared idiotic in its simplicity when he called for fire from heaven to devour a water-sodden sacrifice on a clear day when lightning wasn't forecast. Yet God heard his prayer and acted on it.

His secret was that he understood God's power in the face of intimidation. It was not the strength of Elijah's faith that won through but the supreme power of God, in whom Elijah trusted. Faith is not believing the impossible, but learning to see things from God's perspective, trusting the power of God and relying on his goodness. Or, to put it another way, faith is being certain of realities which otherwise we would not see (Hebrews 11:1).

Summary of 2 Kings

1 Elisha and Jehu's reforms (1-10)
2 Decline and fall of Israel (11-17)
3 Judah alone, the fall of Jerusalem, exile (18-25)

150-153

●Elisha and Jehu's reforms (section 1)

2 Kings opens with the conclusion of Elijah's life story and his dramatic departure. His follower Elisha asks for a 'double portion' of his spirit (2 King 2:9). This reflects the double inheritance of a family estate due to the eldest son; Elisha was asking to become Elijah's spiritual successor.

Elisha

We know little about Elisha except that Elijah sought him out when young from a wealthy family. His ministry was to extend over the next fifty years, covering the reigns of six kings – Ahab, Ahaziah, Jehoram, Jehu, Jehoahaz and Jehoash.

He can be compared to Samuel as seer, counsellor and advisor. He is best known for his miracles (18 are recorded) which demonstrated God's compassion and care for his erring people. Whereas Elijah's ministry parallels that of John the Baptist, Elisha's anticipates the miracle working of Jesus.

His death is recorded in 13:20.

The difficult stories in 2 Kings 1:9-16 and 2:23-25 are included as a warning not to oppose God or his representatives. The destruction of the soldiers seems contrary to Jesus'

81

teaching in Luke 9:54-55; through biblical times God progressively moved his people on to greater understanding. The three-fold repetition is common in ancient dramatic story-telling.

Jehu's destruction of the priests of Baal (2 Kings 10:18-31) was merciless and thorough. But he failed to replace Baal with worship of the true God. There is little value in giving up bad habits if we do not also turn fully to God and allow him to control our lives. An annual moral spring-cleaning is not enough.

29

●Decline and fall of Israel (section 2)

The short accounts of the kings of Judah and Israel can be confusing.

Both kingdoms are seen as God's chosen people, but their rulers tend to rely on foreign powers rather than on God. That compromise resulted in the northern kingdom of Israel falling to invaders. Hoshea, the last king, was little more than an Assyrian puppet. He attempted to save Israel from this pressure by courting the Egyptians – which led directly to the Assyrian invasion. Samaria was beseiged for three years before it fell. Everyone who survived was deported and the Assyrians repopulated the land with other conquered races from Babylon and Syria.

78-79

In 2 Kings 17:7 the author says that 'all this took place because the Israelites had sinned'. His motive for writing is to proclaim this moral. This kind of judgment does not seem to fall automatically on godless regimes today. The principle continues to hold good , however. The collapse of communism and the alarming instability of capitalism in the modern world both point to a need to put God before political ideology.

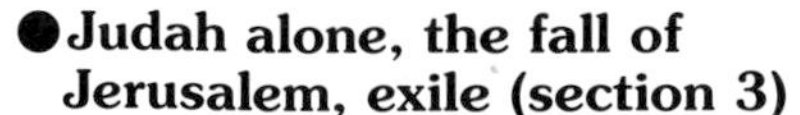

●Judah alone, the fall of Jerusalem, exile (section 3)

Judah existed for another 136 years after the fall of Israel. The writer of Kings would be the first to attribute its survival to three individuals (under God), the godly kings, Hezekiah and Josiah, and the prophet Isaiah whose life spanned four reigns.

Hezekiah (2 Kings 18-20) resisted King Sennacherib of Assyria and thoroughly reformed the religious life of Judah (717-686 BC). Josiah (2 Kings 22-23) reinstated the Passover, after the book of the Law (possibly Deuteronomy) was rediscovered. He reigned from 639-609 BC and also reformed religious life between 686 and 639 BC it had fallen back into paganism once again.

Despite Hezekiah, Josiah and even Isaiah the general slide continued, however. The Babylonians finally conquered Jerusalem, carried away its treasures and its people, and burnt it to the ground in 587 BC. The Lord's people appeared to be defeated at last.

The prophets and few righteous rulers occupied much the same position as Christians in the modern world. A general moral and spiritual decline is continuing, despite some notable exceptions (Mother Teresa in Calcutta and Jackie Pullinger in Hong Kong come easily to mind, who have allowed the love of God to work through them in spectacular ways). Only God can save the world. Our task is to continue to obey him and to bring his truth and justice to bear on our small corner of the world, however bleak the overall situation seems to be.

1 and 2 Chronicles

Another history book?

Like Samuel and Kings, Chronicles is really one book. The books of Joshua to 2 Kings have told the story of Israel from the entry to the promised land to the exile in Babylon, a period of more than 700 years. Chronicles interrupts the sequence and goes back over much of the same ground but with a different purpose.

Chronicles: data

Author and date: Chronicles is part of a series with Ezra and Nehemiah which follow. Author unknown (some have suggested Ezra); probably between 400 and 300 BC, well after the exile of Judah in Babylon.

Purpose: the author assumed that his readers already knew the history so he selected aspects of it to construct a sermon. Chronicles surveys past history in terms that Jews in the fourth century BC would understand. It aimed to give them an understanding of how the Jewish community came into existence and how God had been central to its history, as evidenced in the temple and its worship and in the divine gift of David's line of rulers.

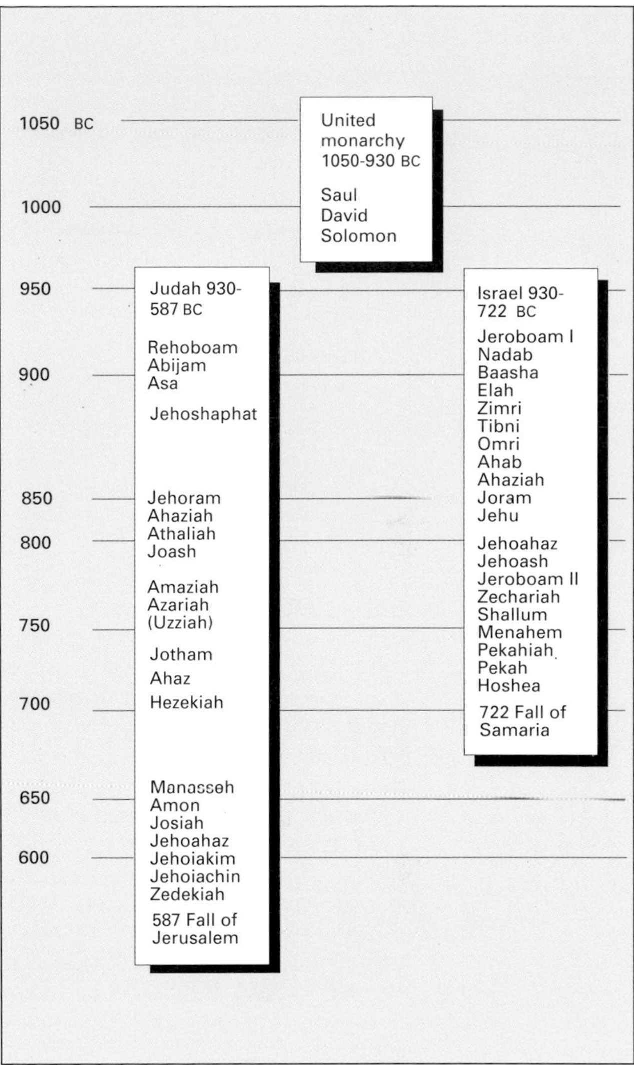

List of the kings of Israel and Judah.

● Themes to look out for

The Israelites needed to learn the hard lessons of history. Prosperity and progress lay in worshipping God. Judgment and exile were in store for those who deserted him. The exile had uprooted the people, and they had lost a sense of national identity. Most of those who returned had been born in Babylon. And now the Persians were controlling international affairs – Babylon had fallen to Cyrus of Persia in 539 BC.

The author addresses the doubts Jews had about their place in the world, and their identity crisis. His answer to this bewilderment is to take his readers back to Adam and show them exactly where they fit in.

The Jews' post-exile confusion of mind is very similar to that of western peoples today. Traditional customs have been dismantled by new ideologies and basic beliefs challenged by massive media bombardment. Where can we turn to find our roots? The chronicler would prescribe a dose of biblical history which would put God back in the centre of our thinking where he belongs.

Summary of 1 Chronicles

1 Genealogies (1-9)
2 Building a temple (10-29)
- David brings the Ark to Jerusalem (10-16)
- David's plan to build (17)
- David's victories and his successor (18-22)
- The Levites (23-26)
- David's departing addresses (27-29)

● Genealogies (section 1)

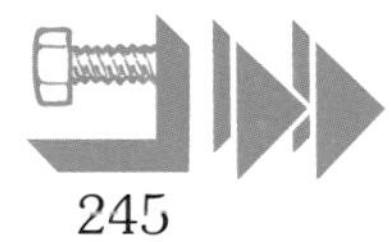
245

Research into family trees is a popular pastime today and careful research can produce accurate information. The chronicler's methods, however, seem to be chaotic. He condenses the first nine chapters of Genesis into ten names, shot as from a machine gun with no explanation. Later on, however, he repeats apparently irrelevant detail about obscure people; did you know, for instance, that Hezron married the daughter of Makir when he was sixty years old? (1 Chronicles 2:21). He uses some biblical sources exactly, others he turns to his own ends, omitting much and adding material from other sources ('these records are from ancient times', 1 Chronicles 4:22). The problem is aggravated by copyists' errors and impossibly large numbers which often vary from the original.

68-69

But these are the wrong concerns if we want to understand what the chronicler is about. His plan is to show how God's grace to his people has continued from creation, through the waters of the flood, the Red Sea, the Jordan and of all kinds of affliction, to the crowning glory of the temple on the summit of Mount Zion.

● Building a temple (section 2)

Solomon actually built the temple but the chronicler is keen to show that David laid the plans for it. David is portrayed here as a cultured urban dweller, not the outlaw turned ruler we met in 2 Samuel. But he is not trying to idealize David. The writer simply ignores events which have no connection with the temple. He traces the temple and its worship activities from its earliest origins to its completion and eventual destruction.

The chronicler is writing religious history as opposed to political history. His concern is to see what God is doing with his people. As we read our newspapers and

Large numbers

Figures sometimes differ between the original source and Chronicles. This is sometimes due to copyists' errors (for instance the words for thousand' and 'paid soldier' were similar and could have been confused; our system of writing in figures was not yet in use. Some apparent problems may disappear if you check other translations. For instance in 2 Chronicles 14:9 Zerah the Cushite commanded 300 chariots 'and a million men'. The New International Version translates this as 'a vast army' because the Hebrew means either 'a thousand thousands' or 'thousands upon thousands'.

The aim of the chronicler is not to furnish his readers with exact figures (they are nearly all 'round' thousands anyway) but to impress them with the great numbers involved.

watch TV telecasts it is easy to forget this dimension to our history-in-the-making. We shall need to keep abreast of both world affairs and church affairs if we are to retain the balanced view of God's activity in the world offered by the Bible through its inclusion of both Samuel-Kings and Chronicles.

Summary of 2 Chronicles

The temple:

1 Constructed (1:1-9:30)
2 Declining (9:31-35:27)
3 Destroyed (36:1-21)
4 Rebuilt (36:22-23)

●The temple constructed (section 1)

The two books of Chronicles hinge on the temple building. So in 2 Chronicles we see less of Solomon as the high financier and more of Solomon as the builder. Construction started in the fourth year of his reign and took seven years. His other activities are recorded in chapters 8 and 9 almost as an appendix.

The nomadic Israelites in their early history had never built a central focus for their worship. They had occasionally commemorated an event at a place by erecting their sacrificial altar. But when Israel became a settled nation God gave Solomon the necessary wealth to build a temple.

●The temple declining (section 2)

The chronicler's assessment of the kings of Judah does not differ from the Kings account, but his emphasis is different. He adds more comments on why things did not always follow the strict cycle of judgment and blessing (*e.g.* 2 Chronicles 12:12). He also suggests reasons which reveal that an unchanging God stands behind the events (*e.g.* 2 Chronicles 20:37).

●The temple destroyed (section 3)

Not even the 'good' kings maintained the temple properly. The treasures of Solomon were plundered by various kings to pay off enemies or to buy allies. Even Hezekiah was guilty.

The 'bad' kings added idolatrous furnishings to the building as symbols of foreign gods. Ahaz replaced the laver with an Assyrian altar to demonstrate his submission to Tiglath-pileser (2 Kings 16; 2 Chronicles 28). This is why by Josiah's time, 300 years after its construction, considerable restoration work was required. Finally in 587 BC King Nebuchadnezzar of Babylon demolished it. The prophet Jeremiah tells us that even after its destruction pilgrims still journeyed to sacrifice at the spot (Jeremiah 41:5).

●The temple rebuilt (section 4)

The chronicler cannot end on the down note of the destruction. The final verses repeat the opening ones of Ezra. Cyrus king of Persia released the exiles to return and rebuild the temple. The fulfilment of this proclamation is recorded, in Ezra and Nehemiah.

We have no final security unless we know the God who created and sustains his world. If the reader is reminded of this today the chronicler would have been well pleased.

Ezra and Nehemiah

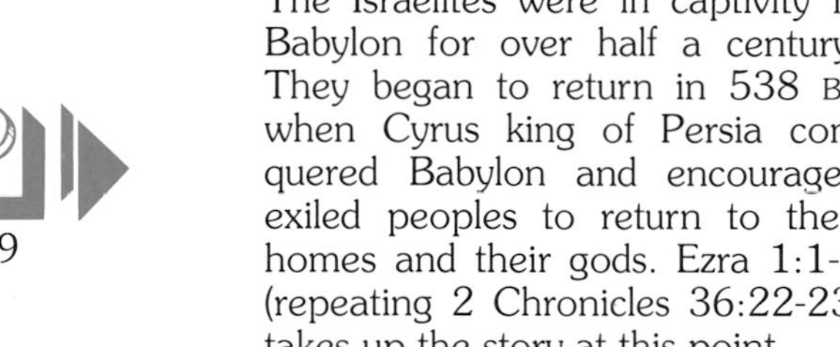

29

The Israelites were in captivity in Babylon for over half a century. They began to return in 538 BC when Cyrus king of Persia conquered Babylon and encouraged exiled peoples to return to their homes and their gods. Ezra 1:1-3 (repeating 2 Chronicles 36:22-23) takes up the story at this point.

Ezra-Nehemiah was originally one book, part of Chronicles. It deals with the 100 years or so between the return of the exiles and the end of Nehemiah's work (about 430 BC).

Persian kings of the period

BC	
559-530	Cyrus
530-522	Cambyses
522-486	Darius I (Hystaspes)
486-465	Xerxes I (Ahasuerus)
465-424	Artaxerxes I (Longimanus)

● The events of Ezra-Nehemiah

Ezra 1-6: Sheshbazzar was appointed first governor of Judah and made a start on temple foundations. The first large group of exiles returned under Zerubbabel in 537 BC. The temple was completed in 515 BC.

Ezra 7-10: The second group of exiles returned under Ezra (the traditionally accepted date is 458 BC).

Nehemiah: Nehemiah arrived as governor in 445 BC and the city walls were rebuilt.

● Themes to look out for

Ezra was concerned with spiritual purity. How could the returning exiles worship as God wanted them to? They were now racially mixed, with foreign wives and often foreign idols.

Another problem was the relation between demands of worship and policies of the state. Ezra, and especially Nehemiah who was himself a high-ranking official, had to try to be loyal to their God and to their government. That problem is often faced today where Christianity is a minority faith in conflict with hostile neighbours and civil authorities. Nehemiah serves as an outstanding model for people in positions of leadership.

Ezra-Nehemiah: data

Author and date: Ezra may have written the whole book Chronicles-Ezra-Nehemiah, but Nehemiah's own contribution was important as he gives much personal detail. It is likely, however, that an unknown author wrote the books in the fourth century BC.

Purpose: to show how God returned Israel to the promised land and how the worship of the temple was restored. The apparently impossible had happened. Israel's hopes were revived.

● The return (section 1)

The return of the exiles was a political move but the writer sees it as controlled by God (Ezra 1:1). The exiles needed much encouragement

Summary of the book of Ezra

1 The return (1-2)
2 The rebuilding (3-6)
- The altar (3)
- Local opposition (4)
- The prophets encourage them to continue (5)
- Completion (6)

3 Ezra arrives in Jerusalem (7-10)

to move back to the ways of their ancestors. They had been comfortable in Babylon and the gods of wood seemed just as valid as the great unknown God described to them by the prophets. Isaiah had denounced their trust in carpentry (see Isaiah 44:9-20 for an amusing but powerful example).

God seems to hide himself. The 'gods' of the world around us seem to be more convincing than the God of the Bible and the preachers. We need to stand back and ask ourselves which, in the long run, has the better credentials.

● The rebuilding (section 2)
Not only were the returning exiles in need of encouragement. The local people, who had not been exiled, were fearful of the rebuilding. They had lost their dynamic faith and were afraid that the re-establishment of Jerusalem would be seen as treason. Then the armies of Persia would attack them as the armies of Babylon and Assyria had in the past. This opposition frequently held up the work, but the prophets were on hand to encourage and inspire the builders.

Prophets of the period

Malachi wrote in about 460 BC.

Zechariah in 520-518 BC.

Haggai in 520 BC.

Their books in the Old Testament throw light on this period.

● Ezra arrives in Jerusalem (section 3)
Ezra was a priest in the family of Aaron. He asked for permission to go to Palestine and was given authority by the Persian government.

'God was not against marriage between those of different race..'

His task was to re-establish the religious life of the community (which had sunk again after the euphoria of the first homecoming, as Malachi vividly describes). He brought with him 'the book of the law of Moses', probably the book of Deuteronomy, and based his reforms firmly on the principles laid down by the God of Israel.

His greatest stumbling-block was the mixed marriages of many of the Jews. These were roundly denounced and repented of (Ezra 9-10). God was not against marriage between those of different race but of different *religion*.

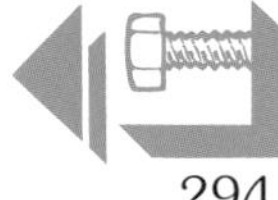

291

Traditionally it is assumed that Ezra arrived before Nehemiah. The date of Nehemiah's arrival can be pinpointed at 445 BC (the twentieth year of Artaxerxes I: Nehemiah 2:1). He too had a strong conviction that God was calling him for a clear purpose, to rebuild the walls of Jerusalem.

Summary of Nehemiah

1 Nehemiah's commissioning (1:1-2:10)
2 Building the walls (2:10-7:73)
3 Living by God's law (7:73-10:39)
4 Residents listed (11:1-12:26)
5 Some disappointments (13)

● Nehemiah's commissioning (section 1)

Nehemiah 2:4 provides a fine example of someone who lives very close to God. The king asked him what he wanted. 'Then I prayed to the God of heaven, and I answered the king ...' Nehemiah was conscious enough of God to remember to ask his advice at a time of great need, and familiar enough with God to exchange a word or two with him in the brief time available.

● Building the walls (section 2)

The Israelites had lost the enthusiasm that they had brought with them to Jerusalem. They had begun to integrate with the local Samaritan population and to build a comfortable life for themselves. Their social and business practices fell short of God's standards of purity, as Ezra had discovered.

Nehemiah knew that Jerusalem had to become independent if its distinctive moral and religious life was to be maintained. This meant rebuilding the city walls. There was fierce opposition, notably from Sanballat (probably governor of Syria) and Tobiah, his secretary. They accused the builders of being revolutionaries. When this failed they ridiculed the building and finally resorted to violence . Nothing deflected Nehemiah from his task, however, and the walls were completed so quickly that even the enemies acknowledged that God must have approved.

The charge of treason, ridicule, the threat of violence; these are all familiar to Christians in many parts of our world today. By following Nehemiah's example of constant prayer, determination to complete the task with the Lord's help, courage and faith, we can fight our battles equally effectively.

● Living by God's law (section 3)

The new city was compact and secure and it gave the Israelites a chance to set their own standards again. Nehemiah concentrated on the business community. His reforms were aimed at those who were exploiting their own people.

Ezra put God's law back into the heart of the Jewish way of life. The people were moved to genuine repentance.

● Residents listed (section 4)

The emphasis on purity demanded a precise list of who belonged to the new regime. The list in Nehemiah 7 includes those in both the first and the main parties of returnees and is practically identical with Ezra 2. The list in Nehemiah 11-12 is very similar to 1 Chronicles 9:2-17. It probably relates to those who stayed in Jerusalem.

● Some disappointments (section 5)

Nehemiah reported back to King Artaxerxes in 433 BC. We are not told how long he remained in Persia before returning to Jerusalem but it was time enough for standards to fall. Many of his reforms had to be started all over again. Tobiah had wormed his way in and had to be ejected; income for Levites had to be raised. The sabbath was being neglected; mixed marriages were on the increase again.

It is a disappointing ending. The author has not varnished the truth. When a person or a church moves forward, regular checks are needed to prevent old sins and bad attitudes creeping back in – sometimes in new guises.

The book of Esther

This book is set not in Israel or Judah but in Persia among those Israelites who did not return to Judah from the Babylonian exile. We know that the Israelites were not always well treated by the Persians from sources such as the book of Daniel. In Esther, though, the threats are even more serious. A plot threatens to destroy the whole Jewish race in the Persian empire.

Summary of the book of Esther

Esther is an action-packed story and does not really break into sections. This summary is a guide to the story:

1 A new queen (1:1-2:20)
2 Mordecai opposes Haman (2:21-3:15)
3 Esther's intervention (4:1-5:8)
4 Haman schemes against Mordecai and the Jews (5:9-6:14)
5 Rescue (7:1-9:17)
6 The feast of Purim (9:16-10:3)

The theme of the story is God's miraculous intervention through the coincidence of events to preserve his people, although God is never mentioned specifically. Like Ezra-Nehemiah it describes conflict between religious convictions and state policy. Esther and Mordecai keep the balance with faith and courage.

● A new queen (section 1)

Herodotus, the Greek historian of the fifth century BC, travelled in Persia and recorded that Xerxes was a changeable, self-indulgent man. Esther's record of his lavish display of wealth, dismissal of his queen and the extended beauty contest to find a new one, fit in with this description. He unwittingly selected a Jewish girl as his queen.

The book of Esther: data

Author unknown. He had a detailed knowledge of Persian culture of the fifth century BC and was obviously a Jew as the book is fiercely nationalistic. Date: the action takes place in the reign of Xerxes I (486-465 BC) in Susa, 150 miles east of Babylon. Nature: Many writers have thought that the book was written as a 'historical novel' in the time of the Maccabees (second century BC) to strengthen Jewish patriotism. There is, however, no convincing evidence to deny that the book is what it claims to be, a factual narrative.

● Mordecai opposes Haman (section 2)

Loyalty to the king does not mean that God must take second place. Mordecai saw public submission to Haman as a form of idolatry and refused to comply. Haman seized his chance to rid the empire of Jews and persuaded the king to brand the offence as treason.

● Esther's intervention (section 3)

Esther was the only Jew who had access to Xerxes and even she risked her life by appearing before

Place in the Hebrew Scripture

The book of Esther is second only to the Torah (Law) in the Jewish faith. In the Hebrew Scriptures Esther is grouped with 'the Writings' such as the Psalms rather than with the history books. This is because it is one of the five festal books which are read aloud on important dates in the Jewish calendar. It is used at the feast of Purim which commemorates their deliverance from exile.

46

him without being summoned. She valued the good of her people more highly than her own safety.

● Haman schemes against Mordecai and the Jews (section 4)

The story unfolds as a black come-
46 dy, with Haman occupying the gallows he had erected for Mordecai.

● Rescue (section 5)

The king issued a second edict, allowing the Jews to defend themselves if attacked under the terms of the first.

It was not easy for the Israelites to preserve their distinctive way of life. When it was threatened they narrowed their loyalty and used the edict to take revenge.

The request for the death of Haman's sons seems harsh to us but in its own terms shows how zealous they were for the Lord and how concerned they were to root out evil. It would be unfair to judge them in the light of the love of Christ of which they could know nothing.

● The feast of Purim (section 6)

The nation was rescued and to commemorate this the 14th and 15th day of Adar (roughly February) were instituted as annual feast days. Though God is not mentioned in the book Jews recognize his hand throughout and give him the glory. Purim is still celebrated today and now also celebrates more recent events of deliverance.

The stirring events of the past, remembered in annual festivals, can do much to hold together people united by race or belief. At best they may celebrate what is good and benefit the participants. At worst, however, festivals can degenerate to a display of bigotry. Discernment is needed.

POETRY, PSALMS AND WISDOM

by Tremper Longman III

Poetry occurs throughout the Bible, though mostly in the Old Testament. It is easily recognized in most modern Bible versions.

The five books in this section of the Bible are written very largely in poetry, which is explained on page 138. The Hebrews were not ashamed to express their emotions and here we find worship, joy, sorrow, anger and love poured out before God.

Poetry, psalms and wisdom
The five books in this section are written chiefly as poetry:
Job, Psalms, Proverbs, Ecclesiastes and Song of Songs

Prophecy
Much of these prophetic books is also written as poetry
Isaiah, Micah, Nahum, Habakkuk and Zephaniah

Parts of Ezekiel, Zechariah and Revelation are in poetry

Other significant poetic passages:

Genesis 49 Jacob's blessings
Exodus 15 Song of Moses
Numbers 23-24 Balaam's prophecies
Deuteronomy 32 Song of Moses
Deuteronomy 33 Moses' blessing
Judges 5 Song of Deborah
1 Samuel 2 Hannah's prayer
2 Samuel 1 David's lament
2 Samuel 22 David's song of praise
2 Kings 19 Isaiah's prophecy
1 Chronicles 16 David's psalm of praise
Jonah 2 Jonah's lament
Luke 1 Mary's song
Luke 1 Zechariah's song
Luke 2 Simeon's song
Philippians 2 The song of Christ's humility and glory

In the New Testament there are also many quotations of poetry from the Old Testament

Where to find poetry in the Bible.

The book of Job

Everyone suffers in this life. No-one can escape the pain of depression, grief, sickness, accident or loneliness. This common experience helps to explain the universal appeal of the book of Job, the story of one man's intense suffering and his search for the reason why he feels the pain.

Job is also one of the most beautifully crafted books in the Bible. It powerfully communicates its message through the art of story-telling. Its literary richness has influenced western writing down to the present day.

There is nothing quite like the book of Job elsewhere in the Bible or in other writings from the ancient Near East. That is not to say that the other peoples of the Near East were unconcerned about suffering. Indeed, the peoples of Mesopotamia and Egypt produced books dealing with the relationship between the

The book of Job: data

Author: unknown.

Date: uncertain. Ancient tradition (as well as modern scholarship) suggests a date as early as before Moses (about 1500 BC) or as late as Ezra (about 500 BC) and everything in between!

The setting of the book is definitely early. Job lives and acts like one of the patriarchs (Abraham, Isaac, Jacob). He is a non-Israelite since Uz is east of the Jordan, an area later called Edom. Thus, Job the person is best understood as living before God made his covenant with Abraham and committed himself to a chosen people. However, the setting of a book does not determine when it was written.

gods and justice. But they differ from Job not only in form but also in the answer they give to the problem of suffering.

Many people consider Job to be a defence of God's goodness in the light of evil and suffering in the world. However, while suffering is central to the book, there is no clear explanation given for it. Job is more of a debate about the source of wisdom. Who is wise? Who has the answers to our deepest questions about life?

There are two themes to look out for in the book. One is the veil of mystery which lies over human life. It provides a corrective to our western belief that everything can be reduced to simple equations; the mind and workings of God cannot be known entirely. The other is the pastoral care of people who suffer; the clumsy theology of Job's friends only rubs salt into his wounds.

Summary of the book of Job

1 Prologue (1-2)
2 Job's lament (3)
3 Dialogue with his three 'friends' (4-27)
4 Job's speech on wisdom (28)
5 Job's concluding statement (29-31)
6 Elihu's speech (32-37)
7 God's speech and Job's response (38-42:6)
8 Epilogue (42:7-17)

●Prologue (section 1)

The first few verses are set on earth and introduce the main character Job. He is a wealthy man with a stable, happy family, and is also deeply devoted to the Lord.

The scene switches to the divine council chamber where an angel acts as accuser against Job's blamelessness. He is called Satan in many English versions, but the word probably should be translated 'accuser'. The accuser's role is minor and he does not appear after 2:7. The conflict in the book is not between Job and Satan, but rather between Job and God.

None the less, it is the accuser who, with the Lord's permission, brings grief and pain into Job's life. He does this first by taking away his possessions and destroying his family (1:6-19) and then by afflicting Job with a horrible disease (2:1-10). The end of the prologue introduces the three friends of Job who are so important to the story: Eliphaz, Bildad and Zophar.

●Job's lament (section 2)

Before the three friends speak, Job pours out his heart in despair. He even bemoans the fact that he was born.

Job is not alone in Scripture to lament his pain. The writers of some Psalms do it, too. And so did Jesus in the garden of Gethsemane (Luke 22:39-44). God is not offended when we cry. In a very real sense, he cries with us because we suffer the effects of a world which has become twisted out of the shape he made it in (see Hebrew 4:15,16).

●Dialogue with his three 'friends' (section 3)

The ailing Job is confronted by three callous friends. They hammer him with their opinion about his suffering. They argue that Job has experienced such evil in his life because he is a sinner (11:13-20). It's as simple as that to them.

Job responds to their attacks with heated denials. He has not sinned in

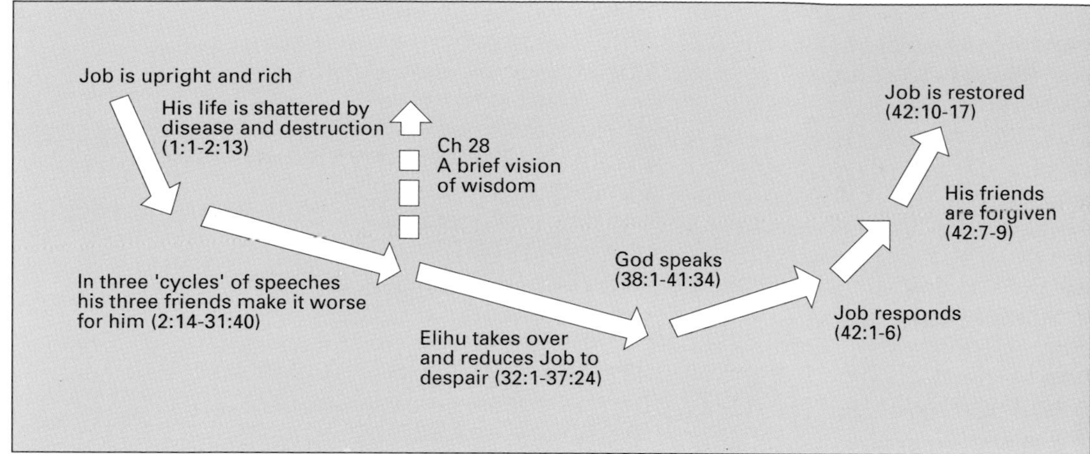

The shape of the book of Job.

such a way as to deserve this intense suffering. He believes that God makes the wicked *and* the blameless suffer (9:21-24). And the reader knows what neither the friends nor Job know for sure, that Job is right; his suffering is not related to his sin. Rather it is initiated by the accuser and permitted by God.

354-357

At the heart of the debate is the question of wisdom. Who is wise? Who has the correct insight into the issue of Job's suffering? The friends on one side and Job on the other set themselves up as wise men with the right answers, and they insult each other's views (11:12; 12:1-3, 12; 13:12; 15:1-13).

There are three cycles of debate. The friends speak in turn against Job: first Eliphaz, then Bildad and lastly Zophar. Job responds to each. However, after the first round the debate tails off until in the last round the speeches are much shorter and Zophar remains silent.

This does not signal the end of the story, however; just the opposite. The friends have simply exhausted themselves. They have beaten their heads against a stone wall and achieved nothing. The only change

The prowling enemy

The figure of Satan makes few appearances in the Old Testament. The doctrine of a personal, spiritual enemy of God and his people is not fully developed until New Testament times. The references in Job may indicate a late date for the book's final compilation.

But even in Job Satan is clearly under God's ultimate authority. He is never pictured in the Bible as equal and opposite to God; tradition suggests that he is a fallen angel bent on destroying God's work but never fully able to succeed.

The ministry of Jesus began after an encounter with Satan who tried to divert him from his task (Matthew 4:1-17). The early Christians had no doubt that Satan existed and was a crafty and formidable opponent. He prowls like a lion stalking its prey (1 Peter 5:8), but in the end is defeated by Christ (Revelation 20:10).

The existence of evil in the world hurts everyone. We look everywhere for the gun to kill it with. But we cannot defeat evil simply by using the weapons of education, politics and social reform. We need the power of God as well, and the spiritual weapons of prayer and the Scriptures (see 2 Corinthians 10:4; Ephesians 6:10-20).

in Job is in the strength of his anger against his friends and, even more crucially, against God.

The three friends come across as unfeeling counsellors who are more concerned to keep their theology straight than to share deeply in another person's painful life. The irony is that their theology is all wrong! God doesn't mechanically and immediately reward obedience with success or judge disobedience with suffering. It is possible to sin and prosper, and to be right and suffer. The three friends warn us against holding doctrines which are too narrow to embrace the whole of God's revelation. In their case, they had no idea of how the 'fallenness' or present imperfection of the world might affect human beings nor of how it might tie in with God's purposes. The friends also warn us that preaching trite beliefs to sufferers can turn them away from God rather than towards him.

●Job's speech on wisdom (section 4)

An abrupt change takes place in Job's thinking in chapter 28. So far he has ridiculed his friends' wisdom and made much of his own. He has grown increasingly impatient with God. But all of a sudden he has a moment of clear vision. In one of the most moving chapters of the Old Testament, Job proclaims his faith in the deep wisdom of God. God alone is wise, and man cannot always see how present experience relates to God's goodness.

If Job had stopped here, the story would have moved quickly to a happy ending. Unfortunately, he soon sinks back into depression.

●Job's concluding statement (section 5)

Job's last words before the momentous conclusion brood on the past when he enjoyed God's blessings (chapter 29). He bemoans his present suffering and complains that God has turned a deaf ear to him (30:20). He appeals to God once again that he is blameless and does not deserve the suffering which has come upon him (chapter 31).

Job is experiencing what some spiritual teachers call 'the dark night of the soul'. He has passed through doubt; he truly believes yet God seems so far away. He is now suffering from the combined effects of physical pain and emotional tiredness. He is worn out, and so his trust in God shatters once again. Can we blame him? What Job and people like him need is human understanding, practical help and the prayers of loving friends.

●Elihu's speech (section 6)

At this point, Elihu steps in. The three friends represented the wisdom of the elders; Elihu is the brash young man who thinks he has all the answers. He has waited patiently out of respect for their seniority, expecting them to resolve the issue with Job. But they have failed and he can no longer remain silent (32:6-9). He hates to see Job complacent in his pride (32:2). So he sets himself up as still another wise man (33:33).

But in spite of his claim to say something new (32:14), he comes back to the same old theology of tit for tat.

●God's speech and Job's response (section 7)

Throughout the debate, Job has hoped for an interview with God

(23:2-7). He finally gets his wish. God appears to him in the form of a storm, an indication that he is coming in judgment (Psalms 18, 29; Nahum 1).

Job had hoped to learn why he was suffering. But God never tells him directly, although he does rebuke Job for casting aspersions on his divine reputation (40:8). Instead, God answers the question about the source of wisdom, the issue which has been smouldering under the surface of the story: God alone is wise.

His first words from the storm set Job's wisdom in its place. God then asks Job a series of questions which only the Creator can possibly answer (chapters 38, 39). They contrast God's full knowledge and control of the natural order, which he created, with Job's ignorance. The implication is that the same principle applies to the moral order as well. God knows, but Job is ignorant.

356

This conclusion is punctuated by a series of unanswered questions which run through the divine speeches and ask more explicitly about the source of wisdom. See 38:36-37; 39:13-18, 26.

Job recognizes the truth of God's speech. He responds humbly, and repents. He submits himself to the Almighty God of the universe and to his will.

● Epilogue (section 8)

The epilogue brings the story to a happy end. Job is reconciled with God and his fortune is restored. God blesses him and allows him to live a long life. Though he grew impatient with God, Job neither 'cursed God and died' nor did he give in to the facile arguments of the friends. As a result, he became an intercessor for his friends who had urged on him a false wisdom which assumed God was like a machine.

If we read some parts of the Bible (such as Deuteronomy and Proverbs) in isolation, we could have a theology like the three friends: if someone is obedient, they will be blessed; if disobedient, then cursed. Some people today believe that God wants all Christians to be permanently healthy and wealthy. The book of Job stands as a judgment on all success-oriented gospels. It proves that we cannot turn the promises of Proverbs into a mechanical, almost magical formula for success in this life.

The book of Psalms

340-344

The book of Psalms has rightly been called the 'Hymnbook of the temple'. It contains 150 of the songs which Israel used to glorify the Lord and also to appeal to him for help. Like some of our hymns, they are also prayers, intimate conversations between God and his people. And like our hymns, the psalms were used both in public worship and in private devotion.

The psalms have had a tremendous appeal to Christians in every generation. They are probably read and studied more than any other part of the Old Testament. Their frequent lack of reference to specific events makes them easy to apply to our lives. They inform us about God, arouse and express our emotions, stimulate our imaginations with powerful images and appeal to our wills, commanding us to obey God.

The book of Psalms: data

Authors and date: the Psalter is unlike other Bible books in that it is a collection of 150 separate poems. According to the titles, the earliest psalm was written by Moses (90), while the content of some psalms indicates that they were written during or after the Babylonian captivity (126, 137). Thus, the psalms were composed over a period of nearly 1,000 years. The Old Testament refers to David's activity (tenth century BC) as a psalm writer, and the titles of individual psalms suggest that he was a major contributor to the book.

Purpose: as there are 150 separate pieces, there are 150 different reasons for writing! Individual psalms were composed in response to God's presence or absence in the life of the psalmist. For instance, when he was aware of God's grace in his life, he wrote a hymn of praise; when he felt abandoned by God, he composed a lament.

A collection of separate poems, Psalms does not have any logical sequence as most other biblical books. There are small groupings of psalms based on content (*e.g.* psalms about kingship, 93-99), authorship (the sons of Korah, 42-49) or use (psalms of ascent sung by worshippers as they 'go up' to the temple, 120-134). There is also an ancient tradition which divides the Psalter into five books, parallel to the first five books of the Bible (1-41; 42-72; 73-89; 90-106; 107-150).

There is some logic behind the placement of psalms at the opening and closing of the book. Psalm 1 is unique and opens the book with a distinction between the righteous and the wicked. The reader must decide which side he or she is on before entering into intimate conversation with God. Psalms 146-150 unite in a great burst of praise as a finale to the book.

But apart from this there is no overall structure of the book. It appears that new psalms were added anywhere, and not always at the end. It is likely that different principles were used by editors during the 1,000-year period in which Psalms was a growing and changing book.

Martin Luther described Psalms as a garden. The beauty of a garden is the result of a variety of shapes, colours and fragrances. Likewise, the overall beauty of the Psalter is in the variety of its writing styles, the emotions it expresses and the situations it describes.

We can use the Psalter in two ways. It is a book to dip into regularly when we are lost for words – or want some new ones – with which to praise God or to express our anxieties. But to do that effectively we need to learn where to

Summary of the book of Psalms

While there is a tremendous variety among the poems, they do fall roughly into seven different types.

1 Hymns of praise (*e.g.* 8, 21, 29, 45, 48, 68, 98, 104, 117, 144-150)
2 Laments (*e.g.* 5, 10, 13, 31, 42-43, 44, 51, 69, 102, 123, 142)
3 Songs of thanksgiving (*e.g.* 18, 30, 32, 34, 75, 92, 116, 124)
4 Prayers of remembrance (*e.g.* 105, 106, 135, 136)
5 Wisdom psalms (*e.g.* 1, 15, 19, 36, 49, 50, 53, 112, 119, 139)
6 Kingship psalms (*e.g.* 2, 20, 21, 95-99)
7 Hymns of confidence (*e.g.* 11,16, 23, 27, 37, 46, 91, 131)

look for such help. So another way to use the Psalter is to read through it regularly, trying to identify with – and learn from – the mood, the concern, the truth, the feeling, of each psalm, whatever our situation at the time. You may find it helpful to make your own list of psalms which are specially powerful or address very specific themes, for specific future use.

340-344

They loved to sing

The people of Israel loved poetry and music. There are passing references in the Old Testament to work songs (*e.g.* Numbers 21:17-18; Isaiah 9:3) and party songs (Isaiah 5:12). Laments were composed when important people died (*e.g.* 2 Samuel 1:19-27).

It is sometimes difficult for people today to read Hebrew poetry because it does not have the kind of rhythm we associate with words set to music. There is no single pattern for Hebrew poetry, although it is clear that rhythm comes largely from the accents or stresses in lines which contain any number of syllables. The writers used a variety of literary devices: picture language is common, and so is 'parallelism' – when an idea is expressed in two different ways.

We do not know if any form of written notation existed for the music. So we do not know what the tunes were like; they were probably more like chants than modern songs. Many musical instruments are mentioned in the Bible, but the difficulty of translation means that they are named differently in some Bible versions.

The main stringed instrument was probably the lyre, with perhaps eight or ten strings. The 'pipe' or 'flute' was probably more like an oboe. Trumpets and horns were first made from animal horns, and later from metal. Cymbals, bells and a kind of tambourine were common. Whatever it was like, Hebrew music must have been popular and designed for participation rather than listening.

● Hyms of praise (section 1)

Ancient Jewish tradition calls the book of Psalms 'Praises', so in one sense it is right to name our first type of psalm after the chief characteristic of the book. There are fewer praise psalms than there are laments, but praise overcomes mourning in the Psalms in two ways. First, almost all of the laments conclude on a note of trust or praise. Secondly, the praise hymns are more numerous at the end of the book, and so become its dominant note.

Hymns are easily recognized by their exuberant praise of the Lord. They are songs to be sung when we are conscious of God's love and help. They usually begin with the psalmist inviting those around him to join in the praise:

> Sing joyfully to the Lord, you righteous;
> it is fitting for the upright to praise him (33:1).

These hymns are never very specific about the original cause for the praise. Historical events are not usually named. So we can apply them easily to ever-new situations of God's blessing. However, the psalmist does not praise God in the abstract. He praises the Lord for his wonderful acts at creation (8), for giving the Law (19), for being king (47), for dwelling in Zion (48), for winning a battle (98), and for many other reasons.

It is easy to praise God when we are conscious of some great answer to prayer. But at other times we want to praise him but find it hard because we have nothing to focus on. The psalms turn our attention to God – who he is, his great acts of creation and salvation, and his constant love

Being specific makes worship more meaningful – and there's always something about God to praise him for!

● **Laments (section 2)**

At the opposite end of the emotional scale are the laments. These are easily recognized by their depressed mood. They are the words of men and women who are sad, bitter, confused, or angry, and who feel alienated from God.

While the psalmist experiences God's absence, he also feels the pressure of other men and women who desire his downfall (the 'enemy'). Furthermore, the psalms contain curses against the enemy. These rather heated statements are difficult for Christians to understand. After all, Jesus commanded his disciples to 'turn the other cheek' and to 'love their enemies' (Matthew 5:38-48). It is not unusual to find a curse like that of 69:28:

> May they be blotted out of the book of life
> and not be listed with the righteous.

To understand these curses, we must remember that God directed his warfare against the human enemies of Israel. He used Israel to execute his judgment against those who, in opposing the nation, were also opposing his truth and his purposes for mankind. These judgments are previews of the future judgment of the world when Christ returns again at the end of history.

The curses cannot be prayed today in the same way, because Jesus Christ has told us to 'put away the sword' (Matthew 26:52). He has directed our warfare against Satan and the powers of evil (Ephesians 6:10-18). However, the laments can help us to cope with our feelings of anger and frustration. Such feelings are natural, and God is surely the best person of all in whom to confide them. He is angry about evil, too – although he still longs for evil people to turn back to him. So we can use the psalms to pray legitimately for the destruction of evil attitudes and the abolition of evil situations – but there is no place in the Christian life for the vehement personal attacks of the politician. Only Satan can be the object of personal hatred.

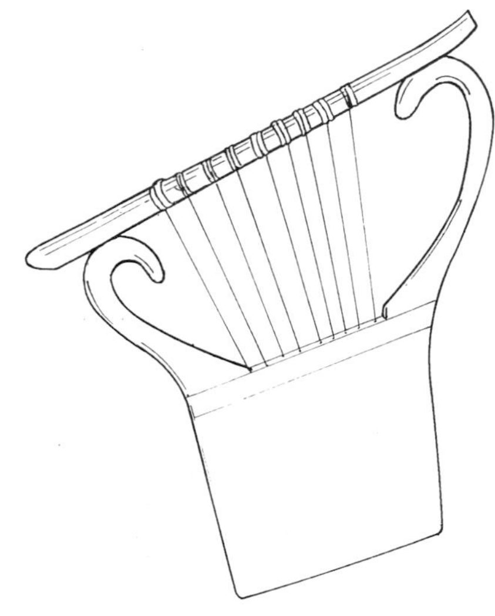

David's harp probably looked something like this kinnor.

● **Songs of thanksgiving (section 3)**

When the psalmist's lament has been answered by the Lord, he turns again to God with a prayer of thanksgiving. Thus, the thanksgivings complete an initial trio of psalm types:

> Enjoying a right relationship with God: hymns
>
> Feeling distant from God: laments
>
> Back to a right relationship with God: thanksgivings.

In fact, the psalmist will often quote

his earlier lament which God has just answered (30:8-10).

Saying 'thank you' to God is an important way of continuing to recognize our utter dependence upon him. His help is a gift, not a right.

●Prayers of remembrance (section 4)

The past plays a crucial role in a number of psalms. Hymns tell of past victories which God has won (98:1-3), while laments often appeal to God's past rescue acts in order to inspire hope in the present (77). Some praise the Lord by listing how he stepped wonderfully in to the affairs of his people, rescuing them from trouble.

156

These psalms give us an important principle for our prayers of intercession. We can look back at how God has stepped into similar situations and with confidence ask him to do it again.

●Wisdom psalms (section 5)

A small but important group of psalms reflect the issues and concerns of the Old Testament wisdom books. Like the book of Proverbs, certain psalms bless the righteous wise and castigate wicked-fools (1). Others describe the virtues of God's law (119). Some are similar to the darker side of wisdom contained in Job and Ecclesiastes. Psalm 49 worries about death, while 73 struggles with the apparent good fortune of the rich and powerful. Even the Song of Solomon finds a parallel in 45.

Jesus Christ reveals himself as the full expression of God's wisdom (Colossians 2:1-5).

●Kingship psalms (section 6)

All the psalms assume that God is king of Israel and of the entire universe. His kingship becomes the major focus of praise in a number of them, for example:

> The Lord reigns,
> let the nations tremble;
> he sits enthroned between the cherubim,
> let the earth shake (99:1).

In other psalms, attention is focused on the human king of Israel. The story of Saul's appointment (1 Samuel 8-12) laid down the principle that the human king should serve the divine king and reflect his greatness. So Psalm 2, for example, magnifies both the divine and the human kings.

●Psalms of confidence (section 7)

Some of the most memorable psalms are those in which the author places his deeply-felt trust in the Lord. They are usually short and simple, and often have a rich picture or symbol at the centre. Two examples are 23 with its well-known and much-loved image of God as a shepherd, and 131 with its striking picture of God as a caring mother.

The psalms are invitations for us to be totally honest with God. The psalmists held nothing back from the Lord; they boldly expressed their love, joy, grief, anger and frustrations to him. As we read the psalms, they become 'mirrors of our soul' (John Calvin) and give us the words to express our heartfelt emotions before God. But even those which plumb the darkest side of our emotional lives, in the end turn to the Lord with either praise or expressions of trust. In so doing, they lead us along the road of repentance and thanksgiving towards Christian maturity.

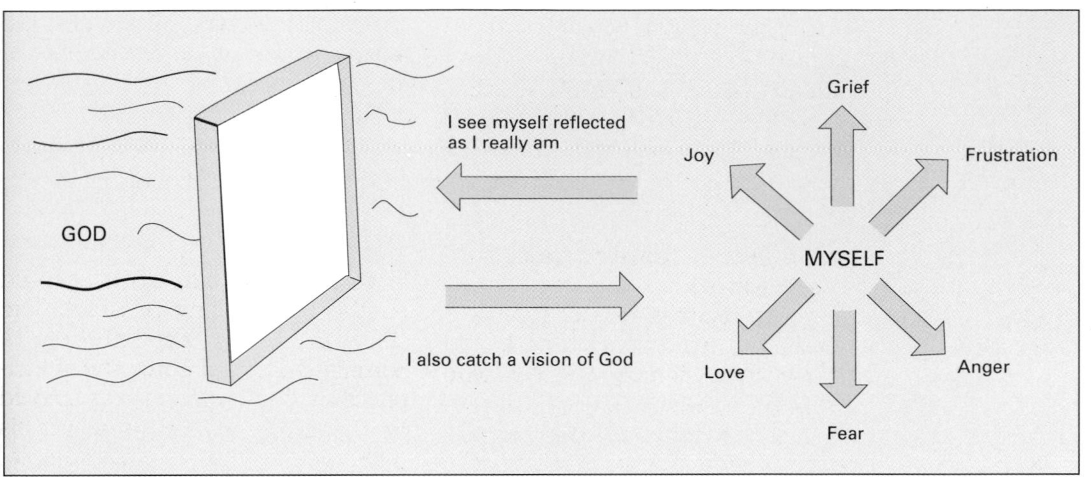

Using the mirror of the Psalms.

The book of Proverbs

The book of Proverbs is becoming one of the most popular books in the Old Testament. Christians seek it out for practical advice on how to live. Its appeal is perhaps linked to the growth of interest in counselling and 'getting to know oneself'.

However, Proverbs is more than a 'how to' book. It raises deep theological questions. Furthermore, individual sayings are filled with imagery which is often difficult to unpack. And apparently contradictory advice occasionally needs unravelling (26:4-5). Understanding the book of Proverbs is not as easy as it appears at first!

While we can find many helpful hints which we can lift straight out of Proverbs into our modern daily life, we shall get the most from the book if we look out for the unchanging principles which lie behind all the instructions – including the ones we cannot apply directly today.

So ask yourself such questions as: 'Why is Proverbs so full of warnings about adultery – what is it trying to protect?' 'What truths about God lie behind the teachings about honesty and integrity?'

The book of Proverbs: data

Author: the opening verse associates the book with Solomon. He was famous for his God-given wisdom (1 Kings 3:1-28). 1 Kings 4:29-34 shows him exercising wisdom internationally; it even numbers his proverbs at 3,000 (only a small proportion of which survive in the book of Proverbs). However, while Solomon is the chief source of the book, there are additional contributors to it. These include the anonymous wise men of 22:17 - 24:34, as well as the short sections by Agur (chapter 30) and King Lemuel (31:1-9). Servants of Hezekiah, a later king, were involved in compiling the book (25:1).

Date: probably completed during Hezekiah's reign (about 715-686 BC), but later additions (*e.g.* chapters 30, 31) possibly inserted during or after Judah's exile in Babylon (sixth century BC).

Purpose: to show how faith in God affected everyday life.

CUTTING OUT THE SECTIONS

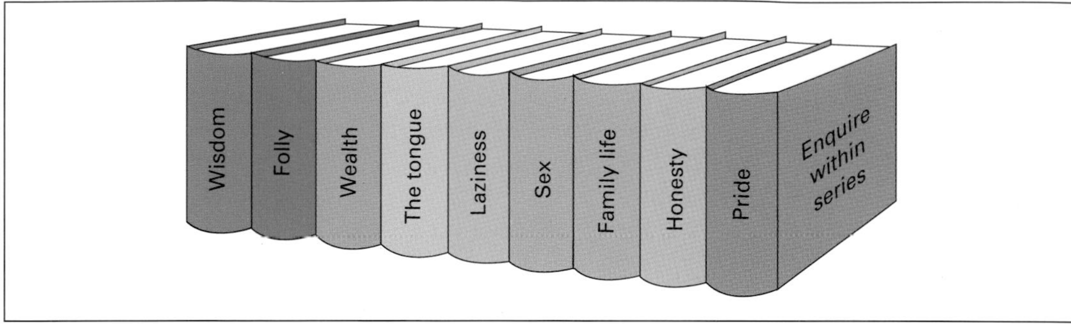

Using the treasury of Proverbs.

354-357

37-38

'What does it tell me about the really important things of life – have I got my priorities right?' 'How should I regard my weaknesses and failings – and those of others?' 'What principles are laid down for happy relationships between people at home, at work and in the church?'

Summary of the book of Proverbs

1 Introduction and motto (1:1-7)
2 Discourses on wisdom (1:8 9:18)
3 Proverbs collection (10:1-29:27)
4 Sayings of Agur (30)
5 Sayings of King Lemuel (31:1-9)
6 Poem to a virtuous woman (31:10-31)

●Introduction and motto (section 1)

The goal of the book is to impart wisdom to the reader. Wisdom in the book of Proverbs has more to do with how we behave than with what we know, and so is about 'what is right and just and fair' (1:3). It is the skill of living in God's way.

The introduction also warns the reader that he or she will not find in the book simple teaching with a plain meaning. On the contrary, it is made up of proverbs, parables and riddles. These teach us by both revealing and concealing the truth, and demand that the wise person digs deeply and meditates carefully on the wisdom found here.

Verse 7 has been called the motto of the book. The source of wisdom is a relationship with the Lord. The reader needs the right attitude toward God if he or she is to have a clear understanding of the world God created.

Many Bible versions translate verse 7 'the fear of the Lord ...'. Fear does not mean terror or dread in this context. Rather, it means awe and respect. If we respect God, then we shall respect his wishes, and live in ways which please him. Perhaps in a world which encourages us to do our own thing we need this spiritual restriction on our freedom as much as people did 2,500 years ago. It is not possible to honour God in our actions if we do not also honour him in our hearts.

●Discourses on wisdom (section 2)

The book changes at the tenth chapter, where the short, pithy proverbs which we usually associate with the book begin. Before that, there are longer discussions about wisdom. They contain a father's advice to his son. Here we learn that wisdom is far more valuable than gems and gold (3:13-15); and it

gives quality of life to the person who has it (3:16-18).

There is a repeated theme about the relationship between wisdom and righteousness on the one hand and folly and wickedness on the other. It focuses most on sexual behaviour, a source of temptation for the young men who are addressed by the book. The wise person avoids adulterous relationships (chapters 5, 6, 7,) and remains faithful to his wife. These opening discussions lay the foundation for the later proverbs.

● Proverbs collection (section 3)

This section makes up the bulk of the book and consists of short sayings about how we should live. It could be divided into two parts, those proverbs which are said to come from Solomon (10:1 - 22:16; 25:1 - 29:27) and those which originate from unnamed wise men (22:17 - 24:34).

The proverbs do not appear to be in any logical order. Occasionally they are grouped together by content, and recent study has suggested some less obvious literary structure.

Taken out of context, many of these proverbs seem to be simple, good and practical advice for living.

> A wise son brings joy to his father, but a foolish son grief to his mother (10:1).

However, such proverbs must be read in the light of Proverbs 1-9.

Who is Madam Folly?

In chapter 9 the writer contrasts Lady Wisdom (verses 1-6), whom he introduced in 1:20-33 and chapter 8, with another woman, Madam Folly (verses 13-17), and asks readers to choose between them. Both women call out to the men who are passing by their mountain-top houses to come in and have a meal and build an intimate relationship with them.

Of course, the writer is using images. As he showed in chapter 8, Lady Wisdom is a poetic symbol of God's wisdom and thus represents God himself. Wisdom's house is the Jerusalem temple, and so Lady Wisdom's appeal to the reader is to enter into a living relationship with God.

But who is Madam Folly? Her house also stands on a mountain, the 'highest point of the city' (9:14). This suggests that Madam Folly stands for all the false gods and goddesses of the surrounding nations who tempt the Israelites away from true worship to their 'high places' or shrines. Folly stands for Baal, Marduk, Ishtar, Astarte and the other gods of the ancient Near East.

By contrasting Wisdom and Folly the writer is asking the reader to make a decision. Whose invitation are you going to accept? Wisdom's or Folly's? The decision is crucial. Those who embrace Lady Wisdom 'will live' (verse 6), while those who dine with Madam Folly will join her victims who are far from God (verse 18). The basic gospel choice comes at a critical point in the book of Proverbs, providing a base on which are built the short, pithy proverbs of the rest of the book.

In the words of one TV talent show, 'it's make your mind up time'. There are not many direct appeals of this kind in the Bible, so when they appear they need to be thought about. Are we spectators on the sidelines; or have we joined the players? Do we just admire the Bible's teaching, or are we actively applying it? Do we merely believe in God, or are we trusting him with our lives? As Jesus said, if we are not for him, we are against him; there's no fence to sit on (Matthew 12:30).

355

There wisdom was shown to be about God. So to be truly wise, and to bring joy to his parents, the wise son needs to be in a right relationship with God. In that sense, the proverbs are deeply spiritual, although they rarely mention God explicitly.

It can be very helpful just to read through the proverbs soaking in their varied teaching. But it is also a good idea to gather together in a notebook the scattered proverbs on each topic in order to study that topic in depth. Some of the most common topics are wisdom, folly, attitudes to wealth, the tongue, laziness and discipline, sexuality, family life, honesty and pride.

- **Sayings of Agur (section 4)**
- **Sayings of King Lemuel (section 5)**
- **Poem to a virtuous woman (section 6)**

Proverbs ends with three separate collections of sayings which form an appendix to the book. The first two come from named but otherwise unknown authors, while the last is anonymous.

The style of these sections is different from the rest. Instead of short proverbs they contain longer poetic statements. However, the general theme of wisdom is the same and many of the same topics are covered. Agur's wisdom looks away from himself and his own abilities, and places firm trust in the 'flawless' word of God (30:2-6). Lemuel repeats wisdom from his mother, who advises him to avoid getting drunk, and to serve his people instead.

The book concludes with a beautiful poem in praise of a good wife. Supportive at home, she is none the less active in the public world as well. She is graceful and charming, as well as being an outgoing and even aggressive person. Her husband and her children love her.

The book of Ecclesiastes

356-357

Ecclesiastes is an unusual book; some people come away from it asking how it ever got into the Bible. After all, the main voice of the book makes some pretty disturbing statements.

Life, he concludes, is utterly 'Meaningless! Everything is meaningless' (12:8). The search for meaning in life is like 'chasing after the wind' (2:26). The task depresses him so much that he 'hates life' (2:17), though he fears death because it is the ultimate end of everything (3:18-21). He even advises his listeners to avoid the extremes of both wickedness and righteousness (7:15-18)! And death renders the otherwise valuable wisdom profitless (2:12-16).

He does find a simple happiness in eating, drinking and working, but this enjoyment is half-hearted in the light of death and the uncertainties of life (2:24-26; 3:12-13,22; 5:18-20; 9:9-10).

The main speaker of the book has been given many different names in English translations. The two most common are 'the Preacher' and 'the Teacher'. The Hebrew word is *Qohelet* and it literally means 'the assembler', that is, someone who assembles a crowd. So the translation depends on what kind of group

is being assembled, a congregation or a class.

There are basically two ways of looking at Ecclesiastes. One is the suggestion that the author is looking at life through the eyes of a doubter, and is taking unbelief to its logical conclusion. Without God, there is no meaning to life. Even materialism fails to satisfy in the end. Always there is death lurking round the corner to spoil our fun. This makes the book a kind of evangelistic tract. At the end, our author unmasks his real opinion, which is a strictly orthodox one.

The book of Ecclesiastes: data

Author: some suggest that *Qohelet* is Solomon, writing during the period when he slid away from God. (The writer of the epilogue (12:8-14) could then be Solomon as a repentant old man.) However, it is more likely that *Qohelet* began to think like Solomon as a kind of mental exercise because 'What more can the king's successor do than what has already been done?' (2:12). That is, if Solomon couldn't find meaning in the pleasures of this life then who can? This explains why the author uses a nickname rather than a real name. He can both associate himself with Solomon and then distance himself at the same time. Notice, for instance, that later in the book he speaks of kings as if he isn't one (5:8-9; 8:2-4).

Date: unknown. There is no historical evidence in the book to tie it to any period. It is often considered to originate from late in the Old Testament period.

The other way of looking at the book is to see it as the work of two speakers, only the second being the author of the book. *Qohelet* is the main writer (or speaker), expressing his doubts. He limits his view to that which is 'under the sun' – that is, to this world. The second writer, who is the author introduces the book (1:1-11) and adds a God-centred perspective in 12:9-14. He uses *Qohelet*'s writing in order to teach his son to avoid scepticism which arises when God's people don't look to God (that is, they restrict themselves to 'under the sun'). He also uses it to instruct his son, to establish a right relationship with the Lord (12:13-14).

Whichever way we take the book (and scholarly opinion is sharply divided), it does serve a valuable purpose. It is a strong reminder of how crazy the cycle of human life is: from birth to death via hard work and passing pleasure. What's the point? The really sad thing is that so few people ever stop to ask the question. So the book asks it for them. And it gives a powerful answer: there is no point. Unless, that is, God gives one. And if he does, that will affect radically what we do and how we think – which, of course, is what the rest of the Bible is all about. So look out for ways in which the attitudes described by Qohelet *are reflected in your culture or circle.*

Summary of the book of Ecclesiastes

Ecclesiastes is difficult to divide up, because the content rambles and is not presented logically.

1 Introduction (1:1-11)

2 Search for meaning in life (1:12-6:12)

3 Advice for living (7:1-11:10)

4 Meditation on death (12:1-7)

5 Conclusion (12:8-14)

CUTTING OUT THE SECTIONS

Life appears meaningless to many people today.

● Introduction (section 1)

These first few verses introduce *Qohelet* and set the mood for his speech. The mood is downcast and sceptical. There is 'nothing new under the sun' (1:9).

● Search for meaning in life (section 2)

What makes life worth living? This question haunts *Qohelet*. He examines in turn pleasures, good deeds, wisdom, foolishness, work, advancement and wealth. But it's no good. While life may have some limited value, death ruins it all. Life is indeed meaningless.

The often-quoted poem in 3:1-8 is not meant to make us shrug our shoulders and say, 'that's life!' It reminds us that certain actions and attitudes are only appropriate at certain times. The wise person knows when, and honours God and helps others by being sensitive.

● Advice for living (section 3)

This section is mostly made up of proverbs and other forms of advice. However, while there is some orthodox advice (7:5-7), much seems contrary to the wisdom of other parts of the Bible (7:1-4,10, 15-18). *Qohelet*'s world-centred advice is much like that of Job's three friends.

132-136

● Meditation on death (section 4)

This brief section compares an ageing person with the slow decay of an uncared-for house. Some of the images of this section become very telling as we grow older. The teeth fall out (the grinders, verse 3); sleep is light ('rise up', verse 4); and hair goes white as almond blossom (verse 5).

In the light of the context of the whole book, the moral is obvious. We'll get the most out of life if we let God direct it. And as our physical powers will slowly decline, it makes sense to give God our best years while we can.

● Conclusion (section 5)

The wise man – perhaps a second author – warns his son (12:12) of the dangers of doubt and scepticism. The last two verses move from the street-wise words of *Qohelet* to the simple gospel. They encourage the reader to have a proper relationship with God ('fear God'), to obey him ('keep his commandments') and to remember his final judgment (verse 14).

Qohelet's world, lacking a knowledge of God, is full of gloom; it is suffering the effects of the fall (Genesis 3). In Romans 8:20 Paul speaks of the 'creation being subjected to frustration'. This may be a New Testament reference to the book of Ecclesiastes, since the word 'frustration' is a Greek translation of the Hebrew word 'meaningless'.

Qohelet wasn't wrong to paint the world in such depressing colours. Many unbelievers can relate to *Qohelet*'s frustrated struggle for meaning in life. The book of Ecclesiastes teaches us that apart from Jesus Christ we will never find it.

Ecclesiastes will probably prompt a different thought each time it is read. It can show up vividly the real difference which faith makes to a person. It can keep a Christian's feet on the ground by reminding him or her of life's complexities. It can inform our 'world-view', revealing how all parts of life suffer when we keep God out of them. Above all, it reminds the person who has grown familiar with being a Christian of all the people who are miles from faith yet need it: how shall we lead them to it?

70-75

The Song of Songs

The Song of Songs: data

Author: an alternative name for the Song of Songs is the Song of Solomon. None the less, Solomon's exact role in the book is uncertain. Since the Song is a collection of love poems, it is possible that Solomon is one of a number of different authors. That would make it like the book of Proverbs which also gives Solomon pride of place (1:1), though he clearly didn't write the whole book (22:17; 24:23; 25:1; 30:1; 31:1).

Purpose: to praise the divinely-given gift of human love and sexuality, and to meditate in wonder on the closeness of our relationship with God.

Date: uncertain. If the basic material does come from Solomon's time, it is likely that later changes or additions were made.

The Song of Songs is both a spiritual and an earthly song. In the first century AD, the famous Rabbi Aqiba said, 'all the Scriptures are holy, but the Song of Songs is the Holy of Holies' – so he banned its popular use as a ditty at the local bars. For centuries scholars have debated its meaning, some emphasizing its spiritual pictures and others its earthly significance.

The title of the book comes from its first verse. The Hebrew term asserts that it is the most beautiful and important song of all.

● Is it a story or a song?

Many people are convinced that the book tells a story. However, they have not been able to agree on even the most basic outline to the plot. Some suggest it is the story of Solomon and his simple country girlfriend. He falls in love with her and she leads him away from the high life of his court and his numerous wives and concubines. Others believe it is the love story of Solomon and the daughter of Pharaoh (1 Kings 11). Still others identify a third major character in the book: a shepherd boy. He is the woman's true lover and Solomon tries to break up their simple relationship. The Song then becomes a lesson in faithfulness in the light of temptation.

But there is little evidence for these ideas. The Song does not have a narrative structure; it is a collection of poems on the single theme of love.

It is not necessary to separate the poems from one another. Like other poetry, we should read it slowly, unpacking the rich imagery and thinking about its truth before applying the content to our lives.

● Human or divine love?

Many Christian commentators have said that the Song is about the love between God (or Christ) and his people. This is the result of an 'allegorical' interpretation of the book. An allegory looks for specific people or events behind the symbols. So the Lover would be Jesus Christ and the church his Beloved.

This was the standard view in the early church and in medieval times. It was hard to understand why an otherwise blatantly sexual message was in the Bible.

But the allegorical approach has no biblical warrant. This, coupled with the discovery of ancient Egyptian love poems, has led most scholars to agree that the Song of Songs is itself a love poem about a woman and her husband. Today, there are few scholars, Protestant, Catholic or Jewish, who would interpret the Song allegorically. It is then rightly classified as a further example of Wisdom literature, which applies God's will to ordinary daily life, in this case human sexuality.

303-305

● What does it teach about sex?

The Lover and his Beloved make love in the garden (4:16-5:1; 6:2-3; 8:5-7), which may remind the reader of the Garden of Eden. The connection is not accidental. The focus of attention in Genesis 2 and 3 is on relationship, a major aspect of which is the sexual relationship between Adam and Eve.

They enjoyed perfect harmony with God and with each other. The intimacy which they experienced is expressed in sexual terms: 'The man and his wife were both naked, and they felt no shame' (Genesis 2:25).

However, when they gave in to the temptation of the serpent they were cut off from God. Their sexual relationship changed too: 'Then the eyes of both of them were opened, and they realized that they were naked; so they sewed fig leaves together and made coverings for themselves' (Genesis 3:7). In the Song of Songs we can see a picture of a restored sexuality.

Marriage is a large part of adult life for the majority of people. In this book the Bible takes time out from simply teaching about it, to celebrating it. It is a good thing, which God has given.

The Bible also teaches us about God by using all kinds of images – one of which is the marriage relationship. God is the husband, the church is his bride.

In the Old Testament 'the wife' is often portrayed as unfaithful to the point of being a prostitute (Jeremiah 2:20; 3:1; Ezekiel 16, 23). One of the most memorable scenes in the Old Testament is when God commands his prophet Hosea to marry a prostitute to symbolize his love for a faithless Israel (Hosea 1, 3). The New Testament likens human marriage to God's union with his people (Ephesians 5:22-23). So Christians may appropriately read the Song of Songs in the light of Ephesians and note – with amazement – the intimate relationship which we can enjoy with Jesus Christ.

3.4

'THUS SAYS THE LORD'
The prophets

by Mary J. Evans

The books of the prophets are grouped at the end of the Old Testament though not in historical order. Other prophets, who did not write books, feature in both Old and New Testaments.

Their task was not to foretell the future so much as to give the people of the time messages from God. They were a vital part of God 's communications link with humanity.

Who were the prophets?

Prophet	Approximate date of ministry (BC)	King(s)	Kingdom
The early, 'non-writing' prophets			
Samuel	1050-1000	Saul, David	United
Elijah	870-852	Ahab, Ahaziah	Israel
Elisha	852-795	Jehoram-Jehoash	Israel
Micaiah	853	Ahab	Israel
The 'writing' prophets of the period of the monarchy			
Joel	810-750	Joash-Uzziah	Judah
Amos	760	Jeroboam II	Israel
Jonah	760	Jeroboam II	Israel
Hosea	760-722	Jeroboam II- Hoshea	Israel
(722 The fall of Samaria)			
Isaiah	740-700	Uzziah-Hezekiah	Judah
Micah	740-687	Jotham-Hezekiah	Judah
Zephaniah	640-610	Josiah	Judah
Nahum	630-612	Josiah-the exile	Judah
Habakkuk	600	Jehoiakim	Judah
(587 The fall of Jerusalem)			
The 'writing' prophets of the period of exile			
Daniel	604-535		
Ezekiel	592-570		
Obadiah	? 587		
Haggai	? 520		
Zechariah	? 520		
Malachi	?450		

SEE ALSO PAGES 123 AND 168

Introduction to the prophets

There are fifteen books in the Old Testament named after prophets and containing accounts of their teachings and their lives. They are the three 'major' prophets, Isaiah, Jeremiah and Ezekiel, and the twelve 'minor' prophets. Daniel is associated with the prophets in English Bibles, but in spite of his gifts in interpreting dreams, he is presented more as a statesman than a prophet and in the Hebrew Bible his book is classified with books such as Psalms in 'the Writings'.

● Who the prophets were

The Old Testament prophets were such a mixture of people that it is hard to find many similarities between them. Some were loners working independently, while others usually worked as part of a team. Some were skilled diplomats, at home in the highest levels of society, while others were blunt countrymen who didn't seem to know the meaning of the word tact. Among them were the quiet thinkers, eccentric dreamers, political activists, fierce accusers and gentle encouragers.

A few generally stayed in one place, perhaps associated with a local worship-centre, but some travelled widely. Some seem to have been called by God for a short-term mission to deliver a specific message; they then apparently disappeared from the public eye. Others could be described as career prophets; they worked for many years teaching, advising, rebuking and comforting the people, and predicting the action that God would take in blessing or punishing them.

But the prophets did have two things in common. The first was their faith in and commitment to the God of Israel. The second was their belief that what they said to the people of Israel did not come from their own minds but from God himself. The messages were as varied as the people who brought them, but behind all of them was the belief that God was concerned for and involved in the world he had made and that he had plans and purposes for people in general and Israel in particular.

Their methods

Most of the prophets were primarily public speakers; writing was a secondary activity. Many prophets are mentioned who seem to have left no written records at all, and much of the material in the prophetic books is a written record of speeches delivered by the prophet at various times. But as the habit of writing down prophecies became more common, so additional written material was included which had not been preached aloud first. You will find, therefore, descriptions of incidents that occurred in the prophets' lives. Sometimes they are vivid first-hand accounts, and sometimes they are reported objectively by an observer or editor. Some books also include what seem like extracts from the prophet's diary, in which he expresses his personal hopes and fears or records his prayers or praises.

As you read the prophets, look carefully to see if the passage is God's message through the prophet, or if it is a personal comment or description. Usually God's messages begin with a phrase such as 'The LORD spoke to me...' (Isaiah 8:11); 'An oracle concerning...' (Isaiah 13:1); 'The word of the LORD came to Jeremiah' (Jeremiah 32:26). Some modern Bible versions use inverted commas for God's message in order to distinguish it from the prophet's comment. In Jeremiah 16, for example, verses 19 and 20 are Jeremiah praying (with a confusing made-up quote from the people!), and verse 21 is God speaking. To help us the New International Version uses inverted commas to mark verse 21 off; the Good News Bible inserts 'says the LORD' which was not in the original Hebrew.

357-360

The prophets used a variety of techniques to get their message across. Sometimes they spoke straight words of condemnation. They did not mince their words in describing exactly what God thought of Israel's attitudes or behaviour, or in warning of the punishment the people would bring upon their own heads. On other occasions they pleaded with the people, using picture language to illustrate the great blessings that would be theirs if only they would turn back to the Lord in obedience and faith.

They sometimes used parables and illustrations. Some prophets reported dreams and visions that God had given them. Several used dramatic visual aids; they built models, broke pots or buried clothes to get their points across. A few were poets and wrote beautiful psalms or laments. Some spoke openly of their personal troubles. Their aim was always the same – to encourage Israel to live in the way God intended, so that the whole world might know that Israel's God was Lord of all.

344-348

Their message

One of the main tasks of prophets was to teach Israel what God was

121

Other Old Testament prophets

More than twenty other named people are described as prophets in the Old Testament apart from many individuals and groups who are mentioned but not named. Some, like Abraham (Genesis 20:7), Moses (Deuteronomy 34:10) and Samuel (1 Samuel 3:20) are well known in other contexts. But of people such as Iddo and Oded (2 Chronicles 13:22; 28:9), we know little more than their names. Although we have information about only a small part of their work, it still gives us a broader view of the prophets and their ministry than the prophetic books can alone.

Nathan was a trusted counsellor of David (2 Samuel 7,12; 1 Kings 1), and Ahijah counselled King Jeroboam I (1 Kings 11-14). They gave advice and support when asked and were not afraid to step in with criticism and rebuke when the king's behaviour fell short of God's standards.

Elijah and Elisha were not just advisers to kings, but also significant leaders in their own right. More than a dozen chapters in 1 and 2 Kings are given over to them and their work. Elijah, the fierce loner, took on the powerful queen and her army of priests and Baal worshippers single-handed.

Elisha, perhaps because Elijah's work had changed the climate of opinion, seems to have been equally at home with kings and with the common people. He often worked with groups of professional prophets and was known as a miracle worker.

Not all the prophets were men. There were several notable women prophets, including Miriam, Deborah and Huldah. Miriam's ministry (Exodus 15:20) seems to have been mainly in poetry and singing. Deborah's chief role (Judges 4) was as judge and national leader. Huldah advised King Josiah on the proper action to take when, during repairs to the temple, the 'Book of the Law' was discovered (2 Kings 22). There are no women among the writing prophets, however, but there is no Old Testament prejudice against God's word being declared by a woman.

The prophets illustrate what the New Testament teaches: that there is no stereotype for God's servants; he uses a variety of people equipped for specific tasks (see Romans 12:4-8).

like. They explained what God's commands and purposes were and reminded the people of the great benefits 'keeping the covenant' and living in right relationship with God would bring – and the painful results of failing to do so. The way they did this differed according to the gifts, circumstances and specific message of each prophet. But it always involved the example of their own lives. There was no room in this job for the 'do as I say but not as I do' preachers.

360

The prophets often spoke and wrote about the future. It was not that they gave detailed timetables of coming events so that Israel would always know exactly what was going to happen next. Their concern was that Israel should understand how God was at work and what he expected from his people now. It was the prophets' job to make sure people realized that their present actions would have certain future results. The predictions they did make were statements about how God was going to bring the promised blessing or punishment.

Those forecasts almost always occurred when the prophets were condemning Israel's current behaviour and calling the people to change their ways. The prophets wanted to change what was going

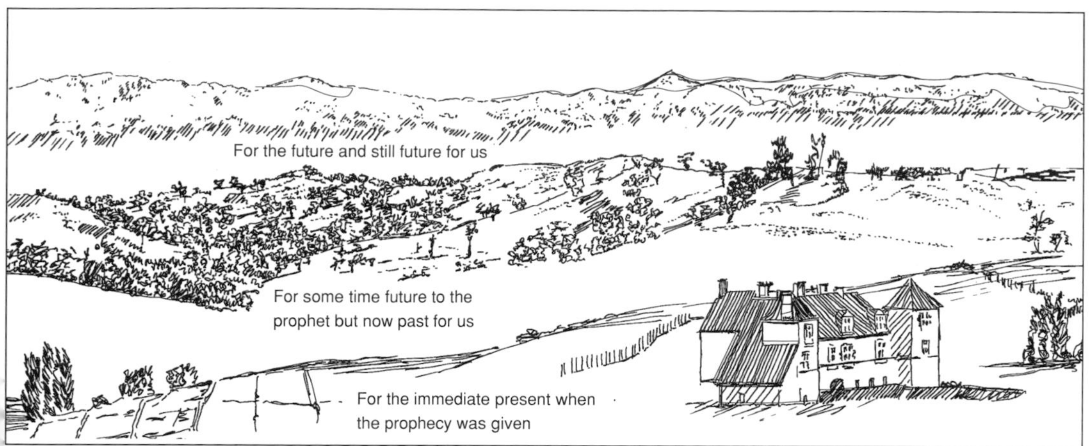

Three applications of prophecy.

on at the time. They certainly did not want Israel to concentrate only on future events. So most of the prophecies about the future depend on how the listeners responded. If the people turned back to God, predicted judgments would not happen. This helps to explain, for example, Jonah's lack of surprise when, after clearly stating that Nineveh would be destroyed, God seems to change his mind and gives them another chance when they repent.

●How to read the prophets

Most of the books were compiled from short, unrelated messages. It is generally best to read a chunk at a time. To help you find your way round them more easily, the sections on individual prophets focus on their major themes and concerns, rather than presenting a chapter-by-chapter outline.

The messages were mostly directed into political situations and everyday problems which existed at the time they were given. But a few grappled, under the inspiration of the Holy Spirit, with God's long-term plans. They especially looked forward to 'the day of the LORD', when God would intervene dramatically in the fortunes of Israel. Generally the people thought it would be a time of triumph over Israel's enemies; Amos had to warn them that it would be a day of judgment (Amos 5:18-20).

The New Testament regards a number of prophecies as being fulfilled in the life of Jesus (*e.g.* Matthew 4:14-16). The book of Isaiah has a series of poetic prophecies which are called the 'servant-songs' and which seem to point especially to the person and work of Christ (Isaiah 42:1-4;49:1-6; 50:4-9; 52:13 - 53:12).

As you read, ask yourself four questions. First, 'What did this mean to the people of the time?' The answer will teach you a lot about God's purposes for the world and for his people. Secondly, ask, 'What specific aspect of God's character is being portrayed? Is it one I make full allowance for in my life?' Thirdly, look for some principles of conduct which you can apply, or which can form the basis for your prayers for the world and for the church. For example, there's plenty to think about in Ezekiel's

166
184

156

prophecy against Israel's 'shepherds' concerning Christian leadership and responsibility (Ezekiel 34). And finally, always be on the look-out for some of the sparkling promises and challenges which pop up unexpectedly. Take Isaiah 40:31 as a starter!

The book of Isaiah

Isaiah, one of the longest and most significant Old Testament books, takes its name from Isaiah of Jerusalem. It divides into three clear sections.

Summary of the book of Isaiah

Within each section the material is not arranged in an orderly structure. It is simply a collection of proclamations, illustrations, poems, historical references and meditations. This means that sometimes there is very little connection between one passage and the next.

1 *The mounting crisis (1-39)*
The crisis described (1-5)
The prophet's call (6)
Coming soon: Assyria and Immanuel (7-12)
Messages for the nations (13-23)
God's final victory (24-27)
The Assyrian crisis (28-31)
Prelude to salvation and Hezekiah's test (32-39)

2 *Hope from afar (40-55)*
Visions of God's greatness (40-48)
The dawn of redemption (49-55)

3 *The glory and shame of Judah (56-66)*

● The mounting crisis (section 1)

Chapters 1-39 relate to the end of the eighth century BC. The background is one of oppression, injustice and religious hypocrisy. But there was a minority who were genuinely willing to listen and respond. (The situation is the same as that seen in Micah.) The main emphasis of the prophet's messages is on the way God will judge and punish the people. However, if they repent and trust God, Isaiah assures them that the future will be less bleak.

● Points to look out for

The main emphases in the account of Isaiah's call (chapter 6) – the holi-

The book of Isaiah: data

Content: the book contains sermons delivered to the people, and also personal reflections about God and his purposes.

Author: traditionally, the whole book has been seen as the work of Isaiah of Jerusalem. However, many scholars today support the view that the three sections were written by different writers. Isaiah of Jerusalem is said to have been responsible for only the first section. The second and third sections may have been produced by later prophets who had been greatly influenced by Isaiah's work.

But there is no strong factual reason to doubt the traditional view. It simply rests on the belief that a prophet, under the guidance of the Holy Spirit, can speak about situations which have yet to occur. Certainly the book as we have it forms a unity, and the glorious picture of hope in chapters 40-55 must be set in the context of the warnings of judgment in chapters 1-39, and the challenging realism of chapters 56-66.

Date: if the book is entirely by Isaiah of Jerusalem, then the original material must date from the second half of the eighth century BC (see the list of kings on page 123). If chapters 40-66 come from prophets in a later 'school' following Isaiah's thought, then some material could be as late as the fifth century BC.

ness of God, the strong awareness of personal sin and unworthiness, and the clear experience of receiving forgiveness and cleansing – are repeated throughout this section.

Isaiah strikes a fine balance between judgment and hope. He makes sure that people who are faithful to God and who accept his sovereignty are supported and encouraged by teaching about the reality of his coming kingdom. Everyone else is shown the reality of judgment so that they are not misled by false hope.

The day of God's action is presented as a time of judgment and destruction, but it also brings in the kingdom of peace and justice. Isaiah seems to have two timescales in mind. On the one hand there are clear historical references to Judah being saved from the Assyrian invasion, but later conquered and exiled by the Babylonians before being finally rescued from exile. On the other hand there are glimpses beyond the present, to the end times when the Messiah will come and God will intervene in history in a dramatic and final way.

Here's an example of how in the Bible history seems to repeat itself. In fact, it doesn't; the Bible's model of history is a straight line from creation to final judgment and re-creation, not an endless cycle of similar events. But prophecy often applies at three levels: to the present time of the prophet; to some long-distance event such as the final judgment, or the coming of the Messiah; and it also embodies principles which are always true. So we can read it expecting God to speak through it about our own situations, without having to jump to (usually wrong) conclusions about it being completely fulfilled in the past or in our own time.

Isaiah also has an interest in other nations. They too will be judged and punished, but not, of course, for breaking the covenant. Their judgment is for general cruelty and oppression (chapters 13-21; 23-24; 34). However, in the glorious future God has in store for his own people, there is also a place for those from other nations (2:2-4; 19:20-25; 25:6). *Here is an early example of God's love being extended to all peoples, whatever their colour or race. The New Testament shows that such unity comes through common faith in Jesus Christ.*

● Isaiah: the man of vision

Isaiah came from a wealthy and influential family; Jewish tradition suggests he may have been of royal or noble blood. He was married (8:3) to a woman described as a prophetess, and they had two sons whose names (Shear-Jashub and Maher-Shalal-Hash-Baz) were symbolic (7:3; 8:1-4, 18).

Isaiah was a gifted poet as well as a preacher. He worked as an adviser to four successive kings of Judah (the southern kingdom after the division of Israel). He was a contemporary of Micah, and worked not long after Amos and Hosea who prophesied largely in the northern kingdom of Israel.

Isaiah's call to prophesy came after a powerful vision in the Jerusalem temple (6:1-13). The vision had two major themes: the greatness of God and the need for personal holiness. *Those themes dominate the whole of the book which bears his name. But part of his purpose is to show how people continually try to cut God down to their size, and to get round his call to obey his laws.*

'Those who hope in the LORD will soar on wings like eagles' (Isaiah 40:31).

29

●Hope from afar (section 2)
Chapters 40-55 relate to a time some 150 years after chapters 1-39. They reflect the viewpoint of one who has seen and understands the situation of the people exiled in Babylon. The judgment has apparently already taken place. The prophet is encouraging the community by speaking of the God who brings salvation, and who will rescue them from exile.

140

●Points to look out for
The greatness of God. More than anything else, this section portrays a majestic vision of God. There is only one God; he is the king of all. He is the holy creator, the lord of the universe. But although he is so great, God is not distant from his people. In fact, he is deeply caring, and is involved in his people's affairs (43:14; 44:6-28; 45:5). He not only has the power to save them, but also the great desire to do so.

This magnificent view of God is rooted in the context of real life. It is not an abstract doctrinal statement. Instead, it stems from both God's and the author's pastoral concern for the people in the situation they faced. Some were filled with guilt and remorse, feeling that the nation had sunk too low ever to be restored or forgiven. Others were disheartened, wondering if the Babylonian gods really were more powerful than the God of Israel. In response to these fears, and in order to expose them as groundless, the prophet simply proclaims God in all his majesty.

The servant of God. There are four 'servant-songs' (42:1-4; 49:1-6; 50:4-11; 52:13 - 53:12). God's purposes are often worked out through people. Sometimes these are unbelieving rulers like Cyrus, sometimes believers like the prophet himself. But sometimes only a messianic figure, a saviour of great power, seems to fit the bill. The task of God's servant is to show what God is like and to bring God's justice.

The New Testament takes it for granted that the 'servant' passages can be applied to Christ, the final sin-bearer. This does not take away their reference to earlier human servants. *Nor does it prevent us from applying the principles to our 'servant' ministry in the church. The calling of all God's people is to serve others' needs before our*

Looking back

There is a creative tension in Isaiah as a whole. It moves from past, to present, to future; from specific historical situations to universal concerns. It narrows down to see salvation given only to a minority in Judah and widens out to see even Gentiles playing a key part in God's kingdom.

Within this creative tension we find the confident assertion of absolute rules. God is king and will judge and punish sin, even among his own people. The New Testament echoes this when it affirms that salvation can be found only in Jesus and that all who reject him will die (John 14:6; Acts 4:12; Romans 6:23; Galatians 6:7-8). But we also find in Isaiah a flexibility which may seem almost like compromise. A heathen king is described as serving God; foreigners can play a full part in God's kingdom.

'My thoughts are not your thoughts, neither are your ways my ways' (55:8). The whole book illustrates that verse. And people in every generation find such creative tension difficult. We would rather everything was black and white. But Isaiah's message to us is to stick to God's rules, and to allow him to make exceptions to our rules.

own. So we also are called to be trustworthy, caring and helpful, totally dedicated to God and willing if necessary to undergo great suffering for the benefit of others.

● The glory and shame of Judah (section 3)

Chapters 56-66 bring both hope and challenge into the period after the Jews' return from exile in Babylon. They were disillusioned because they had arrived expecting to build a new and successful community. Instead, they had found only hard work and opposition.

But the central message of chapters 56-66 is still the glorious hope that should sustain those who live in God's ways and remain faithful to him. God is still the same. The responsibility to serve him by seeking social justice is still the same. The hope for salvation remains. And alongside it come the realization that salvation involves more than physical release from exile and the rebuilding of the nation.

Within the context of the whole book, chapters 56-66 see the great truths of chapters 40-55 as remaining valid even when the hopes they raised were apparently never fulfilled at the time.

The book of Jeremiah

Jeremiah was born at the end of Manasseh's reign, when Assyria controlled the whole region. Judah (the southern kingdom) had adopted much Assyrian religion, and the nation was full of idolatry and moral corruption (2 Kings 21). He lived through Josiah's reforms and saw their failure to change the hearts of the people. He watched Assyria and Egypt fall to the emerging power of Babylon, and Judah come under Babylonian control. He saw the futile attempts to resist this control, and the eventual fall of Jerusalem and the destruction of the temple.

His message was that the Babylonians would destroy Judah and that the people would be deported. This was a direct result of God's judgment on them and not a sign of God's powerlessness, he explained. After the exile the people would go back. He strongly advised the Judean leaders to accept the inevitable and surrender to Babylonian control. This advice was seen as treason because he advocated surrender, and as blasphemous because the people thought he meant that God was too weak to prevent the exile.

29

The book of Jeremiah: data

Author: Jeremiah, a prophet in Jerusalem. His secretary Baruch added material to that which Jeremiah dictated (36:32), but whether this was also originally spoken by Jeremiah is unclear.

Date: Jeremiah worked between 626 and 587 BC, spanning the reigns of five kings. It is not known when the book received its present form.

Summary of the book of Jeremiah

The book is not arranged according to themes or dates. It is more of an anthology than a logically organized thesis. Nevertheless, the different accounts do have clear messages, all consistent with one another and united by the sense of the same character behind them all. The following summary gives only broad themes for each section.

1 The prophet's call (1)
2 Challenge to the nation (2-6)
3 Illusions of the temple's security (7-10)
4 Jeremiah and the covenant (11-12)
5 Warnings of trouble (13-21)
6 Vision of the end (22-25)
7 Glimpses of hope (26-34)
8 Prophecies and events in Jehoiakim's reign (35-36)
9 Prophecies and events in Zedekiah's reign (37-39)
10 Prophecies and events in Judah (40:1 - 43:7)
11 Prophecies and events in Egypt (43:8 - 44:30)
12 Message to Baruch (45)
13 Prophecies against the nations (46-52)

●Points to look out for

The key aspects of Jeremiah's message are summarized in the 'temple sermon' (7:1-29). He condemns the people and their leaders for ignoring the covenant law and for assuming that, because God had given them the covenant and the temple and they observed the set religious rituals, God was bound to protect them. Jeremiah saw this as false hope. He insisted that obedience, not tradition and ritual, was the essence of true faith. All their prayers would go unheeded, the exile could not be avoided, unless they trusted God fully.

34-36

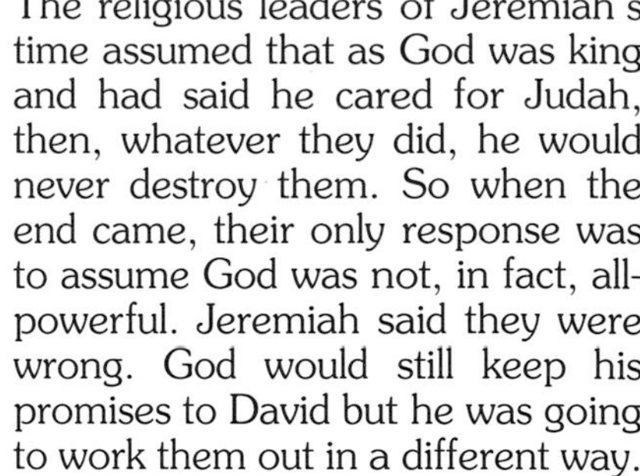
The religious leaders of Jeremiah's time assumed that as God was king and had said he cared for Judah, then, whatever they did, he would never destroy them. So when the end came, their only response was to assume God was not, in fact, all-powerful. Jeremiah said they were wrong. God would still keep his promises to David but he was going to work them out in a different way.

Jeremiah: the weeping prophet

Born into a priestly family, Jeremiah was strongly aware of being chosen personally (1:4-19) by God. But he also felt very inadequate and he hated the thought of the message he had to bring. This reluctance remained with him throughout his ministry, but so too did the awareness of God's presence with him and purposes for him.

He longed for support and companionship, and found only loneliness and rejection. He was a great patriot but was seen as a traitor. He was sensitive and unsure of himself but because of the uncompromising nature of his message was seen as inflexible and hard-hearted. He suffered great personal anguish and was often driven to despair. Yet through it all he found consolation in his own personal relationship with God and in the firm belief that Judah's exile in Babylon, though lengthy, would one day come to an end.

Jeremiah encourages many Christians by showing that God can use sensitive, depressive people as well as confident extroverts. He is also a good example of a relationship with God based on absolute obedience yet which left room for honest questioning and debate. Such trust and security in a God he loved gave him no guarantee of freedom from suffering. Jeremiah had a comparable experience to Jesus, who was also seen as a lamb led to the slaughter (11:19; Acts 8:32). It is part of the cost of discipleship.

Jeremiah thus presents us with two important principles. First, God is not a machine who turns out standard responses to standard rituals. He is a personal God who seeks a loving partnership with his people. So discipline and structure in worship and church life may be important, but if they become all-important then we have missed the point of them. Then secondly, we cannot be overconfident about the ways God will work. He does not have to do things our way; and when he does act differently to our plans, we can't complain. Faith trusts and follows God; it does not dictate to him.

Jeremiah also portrays God as full of compassion and love. He is always ready to respond to people's repentance by forgiving and accepting them (3:12; 9:24; 31:3,20). But he is also just and righteous; he holds them responsible for their behaviour, and he will not compromise in judging evil and unrepentant people (9:23-26; 44:2-6). Jeremiah did not always understand God's actions or plans, and he knew by experience that God was very approachable (20:7-13; 32:17-25). *The Christian life needs that balance. God does not turn a blind eye to our sins. But he understands our frailty. So despite his gloom and doom, Jeremiah offers us reassurance as well.*

AUTOMATIC
PRAYER MACHINE
Insert prayer
JUST THE ANSWER YOU EXPECTED
Wait ten seconds then press
Please take your ticket

What God is not, according to Jeremiah.

As the situation got worse Jeremiah's own hope and vision for the future became stronger. Knowing that the old covenant had not transformed people's lives set him thinking about the future new covenant which God would introduce. Then people would know God for themselves. They would love and obey him naturally and not simply because the law told them to (31:31-34). His vision was partially fulfilled by Jesus, and will reach its completion in God's final new creation.

296-297

The book of Lamentations

The book of Lamentations is not very cheerful reading. It is a series of five laments, or mourning poems, in which the author pours out his desperate sadness over the fall of Jerusalem and the destruction of the temple.

The first four poems are in acrostic form; each verse (or in chapter 3, each three verses) begins with a different letter of the Hebrew alphabet. This form somehow seems to emphasize the great tragedy of the content.

Whereas the book of Job examines the problems of undeserved personal suffering, Lamentations meditates on the suffering resulting from Judah's deserved punishment. The author's sadness is increased because he knows that the tragedy could have been avoided if the people had only obeyed God. He cannot fall back on the excuse of saying 'it's just not fair', because he sensed that it was fair.

The book of Lamentations: data

Author: the book is clearly by an eye-witness of the events leading up to the exile of Judah in Babylon. The Greek version of the Old Testament links the poems with Jeremiah and he is traditionally assumed to be the author, but we cannot be sure of this. Date: probably about 540 BC.

Lamentations is an outpouring of personal feelings. It is not a doctrinal treatise. But it does provide a clear statement of faith in the midst of pain, and even, in 3:21-40, of hope in the midst of despair. *There might not be many occasions when we shall feel drawn to Lamentations. But there are times when tragedies strike, perhaps through carelessness or wilfulness. There are times when governments or directors implement policies which lead to suffering. The New Testament urges us to 'mourn with those who mourn' (Romans 12:15). Lamentations gives us a graphic example of how to do just that.*

The book of Ezekiel

29

292-294

Ezekiel understood the isolation felt by some early Jewish exiles in Babylon. They thought that God's plans were still focused far away on Jerusalem. Others despaired, feeling rejected by God and condemned for the sins of their ancestors. Ezekiel tried to answer their problems and misunderstandings. He was driven by his overwhelming awareness of God's holiness that came when God called him (2:1 - 3:15). Ezekiel became totally convinced that God's glory and power could be experienced in exile just as easily as in the Jerusalem temple.

The Jews needed to learn that God's presence and power is not limited to one place. That may be easier for us to grasp in a mobile society than it was for them in a normally static society. But the reminder is still needed. Mobility, especially when enforced by family or work needs, can cause some people to feel isolated and lonely. Others become insecure and uncertain about God's purposes for them in a strange place. The vision of God's far-reaching purposes – of wheels within wheels (1:15-21) – applies to any kind of physical or emotional 'exile'.

The book of Ezekiel: data

Author: it is generally agreed that the whole book is by Ezekiel, although a few scholars have suggested a second author because of the book's knowledge of situations back in Jerusalem.

Date: the prophecies were uttered between 593 and 566 BC.

Summary of the book of Ezekiel

1 Messages of judgment (1-24)
2 Messages to other nations (25-32)
3 Words of hope and encouragement (33-39)
4 Visions of the new temple (40-48)

Unlike Isaiah and Jeremiah, the book is well structured in four clear sections. The judgment prophecies of chapters 1-24 (section 1) and the messages to foreign nations of chapters 25-32 (section 2) reflect

the prophet's primary task. He was to remove any hope that Jerusalem might yet be saved, and to convince the exiles that Judah's destruction was God's judgment for its sin and not an indication that God was unfaithful, uncaring or powerless.

Once the exiles grasped the lessons about their responsibility and God's judgment, Ezekiel's role changed. In chapters 33-39 (section 3) his message becomes one of hope and encouragement, getting them ready to build a new community after the exile. The vision of the new temple in chapters 40-48 (section 4) gave them added hope.

The style in Ezekiel is sometimes stilted, formal, and a little difficult to read. But the prophet's own enthusiasm and passion more than compensate today's reader.

Ezekiel: the respected eccentric

Ezekiel, like Jeremiah, was born into a priestly family. He was deported from Jerusalem with an early group of exiles, probably in 597 BC. Five years later, now aged 30 and living in Babylon, he was called to be a prophet. He worked among the exiled community for five years up to the fall of Jerusalem, and for at least seventeen years afterwards. He was an odd character, a mixture of the staid lawyer, the hardline critic, the eccentric visionary and the caring pastor. He was respected (8:1; 14:1; 20:1), but his messages were not always well received (3:25; 33:30-32).

Ezekiel is very forward looking. He stresses that the God who has acted in the past will also act in the future. Because of who God is, his action will be both glorious and victorious; but it will also be unpredictable. When Ezekiel talks of the future, it is not always clear when he refers to the immediate return from exile and when to the end times. Perhaps it is unhelpful to separate rigorously the two ideas. *To use Ezekiel's visions today in the attempt to work out exactly how God will act in the long-term future is to miss the point of them. Ezekiel makes full use of picture language and the symbolic images common in his time. Such passages were not intended to be taken literally but to provide a graphic impression of who God is and how he works.*

●Points to look out for

The God of action

Ezekiel stresses that God wants to be 'known'. To make this possible, God shows who he is by what he does. By allowing Judah to be destroyed, he showed that he would not tolerate evil. By releasing the Jews from exile he showed his power and his grace.

152-153

God is seen as both an awesome judge, and also as a kind and loving shepherd (chapter 34). He is able to bring new life even to the 'very dry' bones of sinful Judah (chapter 37). He is not to be played about with or taken for granted, however. Ezekiel shows that attempts to manipulate God are ridiculous; people who worship idols and then consult prophets will be punished (14:1-8).

88

The temptation to add human or superstitious elements to our faith can be surprisingly strong: to consult the horoscope or to cross our fingers 'just in case' there's something in them. Strong too is the temptation to bargain with God: 'do this for me and I'll do that for you'. Ezekiel's message is that such attitudes will always take us further from God, not closer to him.

The importance of human responsibility

Ezekiel taught that everyone was responsible for their own actions. Neither family background nor environment can in the end be blamed for the way a person behaves (18:1-32; 33:7-20). A person's choice to serve God or to ignore him will be respected, and the consequences of it will stand. But no-one, whatever their past actions, is deprived of the chance to repent and receive the forgiveness and new life that God longs to give.

This is a particularly important truth for today. Personal responsibility is sometimes down-played, and people's actions explained only in terms of their genetic make-up or bad experiences in childhood. The Bible never denies the many factors which make us what we are. But it never allows us to use those factors as excuses for sin.

The new life

God still has plans for the future, which include the exiles. But they involve not just physical rescue but a change in their hearts. This inward renewal is God's gift to them (11:19; 36:26), but it also involves their own will and commitment (18:31). Chapter 37 foreshadows the New Testament promise of inner renewal by the Holy Spirit, which is a continuous process in the life of each believer (see Colossians 3:9-10).

The role of leaders

Ezekiel had a keen sense of his own responsibility as a 'watchman' (3:12-21; 33:1-9). He was strongly critical of leaders who did not take their responsibilities seriously (11:1-15; 13:1-23; 34:1-19). Leaders should be dedicated to God and to the task, having a real concern for the needs of the people and not just for their own status. They should not be afraid to speak out, and should make decisions based on truth and justice, not on self-interest or out of fear of giving offence.

Ezekiel foreshadows the New Testament teaching on leadership as serving rather than as ruling (see Mark 10:45; John 13:14-16). *In any task within the church, Christians are called to examine their motives. Our first concern is to minister to others and not to receive the respect we think we deserve. We share the blame if our 'flock' falls by the wayside because we didn't warn it of danger or nurture it carefully.*

The book of Daniel

Daniel was a statesman rather than a prophet and the book bearing his name is not like other collections of prophetic speeches. It is one of the few Old Testament books which is universal in outlook, not being addressed directly to Israel.

The book's purpose is first to encourage faithful believers living in difficult times. It shows them that God and his people will eventually triumph. Secondly it challenges them to be loyal to God and to keep the faith while they are living in a corrupt and oppressive society.

The first section (chapters 1-6) is narrative in form. It tells of Daniel and some of his fellow-exiles from Judah who were trained to become Babylonian government officials.

The book of Daniel: data

This style of 'apocalyptic' writing was very popular in the two centuries before Christ. This, and the fact that Daniel's visions appear to give detailed information about the Greek empire which was in power then, has led many scholars to suggest that the book must have been written around 165 BC and Daniel's name added to give it authority. Certainly the stories of life in Babylon would have encouraged the second-century Jews who were also facing religious persecution, but they fit very well with what we know of life during the exile and there is no strong reason for doubting that the book genuinely comes from that period.

The story of Daniel has captured many people's imaginations. And even if the stories of the fiery furnace and the lions' den stretch your imagination, the point of the book is crystal clear: Daniel and his friends refused any form of compromise despite extreme danger. As you read the book it is worth asking, 'Is my faith that precious to me?' 'Is God that central in my thinking?' Notice too the moral of the story: the person who stands firm is assured of God's power and support (see 3:25).

Summary of the book of Daniel

1 Stories of Daniel and his friends (1-6)
2 Dreams and visions (7-12)

The second section consists of dreams and visions which use signs, numbers and symbolic language. It is very similar to a style of literature known as apocalyptic (from the Greek word for revelation), which developed after the Old Testament period when there were no prophets.

360-362

Apocalyptic books were usually compiled at times when God's people felt oppressed or persecuted. Perhaps for that reason, they stress the future life, and what will happen at and after the end of the world, when the trouble will be over. A major reason for using picture language was that authors writing about monsters, goats and statues could not be accused of treason, even if readers guessed they were referring to nations and rulers.

●Points to look out for

Daniel wants his readers to believe that the God of Israel is in control of all human history, both of individual lives and of world powers. In the end his kingdom will overcome all the pagan empires of the world.

The author is also fascinated by dreams and visions. They occur in the stories about life in exile as well as in the visionary second half of the book. Daniel teaches that the interpretation of dreams about the future could only come from the God who controls history, and not from human insight. When Daniel himself asks for further explanation of one of his visions (7:15-16) the answer given by the angel is very general. This perhaps warns the reader against using these visions to work out exactly what will happen in future history.

The book of Hosea

Israel (the northern kingdom) was prosperous in Hosea's time. But corruption and oppression were common (4:1-3). Towards the end of Hosea's ministry Israel also faced a strong threat from its powerful enemy, Assyria. Amos was concerned with social and political injustice. Hosea, however, was appalled by Israel's idolatry. He had an almost overpowering awareness of God's love for Israel, and so was very sensitive to the fact that their deliberate decision to worship idols would hurt God.

Hosea was convinced that unless Israel repented and the people changed both their attitudes and their behaviour, then the destruction of the nation was inevitable. But above all he was convinced of God's great love and his longing to save and restore them.

The book of Hosea: data

Hosea prophesied in the northern kingdom of Israel about the same time as Amos. He worked through the reigns of four kings (1:1), in the latter half of the eighth century BC.

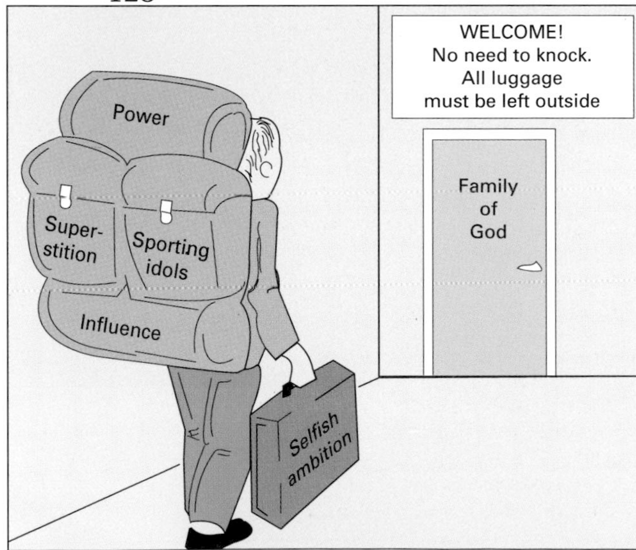

●Points to look out for

Religion is a relationship with God

God's love for Israel is likened to a caring parent (11:1-4), a careful doctor (7:1; 11:3), and a protective shepherd (13:5-6), as well as a loving husband.

All relationships are demanding. If we love someone, then we will want to please them, not just out of a sense of duty but also to avoid hurting them. God wants us to respond to him and to enjoy the benefits of belonging to his family. But his great love does not mean that we can live as we please. He cannot and will not tolerate a rival. The message of Hosea challenges any attempt to share our love and our loyalty with some modern equivalent of the Baal cult, such as sporting idols, political power or selfish ambition.

Hosea's family life

He married a woman who was, or

Summary of the book of Hosea

Most of the book of Hosea is a record of his speeches about judgment, God's love, and also of laments about the fate of Israel because of its refusal to respond to God. Chapters 1 and 3 are rather different, and tell of Hosea's tragic family life.

1 Call and marriage (1-3)
2 Messages of judgment against Israel (4-13)
3 Repentance and hope (14)

who became, a prostitute. She had three children of whom Hosea may or may not have been the father. She ran away and ended up destitute, living like a slave. Hosea loved her, bought her back from slavery and restored her to the status of his wife. Hosea's experience helped him to understand the meaning of love and commitment and also the suffering involved when trust is betrayed. It gave him a vivid picture of how Israel flirted with pagan religions; he called it spiritual adultery.

Hosea's longsuffering love for his wife takes its place alongside such New Testament parables as the lost son, as a deeply moving portrayal of God's patient, forgiving and redeeming love. It forces us to think of God in personal terms rather than as a theological idea. The story of Hosea has also inspired people who find themselves in crumbling marriages, giving them hope to hang on faithfully even when their partner has jilted them. In an age when the general moral tone is one of 'please yourself', Hosea brings a refreshing reminder that principles matter more than pleasures, and that the suffering which comes from personal sacrifice is not in vain.

38

310-311

The book of Joel

The message of Joel is familiar. He condemns Judah's disobedience, not to terrify the people with the thought of future judgment but to encourage them to change their ways and so avoid it. He predicts disaster for Judah (1:2 - 2:11) but also an 'afterwards' when 'everyone who calls on the name of the LORD will be saved' (2:32).

It is not clear whether the invasions of locusts predicted in chapters 1 and 2 were real events or were symbols of an invading army. But Joel does see the disasters as God's judgment and criticizes the people for not responding in repentance and faith.

●Points to look out for

Public worship and personal faith

Joel recognizes that though public religious ritual can never replace a heartfelt personal return to God (2:13), it can be used as a sign of people's response (1:13-14; 2:15-17).

34-36

The book of Joel: data

Date: we do not know the precise date of Joel. The book is relevant to many stages of Judah's history, but Joel probably wrote after the exile, perhaps about 400 BC.

Author: nothing is known about the author except the hints in the book itself. He was clearly very familiar with the temple and its ritual, so some have suggested he was a priest.

Traditional church services often come under fire from people who can see their all too obvious weaknesses. But Joel did not throw the baby out with the bathwater, and offers a creative balance between public and personal faith. A formal service in which people together confess their sins and promise to serve God can have powerful effects. What matters is my attitude as I worship: Am I listening to God and responding humbly to him? Am I making the prayers my own or am I letting the words wash over my head? And do I make music because it feels good, or because it truly lifts me into the awesome presence of God?

The eternal God

Joel portrays God as Lord of creation (1:1-12; 2:21-24); the great judge (1:15; 3:2-16); and as loving and compassionate (2:12-14). He is the king, and whatever else happens he will be honoured (3:17-21). Joel centres his teaching on the coming 'day of the LORD'. Whether his listeners take this as a warning to repent or as an encouragement to hope depends on their relationship to God. In some passages this 'day' seems to be coming immediately and in others it refers to the distant future. This may be a deliberate ploy to show that God is working all the time as well as on specific occasions.

The New Testament presents the final 'day of the LORD' as the day of Christ's return. And in Acts 2, Peter says one part of Joel's prophecy (2:28 32) was fulfilled at Pentecost. He thus confirms that God's plans have been, and are being, worked out through the centuries.

The day of the LORD

This phrase occurs frequently in several of the prophets. Chronologically it was used first by Amos (5:18-20). The people of his time had coined the phrase to signify the time when God would make Israel top of the league of nations. Amos told them that the day would be one of judgment on Israel itself. Other prophets, such as Isaiah (2:12-18) and Joel (1:15) say the same.

However, the day will affect other nations too, such as Babylon (Isaiah 13:6,9), Egypt (Jeremiah 46:10) and many others (Obadiah 15).

People who truly trust God and have turned away from their sins will be rescued from the judgment and will constitute a 'remnant' of people who will remain to serve God (Joel 2:32).

The idea is continued in the New Testament, where it refers to the second coming of Jesus Christ (2 Thessalonians 2:2). It will be unexpected (1 Thessalonians 5:2) although preceded by warning signs (2 Thessalonians 2:2-3).

The book of Amos

Summary of the book of Amos

1 God's judgment on the nations announced (1-2)
2 How Israel has abused its privileges (3-6)
3 Five visions of judgment (7-9).

By the middle of the eighth century BC, both Israel and Judah enjoyed long-term political stability and economic growth. Kings Jeroboam II in the north and Uzziah in the south both reigned for about forty years without any major threats from foreign invaders. Both countries had become prosperous. But as Amos travelled north, perhaps initially on business, he was shocked by what

The book of Amos: data

Author: Amos was a farmer and a businessman, not a professional prophet. He lived in the southern kingdom of Judah (7:14-15). But God called him to go north to Israel and warn the Israelites that unless they changed their behaviour they were heading for disaster.

Date: he probably uttered these prophecies around 760 BC.

Nature of the book: Amos is the first of the 'writing prophets'; the book is a carefully structured work and not simply a random report of his spoken words.

he saw.

The prosperity was not shared by all. Rich and powerful people had taken all the benefit, while other people remained in desperate poverty. Israel's covenant with God had justice and a special concern for the weak and powerless written into it. Those ideals had been abandoned. To make matters worse people believed that their prosperity was a sign of God's approval. An outsider looking at Israel would have assumed that its God tolerated injustice, oppression, dishonesty and immorality, and that his concern was not for the poor but only that he got enough sacrifices.

Amos said that the result of this way of life could only be exile and the end of Israel as an independent nation. His task was to find a way of shaking it out of its complacency and hypocrisy.

●Points to look out for

Amos's methods

He gained his listeners' attention by condemning neighbouring pagan nations and then claiming that they, the so-called 'covenant people', were just as bad. He varied his techniques. He told stories; sometimes he was strongly critical, sometimes gently persuasive. The 'evils' he condemned:

1 Misuse of the legal system by the rich to the disadvantage of the poor (2:7; 5:12).

2 Dishonest trading, including false weights and measures, and charging excessive rents or interest (2:6; 5:11; 8:5-6).

3 Self-indulgence, such as extravagant feasts and drinking parties or owning two houses, when others were starving or homeless (3:15-4:1).

4 Hypocrisy in religion, as extravagant ritual replaced faith and obedience (5:21-27).

'It's not our problem,' we say, that people in our community fall foul of corrupt traders, or fall through the security net of a society which rewards success and is impatient with failure. But it is central to the Christian gospel that those who have been rescued from a fate worse than physical death show practical support for those who suffer in this life – and challenge

294-295

For Joel the locust-swarm was a vivid picture of disaster.

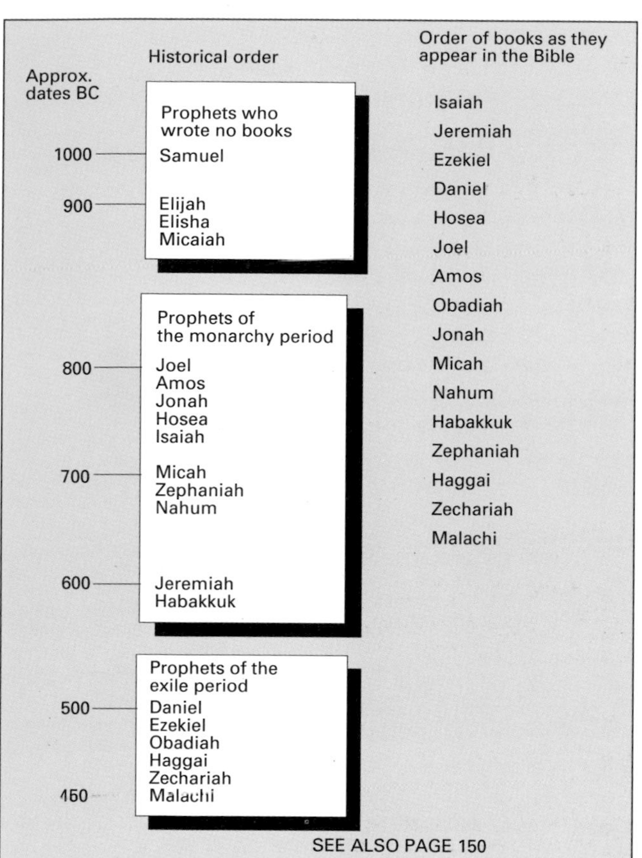

The prophets in order.

the causes of their suffering (see James 2:15-16; 5:1-6).

God's view of daily life

Amos taught that God is interested in every aspect of our lives, and that he holds us responsible for what we do. God hates hypocrisy. People who worship the God of love and justice but do not apply that love and justice in their dealings with others are hypocrites. Such people, Amos said, would be punished by God. But it would be wrong to suppose that his picture of God was that of the judge with the big stick. Amos also spoke of God as loving, deeply concerned for the poor and the mistreated, caring about justice and truth. He would judge them, but with great sadness. There is no hint of gloating in the book. The condemnation of wrong is given in the context of God's offer of forgiveness.

Amos's story leaves us with two sobering truths to consider:

1 God mixes religion and politics. In his sight there is no real difference between a child snatching a toy from another, and a developer inspired by 'the profit motive' buying up land or companies with no thought for the human consequences. Both are examples of selfishness. Nor is there any real difference between the husband who has an extramarital affair and the politician who deceives the electorate with half-truths in order to stay in power or to push through party dogma. Both are breaches of trust.

2 Prophets are not well received. Amos suffered when he faced the power blocs of his time. People will tolerate Christians who offer gentle religious thoughts. They may hate those who challenge their consciences and lifestyles (see 7:10-17).

The book of Obadiah

There is not enough information in Obadiah to tell us its date or the details of its background. It strongly condemns the nation of Edom (descended from Esau), and predicts that it will be totally destroyed. Obadiah's message was delivered to Judah, not directly to Edom.

Judah had been through a time of

great difficulty and disaster. Obadiah does not say if this was the result of Judah's disobedience and sin, but even if it was, it still hurt to see Edom, which also deserved punishment, gloating over Judah's distress. Obadiah puts into words the hurt and anger that the Judeans felt, and assures them that Edom will also be punished for its sin and that Judah will eventually be restored.

Obadiah shows that even nations who do not believe in or follow God are answerable to him for the way they treat people.

This little book offers hope and encouragement to God's people at all periods of history. When unbelievers scorn us in our weakness, when they take advantage of us, God's anger rises against them. After they have had opportunities to turn back to him, perhaps through the witness of the people they mock or persecute, God will ensure that they are justly punished for their sin. So there's no need for us to plot revenge; we can get on with more positive and fruitful activities, and leave God's enemies to God himself. See how St Paul argues this case in Romans 12:17-21.

The book of Jonah

The book of Jonah is different from most other prophets. It is not a collection of sermons given by Jonah, but a story about him. The message of the book is tied closely to the story. A strong reason for regarding it as historical is that Jesus accepted the story as genuine (see Matthew 12:38-41; Luke 11:29-32). He even went so far as to compare his mission with that of Jonah. But modern readers who prefer to see it as a parable will find the message it contains still valid!

The book of Jonah: data

Author: there was a prophet called Jonah in the eighth century BC (2 Kings 14:25) but we know nothing more about him, or if he is the same person as the hero of this story.

Date: it is uncertain when Jonah was written, although it would make more sense if it had been written before the fall of Nineveh in 612 BC.

Summary of the book of Jonah

1 Jonah's call and flight (1)
2 Jonah's prayer from the fish (2)
3 Jonah's visit to Nineveh (3-4)

●Points to look out for

God's compassion for sinners

God does punish evil, but his great compassion means that if there is even the slightest hint of repentance then he is likely to give guilty people another chance.

Jonah knew that (4:2), and yet he really resented God giving the Ninevites, a corrupt and vicious people, another chance.

Who are the no-good people in your community? In some places it will be the Mafia. In others it will be racists. In many it will be violent teenagers, child-molesters, neo-Nazis or gangs roaming city streets. On another level, we may be aware of nations in which our standards of truth and justice are not applied, where corruption is rife and deliberate lies and death squads seem to dominate diplomatic relations. Why should God give them a chance? Look at 4:2 again, compare it with John 3:16, and frame the answer in your own words. After that, it might be appropriate to pray for the people you identified.

God's concern for Jonah

There is great encouragement in the way that God took so much trouble to deal with even such an awkward character as Jonah. He corrected the prophet's wrong attitudes and used Jonah even after he had rejected the first commission.

71

What applies to sinners applies to saints as well: God may give us more than one chance to do what he asks, if we refuse first time. But of course, the real moral of this tale is that we should not need more than one chance. Jonah ends up looking silly because he would not trust God. He makes readers of every generation ask, 'What service for God am I rejecting? What command of God am I refusing to obey?'

What about the 'whale'?

Modern readers often find difficulty in accepting literally that the great fish (not identified as a whale) could swallow a man whole and that he could survive for three days and recover fully.

For those who are not happy to see the book as a parable it is worth bearing in mind that there are accounts of sailors being swallowed by whales and surviving the experience. Even if these cannot be confirmed, God is capable of overruling nature in a unique way if he so purposes. This question should not be allowed to distract the reader from the main point of the book.

The book of Micah

Summary of the book of Micah

1 God's accusations against Israel and Judah (1)
2 Oppression by the rich and rulers (2-3)
3 God's triumph will follow judgment (4-5)
4 God's case against Israel (6)
5 Repentance will lead to restoration (7)

In Judah, as in Israel, there was much greed and oppression in the eighth century BC. 'Justice' was available for the rich but not for the poor, and idols were widely worshipped. Amos's prophecies about Israel had been fulfilled when Assyria defeated it and destroyed Samaria in 722 BC, but the people of Judah had not changed their equally bad ways. They were proud of the Jerusalem temple and the line of kings descended from David. Because of these they believed God would always protect them, however much they ignored his commandments. Micah's main task was to show that this view of God was mistaken. God was able to protect them from the invading Assyrians, but only if they took him seriously and kept their side of the covenant they

The book of Micah: data

Author: Micah of Moresheth, a rural town in the southern kingdom of Judah. He is the fourth of the 'eighth-century prophets' (the others being Amos, Hosea and Isaiah).

Date: he worked between 725 and 701 BC.

had made with him. Otherwise, far from protecting them, God would allow *them* to be taken into exile, too.

●Points to look out for

The responsibilities of leaders, whether prophets or political governors

For them to behave like butchers rather than like shepherds is totally unacceptable to God (3:1-12). The main corruptions which the leaders either tolerated or practised are listed in 2:1-5; 3:1-4, 9-11; and 6:9-12. But it was not just a social problem. It was a spiritual one, too. The prophets, the preachers of God's word, were giving out a false message (2:6-11; 3:5-7).

We all like to hear things that make us feel good, and we dislike hearing messages which suggest that we're not so good. Preachers and teachers face a huge temptation to say what they think we want to hear, rather than to say what God wants us to hear. Before we accuse them of lacking courage, we first have to ask if we are more willing to hear God's message, whatever it is, than to criticize or reject the messenger who brings uncomfortable words. The listeners' desire to hear God's word helps the preacher to remain faithful to it.

Hope for the future

Amos and Hosea both encouraged repentance, which would lead to great hope for the future, but neither seems to have expected that the offer would be taken up. Micah, however, was much more optimistic. Perhaps encouraged by the religious renewal led by King Hezekiah, Micah was confident that at least a minority would respond to God and enjoy the future of which he spoke.

The gap between rich and poor is well illustrated in Hong Kong harbour.

Note especially the vision of peace in 4:3-4, which is almost identical to that in Isaiah 2:3-4. Perhaps this is a good example of how God gave the same message to more than one person, in order to emphasize it and also to reinforce the claim that it was genuine. The prophecy about Bethlehem (5:2) is taken up in the New Testament (Matthew 2:6) and refers to the birth of Jesus.

Heaven on earth! That's what the promise of peace in 4:3-4 seems like. It sounds so impossible, as more nations get nuclear weapons and firms making home security systems enjoy a boom in sales. Micah and Isaiah put into words the deep longings most people feel. They make sure that we understand that only God can bring about this universal peace – and Revelation 21:1-4 describes it as 'a new creation'. But meanwhile, what do we do? Hopes and dreams are not enough. Jesus said, 'Blessed are the peacemakers, for they will be called sons of God' (Matthew 5:9). God's people are called to sow the seeds of peace in all their relationships – with one another and within their society. It is part of the gospel.

184

169

294-296

The book of Nahum

Nahum and Jonah both focus on Nineveh, capital of Assyria. They give two sides of the same picture. Nahum tells us that God will certainly punish people outside of Israel if they do not repent, Jonah that forgiveness is possible even for those outside of Israel if they do.

Nahum condemns Assyria as an oppressive and evil colonial power. He asserts that God will not tolerate its oppression and injustice and that Assyria will therefore be destroyed. There will be no regret, only rejoicing (3:19) when this happens.

The main theme of the book is that God 'is slow to anger and great in power', and he 'will not leave the guilty unpunished' (1:3). The destruction of Nineveh simply proves God's kingship, his hatred of injustice and also his protecting care for those who turn to him (1:7). Assyria's defeat brought the southern kingdom of Judah at least temporary relief from outside pressure.

Nahum's rejoicing over Nineveh's downfall may seem a bit unforgiving and 'unchristian' to us. Personal revenge can never be right. And yet in God's scheme of things there has to be an end to evil. When evil people and nations press on regardless of the hurt they cause, ignoring both divine and human pleas for reform, joy and sadness will be right reactions on the day their power is finally broken. There will be joy because justice is seen to be done, and because at last relief has come to people who have suffered horribly. And there will be sadness because it had to end this way, that people were so cruel and bad. God's power is seen most in his triumph over evil; it is in him that we rejoice most of all.

The book of Nahum: data

Author: we know nothing about Nahum himself. Nahum means 'comforter', but there is little comfort in his message.

Date: this prophecy of doom on the powerful and cruel Assyrian regime, symbolized by its capital city, Nineveh, dates sometime between the defeat of Thebes (663 BC, 3:8) and the destruction of Nineveh (612 BC).

The book of Habakkuk

The book of Habakkuk: data

Author: unknown.

Date: around 600 BC, when the Babylonians had overthrown the Assyrians and were threatening the southern kingdom of Judah.

The book of Habakkuk is not a prophetic statement. It is a record of Habakkuk's personal struggle with the problems of suffering and evil in the world. He believed that God was powerful and just, yet at the end of the seventh century BC Judah was full of violence and injustice and he could not understand why God seemed to be doing nothing about it.

The answer Habakkuk was given, that after a time God would use the Babylonians to punish Judah (1:5-11), was no help at all. The Babylonians were themselves evil, so how could a holy God use them (1:12-17)? God replies that he will deal with the Babylonians too, who

would be betrayed by their own power-seeking (2:5). This does not actually solve Habakkuk's problem of how God could ever choose to use such people, but it does help him come to terms with the situation. The book ends with a prayer of confident trust.

Habakkuk is realistic; the problems didn't go away but he found a way of coping with them. In the process, he had no qualms about questioning God over things that he did not understand. In the 'taunt-song' of 2:6-20 Habakkuk vents his feelings about Babylon and revels in their doom. This helps him reaffirm his faith in God even when there is still no sign of God doing something (3:16).

When we face the problem of evil in the world, and have no clear sign that God is concerned about it, we have two options: to deny our faith or to keep on believing that God will act, but without proof. Habakkuk opted for the second, and his book left future readers with two good examples to follow:

1 He is honest with God. 'Why don't you listen?' he cries (1:2). He is not being irreverent. His desperate prayer is based on his belief that God does care deeply about the situation. That sort of prayer never gives up and is guaranteed an answer (1 John 5:14-15).

2 He learns to be patient. The answer 'will certainly come'; 'though it linger, wait for it' (2:3).

Both examples, of course, apply to many aspects of Christian living.

139

The book of Zephaniah

The book of Zephaniah: data

Zephaniah prophesied in the time of King Josiah (640-609 BC), and was perhaps someone who encouraged Josiah to make his reforms (2 Kings 22-23).

There is not a great deal of original material in Zephaniah. It reflects the teaching of Micah, Isaiah and other prophets, forming a good summary of general prophetic teaching on judgment and salvation.

Zephaniah's teaching centres on 'the day of the LORD'. He picks up Amos's idea (Amos 5) that it will not just be a time of rejoicing because God will wipe out Israel's enemies, but also a time to fear because Israel and Judah themselves will be judged. Even the believers who repent have no guarantee of escaping the disaster altogether, although there is real hope for them. After the judgment, God will restore to Israel faithful people (called 'the remnant') and enable them to live in his way (2:1-3,7). Their two-way relationship with God will bring real joy and delight to both parties (3:9, 17, 20). The New Testament explains how this two-way relationship can come into being, through the death of Jesus Christ (Romans 5:1,2).

In looking forward to a new kind

38

Summary of the book of Zephaniah

1 A challenge to Judah (1:1 - 2:3)
2 Condemnation of evil in the world (2:4-15)
3 A message of hope for Jerusalem (3)

166

of relationship with God, Zephaniah also looks forward to a new kind of relationship with God's people: they will serve the Lord together 'shoulder to shoulder' (3:9). Human barriers should fall away once people from different countries and backgrounds become members of God's single family (see how Galatians 3:26-28 and Ephesians 2:14-18 describe this). So there should be no racism in the church. But by the same principle, there should be no personal rivalry or envy of any kind.

The book of Haggai

The book of Haggai: data

Author: Haggai is the earliest known prophet to have worked among the exiles who returned to Jerusalem from Babylon in 539 BC. He is unknown except for references in Ezra 5:1; 6:14.

Date: the prophecies are dated precisely (1:1; 2:1, 10, 20), which is 520 BC.

The Persian emperor, Cyrus, enabled a group of exiles, enthused by the prophecies of Jeremiah and Ezekiel, to return to Judah and begin to rebuild the nation in 539 BC. They began well, but were soon disheartened by the huge task, and by the hostility of neighbouring states. There were apparently no major moral or religious problems, just a general apathy. Work on rebuilding the temple never got above the foundations.

Around 520 BC the prophets Haggai and Zechariah both began to speak out. Haggai challenged the people to make finishing the temple their first priority. He knew the temple could not replace personal faith, but it could serve as a focus of national unity. Building it was evidence of the people's obedience and faith. They had allowed difficulty, discouragement, and concern for their own legitimate needs to prevent them from completing what God had told them to do. They listened and responded; by 516 BC the temple was completed.

Home making is a priority for most people. Not only do we want a roof over our heads, we want it comfortably furnished and pleasantly decorated. And the work on it never seems to stop; there's always more to do. That's what the people in Jerusalem found. They made their homes good ('panelled', 1:4). But they did it at the expense of God's house. Haggai had to teach them to distinguish between what is important (making a home) and what is necessary – doing God's work. In other words, to 'seek first God's kingdom and his righteousness' (Matthew 6:33). Many things that are good in themselves can actually hinder God's work when we let them assume a priority they don't deserve.

●Points to look out for

The message is from God

Thirty-two times in this short book we are told that God's word was being spoken.

The vision of the future

Prosperity in the land, David's descendant, Zerubbabel, as messianic ruler, and the shaking of creation (2:6-9) until God's purposes are carried out, are all promised.

Haggai was probably looking ahead to much later times, seeing Zerubbabel as a symbol that the Davidic covenant will continue. 'In a little while' (2:6) may be deliberately ambiguous; God will fulfil his own word in his own time.

The book of Zechariah

The book of Zechariah: data

Author: nothing is known for certain about Zechariah. His ancestor Iddo (Ezra 5:1; 6:14) was head of a priestly family which returned to Jerusalem from Babylon (Nehemiah 12:4), so Zechariah may have been a priest too. Chapters 9-14 seem to have lost the sense of encouragement of chapters 1-8 and see only disobedience and bad leadership in Judah; they are sometimes seen as the work of a different, unknown prophet.

Date: he worked at the same time as Haggai, about 520-518 BC.

Zechariah wrote at the same time as Haggai but in a very different style. Haggai brought a straightforward, clear message. Zechariah was a visionary, and his book uses a wealth of symbols and images.

Haggai is like a blueprint setting out God's plan for the community; Zechariah is like an abstract painting in which the meaning is expressed more by colour and texture than detail. The canvas is wide. He moves from considering events in Judah's history and the relationship between good and evil to thinking about good and evil in general and about events at the end of time, when God would send a messenger to usher in his kingdom.

The angel who leads Zechariah through his visions (1:7 - 6:8) only gives a very general interpretation of their meaning. It is usually linked to the challenge to repent from sin and obey and trust God, which precedes and follows the visions (1:3-6; 6:9 - 7:14). *The reader is clearly not meant to press all the details, but to receive an impression of God's will and respond to it. The book thus becomes relevant for every age, and not just the author's time or the end of the world.*

●Points to look out for

Zechariah brought good news, that God was going to bless the people. He also issued a challenge to live in a way that matched up to God's concern for justice and care for the poor, and to wait with confident excitement for God to work in the future.

Zechariah provides a very positive view of the future, but recognizes that final victory will come only after fierce struggle and even apparent

Summary of the book of Zechariah

1 Prophecies during the rebuilding of the temple (1-8)
- Eight visions (1:1 - 6:8)
- Joshua is crowned as a symbol of the Messiah (6:9-15)
- Questions about fasts and feasts (7-8)

2 Undated later prophecies (9-14)
- The Prince of Peace (9)
- Bad shepherds and the Good Shepherd (10-11)
- Jerusalem repents (12)
- Sin will be cleansed (13)
- Blessings and judgments of God's kingdom (14)

defeat. He also takes seriously the spiritual forces of evil which oppose God's work.

185

The New Testament uses Zechariah as a major source of prophetic information about the Messiah and his work. Zechariah's picture of the messenger to come (2:4,10; 6:12-13; 9:9-10; 11:12-13; 14:4,9,16) relates both to what happened to Jesus and to New Testament predictions about his second coming.

The book of Malachi

The book of Malachi: data

Author: he is unknown apart from this book.

Date: Malachi probably worked around the time of Ezra and Nehemiah (460 BC) about 100 years after the first return to Jerusalem from exile in Babylon in 539 BC.

Malachi has a hard-hitting message balanced by a deep pastoral concern. He was certain that God would judge the Judeans who rejected the terms of the covenant, but he wanted to make absolutely sure that both those who responded to the message and those who did not, really understood about God's love and the practical results of knowing him. The book provides a fitting end to the Old Testament. It gives a clear summary of the prophetic message and ties this to the law of Moses (4:4).

207-208

34

●Points to look out for

The covenant

Malachi picks up the teaching of Deuteronomy. God is just, righteous, loving, glorious and awesome. Curses and blessings result from breaking or keeping the covenant.

The people's unfaithfulness

There was oppression and immorality (3:5). But the heart of the problem seemed to be that they believed in God, but acted as if he was to be pacified and manipulated, rather than honoured and obeyed. Their religion had no impact on their behaviour.

The future

There would be a day of reckoning, when those who rejected God would be destroyed by the refining fire (3:2-3). There would also be many who responded to God, and they would be overwhelmed by the blessings they received as God's treasured possession (3:10-12,17).

Malachi focuses on principles of worship which can be extracted from their Old Testament context and applied equally well to our own. Look at these:

1 The principle of perfection (1:7). God wants the best we can offer, not the left-overs of our resources.

2 The principle of faithfulness (2:14). There was easy divorce then, as there is now. God looks for commitment in marriage, not easy-come-easy-go relationships.

3 The principle of giving (3:8). The offering of one-tenth of resources to God in the law of Moses was obligatory. The New Testament never fixes a standard (except that of cheerful generosity, 2 Corinthians 9:7) but with so much to be grateful for, Christians often argue that their proportion cannot be less than that.

3.5

THE LIFE OF CHRIST AND THE ORIGINS OF THE CHURCH

Gospels and Acts

by David Stone

There is a gap of around five hundred years between the writing of the last Old Testament book, Malachi, and the first New Testament letter, probably to the Galatians. The New Testament books do not appear in historical order however.

They begin with four versions of the life of Christ, 'gospels' or 'good news', and continue with their sequel, the Acts of the Apostles, written by Luke, and describing the birth of the church and the ministry of the apostle Paul.

This section is the focus of the whole Bible. The Old Testament looks forward to it and the letters and Revelation are developed from it.

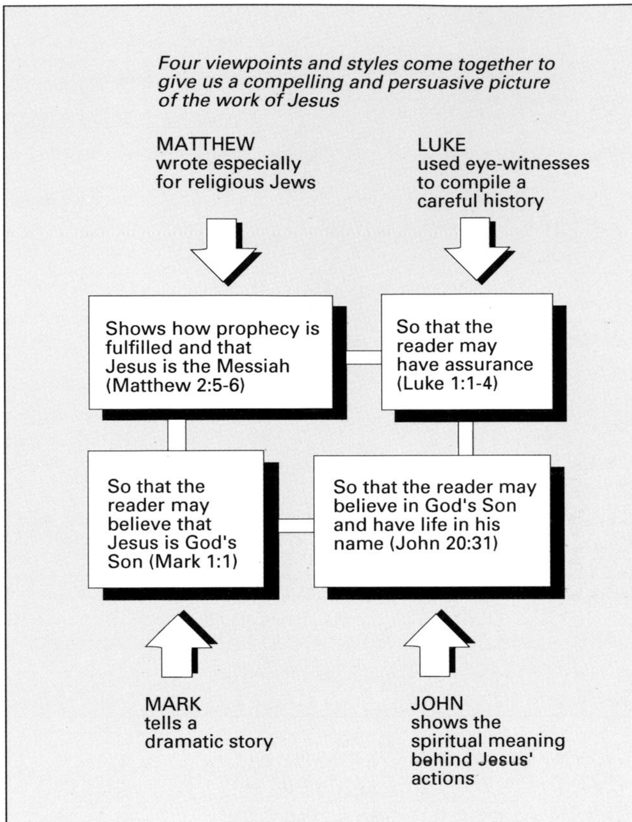

Four gospel viewpoints.

Introduction to the gospels

The New Testament begins with the four gospels. 'Gospel' simply means good news and that is exactly what these four books are: the written good news of who Jesus is and what he has done.

336-339

Until the time of Jesus, God had made himself known 'at many times and in various ways' (Hebrews 1:1). The Old Testament records events through which God began to show what he was like to his chosen nation of Israel. But like a trailer to a forthcoming film, the Old Testament gives only a taste of what is to come. It looks forward to the time when God will come in person and start a revolution that will bring to an end the mess the world is in.

270-272

The good news of the New Testament is that God himself, in the person of his Son Jesus, *has* visited us. The revolution is under way! As John says in his gospel, 'God did not send his Son into the world to condemn the world, but to save the world through him' (John 3:17). That is why the gospels, which tell us about Jesus, are worth getting to know for ourselves and for passing on to others.

What was Jesus like? What did he do? What happened to him? Why did these things take place? These are the questions which the gospels set out to answer. But they are not like modern biographies which present a complete picture of someone's life. For a start they ignore most of what happened during Jesus' first thirty years. They concentrate instead on the three years of his public ministry. They do not always set out events in the order in which they happened, either. Other factors seem to influence the way they are arranged – for example, some of Jesus' teaching or actions on different occasions may be grouped together if the writer wants to emphasize an overall theme.

The gospels tell us the sort of things Jesus said and the amazing things he did. We learn about his twelve disciples, the men he chose as his special followers, and the way they came to discover who he was. We discover in detail the circumstances surrounding his death: how people who rejected the evidence that he was God's Son and charged him with blasphemy arranged his execution. The gospels also draw attention to the deeper significance of Jesus' death on the cross, seeing it

How they chose what to put in

How did the gospel writers select their material? Part of the answer is that these stories about Jesus formed the foundation of the preaching of the Christian good news that has gone on ever since Jesus began it. The writers of the gospels set out their belief that through these events God put into effect his plan to rescue us. They link the discovery of salvation which Christians in every generation have made with the historical life of Jesus of Nazareth.

Matthew, Mark and John bring the story of Jesus to its conclusion after his resurrection and ascension. But Luke, the author of the third gospel, goes further and writes a sequel. The Acts of the Apostles is his account of how the Christian church came into being and how, under the direction of the Holy Spirit, the good news about Jesus began to spread throughout the world.

The rest of the New Testament takes much of the information in the gospels for granted and does not tell us much more about the life of Jesus. Other writers from the time (like the historians Tacitus and Josephus) mention him, but we would know very little if we did not have Matthew, Mark, Luke and John to turn to.

as God's way of bringing salvation to the whole human race. They conclude with the victory of his being raised from death and his return to heaven, leaving his followers to take the good news of what he has done out into the whole world.

●Why the gospels were written

Writing was not as common in the first century AD as it is now and, of course, printing had not been invented. To begin with, the stories about Jesus and his early followers were passed on by Christian teachers who travelled from place to place. People then were used to committing such things to memory – this was especially true of those who became Christians from a Jewish background.

But as the actual eyewitnesses of Jesus' life began to die out and as Christianity began to spread among non-Jewish groups, it became necessary to write down what had happened. In fact, many different 'gospels' were written in the first few centuries, most of which have since been lost. Only the four we have in our Bibles were recognized universally as authoritative accounts of Jesus' life.

No two friends, artists or biographers will record exactly the same details about a person. So to get a full picture of him or her, we need to build it up from different points of view. That is what the gospels do. They are like four portraits of Jesus. Each is very different (though, as we shall see, there are also great similarities between them, especially Matthew, Mark and Luke) but each is about the same person, Jesus. Each contributes a different perspective to help us grasp more fully who Jesus is and what he was like. As you read, look out for the differences of viewpoint. Notice how Matthew is concerned about Jewish questions and the Old Testament background for Jesus, and how John focuses on the spiritual meaning of Jesus' actions. Use Mark as a brief overview of Jesus' life, and Luke as an objective collection of eyewitness reports welded into a balanced selection of events and sayings.

Mark makes his intention very clear in the heading to his gospel: 'The beginning of the gospel about Jesus Christ, the Son of God' (Mark 1:1).

187

344-348

Parables

When Jesus taught, people listened. To help them remember what he said, he often used vivid picture language, stories, riddles and striking illustrations. These are all examples of parables.

Sometimes Jesus taught in this way to *reveal* truth clearly and bring home the full force of what he was saying. This does not always come across in quite the same way to the modern reader. For example, the story of the Good Samaritan (Luke 10:25-37) is so well known that is difficult for us to think 'Samaritan' without also thinking 'good'. Yet orthodox Jews in Jesus' day regarded Samaritans as anything but good. A story in which a Samaritan comes to the aid of a victim who had been disregarded by a priest and a Levite would have been a great shock to them.

One way of regaining the original impact of the parables is to think of modern equivalents (e.g. instead of 'Samaritan' perhaps read 'terrorist'). Another is to let our imaginations rove over the scene – bearing in mind that the report in the gospel is probably abbreviated and in any case loses some of the impact a live story-teller would have. The woman searching for the lost coin (Luke 15:8-10): see her on her hands and knees feeling into every corner. The father looking into the distance in case his son should return (Luke 15:20): his eyes straining, tears running from them. By recapturing the drama, we can begin to understand the message – that God leaves no stone unturned in his search for us; that he longs deeply for us to return to him.

Another reason Jesus taught in parables was to *conceal* truth (Mark 4:9-12). Parables have a dual function. They communicate truth about God only to people who have been given the spiritual ability to understand their deeper meaning. These are people who, like the disciples, are serious about trusting and obeying him. Parables may obscure the truth about God to those who, because of their refusal to believe and to apply what he says, have been left in the dark.

He has no doubt about the true identity of Jesus. His aim in writing is to present the story of Jesus in such a way that his readers too will be convinced that Jesus is God's Son.

191

Luke (1:1-4) claims to have investigated the eyewitness evidence of what actually happened. This is important: the gospels are accounts which have been selected to help people relate the Jesus they believe in to the Jesus who lived in Palestine in the first century.

So in his gospel, John says that he intends it to give information about Jesus which will lead us to 'have life in his name' as we accept for ourselves what he tells us about him (20:30-31). In other words, the gospels are not intended *merely* to tell us what happened. In aiming to persuade us about Jesus *and* to affect the way we live, they are more like good sermons. These stories have been preserved so that, like Jesus' first followers, we can know about him in theory *and* believe in him in practice.

For nearly two thousand years, countless people all over the world have done just that as they have heard and seen Jesus for themselves through the gospels. The authors' concern with the way Jesus related to ordinary people in real-life situations makes what they have written ring true with people of every culture and generation.

For example, if we want to know what 'being holy' means, then the gospels tell us in simple terms: it means getting our thoughts cleaned up (Matthew 5:28). If we

want to know how to deal with difficult people, then Jesus tells us clearly: we must love our enemies and do good to troublemakers (Luke 6:35-36). That may not be what we want to hear, of course, which is why it is impossible to sit on the fence when we read Jesus' teaching; we can either accept and apply it, or reject it.

●A common point of view

Because Matthew, Mark and Luke look at the life of Jesus from similar viewpoints, they are sometimes called the 'synoptic gospels'. They have much in common (*e.g.* 95% of Mark's gospel appears also in Matthew and Luke) and they share the same basic outline of events. They also describe many events in almost exactly the same way. (Look at Matthew 14:13-21, Mark 6:32-44 and Luke 9:10-17 for an example, then compare these accounts with John 6:1-15 to show how differently he reports the same incident.)

71

Miracles

Start reading a gospel and it isn't long before you come across Jesus doing a 'miracle'. Most are miracles of healing, in which Jesus makes a sick person well or casts out evil spirits. There are also three occasions when he raises someone from the dead and a number of instances where he demonstrates his power over nature – such as calming a storm (Mark 4:35-41) or turning water into wine (John 2:1-11).

Why did Jesus do these things? His actions stemmed from who he was: God's Son. First, he expressed *God's love* for people in need. Matthew tells us that 'when Jesus landed and saw a large crowd, he had compassion on them and healed their sick' (Matthew 14:14). Secondly, since the coming of Jesus heralded the arrival of God's kingdom in power, he also expressed *God's rule*. An example of this is where Jesus heals a woman 'whom Satan had kept bound for eighteen long years' (Luke 13:16). The miracles take place as Satan's stranglehold begins to be broken.

So miracles are signposts which point to Jesus' true identity, as the Messiah. In Luke 7:18-23, Jesus reminds John the Baptist that the miracles he has been performing are just what the Old Testament prophecies about the Messiah (in this case Isaiah 35:5-6 and 61:1-3) said he would do. Another example is in Mark 2:1-12, where Jesus heals a paralysed man in order to show the truth of his earlier claim to forgive sins.

Notice that the miracles do not *compel* people to believe. They are not absolute proofs of who Jesus is; another explanation for them can always be found by those who want one (see Mark 3:22). But they are helpful pointers to the truth for people who are willing to allow Jesus to become Lord of their lives.

The greatest miracle, of course, was the resurrection of Jesus from the dead. The New Testament provides such powerful evidence that this took place that it is difficult to reach any other conclusion. This can help us to accept other miracles which we may find hard to believe. For if the miracle of the resurrection of Jesus *did* happen then other miracles are at least possible. In addition, since the resurrection can be seen as God's seal of approval on Jesus' ministry, this must include the miracles he performed.

An important question now is: 'Do miracles happen today?' Clearly, the signs (as John calls them, e.g. 2:11), pointed distinctively to the physical person of Jesus. The New Testament does encourage us to expect to see God working powerfully through the church (John 14:12). But it also warns us not to seek spectacular miracles for their own sake (Mark 8:11-12). We can ask God to intervene but we cannot tell God how to do it. He remains in charge, working for his own glory, not our gratification.

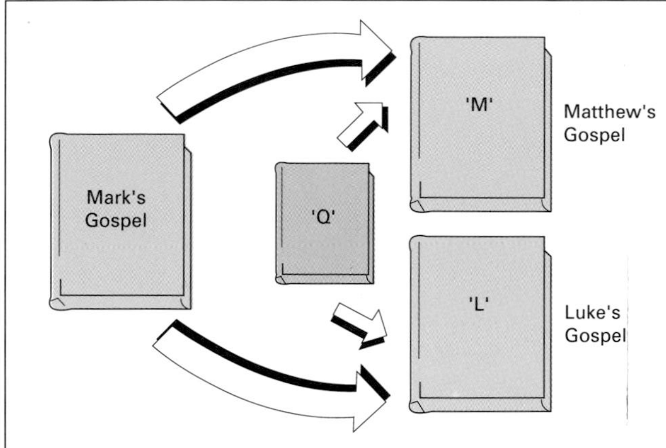

Possible sources of the 'synoptic' gospels, Matthew and Luke.

Most scholars think that Mark was the first to be written and that Matthew and Luke based their gospels on Mark, rewriting it and adding material from their own research. In addition, some of the sayings of Jesus which are not in Mark are very similar in Matthew and Luke. This had led scholars to suggest that they each made use of an early, now otherwise unknown, collection of Jesus' teaching. They label this possible source 'Q', and the material which is unique to Matthew and Luke is known as 'M' and 'L'.

The gospel writers were committed to telling the story of Jesus and so pass on a reliable account of his life and ministry. But each has done so differently, in line with their individual purposes.

For example, look at Mark 11:12-25 and compare it with Matthew 21:18-22.

Both passages describe an incident where Jesus cursed a fig tree which subsequently withered. In Mark's account, the two halves of the story form a sandwich round another incident (something he does quite often), in which Jesus evicts those who were in effect stopping people from using the temple as a place of prayer. Mark uses the cursing of the fig tree to illustrate God's judgment on religious hypocrites. But Matthew uses the story primarily to illustrate God's power available to those who trust him. He therefore puts the cursing and the withering together in order to emphasize this point, with the temple incident coming just before in verses 12-17.

When reading a gospel passage, find out if one of the other gospels has a parallel account. Studying this as well may help you to understand and apply its truth more effectively.

●Understanding the gospels today

The gospels are about people who lived in first-century Palestine. Their life was very different from that of today's world. For example, we would not think it wrong for Jesus to talk to a woman from Samaria (see John 4:4-42). But the orthodox Jews of his time would have been scandalized. Not only was she a woman (which in a male-dominated society would have been bad enough!) but she had a doubtful reputation, and was also from a despised race.

As you find incidents like this which reflect a different way of life from your own, you will get more out of the passage if you first stop to ask yourself what lasting truths are illustrated by it. (In this case, Jesus is giving an example of how God treats all people with equal concern, whatever their background.)

In the sections which follow, each gospel is summarized, and then 'points to look out for' are suggested. This is to avoid undue repetition.

The Gospel of Matthew

Summary of the Gospel of Matthew

It has been suggested that just as the Old Testament begins with the five 'books of Moses', so Matthew arranges the teaching of Jesus in five sections, set as neat blocks in the middle of his other material. Notice that each section ends with a distinctive 'when Jesus had finished ...'.

1 The ancestry, birth and early life of Jesus (1-2)
2 John the Baptist; Jesus' baptism, temptations and start of ministry (3-4)
3 Teaching block 1: The Sermon on the Mount (5:1 - 7:27)
4 Jesus at work in Galilee (8-9)
5 Teaching block 2: Instructions for the disciples' ministry (10:1 - 11:1)
6 Some people accept Jesus and other reject him (11:2 - 12:50)
7 Teaching block 3: Parables about the kingdom of heaven (13:1-53)
8 Conflict with the Pharisees deep ens (13:54 - 17:27)
9 Teaching block 4: How disciples should behave towards each other (18)
10 Jesus travels to Jerusalem (19-22)
11 Teaching block 5: The shape of the future (23-25)
12 The death and resurrection of Jesus (26-28)

Although Matthew's gospel was probably not the first to be written, its place as the first of the four emphasizes its role as a bridge between the two Testaments. For Matthew, the fact that Christianity has its roots in the Jewish faith is especially important. This shows that the God who came to earth in the person of his Son Jesus is the same as the God of the Old Testament.

Part of Matthew's purpose in writing the gospel seems to have been to reassure Jews who had become Christians that their new faith filled out rather than cancelled out their old faith. So he answers some of the objections that Jews were raising against Christianity. For example, in order to refute claims that Jesus was illegitimate, he records the circumstances of his birth. But his special and repeated emphasis is on how Jesus fulfils the Old Testament predictions of a coming Messiah.

86

●Points to look out for

The family tree

Matthew begins with a list of the ancestors of Jesus, something which modern readers sometimes find a bit daunting! But since the Messiah was to be a descendant of David, Israel's greatest king, Matthew needs to establish that Jesus comes from David's line. (Luke's family tree (3:23-38) differs from Matthew's. It may be that Matthew gives the *legal* line of descent from David, stating who was the heir to the throne in each case, while Luke lists the *actual* descendants of David through the branch to which Joseph belonged.)

The genealogy also shows Matthew's interest in numbers generally (*e.g.* 1:17) and his neat arrangement of events in threes

The Gospel of Matthew: data

Author: the gospel itself does not tell us who wrote it, but early tradition states that it was Matthew the tax collector, also called Levi (*e.g.* Luke 5:27). In this gospel, he is mentioned by name only in 9:9 and 10:3.

Date: Matthew's gospel was probably written after Mark's, at some time between AD 50 and 90, but we do not know exactly when.

(*e.g.* three groups of fourteen generations in 1:1-17, three temptations in 4:1-11, three good things in 6:1-18, three 'do not ...' sayings in 6:25 - 7:6, three commands in 7:7-20). We also find groups of seven (*e.g.* seven parables in chapter 13, seven 'woes' in chapter 23).

Matthew would not want his readers to think that God works mechanically. But he would want us to notice that God works methodically. He is concerned with details, and he achieves his purposes without rushing. That may encourage Christians who are waiting for answers to prayer. It may also warn us against taking short cuts in our enthusiasm to get things done in the church.

Old Testament prophecies fulfilled

Matthew shows how many details of Jesus' life were predicted in the Old Testament. Both in the way he comments on things that happen (*e.g.* 1:22-23; 2:15) and in his quotations of what people say (*e.g.* 2:5-6; 3:15), he shows how many of the lines of Old Testament prophecy converge and are fulfilled in Jesus. Here are just a few:

Prophecy	Subject	Fulfilment
Isaiah 7:14	Born of a virgin	Matthew 1:18-23
Micah 5:2	Place of birth	Matthew 2:1-6
Hosea 11:1	Escape into Egypt	Matthew 2:14-15
Jeremiah 31:15	Slaughter of infants	Matthew 2:16-18
Isaiah 9:1-2	Ministry in Galilee	Matthew 4:12-16
Isaiah 53:4	Healing the sick	Matthew 8:16-17
Psalm 78:2	Teaching in parables	Matthew 13:34-35
Zechariah 9:9	Riding a donkey	Matthew 21:1-9
Zechariah 11:13	Potter's field	Matthew 27:6-7

He had a very practical reason for this. 'How can Jesus be the Messiah?' people asked. 'He comes from Galilee, whereas the prophets tell us that the Messiah will come from Bethlehem' (see John 7:52). Matthew answers by showing that although Jesus was indeed *brought up* in Nazareth (a town in the district of Galilee), he was actually *born* in Bethlehem and so fulfils the prophecy after all.

To many people, the Old Testament seems so inferior to the New when it comes to understanding Christian faith. Matthew's gospel, with its sixty-five references to the Old Testament, shows the value of these books. They point forward to and shed light on the life and ministry of Jesus. They show that God had kept his promises; we can therefore trust him to keep

those he made through Jesus.

God's Law

The Messiah was expected to rule justly and according to the Law of God. Matthew concludes that Jesus is qualified on these grounds, and to prove it he shows how deeply Jesus understood the Old Testament laws and God's true intentions behind them. He sees Jesus as a sort of second Moses – though much greater than Moses ever was – teaching God's Law to the people.

So he quotes Jesus' view of the Law: 'Do not think that I have come to abolish the Law or the Prophets; I have not come to abolish them but to fulfil them' (Matthew 5:17). Then he goes on to show how Jesus fulfils them in the rest of chapter 5. For example, people were taking the commandment 'Do not murder' and twisting it to mean 'hitting someone is allowed as long as you don't actually kill them'. Jesus exposes this misuse of the Law and explains what God intended – that his people should avoid anger and insulting language, as well as physical violence (Matthew 5:21-22).

It is not difficult for most people to avoid killing, stealing and even committing adultery. Nor is it very difficult to give time and resources to charity work. But Matthew's report of the Sermon on the Mount shows that the Christian life is a much more difficult matter of getting our thoughts and attitudes to match up to God's. Loving our enemy means being concerned for his welfare, not simply avoiding an opportunity to stab him in the back.

Life as a follower of Jesus

The Sermon on the Mount in chapters 5 to 7 sets out the standards which members of God's kingdom are to aim for. They are to be like lights in a dark world, leading others to discover God (5:14-16). In chapter 18 Matthew shows Christians how they are to behave towards one another as members of the church. (Only Matthew's gospel uses the word 'church'; see 16:18; 18:17). Jesus' teaching on what will take

The promised Messiah

Messiah (a Hebrew word) and Christ (its Greek equivalent) mean 'anointed one'. In Old Testament times, kings were anointed with special oil to show that they were set aside by God to rule on his behalf. By the time of Jesus, the Jews expected the Messiah to come as a successor to King David. He would free them from their Roman oppressors and usher in the golden age of God's rule. Jesus acknowledged that he was indeed the Messiah (*e.g.* Mark 14:61-62). But for him, being the Messiah involved suffering on the cross to bring about complete *spiritual* renewal, not the merely political freedom which many of his fellow-Jews were expecting (see Matthew 16:16, 20-21). In order to avoid misunderstanding, Jesus tended to use the more cryptic term 'Son of Man' when talking about himself. Only later did 'Christ' become used as a surname of Jesus. (See also the section headed 'Salvation' under Luke on page 193.)

It is still possible to overstress the Messiah's concern for justice (which Jesus promised to fulfil at his second coming and which his people are to work for now) and to undervalue personal salvation. On the other hand, the personal salvation which is so central to his work can be misused to imply that Jesus is not interested in the structures of the world today. The New Testament holds both truths in balance: we cannot have one without the other.

33

193

294-296, 299-301

place at the end of time in chapters 24 and 25 is included not to satisfy our curiosity but to encourage us always to be living in ways that bring honour to him.

275-276

Notice how Jesus, in his practical teaching about Christian living, is always stressing motives. And one motive stands out above all the others: we are to be more concerned about drawing attention to God than about what others think of us, and more ready to serve him and others than to please ourselves. Think about the blows to pride in passages such as 6:1 and 25:44-45.

The gospel for all nations

Although Matthew's gospel has a strong Jewish flavour, it also contains more than a hint that Jesus the Messiah is the king of the whole world. Right at the beginning, Gentile (*i.e.* non-Jewish) women are included in the family tree and Gentile wise men recognize and worship the infant Jesus as king. At several points, Gentiles are commended for having more faith than

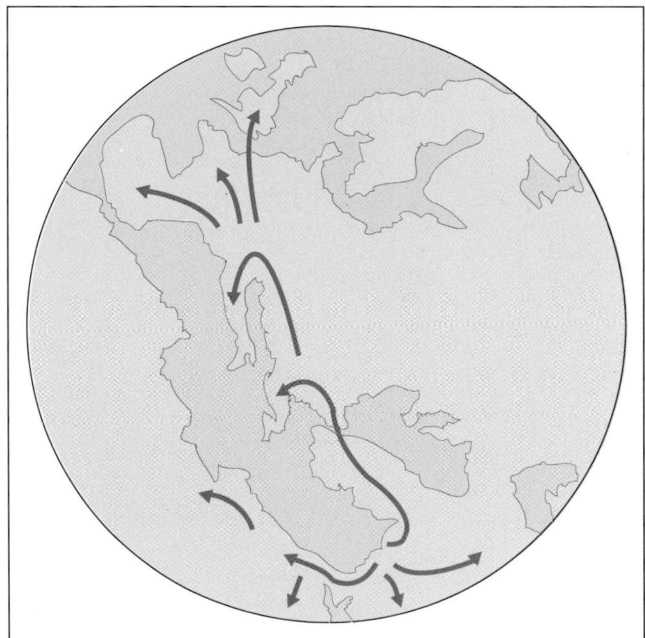

'Make disciples of all nations' (the first centuries AD*).*

The kingdom of heaven

A central theme in the teaching of Jesus is what Mark and Luke call the 'kingdom of God' and Matthew, observing Jewish scruples about using God's name, calls the 'kingdom of heaven'. John does not use the phrase very often but refers instead to 'life' and 'eternal life' (see John 17:3); this would have made more sense to his non-Jewish readers. The phrases mean much the same sort of thing – as shown by Mark 9:43-47.

Jesus' hearers expected the Messiah to bring about God's perfect rule over the whole world. He stressed this *future* dimension in his teaching (*e.g.* Matthew 24 and 25). But Jesus also taught that his coming into the world made the kingdom a *present* reality. Jesus the king has come to reign – as demonstrated by his miracles of healing and exorcism (*e.g.* Matthew 4:17; 9:35; 11:11; 12:28; 18:1).

But this may not always seem to be the case. The enemy has been dealt a decisive and mortal blow but he continues to struggle. Despite this, we are to be in no doubt that God will triumph openly when Jesus returns and evil finally will be overthrown (Matthew 13:36-42). Meanwhile more and more people enter the kingdom by turning to Jesus and allowing him to rule their lives.

Living as a Christian is never easy. The teaching about 'the kingdom' shows why. The church is like an army sent into occupied territory to restore it to its rightful king. The king is with us, but there are pockets of stubborn resistance. And the battle begins inside us – bringing under God's rule every attitude and action – which is often harder than standing up to wrong things in the world around us.

Jews (*e.g.* 8:10; 15:21-28). And Matthew ends his gospel with the logical conclusion: since Jesus is king over all, the one to whom all authority in heaven and on earth has been given, the message of the good news needs to be taken all over the world (28:18-20).

This instruction, sometimes called the 'eleventh commandment', is easy to overlook today. Surely with so many churches all around the world it is not the priority it once was? In fact, there are many places where there are not enough Christian workers (9:36-38). Besides, every generation needs to hear the gospel of Christ in its own language and terms. The missionary task is central to the church, and everyone is meant to be involved – sharing their faith locally, praying for and supporting people who take it further afield.

The Gospel of Mark

Summary of the Gospel of Mark

Mark shares with Matthew and Luke a similar overall framework in his account of Jesus' ministry. His aim is to set out the good news about who Jesus is (which he establishes in chapters 1 to 8) and what he came to do (chapters 9 to 16).

1 Introduction: John the Baptist, Jesus' baptism and temptations (1:1-13)
2 Jesus' ministry in Galilee and its surroundings (1:14 - 9:50)
3 Jesus' ministry in Judea and the journey to Jerusalem (10)
4 Jesus' ministry in Jerusalem and visits to Bethany (11-13)
5 The trial and death of Jesus (14-15)
6 The resurrection (16)

Note

Many scholars think that 16:9-20 was not part of the original gospel but added later to round off the otherwise rather abrupt ending at 16:8. Some early manuscripts include these verses and others do not. Because of this uncertainty, some Bibles have them in smaller print.

Mark's is the shortest of the four gospels and was probably the first to be written. Unlike Matthew, it seems to have been written for a mainly non-Jewish (Gentile) readership. Mark takes care in explaining religious customs which would have been familiar to Jews but unknown to Gentiles (*e.g.* compare 7:1-5 with Matthew 15:1-2).

197-198

This gospel is a series of exciting events which tumble out on top of one another, leaving the reader

The Gospel of Mark: data

Author: Early church tradition suggests that this gospel was written by John Mark, whose mother Mary lived in Jerusalem (Acts 12:12). He is also mentioned in Acts 12:25; 13:13; 15:36-40; Colossians 4:10; 2 Timothy 4:11; Philemon 24 and 1 Peter 5:13. He may be the young man referred to in Mark 14:51-52.

Date: Tradition also tells us that Mark wrote his gospel after Peter's death (which occurred around AD 64-65) and based it on what the apostle had told him about Jesus. Since chapter 13 shows no awareness of the events of the Jewish war which ended in the destruction of Jerusalem in AD 70, a date for the gospel of around AD 65-70 seems most likely.

almost breathless as the author races through. The action is fast and furious – one of his favourite words in 'immediately' as he hurries from one event to the next. It is also full of vivid descriptive detail, like the fact that Jesus was asleep 'on a cushion' (4:38) and that the grass, normally parched for much of the year, was 'green' (6:39). Look out for the way Mark emphasizes points by repeating them three times (*e.g.* the way tradition hinders obedience to God's Word in 7:8, 9, 13, and the predictions of Jesus' death in 8:31; 9:31; 10:32-34).

Mark gets straight to the point in telling the story of who Jesus was and what he did. He begins with the ministry of John the Baptist and does not bother with Jesus' birth and upbringing.

266-270

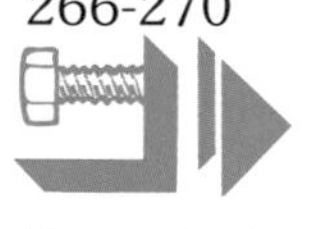

Who else but God has the authority that Jesus exercised? Examples from Mark's gospel.

●Points to look out for

Who is Jesus?

The first half of the gospel records incidents which show that Jesus is the Son of God. As you read through, notice the ways in which his ministry is marked by the authority of God the king:

Mark uses these to point to Jesus' identity as the Son of God. He also makes that claim at three key points in the story: Jesus' baptism (1:11), the transfiguration (9:7) and the crucifixion (15:39).

But it is clear that not everyone made the correct link between what he did and who he was. His opponents joined forces early on (3:6). Some of his family decided that he was mad (3:21), and the religious leaders concluded that he was possessed by Satan (3:22). In addition, Mark records several occasions when Jesus himself discouraged publicity (*e.g.* 1:24-25, 34; 3:12). He used the rather mysterious term 'Son of Man' to describe himself, a title which hinted at his divine nature (see Daniel 7:13) but could also be taken as referring simply to his membership of the human race (as in Psalm 8:4). This was partly so that only those who were committed to obeying him would understand fully who he was (see 4:34).

The evidence concerning Jesus' identity which Mark and the other gospel writers set out is sufficient for faith but not so overpowering

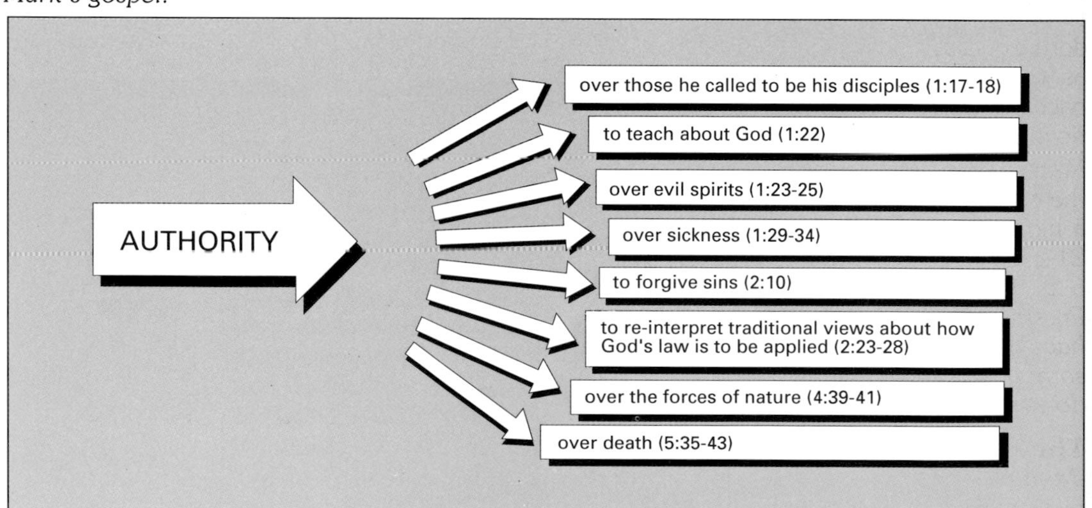

that we are forced to believe. When talking to non-Christian friends about our faith and inviting them to look at the evidence for themselves, our reasoned arguments will never be enough to convince them. We need also to pray that God will use other ways to draw them to himself as well.

Mark is convinced that Jesus is divine, the Son of God. But he also stresses the fact that Jesus is fully human, by recording examples of Jesus' human limitations (*e.g.* 6:5-6; 13:32). Matthew and Luke, concentrating on other aspects of Jesus' life and ministry, omit some of these details.

Studying Mark's portrait of Jesus helps us to see clearly that he shared fully in our human nature and so understands what we go through too. As the writer to the Hebrews puts it, 'Because he himself suffered when he was tempted, he is able to help those who are being tempted' (Hebrews 2:18).

Jesus the teacher

Jesus' ability to heal and cast out demons made him very popular (*e.g.* 1:32-34). But his mission was to proclaim the arrival of the kingdom of God through what he *said* as well as what he *did*. His miracles backed up his preaching but were no substitute for it.

Mark shows how teaching (both to the crowds and to his disciples) was a high priority for Jesus (see 1:14, 21-22, 27, 38; 2:2; 3:23; 4:1-2, 33; 6:2, 6, 34; 8:31; 9:30-31; 10:1). *Passing on to others what they have first learned from Jesus is something that his followers are to do as well (see 3:14; 5:19; 6:12-13).*

The suffering and death of Jesus

Having dealt with the question of who Jesus is, Mark turns to the question of what he came to do. Once his disciples have begun to grasp exactly who he is (8:27-30), Jesus begins to teach them 'that the Son of Man must suffer many things ...' (8:31), a prediction which, for emphasis, is made on two further occasions (9:31; 10:32-34). It is not enough to know who Jesus is without also understanding what he came to do – 'to give his life as a ransom for many' (10:45). The events surrounding Jesus' death occupy a third of the book and cast their shadow on his life from an early stage (*e.g.* 2:20 and 3:6).

Mark stresses that Jesus the Messiah's victory will be won through suffering and death. Jesus was rejected by his friends (*e.g.* 14:50, 71) and his enemies (*e.g.* 14:64; 15:11-14), and was even abandoned by God his Father (15:34). And yet the very rejection that seemed to mark his downfall turned out in the end to be the means of his triumph. Things are not always what they seem!

Life as a follower of Jesus

Jesus warns that those who accept the challenge to follow him must not be surprised if they suffer and face rejection just as he did. As 'even the Son of Man did not come to be served, but to serve' (10:45), so his followers must not aim to be served (like the teachers of the law in 12:38-40) but instead to serve with all they have (like the widow in 12:41-44). It may well be that this gospel was first sent to Christians in Rome who were being persecuted by Nero following the fire of AD 64. *Mark's gospel is a training manual for people who want to follow their Master and live as a servant, just as he did – despite the pressure of persecution.*

275-276

Final victory for us is certain, as it was for him. Each prediction of Jesus' sufferings in chapters 8, 9 and 10 ends with the confident claim that he will rise again. But in the meantime, truly to follow Jesus is not easy; self-denial and carrying a cross (8:34; 15:21) come before resurrection (16:6).

Power in weakness

In chapter 4, Mark sets out three parables about seeds, all of which emphasize that God's power works through apparent weakness. Despite opposition (verses 3-20), delays (verses 26-29) and small beginnings (verses 30-32), the kingdom's growth and fruitfulness is guaranteed. Despite the rejection and setbacks, God's purposes cannot fail.

The disciples of Jesus

Mark tells us that Jesus chose twelve disciples, '... that they might be with him and that he might send them out to preach and to have authority to drive out demons' (Mark 3:14-15).

Simon Peter, known as 'the rock' (John 1:42), was appointed by Jesus to lead the church (Matthew 16:18; Acts 1:15). He made mistakes (Matthew 16:22-23) and once denied that he even knew Jesus (Mark 14:66-72), but he was later forgiven and restored (John 21:15-19). The two New Testament letters in his name contain many passing references to the events described in the gospels.

James and John were two brothers to whom Jesus gave the nickname 'sons of thunder' (Mark 3:17). See Mark 9:38; 10:35 and Luke 9:54 to find out why! They had an ambitious mother too – see Matthew 20:20-21. Peter, James and John were the disciples who were closest to Jesus; he often took them away without the others (*e.g.* Mark 5:37; 9:2; 14:33).

Andrew, like his brother Peter, was a fisherman. He was responsible for bringing Peter to meet Jesus in the first place (John 1:41). See also John 6:8 and 12:22.

Philip was from Bethsaida, the same town as Peter and Andrew (John 1:44). See also John 6:5-7; 12:21-22; 14:8-9.

Bartholomew (also called ***Nathanael***) features in John 1:45-49 and 21:2.

Matthew (also called ***Levi***), was a tax official. Mark 2:14 tells us that his father was Alphaeus. See also Matthew 9:9; 10:3; Luke 5:27-32.

Thomas (also called ***Didymus**, the Twin*), famous for his doubt, features in John 11:16; 14:5; 20:24-29 and 21:2.

James *son of Alphaeus* (and therefore perhaps Matthew's brother) and ***Simon the Zealot*** are only known from the lists of the twelve disciples (Matthew 10:2-4; Mark 3:16-19; Luke 6:13-16; Acts 1:13). The Zealots saw obedience to Roman rule as treason against God and so resisted it fiercely.

Judas son of James (or ***Thaddaeus***) features in John 14:22.

References to ***Judas Iscariot***, the disciple who betrayed Jesus, are found in Matthew 26:14, 25, 47; 27:3 (and the parallel passages in the other gospels); also John 6:71; 12:4; 13:2, 26-30; Acts 1:16. After his death, Judas was replaced as one of the twelve apostles by *Matthias* (Acts 1:21-26).

What a mixed bunch! Who in their right minds today would select them as a team of potential leaders? It shows that Jesus can make great use of all sorts of people. It also reveals how great a unity he can forge in the church: it is about the only place where a former Zealot (violent patriot) could work together with a former tax collector (traitor in the eyes of the Jews).

Christians have always been a minority group. And sometimes that causes us to feel discouraged. Our view of church life becomes negative; we spend more time and resources on maintaining our church than in mission to those outside. Mark encourages us to think positively. The seeds of faith which we sow must one day produce a harvest. Indeed, it is when we are most aware of our own weaknesses that God is most able to use us; there's no pride or prejudice to get in his way.

The Gospel of Luke

Luke's gospel is the longest of the four (1,151 verses) and gives the fullest account of Jesus' life. About half its material is not found in the other gospels. Both Luke's gospel and its sequel, the Acts of the Apostles, were written so that people like Theophilus, to whom they are dedicated (1:3, Acts 1:1), could be more certain about what they had previously been taught about Jesus.

The name Theophilus means 'lover of God' or 'loved by God' and may be a code-name. The way he is addressed as 'most excellent' (1:3) suggests that he was a person of some social standing, perhaps a Roman official who had become a Christian. Some people have taken this to suggest that one of Luke's reasons for writing was to show the Roman authorities that the Christian faith was not the threat to their political power which others had suggested.

●Points to look out for

A universal vision

Luke's main concern is to show Jesus as the Saviour of the whole world. God is interested in *all* types of people, especially those who are poor and helpless, whom others regard as insignificant. This is good news indeed! It means that Christianity is not reserved for some exclusive group: it is for everyone. So Jesus begins his public ministry by quoting Isaiah 61 and applying it to himself: 'The Spirit of the Lord is upon me, because he has anointed me to preach good news to the poor ...' (4:18). All the gospels bring out this concern shown by Jesus for the outsider, but Luke takes a special delight in it (*e.g.* 14:15-24; 19:1-10).

Who would be the 'outsiders' compared with your church membership? Often they are people with different languages or cultural backgrounds. Sometimes they are people who come from a different social group to that of most church-goers. What about the peo-

ple with reading difficulties who find the prospect of hymnbooks and service books a problem? And those with handicaps – or those with criminal records – would they be welcome? Think about how you could express Luke's gospel-for-all in practical, visible ways.

Summary of the Gospel of Luke

1 Introduction and the infancy narratives (1-2)

2 John the Baptist, Jesus' baptism, ancestry and temptations (3:1 - 4:13)

3 Jesus' ministry in Galilee (4:14 - 9:50):

- Jesus begins his ministry (4:14-44)
- Jesus calls his disciples (5:1 - 6:16)
- Jesus teaches his disciples and the crowds (6:17-49)
- Jesus works in Capernaum (7-8)
- Incidents centring on his twelve disciples (9:1-50)

4 Jesus travels from Galilee to Jerusalem (9:51 - 19:44):

- Ministry in Samaria (9:51 - 10:37)
- Jesus teaches about prayer (10:38 - 11:13)
- Jesus in conflict with the Pharisees (11:14-54)
- Jesus continues to teach and heal (12:1 - 19:44)

5 Jesus in Jerusalem (19:45 - 21:38)

6 The trial and death of Jesus (22-23)

7 The resurrection and ascension (24)

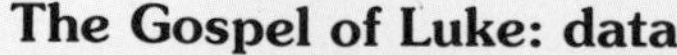

The Gospel of Luke: data

Author: early tradition suggests that Luke wrote the gospel that bears his name and the Acts of the Apostles, which is a reasonable assumption.

Date: the Acts of the Apostles ends with Paul under house arrest in Rome (around AD 62) and has no particular interest in the fall of Jerusalem in AD 70. Assuming Luke would have referred to this if it had happened by the time he was writing, it seems that Luke's first volume, the gospel, was written between AD 60 and 70, after Mark.

294-296

Rich and poor

Luke has quite a lot to say about rich people, much of which seems rather negative. For example, Mary's reaction to the forthcoming birth of Jesus is to sing, 'He has filled the hungry with good things but has sent the rich away empty' (1:53). See also 6:24-25; 12:13-34; 16:19-31; 18:18-27; 21:1-4. But it is not that wealth itself is necessarily a bad thing; the problem is with what wealth can so easily lead to. Rich people run the risk of becoming satisfied with themselves, thinking that they do not need God, and concentrating all their time and effort on getting and managing material things. So in effect they cut themselves off from him and shut themselves out of his kingdom. It is easier for poor people who have few resources to recognize that they depend completely on God's grace. But rich or poor, only those who repent of their self-centredness are able to receive God's gift of salvation as they submit themselves to him (9:23-26; 14:25-35).

The incident of the rich young ruler who could not face up to losing his wealth (18:18-30) is yet another warning about attitudes. The man's money hindered his quest for eternal life only because his money was more important to him than life itself. Luke reminds us we can be rich in religion, too – an equally dangerous state (18:9-14). Anything which I am proud of, cherish and cannot bear to lose – wealth, status, knowledge, power, even relationships – makes me 'rich' in this broader sense.

Salvation

The word used for 'save' also means 'heal' (*e.g.* 8:36), which may explain Luke the doctor's interest in the whole idea. He emphasizes several times that Jesus came to *save* the world (1:69, 71, 77; 2:11, 30; 3:6), as foretold in the Old Testament (4:18-21; 10:23-24; 24:26-27, 44-47). But what does the world need to be saved from? Luke records these words of Jesus: 'It is not the healthy who need a doctor, but the sick. I have not come to call the righteous, but sinners to repentance' (5:31-32). Jesus saw that our basic need is to be saved from the consequences of our sin, our self-centred rebellion against God. We need God's forgiveness.

So Jesus came that people might have 'knowledge of salvation through the forgiveness of their sins' (1:77). He did this by allowing himself to be crucified, refusing to save himself but choosing instead to save others (23:35-43). He explained to his disciples after his resurrection that the Old Testament had forecast that he would '... suffer and rise from the dead on the third day, and repentance and forgiveness of sins will be preached in his name to all nations ...' (24:46-47).

The ministry of Jesus marked the beginning of the promised end for all the sin, suffering and evil. So Luke recounts many different events which show Jesus the rescuer in action – healing disease, casting out demons and raising the dead to life.

The double meaning of the word 'save' reminds Luke's readers that God's concern is to bring us to 'wholeness'. In a world where sin, death and decay still exist, that wholeness can never be complete until Jesus returns. But Luke would have expected church life to reflect that concern, by praying for and supporting those who have physical needs as well as inviting people to find spiritual renewal through faith in Jesus.

'Our dear friend Luke, the doctor'

Paul writes about Luke the doctor as one of his valued colleagues, a Gentile believer who accompanied him on some of his travels (Colossians 4:14; 2 Timothy 4:11 and Philemon 24). His medical background is suggested by the way he includes details which the other gospels omit (*e.g.* 4:38: ' a *high* fever'; 5:12: '*covered with* leprosy'; 6:6: 'whose *right* hand was shrivelled'). Perhaps out of sympathy for his profession, he omits the detail given in Mark that the woman suffering from chronic bleeding had 'suffered a great deal under the care of many doctors' (compare Mark 5:26 with Luke 8:43)! Luke's Greek is much more polished than Mark's and his style shows him to have been a cultured and educated man. He was a careful researcher (1:1-4).

265

Jesus' love for people

Luke emphasizes the love of Jesus, by reporting many of his contacts with individuals. Parables quoted by

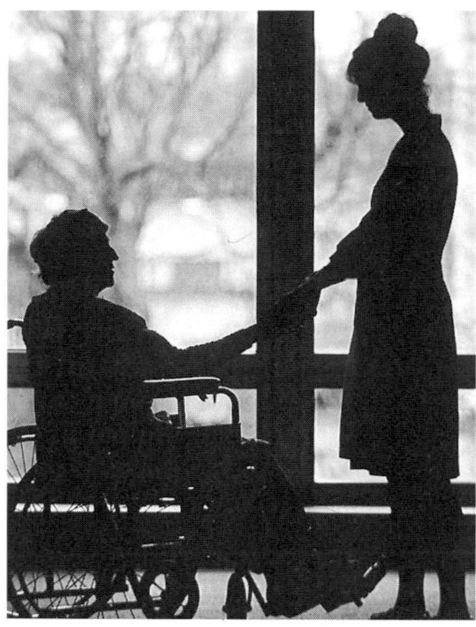

317-318

Matthew tend to be about the kingdom of heaven but Luke focuses on those dealing with people, such as the Good Samaritan (10:25-37) and the Lost Son (15:11-32). To those who object to Jesus spending so much time with people at the poorer end of society, Jesus points out that they are the ones who both need and are open to receive God's help (*e.g.* 18:9-14).

Luke also records Jesus' compassion towards women (*e.g.* 7:36-50; 8:1-3; 10:38-42). They were normally treated as inferior beings. They were not even considered worth educating, and could not give evidence in court – which is why it is rather ironic that women were the first to discover that Jesus had been raised from the dead (24:1-12: note especially verse 11!). Children are another group for whom Jesus has a particular concern in Luke (8:40-56; 9:37-43, 46-48; 18:15-17).

People mattered more than things to Jesus. He gave them whatever time they needed, however 'unimportant' the people were reckoned to be. Look at the time he gave to the old woman while he was already on a mission of mercy to save a young girl (8:40-56). In our hurrying world, it is easy to brush such people aside.

Joy

Luke's gospel is characterized by joy and laughter (*e.g.* 1:14, 44, 58; 2:10, 10:17, 21). Passages such as the *Magnificat* (1:46-55), the *Benedictus* (1:68-79), the *Gloria in Excelsis* (2:13-14) and the *Nunc Dimittis* (2:29-32) have been used in Christian worship for centuries and are still used in some churches today.

The Holy Spirit

Luke shows that Jesus was always dependent on the power of the Holy Spirit, from the time of his conception onwards (1:35; 3:22; 4:1, 14, 18; 10:21). So, too, were others who were part of God's purposes, like Mary (1:35), John the Baptist (1:15), John's parents Elizabeth and Zechariah (1:41, 67) and Simeon (2:25-27). His disciples too, both then and now, are taught to ask their heavenly Father for the gift of the Holy Spirit (11:13) to help them as they stand firm for their Master (12:12).

Prayer

Of the gospel writers, Luke reveals most about the high priority Jesus gave to prayer (*e.g.* 3:21; 5:16; 6:12; 9:18, 28; 11:1; 22:32, 44; 23:46 *etc.*). *But Luke does not limit himself to showing the example of Jesus in prayer. His is the gospel to turn to for the teaching of Jesus about this important subject as well (e.g. 11:1-13; 18:1-14). Look up some of these references if you want your own prayer life enriched.*

The Gospel of John

Summary of the Gospel of John

1 Introduction (1)
2 Jesus' public ministry (2-12)
3 Jesus' ministry to his disciples (13-17)
4 Jesus' suffering and glory (18-20)
5 Conclusion (21)

John's gospel is very different from the others. He describes very few of Jesus' miracles. And instead of parables and short sayings, the teaching of Jesus comes in long speeches and is mainly about himself and his relationship to God his Father. In the other three gospels, Jesus seems to spend most of his time in Galilee. But John focuses mainly on the occasions when Jesus visited Israel's capital city, Jerusalem.

Most scholars think that John was the last of the four gospels to be written and that he assumes that his readers are familiar with the basic facts about Jesus' life given by Matthew, Mark and Luke, if not with the gospels themselves. An example of this is 3:24, where he assumes that his readers know why and how John the Baptist ended up in prison.

●Points to look out for

Jesus the Son of God

John begins with a magnificent introduction (1:1-18) about who Jesus is. He sets out the evidence for these claims in the rest of his gospel. As you read through, look out for the conclusions that people came to as they saw and heard Jesus. Notice, for example, how Jesus' identity is unfolded in chapter 1. He is seen first as a great 'rabbi' or teacher (1:38), then as the Messiah foretold in the Old Testament (1:41, 45) and finally as the Son of God and king of Israel (1:49).

John's gospel describes Jesus as the eternal Word of God who 'became flesh' (1:14). He is the 'Son of Man', the bridge between heaven and earth (3:13). He is the long-awaited Jewish Messiah (7:42), the 'Lamb of God, who takes away the sin of the world' (1:29). He is the fully divine Son of God (3:16), the one who makes his Father known (1:18).

Jesus the man

John is anxious to portray a true and balanced picture of Jesus, so he also emphasizes his genuine humanity (*e.g.* his tiredness at Sychar in 4:6 and his reaction to the death of Lazarus in 11:33-35). This would counter the claims by some early opponents of Christianity that the divine Jesus was a sort of ghostly figure who only *appeared* to be human.

270

It is also important for Christians today not to lose sight of the fact that, though fully God, Jesus was also fully human (see Hebrews 2:14-18). Sometimes, for person-

The Gospel of John: data

Author: John 21:20-24 indicates that this gospel derives from 'the disciple whom Jesus loved'. Although he is not named in the gospel, many early traditions identify him as the apostle John (not to be confused with John the Baptist). The gospel is full of eye-witness details which make this highly likely.

Date: Early tradition indicates that this gospel was written after the others, perhaps between AD 90 and 100, though some scholars think it may be earlier and entirely independent of Matthew, Mark and Luke.

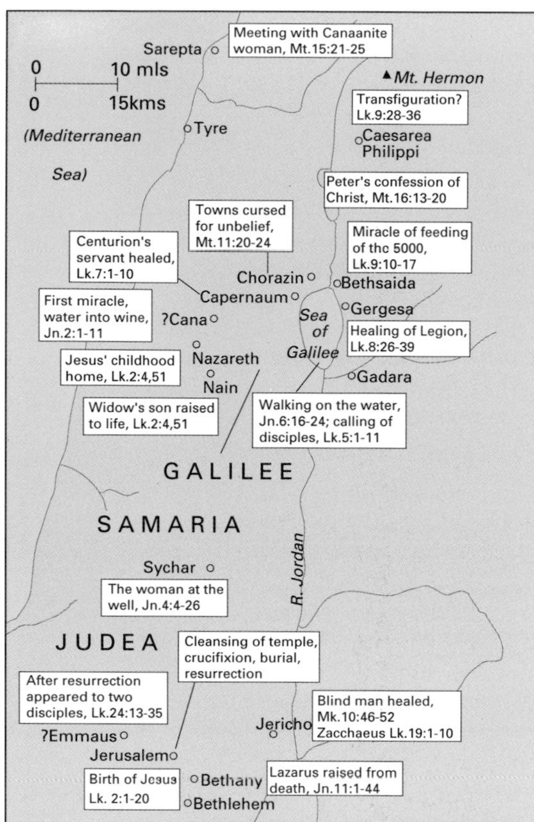

Where Jesus went.

270-272

al reasons or in our discussions with others, we may need to focus on one aspect of Jesus' nature more than another. For example, faced with spiritual need, we will stress the work of Jesus as God's Son dying on the cross in order to open up the way to eternal life. But aware of human weakness, we may want to draw comfort from his first-hand experience of it. However, if we so stress one that we ignore the other, we shall be making Jesus in our image.

181

Signs and sayings

To help his readers make up their minds about who Jesus is, John sets out seven of the miracles performed by Jesus. He calls them 'signs' because they are significant events, intended to point to Jesus' true identity (see 2:11). The whole message of the gospel is an invitation to come and see (1:39) if the claims are true and if they are, to stay and find God's life through Jesus.

The seven signs are:

Sign 1: Water turned into wine (2:1-11).

Sign 2: The healing of a royal official's son (4:46-54).

Sign 3: The healing of a lame man on the sabbath (5:2-9).

Sign 4: The feeding of 5,000 people (6:1-14).

Sign 5: The healing of a man born blind (9:1-7).

Sign 6: The raising of Lazarus from the dead (11:1-44).

Sign 7: The miraculous catch of fish (21:1-14).

Each sign illustrates a theme in Jesus' teaching about himself. In addition, the teaching passages include seven sayings of Jesus which begin with the phrase 'I am ...', which is itself a veiled claim to be God in human form (see Exodus 3:14). These, too, offer fresh pictures of who he is and what he does:

Saying 1: 'I am the bread of life' (6:35).

Saying 2: 'I am the light of the world' (8:12).

Saying 3: 'I am the gate for the sheep' (10:7).

Saying 4: 'I am the good shepherd' (10:11).

Saying 5: 'I am the resurrection and the life' (11:25).

Saying 6: 'I am the way and the truth and the life' (14:6).

Saying 7: 'I am the true vine' (15:1).

Several of the signs and sayings link up directly. For example, Jesus talks about himself as the bread of life

(6:35) after he has miraculously fed 5,000 people (6:1-14). John includes the healing of a blind man (9:1-7) to illustrate Jesus' declaration that he is the light of the world (8:12). And to show that his claim to be the resurrection and the life (11:25) is more than just talk, Jesus raises Lazarus from the dead (11:38-44).

The seven 'I am' sayings bring theology into human experience. They make truth very personal, not only because they tie important ideas to the real-life figure of Jesus, but also because they invite a response. There is only one thing to do with bread: eat it! Only one use for a gate: to go through! John does not want his readers to observe Jesus from a distance, but to experience him personally.

The true nature of faith

John's intention (see 20:30-31) is that his readers should themselves accept Jesus as the Messiah, the Son of God rather than reject him, as did so many of those living at the time (1:10-12).

185

Notice that John makes a distinction between belief that a statement is true (*e.g.* 11:42) and belief in the person of Jesus (*e.g.* 3:16; 9:35-38). The former is simply agreeing intellectually that Jesus is who he claims to be. Christian faith is the latter. It means trusting ourselves to Jesus, trusting in his power and purposes for us.

The Holy Spirit

John's gospel draws attention to the role of the Holy Spirit in the life of the Christian. He comes not just to be with the disciples (as Jesus had been) but to live within them (14:17). This is why Jesus can say that it is actually to their advantage that he should leave and be replaced by the Spirit (16:7). See also 3:5-8; 4:13-14; 7:37-39; 20:21-23.

194

The Acts of the Apostles

Luke describes his first volume as setting out 'all that Jesus began to do and to teach' (1:1). Acts is all about what Jesus continued to do and teach as his Holy Spirit acted in power through the early church. It tells how the Christian faith began in Jerusalem and was then driven across the Roman empire, finally reaching Rome.

●Points to look out for

The spread of the Word

Each section in Acts (see summary above) marks a further movement forward in the church's mission. The disciples, led and empowered by the Holy Spirit, obey Jesus' commission to be his witnesses 'in Jerusalem, and in all Judea and Samaria, and to the ends of the earth' (1:8). This is what Luke is interested in and so he leaves out many details of early church life which his readers, past and present, would find interesting.

191

Jews and Gentiles together

One of the problems faced by the young church was the conversion of non-Jews (Gentiles) into what had started as an exclusively Jewish movement. Luke charts how the apostles slowly realized that the privileges of the gospel were for both Gentiles and Jews.

The slow breakdown of apartheid in South Africa in the late twenti-

eth century is a modern example of how difficult people find it to abandon class or racial prejudice. The first Christians did not find it easy, either. They succeeded in the end only because they recognized the power of God working equally in both groups. So their social unity grew out of a new-found spiritual unity. The church, therefore, may be able to lead the way in breaking down human barriers. We have the spiritual power gradually to change our inner attitudes so that we no longer 'call anything impure that God has made clean' (see 10:9-20, 34-36).

Luke stresses the equality of Jews and Gentiles in a number of ways. One of them is to show how similar was the ministry of Peter (primarily an apostle to the Jews) and Paul (apostle to the Gentiles):

	Peter	Paul
Both heal a man lame from birth (note the close parallels between these accounts)	3:2-8	14:8-10
Both pronounce judgment	5:1-5	13:11
Both perform miracles by unusual methods	5:15	19:12
Both exercise a ministry of healing	9:34	28:8
Both have a Gentile convert from a noble family	10:1	13:12
Both are led by a vision to minister to Gentiles	10:9-20	22:17-21
Both are reverenced	10:25	16:29
Both experience the Holy Spirit confirming their ministry	10:44	19:6
Both are rescued from prison	12:7	16:26

The places Paul visited and then wrote letters to, mentioned in Acts.

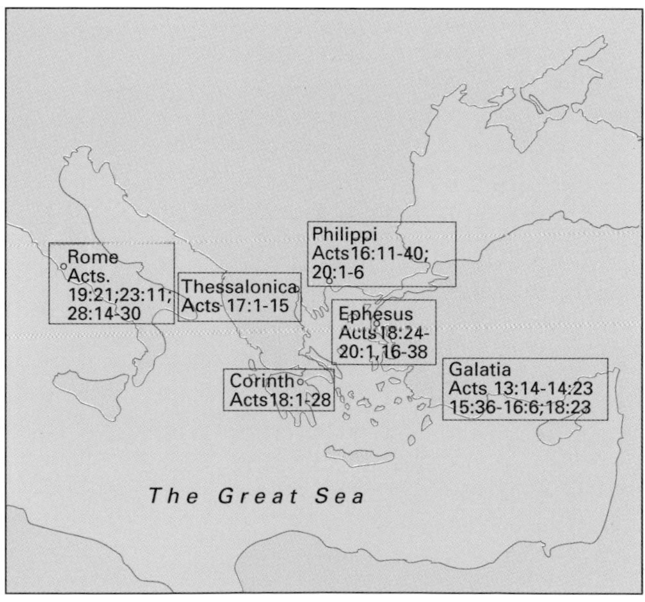

All part of God's plan

Luke tells his readers that the coming of the Holy Spirit, and the worldwide mission of the church which he inspired, fulfil Old Testament prophecy (*e.g.* 2:17-21; 13:47; 15:16-18). Far from being a distortion of what God intends, Luke shows the church's missionary work has been central to his purposes all along. But sadly, many of the Jews, God's chosen people, were to reject Jesus as their Messiah (again, the fulfilment of prophecy – see 28:25-27). They became some of the church's most active opponents.

Not always easy

The early church saw spectacular growth at first (6:1, 7; 9:31; 12:24;

Summary of the Acts of the Apostles

The book is divided into six sections, separated by a short summary about the spread of the word and the growth of the church (see 6:7; 9:31; 12:24; 16:5; 19:20).

1 The birth of the church (1:1 - 6:7):
- Introduction; the ascension of Jesus (1)
- The coming of the Holy Spirit; church growth in Jerusalem (2:1 - 6:7)

2 The start of persecution (6:8 - 9:31):
- The martyrdom of Stephen (6:8 - 8:3)
- The church scatters and the word spreads (8:4-40)
- The conversion of Saul (9:1-31)

3 Christianity spreads to the Gentiles (9:32- 12:24)

4 Paul's first two missionary journeys (12:25 - 16:5):
- Paul's first missionary journey (12:25 - 14:28)
- The Jerusalem council (15:1-35)
- Paul's second missionary journey (15:36 - 16:5)

5 Paul's journeys continue (16:6 - 19:20):
- Paul's second missionary journey continued (16:6 - 18:22)
- Paul's third missionary journey, up to his decision to return to Jerusalem (18:23 - 19:20)

6 Paul's arrest, trial and journey to Rome (19:21 - 28:31):
- Paul's third missionary journey cotinued (19:21 - 21:17)
- Paul's arrest and trial in Jerusalem (21:18 - 23:35)
- Paul's trial at Caesarea (24-26)
- Paul's journey to Rome and activity there (27-28)

For data, see under the Gospel of Luke.

14:21; 16:5; 19:20); 'the Lord's hand was with them' (11:21). The work of the Holy Spirit in giving guidance and power to the disciples was very evident. But this did not make life easy. Far from it! There were setbacks, disagreements and much opposition. Tragedy overtook Ananias and Sapphira (5:1-11), and Paul and Barnabas split up after disagreeing about John Mark (15:36-40).

Although the disciples were sometimes miraculously rescued (*e.g.* 12:1-11), they were often not. Paul was often persecuted (*e.g.* 14:19). Some disciples, including Stephen, were even put to death (7:54 - 8:3). There were enemies outside the church (*e.g.* 13:49-52) and within it (*e.g.* 20:29-30). But through it all, God accomplished his purposes of spreading the gospel all over the Roman world.

This is true for every generation of Christians. Even when God is powerfully at work in our lives or churches we will still be opposed – perhaps more than at other times because Satan's power is more visibly undermined.

●Using Acts today

Luke describes some patterns of the life of the early church. For example, some of them lived in 'community', sharing their possessions (2:44). But does what happened then necessarily indicate what must happen now? The answer depends on whether Luke intended to set a precedent for the church to follow. This is not easy to discover and equally sincere Christians may come up with different answers. But it is important to avoid taking Acts in isolation. Instead, we need to find out which of Luke's concerns are taken up by other New Testament writers in their instructions to the

Next page: one response to the gospel is to care for the world God made. Here Scripture Union volunteers help the National Trust with conservation work.

churches around the ancient world. This takes seriously the fact that God has given us the whole of the New Testament, not just the gospels and Acts.

As you read through Acts, you will discover a great deal about the Christian life. Look carefully to find out what Luke intends to establish as principles which are still relevant today. Here are some other New Testament references to check your conclusions against as you explore Luke's themes:

– The day-to-day life of the church (2:42-47; 4:32-37. See also Romans 14:1-23; 1 Corinthians 5:1-13; 16:1-8; James 2:1-8.)

– How the disciples went about spreading the good news of Jesus, and the strategies they adopted (11:19-30; 13:1-4; 14:21-28; 21:10-14. See also 1 Corinthians 2:1-5; 2 Corinthians 4:1-6; 5:11-21.)

– The qualities church leaders need to do the job God has called them to (6:1-6; 14:23; 16:-3. See also 1 Timothy 3:1-13; 1 Peter 5:1-4.)

– The opposition faced by the church. What could they have done to lessen it? (4:1-22; 6:8-15; 8:1-3; 14:4-7; 16:19-24; 21:27-36. See also 2 Timothy 2:1-13; Hebrews 12:1-13; 1 Peter 4:12-19.)

– The use made of prayer by leaders and church members (4:23-31; 7:60; 10:9; 12:5; 13:2-3; 16:25; 20:36. See also Romans 15:30-32; Ephesians 6:19-20; Colossians 4:2-4; 2 Thessalonians 3:1-5; 1 Timothy 2:1-4.)

– The results of the Holy Spirit's activity. (2:1-4, 41; 4:8, 13, 31; 8:15-20; 10:44-46; 13:2, 9-11; 16:6-7; 19:6, 11-12. See also Romans 8:5-17; 1 Corinthians 12:1-31; 1 John 4:1-3.)

3.6

GUIDELINES FOR CHRISTIAN LIVING
The letters

by Paul Beasley-Murray

Most of the New Testament letters were written in response to specific needs in the new churches. They assume the knowledge of the gospel, though in most cases the gospels had not yet been published.

The needs of the churches in the first century were not always the same as ours, though many are startlingly similar

Page

348-352

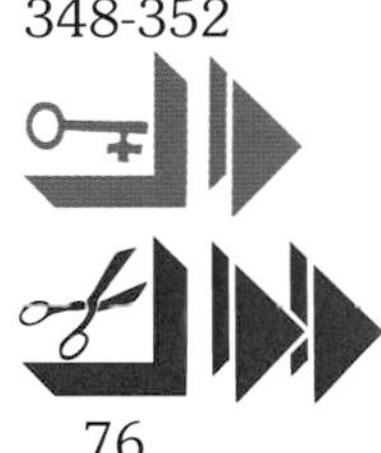

76

Background to the letters

Most of the 'books' of the New Testament are letters (in fact 21 out of 27). Thirteen of them are by Paul while the rest were written by James, Peter (2), Jude, John (3) and an unknown author (to the Hebrews).

In the ancient world letters were usually what we might expect them to be, simple communications between one person and another, or a group. The chief difference between first-century letters and those we send to each other today is that the sender's name came at the beginning. There usually followed a few lines of formal greeting, often mentioning the gods. Greetings and love to others were listed at the end.

First-century letters were sometimes more formal affairs; the 'letter' was used to convey important theories or opinions, perhaps as we might write to a magazine or newspaper. The New Testament letters are more like sermons than letters. Some of them were written to a general audience, not specific individuals or churches. Most of the letters written by people other than Paul are general in this sense.

●God's word for their day

If this comes as a surprise, consider the following. The letters were not written to us! We are privileged to read them but the writers did not know that we would. They expected them to reach their addressees and stay there.

It follows therefore that the New Testament letters were not written as Scripture. The authors probably had no idea that their letters would form part of a 'New Testament' which in turn became part of the Bible itself.

However, they were conscious that they had apostolic authority and under the guidance of the Holy Spirit were writing God's word for their day. These letters usually begin with the sender's credentials, just as other ancient letters did, but they are more than human qualifications. The opening of Colossians is typical:

> Paul, an apostle of Christ Jesus by the will of God, and Timothy our brother, to the holy and faithful brothers in Christ at Colosse: Grace and peace to you from God our Father.
>
> (Colossians 1:1-2)

These letters must have been read and reread and kept most carefully. They were the only Christian writings available until the gospels were written. (Despite the order in the New Testament as we have it, the letters were mostly written *before* the gospels.) They would then have been collected and later bound together with the gospels and Revelation to form what we know as the New Testament.

●How to read them today

They are to be read as whole letters, because most of the recipients could not read and the letters would have been read aloud to groups of people. It would not be possible to pause and consider every phrase or word. In fact many hearers would not have understood them all (just as we don't, unless we have a commentary). But the general impact of the letter would get across and the hearers would have a grasp of its themes. They would feel its impact. They would hear the love and con-

cern of Paul as he strode up and down, dictating to his secretary, letting his hearers know how God's grace in Christ could solve their specific problem.

Try reading each of these letters at one sitting in a modern version. It will give you an idea of the whole message, which we so easily miss by hearing or reading extracts. There is a place for detailed study of each verse of course, but that is best done when you have an overview of the whole letter.

The letters are also to be read against the proper background. Each letter is addressed to a specific, real audience to help with particular problems that had arisen in their church life. To understand the letters we need to know what the problems were.

Unfortunately this is sometimes difficult. It is rather like listening to one end of a telephone conversation. We hear the replies but not the questions. We have to piece together the problems in order to understand the answers. Sometimes Paul seems to quote snippets of his readers' questions (as in 1 Corinthians 6:12 - 7:1), but as there were no inverted commas in the original Greek it is not clear whether Paul is making a statement of his own or quoting his readers' question. For instance in 1 Corinthians 7:1, 'Now for the matters you wrote about: It is good for a man not to marry.' Should the second part of the verse be a quotation (as in 6:12,13) or not? It makes a lot of difference!

The New Testament letters then are first-century letters, addressed as a whole (not chopped into chapters and verses) to real people with real problems which we need to understand if we are to learn from the answers. For this reason we have described the background to each letter in this section. The problems faced by first-century Christians are uncannily like those of our own day. The letters are therefore very relevant to us.

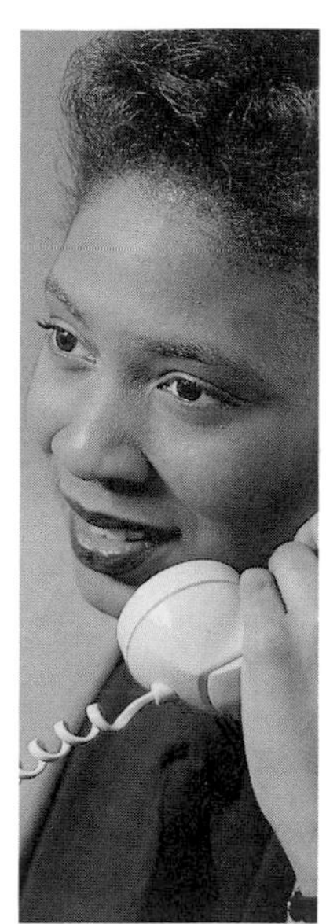

Letter to the church in Rome

'The chief book in the New Testament and the purest gospel.' That was Martin Luther's assessment of Romans. It is certainly one of the most significant of Paul's letters. It is unique in that the author was not trying to sort out specific problems in the church, as he was in his other letters. He is introducing himself to a church he had never visited, and gives a clear statement of the essence of the good news he preached.

Romans: data

Date: The apostle Paul wrote this letter around AD 57, towards the end of his 'third missionary journey' (Acts 20:3). Place of origin: He wrote from Corinth on his way to Jerusalem (15:25) and where he had reviewed his missionary strategy. He was looking for new territory in which to plant the gospel and had his eye on Spain (15:28), the oldest Roman colony in the west. Rome was an obvious place to call at on the way, especially as he had long wanted to visit the Christians there (1:13-15). This letter paves the way for his visit.

CUTTING OUT THE SECTIONS

53-54

First-century Rome was the capital of a powerful empire which sprawled across the known world from Britain to Arabia. It was a large city, even by modern standards, with a population of about a million, of whom perhaps 40,000 to 50,000 were Jewish.

Summary of Romans

1 Introduction (1:1-16)

2 The gospel according to Paul (1:17 - 8:39)

3 The 'Jewish question' (9-11)

4 A pattern for living (12-15)

5 Conclusion (16)

●The gospel according to Paul (section 2)

His statement about what he believes and teaches has two parts.

First the bad news

Paul's 'gospel' begins with bad news. God's anger is directed at all human sin and wickedness. God's 'anger', unlike ours, is not passionate rage, but the inevitable hostility of a loving God to evil in any form (1:18). And it is directed towards everyone, for all are held in the iron grip of sin (3:23).

280

312-313

Look at what mankind has achieved since Paul's day. International air travel covers distances in a couple of hours that would have taken Paul a couple of months. Semiconductors have made washing machines automatic, given telephones memories, and through computers have transformed the way we live, move and have our being. Yet we are no nearer solving basic human problems. Murder, rape and theft stalk the streets of the so-called civilized world while its more law-abiding citizens quarrel and cheat and try to outdo each other. Truly, 'all have sinned and fall short of the glory of God' (3:23).

Then the good news

Paul then introduces God's way of putting people right with himself (3:21). He uses the technical term, 'justification by faith'. When sinful men and women put their trust in Christ who died for them, God forgives them and places them in a new relationship with himself; his anger is replaced by mercy. This new relationship may be described as 'life in the Spirit'.

●The 'Jewish question' (section 3)

Between the sections of Romans on the gospel and its application are three chapters devoted to the destiny of the Jews. Paul is convinced that God has not given up on his chosen people. They have rejected Jesus, it is true, but that is all part of God's plan for bringing all mankind within reach of his grace. Paul, a great believer in the providence of God, believes that in the end the Jews will come to accept Jesus as Messiah (the Christ).

●A pattern for living (section 4)

The third main section returns to the 'life in the Spirit' set out in section 2 and works out some of its practical implications. Paul also spells out Christians' duties towards one another and to the state, stressing the importance of supporting the principle of law and order. His comments in chapter 13 have provoked much debate, but it has to be remembered that they were written at a time of growing persecution for the church. Paul seems to be applying Jesus' teaching about turning

the other cheek (Matthew 5:38-42) even to officials who want to stamp out our faith.

Most people find chapters 12-16 easier than chapters 1-11; we prefer practical advice to theological teaching. But Paul saw no distinction between the two parts: chapter 12 begins with 'Therefore ...': how we live has to be based on what we believe. And it is only as we get into a right relationship with God (which is hardly a theoretical matter!) that we can begin to live in a way that pleases him.

Letters to the church in Corinth

Paul wrote to the Romans as a theologian; he wrote to the Corinthians as a pastor. But what a church he had to pastor! If we are tempted to think of the 'early church' as an ideal pattern for today, 1 Corinthians will make us think again.

Corinth was the most strategic place in all Greece for a church. Situated on the narrow isthmus that connects the mainland with the Peloponnesus peninsula, it was a focal point for trade north-south as well as east-west. It was the capital of the province of Achaia; the Roman proconsul lived there (Acts 18:12).

Along with fame, however, went infamy. The city was dominated by the temple of Aphrodite, goddess of love, and its streets were thronged with temple prostitutes who offered their services to 'worshippers'. To 'corinthianize' was a word which meant having sex outside marriage. The permissive society is not an exclusively modern trend.

● Divisions in the church (section 2)

Even if our own congregation is united our churches are still split into denominations. Paul sees the root cause of division as *arrogance*. The apostles, by contrast, were willing to be treated as the dregs of society for Christ's sake. The spirit of unity is the spirit of humility (chapter 4).

Summary of 1 Corinthians

1 Introduction (1:1-9)
2 Divisions in the church (1:10 - 4:21)
3 Sexual morality and family life (5-7)
4 Christians and pagans (8:1 - 1:1)
5 Church life and worship (11:2 - 14:40)
6 The resurrection of Christ and of believers (15)
7 Christian giving (16:1-4)
8 Personal matters and conclusion (16:5-24)

198

Paul was educated. But he never tried to 'be clever'. He was not interested in winning people to his 'side', only in winning them for Jesus Christ. So when he preached, he did not use brilliant arguments or impressive words. He spoke plainly about the Jesus who died on the cross and rose again (2:1-4). He knew that without such a Christ-centred spirit, the church would split and lose its power. History ever since has shown him to be right.

● Sexual morality (section 3)

In a sex-ridden society, Paul gives teaching as clear then as it is today. Extramarital sex is wrong because

304

the sex act unites the couple in a very deep way (he quotes Genesis 2:24). To treat it casually is to ruin one of God's greatest gifts (6:12 - 7:40).

This is where God's law relates directly to our concept of love. It can never be truly loving to go beyond the bounds of his rules.

55

● Christians and pagans (section 4)

In a pagan city most of the meat on sale had been slaughtered in a religious ritual, and this caused a crisis of conscience for some Christians. So Paul tells them that frankly it doesn't matter – but our main concern should be to treat kindly the Christian who feels it does matter (8:8-9).

This seems irrelevant to us! Yet the principles governing Christian freedom are in fact for all times. We are free from petty regulations but not free to wound each other. As someone has said, 'Your freedom to swing your fist ends at the tip of my nose.'

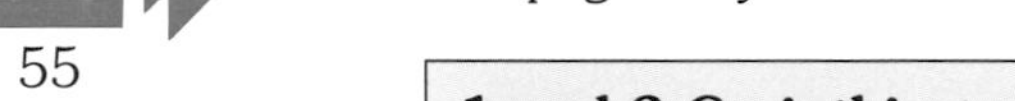

1 and 2 Corinthians: data

Paul may have visited Corinth three times and possibly wrote *four* letters to the Christians there. The pattern may be as follows:

1 *First visit*, AD 50-51. Paul founded the church in Corinth (Acts 18:1-8).
2 *First letter*, referred to in 1 Corinthians 5:9. Perhaps 2 Corinthians 6:14 - 7:1 is a fragment of it.
3 *Second letter*, our '1Corinthians'. Paul had received worrying news (1:11; 16:17) and requests for advice (7:1). So he wrote 1 Corinthians, probably in AD 54, to remedy the situation.
4 *Second visit*, sometimes called his 'painful visit'. Paul was humiliated for some reason (2 Corinthians 12:14, 21; 13:2).
5 *Third letter* or 'severe letter' (2 Corinthians 7:8), written in response to the painful visit (2:4, 9). 2 Corinthians 10-13 may form a fragment of that letter.
6 *Fourth letter*, our '2 Corinthians'. Titus had brought news that the 'severe letter' had done its work so Paul wrote a letter of reconciliation, perhaps in AD 56.
7 *Third visit*, a three-month stay during his third missionary journey (Acts 20:2-3).

● Church life and worship (section 5)

The Corinthian church was almost in a state of anarchy. Paul highlights three areas of concern:

Unisex fashions (11:2-16) Men and women depend on one another but should dress distinctively.

The Lord's Supper (11:17-34) The Corinthian church was guilty of a casual, even flippant approach to this sacrament. Paul warns the Corinthians, and us, that it is possible to 'eat and drink judgment' on ourselves if we do not take it seriously.

Worship and spiritual gifts (12-14) Charismatic renewal has put these items high on the church's agenda. The central chapter of the three here points to the eternal principle governing all such matters – self- giving love.

There is often a conflict in churches today between 'order' and 'freedom' in worship. It was there in Corinth too. Paul says that orderliness is an important witness (14:40) – it reflects God's nature. But it need not stifle freedom.

Indeed, 'free worship' is usually more helpful when it is gently 'led' by someone who is sensitive both to God's Spirit and to all the worshippers.

●Resurrection (section 6)
Christ's resurrection is the positive guarantee that people who died trusting in Christ will also be raised. For them, death is but a step into new creation (15:53).

●Christian giving (section 7)
The organized setting aside of a specific proportion of one's income was established in the Old Testament. Paul encourages us to continue it.

Summary of 2 Corinthians

1 Introduction (1:1-11)
2 Paul's ministry (1:12 - 7:16)
3 The offering for the Christians in Judea (8-9)
4 Paul defends his authority (10:1 - 13:10)
5 Conclusion (13:11-14)

Of all Paul's letters 2 Corinthians is the most personal. Here above all he shares his feelings with his readers. Paul, the great apostle, stands revealed as a man of flesh and blood who knew what it was to be hurt and to be depressed, to protest and to argue. Ministry, then as now, has its low as well as its high points.

The three major themes have a clear relevance to the Christian church of today:

●Ministry (section 2)
These chapters underline the suffering as well as the glory involved in Christian ministry. There is a constant temptation for a minister to long for power and influence. Paul's ministry, however, was patterned on that of Jesus the Servant.

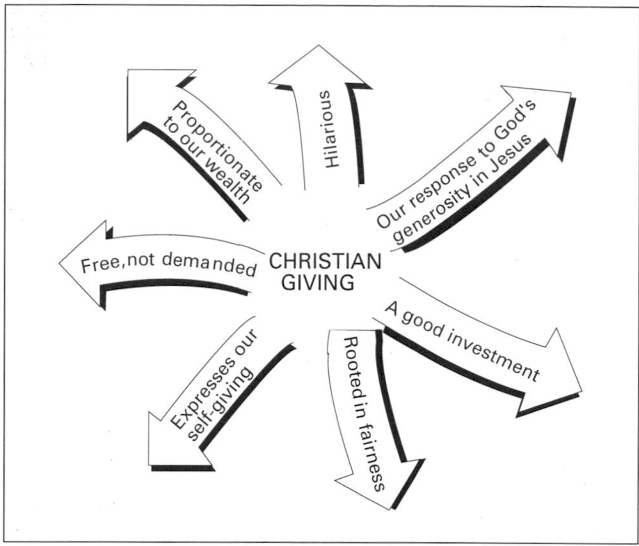

Every reader of 2 Corinthians will find some message of encouragement or challenge which relates to their experience, so wide-ranging is it. But here are some points to look out for in this section:

* The need to forgive each other (2:5-11)
* The minister's need for human support (2:12-13)
* God's glory is reflected by his people (3:7-18)
* Weakness keeps us dependent on God (4)
* Keep looking towards the goal of heaven (5:1-10)
* Beware of mixed marriages with unbelievers (6:14-18)

●Christian giving (section 3)
Paul urges his readers to allow their generosity to overflow. He writes as both a theologian and a fund-raiser, and lays down a number of principles for Christian giving. It is an expression of our total self-giving to

176

the Lord (8:5). It is always 'free-will', it is not something which can be demanded (9:7). It is always proportionate to what one has; there is no set 'flat-rate' amount (8:12). It is always a good investment (9:6). It is rooted in the principle of fairness (8:13-14). And above all it is rooted in our response to God's generosity in Jesus (8:9).

● **Authority (section 4)**
Here we have a fierce denunciation of Paul's opponents and an equally fierce defence of his own authority as an apostle. Is he denying his servanthood as described above? No. His ferocity is used to defend principles, issues and truth, not his hurt pride; it is not an easy balance to achieve.

48-49

34

Paul the traveller and theologian

Paul (originally named Saul) was born in Tarsus as a Roman citizen to parents who came from the tribe of Benjamin. He became a Pharisee, the strictest party of the Jews. He was given the task of rounding up the Christians while still a young man (see Acts 7:58).

But it was while he was on one of his journeys to rid the land of the Christian menace that he was confronted by Jesus in a spectacular vision (Acts 9). After his conversion he spent three years in Damascus and ten in Tarsus, before Barnabas finally invited him to share in the ministry at Antioch. After that he began his globe-trotting ministry in which he planted churches in mostly Gentile areas.

Nothing is known of what Paul looked like, although one ancient writing suggests he was short, balding and with crooked legs. His 'thorn in the flesh' (2 Corinthians 12:1-10) may have been short-sightedness or some form of physical handicap. He certainly suffered a great deal (2 Corinthians 11:22-33).

He was a tireless evangelist, a deeply caring pastor and a brilliant and clear thinker. He was not a hit-and-run preacher who set up churches and left them to fend for themselves, but trained up new converts for ministry and regularly checked up on their progress through personal visits and by sending his messengers and assistants.

He gave to Christianity its rational basis. He spelled out in his letters exactly what the death of Christ achieved, and how a person could become right with God. He clarified the relationship of the Old Testament Law to the new covenant made by Jesus on the cross, and helped the churches to understand the promise of Jesus' return. But his theology was not arid; it pulsated with pastoral concern. To him, doctrine was uesless if it did not result in a life which honoured Jesus.

Letter to the churches in Galatia

This passionate letter was written to the churches in the Roman province of Galatia, the area which we now know as southern Turkey. Here were the churches of Antioch, Iconium, Lystra and Derbe, which Paul together with Barnabas had founded on his first missionary journey (Acts 13-14). Unfortunately these young churches were visited later by some Jewish Christians. They began to persuade the Christians of Galatia that circumcision and obedience to the law of Moses were essential for salvation.

Summary of Galatians

1 Introduction (1:1-10)
2 Paul's defence of his authority (1:11 - 2:21)
3 By grace alone (3-4)
4 Christian freedom (5:1 - 6:10)
5 Conclusion (6:11-18)

● By grace alone (section 3)

The first four chapters are argued tightly and in a way modern readers may find difficult. The clue is Paul's concern about circumcision, an example of an addition to the means of salvation. Paul argues that we are made right with God by his undeserved grace ('favour') not by any other additional acts or ceremonies we might perform.

The value of ceremonies (such as particular forms of baptism, confirmation or ordination) and of personal disciplines is in what they remind us of rather than in what they do.

Galatians: data

Date and purpose: Paul wrote to correct wrong teaching about Jewish customs. The gospel itself was at stake, which accounts for his passionate writing. Paul probably wrote it just before the great council of Jerusalem which met to resolve this issue (Acts 15). Galatians is therefore Paul's earliest known letter, dated around AD 49.

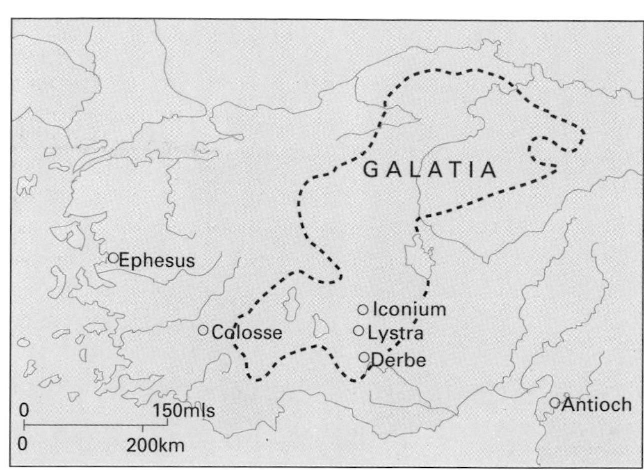

Galatia.

279

● Christian freedom (section 4)

Paul writes here of the fruit of the Spirit: 'love, joy, peace, patience, kindness, goodness, faithfulness, gentleness and self-control' (5:22). Note that Paul does not describe these as 'fruits', but as 'fruit'. *The implication is that all these qualities are to be found 'growing' in the life of every Christian as the Holy Spirit slowly makes us more like Jesus.*

In these last two chapters Paul also works out the implications of Christian freedom. On the one hand Christians should be free to live their lives without being hemmed in by a host of rules and regulations. On the other hand, Christians are not free to do what they like. The key to Christian freedom is found in a readiness to serve God and to serve others.

Letter to the church in Ephesus

Ephesians is in some ways the most impersonal of all Paul's letters. For instance, it contains no personal greetings. This is strange, for Paul spent longer in Ephesus than in any other city (Acts 19:8-10). However the oldest and best Greek manuscripts of this letter omit the words 'in Ephesus' found in 1:2. In the light of these twin facts many believe that Ephesians is a circular letter written to all the churches in the Roman province of Asia, of which Ephesus was the most important city.

Summary of Ephesians

1 Introduction (1:1-2)

2 Paul's vision of the church (1:3 - 3:21)

3 Relationships in the church and in the home (4:1 - 6:20)

4 Conclusion (6:21-24)

●Paul's vision of the church (section 2)

At the beginning of this letter Paul develops the theme of unity in breathtaking manner, as he looks forward to the day when God will 'bring all things in heaven and on earth together under one head, even Christ' (1:10). Paul is not dreaming here of a 'United Nations', but of a 'United Universe' – even those superhuman forces of evil currently working against God and his purposes will submit to the lordship of Christ.

As a prelude to this great event Paul speaks of Christ bringing together Jew and Gentile alike: 'For he himself is our peace, who has made the two one and has destroyed the barrier, the dividing wall of hostility' (2:14). *This principle can be applied more widely to the bitter divisions that mark our day: racial (black and white), religious (Protestant and Catholic), political (socialist and capitalist), social (rich and poor) and even sexual (men and women). The message of Ephesians is that the highest of barriers fall down before Christ. The bond of simple trust in Jesus is strong enough to resist all human or devilish attempts to pull people apart.*

133-134

●Relationships in church and home (section 3)

The second half of the letter is devoted to practical teaching on relationships. Some of the teaching was revolutionary for Paul's day. Instead of simply reinforcing what was believed to be the duty of wives, children and slaves to 'obey' their husbands, parents and masters, Paul proposes something unthinkable: that the 'power-holders' should uphold the dignity of women, children and slaves (5:22 - 6:9). Husbands, for instance, should 'love their wives, just as Christ loved the church' (5:25). This self-giving was – and still is – revolutionary. But in Christ relationships are transformed.

Ephesians: data

Paul clearly wrote this letter from prison (6:20), probably in Rome in the early 60s. Written at the same time as his letter to the Colossians, it is not surprising that a number of thoughts and themes are to be found in both letters.

The letter concludes with a call to arms: 'Put on the full armour of God, so that you can take your stand against the devil's schemes' (6:11). Christians need to be on their guard and not let their relationships be spoilt by the Evil One. The Christian life is not a picnic. It is drawn into a deadly battle between God and the powers of evil, which God will win totally but which his people will not find easy.

Although only short, Ephesians is packed with some memorable passages which will repay careful thought and prayer. Here are some, in addition to those mentioned above:

God's lavish love and rich power made available to us (1:7,8,18,19; 3:8, 16-19)

The Holy Spirit as a 'down payment' of heaven to come (1;14, 4:30)

Saved by God's grace but called to do good deeds (2:8-10)

Gifted leadership is needed to bring us to mature faith (4:12-14)

Mind your language and temper! (4:26-32)

Make the most of your time (5:15-17)

Some memorable extracts.

Letter to the church in Philippi

Philippians is Paul's 'letter of joy'. Sixteen times the words 'joy' and 'rejoice' appear.

Philippi had been built in 358-357 BC by Philip II of Macedon, father of Alexander the Great, and named after himself. Later Philippi was made a Roman 'colony', the home of many former Roman soldiers. A colony had the same rights and privileges as if it was on Italian soil. Thus in Acts 16:21 the people saw themselves first and foremost as Romans.

Philippi was Paul's first European church. Luke tells the story of its formation in Acts 16. In a night vision Paul heard someone saying, 'Come over to Macedonia and help us' (Acts 16:9). With Silas and Timothy he crossed the Aegean Sea and took the gospel to Philippi.

In addition to the theme of joy, Philippians sets out a pattern for living which has lost none of its relevance down the years. Here are three examples:

●Paul's deep spirituality

Many a man in prison might have felt sorry for himself – but not Paul. 'For to me, to live is Christ' (1:21). Paul's relationship with his Lord was such that he could say, 'I have

Philippians: data

Purpose: Philippians is basically a thank-you letter. The church there had sent Paul money and also one of their members, Epaphroditus, to care for his needs (2:25; 4:10,14-19). Characteristically he took the opportunity to encourage and instruct his readers. Date: There is no general agreement about when and where Paul wrote Philippians. Clearly he was in prison (1:7, 13, 17), but was it in Rome around AD 61-63, or in Caesarea around AD 59-61, or in Ephesus around AD 54? We do not really know. Epaphroditus had been ill but was now recovered and was able to take Paul's letter home with him.

Summary of Philippians

There is no clear structure. The letter has been compared to a chat between friends. One possible division is as follows:

1 Introduction (1:1-11)

2 News (1:12-26)

3 Encouragement and instruction (1:27 - 2:18)

4 Plans for Timothy and Epaphroditus (2:19-30)

5 Warnings against enemies and dangers (3:1 - 4:9)

6 A final thank-you (4:10-20)

7 Conclusion (4:21-23)

learned the secret of being content in any and every situation' (4:11).

● Salvation includes suffering
Paul declares that the experience of sharing in the power of Christ's resurrection cannot be separated from that of sharing in Christ's sufferings (3:10). The Christian faith is not all happy celebration; Jesus suffered at the hands of sinful people, and so shall we.

● Jesus is the pattern for Christian living
Philippians contains one of the greatest of 'Christ-hymns'. In the course of urging his readers to be 'like-minded, having the same love' for one another (2:2), Paul cites an early Christian hymn, which celebrates the life of the Servant-King, who for our sakes 'made himself nothing...humbled himself and became obedient to death', and whom God therefore exalted 'to the highest place' (2:6-11). Here is a profound Christian truth linked closely to practical advice on how to live.

270

Not many people who are in prison, with no immediate hope of release, would have Paul's attitude to the Christian life! Look at two phrases in chapter 3 which sum it all up: 'I have lost all things' (verse 8) and 'I press on towards the goal' (verse 14). He is not saying that his place in heaven is in any doubt. But he is saying that he wants to live now in a way that will be worthy of that place in heaven. Every hindrance to knowing God is thrown away; every opportunity to serve him is eagerly taken. Perhaps the secret of his dedication is the sheer joy he has because of what Jesus has done for him. Think about it as you read the letter through. If our dedication is less than his, perhaps it is because we have forgotten the thrill of being a child of God.

Letter to the church in Colosse

In Colossians Paul confidently depicts Christ as lord of the universe. Nothing is outside his control (1:15-18).

The city of Colosse in Paul's time was relatively insignificant. Situated a hundred miles to the east of Ephesus, in the valley of the Lycus river, it was on the main trade route from Ephesus to the east. Although it had been a town of some importance, it was now in decline.

It would seem that Paul had never visited Colosse. The church there had probably started during his three years in Ephesus, when Luke tells us, 'all the Jews and Greeks who lived in the province of Asia heard the word of the Lord' (Acts 19:10). Epaphras, called by Paul 'our dear fellow-servant, who is a faithful minister of Christ on our behalf' (1:7; 4:12) was perhaps converted at that time – he seems to have been responsible for founding the church at Colosse.

Summary of Colossians

1 Introductory prayer of thanksgiving (1:1-14)

2 The person and work of Christ (1:15 - 2:5)

3 Warnings against false teachers (2:6-23)

4 New life in Christ (3:1 - 4:6)

5 Concluding greetings (4:7-18)

Colossians: data

Date: Paul was in prison when he wrote this letter (4:18), probably in Rome about AD 61. Purpose: Epaphras had told him that false teachers had been insisting that for full salvation one must worship certain spiritual 'powers', submit to circumcision and observe set festival days (2:6-23). In response Paul emphasizes that Christ is all-sufficient.

● The person and work of Christ (section 2)

In applying the message of Colossians to our own situation the key is the hymn to Christ (1:15-20). There, Jesus is proclaimed not only Lord of the church but Lord of the world, of 'all things'. A young man, recently crucified, is Lord of all.

How can Jesus be Lord when so much seems to be wrong in the world? Paul gives, or implies, the answer in 1:15-20. The world is out of harmony with God and needs to be reconciled to him. He has begun that work of reconciliation on the cross. So how does that affect me? Quite simply, it means that everything I touch or am involved with in the world is to be brought under his lordship. Therefore I cannot as a Christian waste its resources or damage its structure; I cannot allow greed and injustice to continue unchallenged; I cannot fritter away my money and time. Otherwise, I am not recognizing his lordship over 'all things'.

278

● Warnings against false teachers (section 3)

We cannot be sure what the teachers were saying. But from Paul's criticism it would seem that they were making a three-pronged attack on the church:

55

Three marks of a cult as described in Colossians.

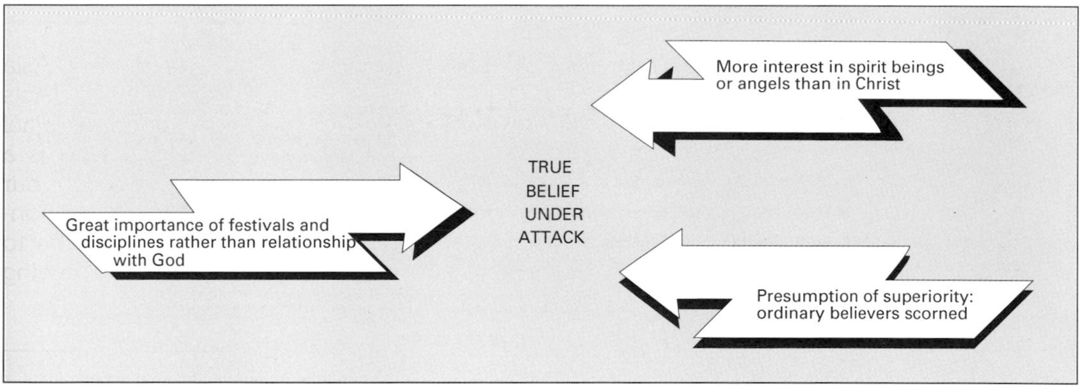

Letters to the church in Thessalonica

Thessalonica (now Salonika) was a thriving seaport on the coast of north-east Greece. It was founded about 315 BC by the Macedonian king, Cassander, and named after his wife, a half-sister of Alexander the Great. In 167 BC it became the capital of the Roman province of Macedonia. From 42 BC it enjoyed the status of a free city, governed by five or six 'politarchs' (see Acts 17:6).

198

1 and 2 Thessalonians: data

Purpose: Timothy reported that some of Paul's Jewish opponents were running a vigorous smear campaign against him. They seem to have been suggesting that Paul's chief motive as a missionary was to make a financial profit out of his converts (1 Thessalonians 2:1-16).

There were also several matters on which the church needed more teaching: on sexual morality (see 1 Thessalonians. 4:3-8), on work (see 4:11-12), and on Jesus' return (see 4:13 - 5:11).

Date: To answer these concerns Paul wrote 1 Thessalonians, which may be dated around AD 51.

The church was founded about AD 50 after Paul, together with Silas and Timothy, had left Philippi on the second missionary journey. Luke tells us how, after only three weeks of preaching, Paul and his companions were forced to leave, such was the opposition from the Jews. About eighteen months later Paul, by that time in Corinth, sent Timothy back to Thessalonica to find out how the young church was getting on (1 Thessalonians 3:15). Timothy returned with a most encouraging progress report.

224

Unfortunately this first letter did not achieve all that Paul had hoped. What he had said about the second coming of Christ was interpreted as a warning that it would happen any minute. As a result some of the church members had stopped work and were excitedly preparing for the end (see 2 Thessalonians 3:6-13). So Paul had to calm them down by reminding them that the signs that must come before the end have not yet happened (see 2 Thessalonians 2:1-12). This second letter was written probably only a matter of weeks after 1 Thessalonians.

Summary of 1 Thessalonians

1 Introduction and thanksgiving (1:1-10)
2 Paul's defence (2:1-16)
3 Paul's desire to revisit Thessalonica (2:17 - 3:13)
4 Some pastoral advice (4:1 - 5:11)
5 Final instructions and greetings (5:12-28)

Summary of 2 Thessalonians

1 Introduction (1:1-2)
2 The judgment to come (1:3-12)
3 Signs of the end (2:1-12)
4 Words of encouragement (2:13-3:15)
5 Conclusion (3:16-18)

The emphasis on the second coming makes the Thessalonian letters distinctive. For many twentieth-century Christians the imagery that Paul uses here is strange. The possibility of the second coming is no longer a burning issue for us. Yet perhaps this is the very reason why we should value these letters.

Although we may not press the details of the imagery, which for the most part was drawn from the Old Testament, the fact remains that there will be a day when the Lord will come down from heaven (1 Thessalonians 4:16). On that day he will bring with him those who have 'fallen asleep in him' (1 Thessalonians 4:14) and also 'punish those who do not know God and do not obey the gospel of our Lord Jesus' (2 Thessalonians 1:8). *On the one hand, here is encouragement for Christians who remember people they loved who have*

died safely in Christ, or as we ourselves come face to face with death. On the other hand, here too is motivation for mission. For without Christ, people will be lost and 'shut out from the presence of the Lord' (2 Thessalonians 1:9).

The pastoral letters to Timothy and Titus

Since the eighteenth century the two letters to Timothy with the letter to Titus have been known as the 'pastoral' epistles. This is because for the most part these letters consist of guidance to two younger pastors, Timothy and Titus, whom Paul had left in charge of the churches in Ephesus and Crete respectively.

The historical information which these letters supply cannot be fitted into the life and ministry of Paul as we have it in Acts, so it appears that they were written probably after Paul's release from the Roman imprisonment described in the last chapter of Acts.

It seems that after his release Paul went to Crete with Titus and probably with Timothy. There they evangelized most of the towns, but encountered some opposition from Jews of Greek origin. Paul therefore left Titus on the island to supervise the ongoing work of the church.

From Crete Paul and Timothy went to Ephesus, where some false teachers – probably elders of the church - were seeking to gain control. Paul expelled two of the ringleaders, Hymenaeus and Alexander (1 Timothy 1:19-20) and left Timothy in charge.

Paul himself returned to Macedonia, from where he wrote the letters we know as Titus and 1 Timothy. Paul, however, did not remain in Macedonia for long. At some stage on his travels he was arrested – perhaps at Troas at the instigation of Alexander the metalworker (2

Timothy: the timid pastor

Timothy was the child of a mixed marriage. His father was Greek and his mother Jewish. His home was in Lystra, a town in the Roman province of Galatia, which Paul had visited on both his first and second missionary journeys (Acts 14:8-18; 16:1-3). On his second visit Paul invited Timothy to accompany him on his travels. Timothy became Paul's constant companion and loyal assistant. Not perhaps the bravest of men (2 Timothy 1:7), Timothy appears to have needed a good deal of encouragement.

The pastoral letters: data

Author: Since the beginning of the last century there has been much debate as to whether these three letters are indeed by Paul. It has been suggested that on grounds of style and content they must be the work of a later writer, who perhaps incorporated some genuine 'fragments' of Paul's writing. However, there may well be a simple reason for the differences between the pastoral letters and Paul's other letters. Paul probably dictated his letters to a trusted secretary, who was allowed a certain freedom of expression.

Date: It is hard to arrive at a precise date for these letters, but 1 Timothy and Titus were written probably around AD 64 and 2 Timothy later, perhaps about AD 67.

The Far East Broadcasting Association sends the good news of Christ over the airwaves.

Timothy 4:14). Eventually he was brought back to Rome, where he had a preliminary hearing before a Roman tribunal (2 Timothy 4:16-18) and was bound over for a full trial.

Summary of 1 Timothy

1 Introduction (1:1-2)

2 False teachers (1:3-20)

3 Church worship (2:1-14)

4 Qualities and duties of leaders (3-4)

5 Pastoral issues and advice (5:1 - 6:10)

6 Personal instructions (6:11-20)

Two important emphases stand out in 1 Timothy.

First, the gospel is for all people (1:1, 15; 2:3-4; 4:10). Even as an old man Paul still passionately wanted to make the gospel known. 'God our Saviour ... wants all men to be saved and to come to a knowledge of the truth' (2:3-4), he declared. Paul had a worldwide vision. Concern today for church growth and even church planting is good as a means to an end, but even a full church is not the same as the whole world won for Christ. Paul's vision is all the more astonishing considering the contrast between ancient and modern methods of communication.

At the beginning of the twentieth century delegates at a missionary conference in Edinburgh vowed to reach 'the whole world for Christ in our generation'. At the end of the twentieth century Christians around the world were setting the year 2,000 as a target for total evangelization. We may not always reach such targets, but if we aim for nothing we shall achieve nothing. Where is world mission on your church's agenda – and on your prayer list?

Secondly, Christian leaders are to live out the gospel. It is noticeable that Paul speaks a lot about what leaders are to be, but tells us very little about what they are to do (see, *e.g.* 3:1-13).

The gifts of the Spirit are intended for people who are bearing the fruit of the Spirit. Paul knew that the authority leaders can exercise is intimately bound up with what kind of people they are.

Summary of 2 Timothy

1 Introduction (1:1-2)

2 A call to suffer (1:3 - 2:13)

3 A charge to Timothy (2:14 - 4:5)

4 Paul's own situation (4:6-18)

5 Conclusion (4:19-22)

It may well be that no more than a year or so had elapsed since Paul wrote his first letter. The tone, however, is different. A note of loneli-

ness runs through the apostle's final letter. Paul was anxious that Timothy, his dear 'son' in the faith, should come to him as quickly as possible (4:9). Deserted by his friends (4:9-13), opposed by Alexander the coppersmith (4:14-15) and unsupported at his first trial (4:16-18), Paul felt isolated. Friendships were clearly important for Paul. For all his strength of character, Paul was never a loner.

This was not simply a matter of personality. From the call of the first disciples by Jesus, the principle of togetherness was established as central to the life of the church. Jesus sent them out in pairs. And Paul described the church as a body of closely-knit parts, each dependent on the others. No Christian is self-sufficient. It is one of God's tactics to keep human pride at bay.

This letter also breathes confidence in the gospel, however. Although Paul sensed that he was close to death, he showed no trace of self-pity. Paul could face death without fear. The race was almost over: 'now there is in store for me the crown of righteousness, which the Lord, the righteous Judge, will award to me on that day – and not only to me, but also to all who have longed for his appearing' (4:6-8).

If Paul was confident in the gospel, he was also confident in the Word of God. 'All Scripture is God-breathed and is useful for teaching, rebuking, correcting and training in righteousness' (3:16). Although penned with the Old Testament in mind, these words can be applied to the New Testament as well.

Care is needed in handling the Bible. It is all too easy to twist the meaning of a passage to make it say what we want it to say – and to ignore other passages which challenge our view. Notice that the purpose of Scripture according to Paul is to rebuke and correct our views; he does not say 'confirm'. There is always more to learn.

58-59

Summary of the letter to Titus

1 Introduction (1:1-4)
2 Church leaders (1:5-16)
3 Duties of various groups (2)
4 Exhortation and warnings (3:1-11)
5 Conclusion (3:12-15)

Titus had been left behind in Crete to sort out the situation there. In particular he was to appoint elders in the church over the whole island (1:5). As distinct from their fellow-Cretans, whom Paul brands as 'always liars, evil brutes, lazy gluttons' (1:12) these elders were to be of far better character (1:6-9).

Titus the man

Titus is not mentioned in Acts. From Paul's letters we learn that he was a pagan convert of Paul's, who came to enjoy the apostle's fullest confidence. Thus when trouble broke out at Corinth, Paul sent Titus to sort out the matter (2 Corinthians 7:6-16; 12:18).

If there is one dominant theme in Titus it is that of 'good works' (1:8, 16; 2:7, 14; 3:1, 8, 14). In his earlier letters Paul had attacked people who tried to make themselves right with God on the basis of 'works of law' (see, *e.g.* Philippians 3:9). But nonetheless he expected Christians to respond to God's grace with lives full of good works. Indeed, accord-

221-222

80

279-280

ing to 1:16 the acid test for claims to know God is the way we live.

When we become Christians by submitting our lives to Christ's control, he begins to change us so that we may reflect his purity and love. But it is not something he can achieve without our cooperation; we have to want to be changed. As you read Titus, see how Paul urges the Cretans to put right what is bad in their natural character. Compare that description of them in 1:12 with Paul's instructions in 1:7-8; 2:1, 12; 3:2.

Letter to Philemon

302

40-41

This, the shortest of Paul's letters – only 335 words in the original Greek – is also the most personal. As the opening verses show, however, this was not so much a private letter, as an apostolic letter about a personal matter. It was a letter written for others to read.

Paul wrote to Philemon, a leading member of the church at Colosse (verses 1-2) concerning Onesimus, one of his slaves who had run away and later come into contact with Paul in prison at Rome. As a result of Paul's influence Onesimus had become a Christian. Paul now writes to Philemon to ask him to welcome Onesimus back, not only as a forgiven slave, but also as a Christian brother (verse 16). Indeed, Paul seems to ask for more than forgiveness, for verse 21 seems to contain the hope that Philemon might agree actually to release Onesimus from slavery.

The letter was written at about the same time as the letter to Colosse, AD 60 or 61. As an apostle Paul could have insisted that Philemon welcome back Onesimus. However, he preferred to allow Philemon to respond freely, and presumably the very fact that this letter is preserved is an indication that he did. One attractive suggestion is that Onesimus, Bishop of Ephesus some forty years later and termed by Ignatius 'a man of inexpressible love', was in fact the same Onesimus as in the letter. If so, then Paul's confidence in Onesimus was well and truly justified.

A striking feature of this letter is Paul's attitude towards slavery. Although Paul nowhere condemns the institution of slavery, he writes of it in such a manner that it may be argued that he sows the seeds of its destruction. Not without reason has this letter therefore been called 'the Magna Carta of the Slave'.

Paul's indirect approach is instructive; it probably helped Philemon change his mind more readily than he would have done in the face of an outright request

and strong condemnation of slavery. To change people's actions requires a change of mind, and that often requires a change of heart. Paul set out to win Philemon's heart; the change followed. It is an example of sensitive pastoral care – and patience.

Letter to the Hebrews

The author of Hebrews gives us perhaps the finest of all New Testament descriptions of the person and work of Christ. Two emphases stand out:

1 The humanity (2:14; 4:15; 5:7) and divinity (1:3, 8) of Christ. Jesus is portrayed as both totally human and totally divine.

2 Jesus fulfils and completes all the Old Testament promises. He is both the high priest and the sacrificial victim and has therefore opened for us a new and living way into the very presence of God (10:19-20). Jesus has bridged the gulf between God and man (2:17; 3:1; 4:14-15; 6:20; 7:26; 8:1).

Hebrews: data

Author: Nobody knows who wrote Hebrews; almost certainly not Paul. Barnabas, Luke, Silas, Clement of Alexandria and Priscilla have been suggested but there is little evidence for any of them.

Date: The letter seems to reflect the years of crisis just preceding the destruction of the Jerusalem temple in AD 70. If the letter was written to Rome (see 13:24: 'Those from Italy send you their greetings'), then it is possible that the persecutions referred to in 10:32 refer to Nero's. This places it somewhere between AD 64 and AD 70. Purpose: The title, 'Hebrews' is not original to the letter, but a second-century addition. However, it is appropriate, for the letter seems to have been written to a group of Jewish Christians, tempted to return to their ancestral faith. Hence the emphasis on Christ's superiority over Moses and the old covenant.

Summary of Hebrews

1 Christ the complete revelation of God (1:1-3)

2 Christ's superiority over the angels (1:4 - 2:18)

3 Christ's superiority over Moses (3:1 - 4:13)

4 The superiority of Christ's priesthood (4:14 - 7:28)

5 The superiority of Christ's covenant (8-9)

6 The superiority of Christ's sacrifice (10)

7 The life of faith (11:1 - 13:17)

8 Personal messages (13:18-25)

195

War clouds were gathering over Palestine and an appeal was being made to Jews to stand together 'for faith and for fatherland'. Such an appeal was deeply emotive, for a patriotic Jew was almost by definition a practising Jew. Against such a background the author urges his readers to remain faithful to Christ. The seriousness of turning back from him into pre-Christian Judaism is emphasized: 'We have come to share in Christ if we hold firmly till the end the confidence we had at first' (3:14).

40

Hebrews is not a letter in the con-

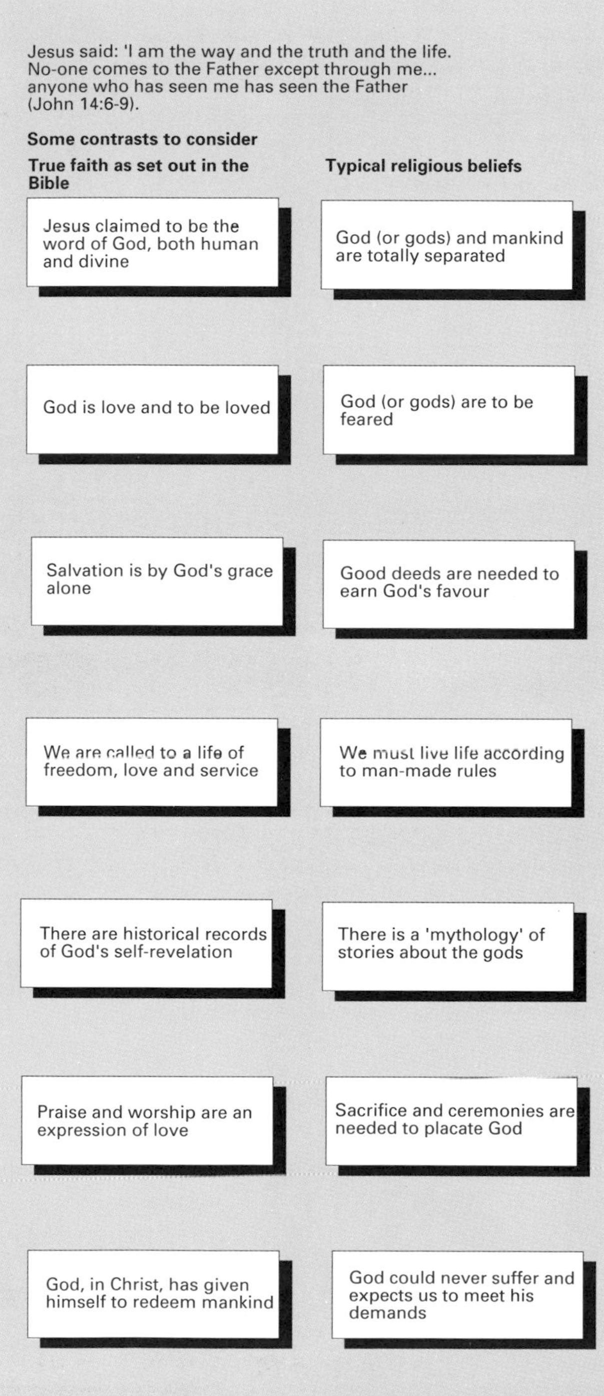

ventional sense. It is more like a sermon, with some personal messages added on at the end (13:18-25).

The author builds up his argument slowly, and today's readers may find it hard going at first. Having stated his case, that Jesus Christ is God's final word to mankind (section 1), he then sets out to demonstrate just how superior Jesus is.

He is superior to the angels (section 2) who, being spiritual beings, were normally considered to be better than people. He is superior even to Moses, the great founder of the Jewish faith (section 3). And he is superior to the Jewish priests (section 4). They had to offer sacrifices for their own sins as well as for the people's sins; Jesus, by contrast, was perfect and had no need to deal with his own sins (5:3; 7:26-28). (The author uses a complex comparison in chapter 7; Melchizedek had no ancestral right to be a priest but received the priest's dues for his service to the father of the Jewish race, Abraham).

So, if Jesus is superior to spiritual beings, to Moses and the priesthood, it follows that the covenant between man and God which he forged by his own death is far superior to previous covenants (section 5). And then comes the crunch: his sacrifice is so superior that it need never be repeated. Jesus died once and for all to deal with the problem of sin for all ages (section 6).

Is Christianity merely one of many ways to God? The author of Hebrews had no doubt that Jesus was the only way (10:12). Remember the context in which he wrote: there were many religions at the time, and the Jewish

Do all religions lead to God?

religion could already lay claim to being a 'great world religion'. It was not so different from our own day. The fact may offend some people. But it is the one fact which Christians cannot bend, and the 'offence of the cross' is one we have to bear graciously but firmly.

Faith that is genuine results in vigorous action (section 7). Chapter 11 lists the exploits of many of the heroes of faith. Christians are to refuse to settle back into false security. God's people, living in a society which largely ignores or rejects God, are like 'aliens and strangers' (11:13). Solidarity with the heroes of faith is not a romantic pastime; it demands a positive commitment to personal holiness (12:1-12).

In addition to the practical instructions in section 7, look out for gems of spiritual encouragement in the earlier parts of the book:

* *Jesus' suffering through temptation means he can help us when we are tempted (2:18; 4:14-16)*
* *God's Word can penetrate the thickest skin (and hardest heart, 4:12-13)*
* *Jesus saves us fully (7:23-25)*
* *Jesus will return to complete our salvation (9:27-28)*
* *We can come to God with confidence (10:19-22)*
* *Stand firm! (10:32-39)*

The letter of James

Practical religion is the theme of James. More than any other New Testament book, James concentrates on how the Christian life should be lived.

Summary of the letter of James

James is notoriously difficult to organize. It seems to be made up of short sayings, with scarcely any apparent relationship between them.

One commentator, A. M. Hunter, has arranged the letter by themes into 'five little sermons':

1 Trials and temptations (1:2-8, 12-18)

2 Riches and poverty (1:9-11; 2:1-13; 5:1-6)

3 Faith and works (1:19-27; 2:14-26)

4 The control of the tongue (3:1-12; 4:11-12; 5:12)

5 Patience and prayer (5:7-11, 13-20)

James spells out the demands of the kingdom. This explains why James the pastor does not so much seek to inform his readers, as to command, exhort and to encourage.

Two aspects of this letter are particularly relevant to the church of today:

● Faith must be expressed by action (section 3)

Faith without works, says James, is dead. Much has been made of his apparent conflict with Paul. Paul says that Abraham was justified by faith (Romans 4); James says that Abraham was justified by his works (2:21). But they both quote the same verse, 'Abram believed the LORD, and he credited it to him as righteousness' (Genesis 15:6). Paul is emphasizing that we cannot earn our own salvation. James agrees,

217

but adds that faith is useless if it is not applied to daily life.

James is saying that faith can be blind. We can rejoice in our relationship with God and yet be thoughtless when it comes to a fellow-Christian's personal needs. We may stress the importance of knowing what we believe, and simply forget that every belief touches some part of our behaviour. James' advice is if you believe in God's love, get on with being loving. That way, the critics can't claim that there are better people outside the church than in it.

231

The letter of James: data

Author: Traditionally this letter has been ascribed to James, 'the Lord's brother' (see Mark 6:3; Galatians 1:19). He became leader of the young church and chaired the council of Jerusalem (Acts 15). Date: It must have been written before that council or he would probably have mentioned it. A date around AD 45-49 is suggested.

Purpose: One attractive suggestion is that James 1:1 should be linked with Acts 11:19, where Luke tells that many Jews were 'scattered' and travelled as far as Phoenicia, Cyprus and Antioch, 'telling the message only to Jews'. James could then be seen as a pastoral letter from the head of the Jerusalem church to his members scattered throughout the Near East. This would account for the Jewish tone of the letter.

● James is concerned lest the world perverts the church

'Friendship with the world', he wrote, 'is hatred towards God' (4:4). But the holiness which James longs for is not the inner cultivation of the soul – spiritual 'navel-gazing' – but the holiness which controls the tongue (3:1-12), cares for the widow and the orphan (1:27) and refuses to play up to the rich (2:1-4). James is concerned for practical holiness, which results in Christians demonstrating a fresh quality of living.

The letters of Peter

56

1 Peter

1 Peter is a letter of encouragement (5:12) to those who were suffering persecution. Key words in it are 'suffering' and 'glory'.

Summary of 1 Peter

1 Introduction (1:1-2)

2 The certain hope (1:3-12)

3 A call to holy living (1:13 - 2:12)

4 A Christian response to suffering (2:13 - 4:19)

5 Christian humility and service in the church (5:1-11)

6 Conclusion (5:12-14)

Three themes:

● Suffering (section 4)

Christians were being persecuted for their faith. Peter's attitude toward suffering is remarkably positive. Suffering tests the reality of a person's faith; it is a sharing in Christ's sufferings; it is a reason for joy (4:12-14). This is an uncomfortable thought to those of us who live relatively comfortable lives today.

For most people in the west, suffering for our faith is an exception to the normal rule of indifference shown to it by people around us.

'Ready to give an answer...'

So we find it hard to cope with when it comes. We can use 1 Peter to prepare ourselves for the unexpected. It is just at such times that we can suddenly let our Lord down – just as Peter once did, despite his promise not to, at Jesus' trial (Mark 14:27-31,66-72).

1 Peter: data

Author: Peter the apostle writes of being a witness of Christ's sufferings. Date: He seems to have written from Rome, in about AD 67 , during the persecution by Nero and perhaps just before his own death. Purpose: He wrote to encourage the churches of what now would be the greater part of Turkey (1:1). The high quality Greek in which the letter is written may have been the style of Silas, Peter's secretary (5:12).

●Right behaviour (section 3)

The implication of 1 Peter is that if Christians paid more attention to living as Jesus did, opportunities of talking about him would come quite naturally. Hence Peter's advice to Christian wives, who long for their husbands to share their faith: it will be winsome behaviour which will convert them, not words alone (3:1-6).

People who have just become Christians are sometimes so full of their discovery that they rush in where angels fear to tread. People whose faith is older and supposedly wiser sometimes fear to tread where the angels have already rushed in! Everyone is called to witness to their faith. Our life must be an open book; but we must also be ready to explain to people what they see (see 3:15).

●Relationships (section 5)

Leaders are not to act as 'lords', but as servants. The true pastor leads rather than drives his flock. All God's people are to put on the 'apron of humility' (a reminder of Jesus washing his disciples' feet at the Last Supper) as they serve one another (5:5).

162

2 Peter

The emphasis in 2 Peter is on growth to Christian maturity (3:18).

2 Peter : data

The style of 2 Peter is different from 1 Peter and there is much debate about the authorship. If we take it as Peter (1:1 and 3:1 suggest this) it must have been written from Rome, soon after 1 Peter, to the same churches and mostly Gentile Christians.

Summary of 2 Peter

1 Introduction (1:1-2)
2 The Christian calling (1:3-21)
3 False teachers (2)
4 The second coming of Christ (3)

● The reliability of the gospel (section 2)

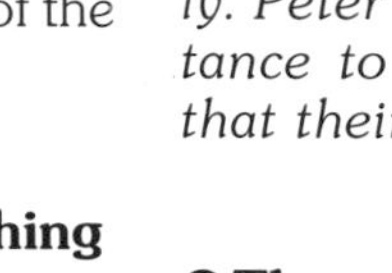
247

Peter underlines the reliability of the gospel by stressing that the Christian message does not rest on myth and legend, but on the evidence of eyewitnesses (1:16). The *historical* Jesus is at the heart of the Christian faith.

● The danger of false teaching (section 3)

214

The immorality, greed and arrogance of false teachers all contribute to a denial of the gospel. This is a sobering thought. Viewed from this perspective the sins of the false teachers are still very much with us. *False teachers, whether they are members of the cults who persist in visiting homes of people around our church or members of our own church or denomination who hit the headlines with outrageous claims, have always been a thorn in the side of faithful believers. It is hard to know what to do about them. Obviously the teaching has to be countered. Sometimes it is possible to put false teachers out of the church – although that often only creates more problems. Peter here gives us some extra crumbs of comfort. He says God will judge these people in no uncertain terms. There is no sin worse than leading people astray; God does not view it lightly. Peter wants to encourage resistance to them in the knowledge that their efforts are doomed.*

● The certainty of Christ's return (section 4)

The apparent delay in Christ's coming is not due to God's weakness, but to his mercy (3:9). The delay is really an illusion – for God sees time differently (3:8). The timing of the Lord's coming may surprise us, but not the fact of it. Therefore believers should 'live holy and godly lives' now (3:11), in readiness for Jesus' return.

The letters of John

1 John

A group of people had left the church or churches and set up their own (2:19). They were trying to persuade others to join them (2:26). This breakaway group denied Christ's human nature (4:2), failed to take sin seriously (1:8,10) and boasted of their 'super-spirituality' (2:4; 4:8). This was the situation that John addressed.

The letters of John: data

Author: 'John the elder', the apostle who wrote 2 and 3 John, probably wrote 1 John as well. The style is similar to the Gospel of John and so are many of the themes: good and evil, life and death, light and darkness, love and hate.

Date: around AD 85-90.

Purpose: To reassure Christians who had believed the gospel that they really did have new life (John 20:31, see 1 John 5:13).

Summary of 1 John

Themes overlap and are repeated but this is one way of dividing the letter:

1 Introduction (1:1-4)
2 What is Christianity? (1:5 - 2:28)
3 Life in the family of God (2:29 - 4:12)
4 The certainty of the faith (4:13 - 5:12)
5 Conclusion (5:13-21)

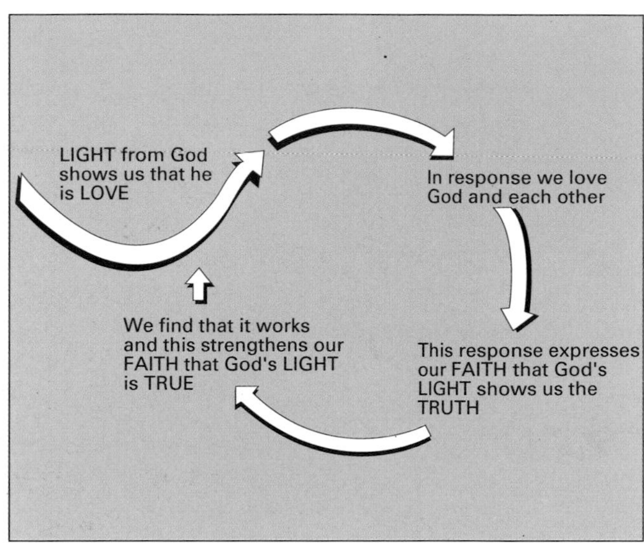

The circle of truth according to John.

● What is Christianity? (section 2)

Light is the key word here. God is light (1:5) and those who deny him live in darkness. But real faith is not mere orthodoxy. True faith takes sin seriously and receives forgiveness, then, in obedience to the 'light' of God's love, loves others as a sign of new life. Anyone who goes on breaking God's law cannot be a Christian (3:6-9).

But I can't stop sinning! John seems to threaten our confidence that we are and shall remain God's children. A question like this needs to take into account the whole teaching of the letter, and the rest of the New Testament. John knows that we go on sinning (1:8-9). But he also wants us to know that no-one filled with God's Spirit can continue deliberately in his or her old sinful way of life. There is power to overcome sin (3:9); there is forgiveness when we fail.

● Life in the family of God (section 3)

Love is again the sign of the reality of the life of faith. The key test as to whether or not a person is walking in the light is, according to John, the test of love. This love consists not in words but in actions: Jesus is our model (3:16).

● The certainty of faith (section 4)

Truth is the key word now. 'If anyone acknowledges that Jesus is the Son of God, God lives in him and he in God' (4:15). 'We know that we live in him and he in us because he has given us of his Spirit' (4:13). When the fact of God, who is love and light, living in us, is expressed in our loving others, the circle of love and truth is complete.

2 John

The themes of 1 John reappear in 2 John. Indeed, 2 John may be seen as a summary of 1 John. The longer letter seems to have been intended for a group of churches, whereas 2 John was intended for one church in particular. The 'chosen lady' (verse 1) to whom 2 John is written may be a term for a church – her 'children' (verse 13) then would be the members of that church.

Perhaps somewhat surprisingly in view of his emphasis on love, John urges the church to have nothing to do with the breakaway group – they are not even to be welcomed into

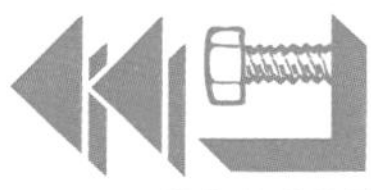

296-297

people's homes – for they are 'deceivers' (verse 7).

The important question to ask is if, in meeting regularly with such false teachers, we would appear to be condoning what they teach.

3 John

This letter is a private note concerned about one particular individual. Yet, as in Philemon, there is a local church 'listening in'. Tradition has suggested that this was the church at Pergamum.

Four people are mentioned in the letter: John the elder, who wrote it; Gaius, who received the letter, and was presumably a man of influence in the church; Diotrephes, whose actions were causing all the trouble; and Demetrius, who appears to have acted as postman.

Diotrephes is the centre of interest. Described as one who 'loves to be first' (verse 9) he was refusing to have anything to do with John and John's followers.

The letter of Jude

This letter is a passionate defence of Christianity against those who want to alter 'the faith that was once for all entrusted to the saints' (verse 3).

The letter of Jude: data

Author: The brother of James (1) and therefore of Jesus.

Date: Probably between AD 70-80. The letter was written to a church or group of churches familiar with the Old Testament.

Jude is 'a tract for the times'. The church was being threatened by a group who had 'secretly slipped in' (verse 4). Evidently their understanding of God's grace left them free to indulge in all kinds of sexual misbehaviour.

Jude responds to this threat in eighteen verses of denunciation. His language is extremely strong. These 'godless men' are marked out 'for the punishment of eternal fire' (verse 7).

Today we don't usually use that kind of language of people with whom we disagree! However, two things should be noted: first, Jude is not addressing his opponents directly, but rather warning the believers of the dangers of the new teaching. Secondly, strong language may indeed be called for when the gospel itself is at stake. Some Christians are wrongly dogmatic about minor issues, but there is also a danger of being far too open and uncritical of dangerous trends in the church.

Jude, however, is not all negative. He concludes by urging his readers to secure their own salvation by keeping themselves in the love of God (verse 21). God in his love may draw us to himself (verse 1), but, as the false teachers show, it is possible for us to turn our backs upon the love of God. God is able to keep us from falling (verse 24) as we work at our relationship with him.

Summary of the letter of Jude

1 Introduction (1-2)
2 False teachers denounced (3-16)
3 A pastoral word to the church (17-23)
4 Benediction (24-25)

3.7 A VISION OF JUDGMENT

Revelation

by Michael J. Wilcock

The book of Revelation is in a section of its own because it is quite different from the other books of the New Testament. It is a book of visions and is similar to parts of the book of Daniel and other books not in the Bible as we have it.

The theme of Revelation is the risen Christ. Much of the book stirs the imagination, intrigues, even terrifies, but the focus always returns to the Lamb of God, sacrificed, yet on the throne of history past and future.

The book of Revelation

Nobody knows the exact order in which the books of the Bible were written. But it is generally agreed that the one we find printed last was also produced last. Revelation stands out at the far end, not quite like any other part of the Bible. A random dip into it may turn up something unexpectedly familiar, or on the other hand something totally outlandish. But it grows on you. As you get to know more of Christ, and more of the rest of Scripture, so you are likely to find Revelation increasingly worth reading.

Revelation, even more than any other Bible book, must not be narrowed down to one particular place or time. The churches to which John was writing represent the Christian church as a whole. By AD 90 many churches around the Roman empire had been in existence for quite a long time.

Their fortunes varied. Some were struggling, some were flourishing.

Revelation: data

Author: Most people take it that the John who wrote Revelation was *the* John, Jesus' friend and one of the original twelve disciples. He is believed to have lived to a great age, and to have been leader or overseer of the church in Ephesus, chief city of the Roman province of Asia.

Date: Late in his life, perhaps in the early nineties of the first century, John was arrested and sent into exile on the island of Patmos (1:9). While he was there God gave him this series of remarkable visions. He wrote down a description of them, and sent it as a circular letter to several of the churches on the mainland (1:11).

360-362

Summary of the book of Revelation

1 Introduction (1:1-8)
2 Seven letters to the church (1:9 - 3:22)
3 Seven seals broken open (4:1 - 8:1)
4 Seven trumpets of warning blown (8:2 - 11:18)
5 God's view of human history (11:19 - 15:4)
6 Seven bowls of punishment poured out (15:5 - 16:21)
7 Babylon the prostitute (17:1 - 19:10)
8 The real conflict (19:11 - 21:8)
9 Jerusalem the bride (21:9 - 22:19)
10 Conclusion (22:20-21)

Some had lost their edge and were scarcely distinguishable from the pagan world around them. Some were facing fierce opposition. All were under attack in one way or another from the great Enemy of the people of God.

Because these spiritual facts are always true, Christians in all ages have found the book an eye-opener – a real 'revelation' – as to the way things actually are, behind the scenes. Revelation is a book for today; it is not just about the future.

● Introduction (section 1)

This tells us who the book is for and who it is from. It is officially addressed to the seven churches of Asia, but it is really an open letter intended for all God's people. So if we belong to him, then it is for us too.

● Seven letters to the church (section 2)

It is sometimes taken for granted

The seven churches

The places mentioned in Revelation are in an area of western Turkey referred to also in the book of Acts. Today, it is possible to include in the regular tourist trail the island of Patmos and the locations of the seven churches.

Ephesus was a large city and the centre of Roman administration in the province of Asia. It was famous for its temple to Artemis (Diana). Paul founded the church there (Acts 19).

Smyrna was a prosperous city and port, famed for its beauty and the fertility of the surrounding area. It is modern Izmir, a large city. The church was probably founded about the same time as that in Ephesus.

Pergamum was full of pagan temples, hence 'where Satan has his throne' (2:13). It was also the centre of emperor worship. The town of Bergama stands near the site today.

Thyatira was the smallest of the seven cities mentioned. It was an industrial centre with trade guilds operating a 'closed shop' employment policy. Lydia, the purple-dye merchant converted under Paul (Acts 16:14-15) came from this city.

Sardis was well known for its textile industry and for the shameless behaviour of its people. Christians appear to have been sucked back into their bad ways. Both city and church had become apathetic.

Philadelphia had a small population (in an area afflicted by earthquakes) but was on the threshold of a prosperous and fertile area. Alasehir now stands on its site.

Laodicea was a large commercial and administrative centre, wealthy, with clothing factories and a medical school. Water was piped to it from hot springs (near the present-day Denizli) and probably arrived lukewarm.

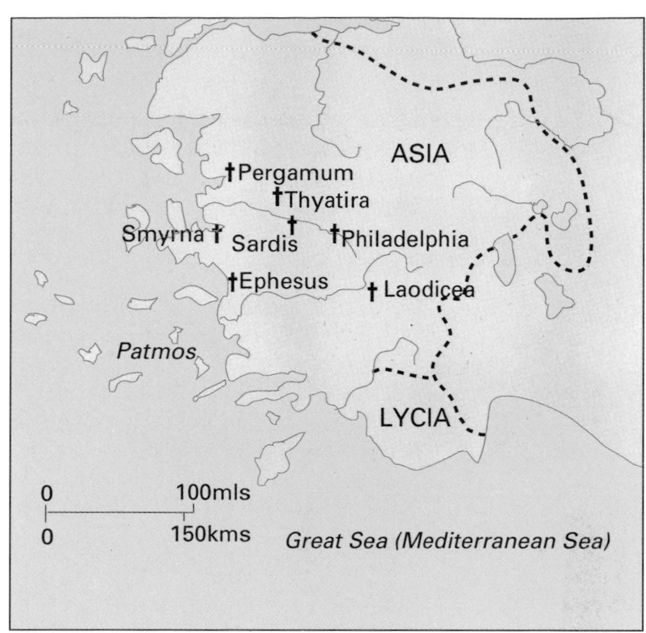

The 'seven churches' who received the letters.

that Revelation is all about the future. And certainly the last of its eight scenes is set entirely in the next world. But the first one is all about this world, and only as the drama progresses do we gradually see more of the next.

Jesus appears to John, and dictates to him a letter for each of the Asian churches. His messages are not only *to* them but also *about* them, and hold up a mirror to the Christian church of all times and places. He does say in each case what he has in store in the future life for those who win through to it. But the letters are really about how God's people cope (or fail to cope) with this life, its pressures and its challenges.

● Seven seals broken open (section 3)

What is the 'heaven' into which John now looks? There are bad things as well as good things in it. It might better be defined as 'the

282-284

sphere of spiritual reality', where things are seen for what they really are. Jesus, the Lamb, is at the centre of everything, and only he can break open the row of seals along the edge of the scroll of history so that it can be opened up and seen as a whole.

Here we begin to glimpse something of the future, because when the sixth seal is opened the end of the world is shown to us. For the moment, we hear nothing of what will follow that (8:1). But first, as the earlier seals have been opened, we have seen that the world is full of suffering, and that God's people are caught up in it – though the church will never actually be destroyed.

There is one image in this section that has caused much debate. The '144,000 Israelites' (7:4) are a symbolic group, standing for the numberless crowd from every nation which belongs to God for ever, in spite of all the trouble that comes their way in this world.

245

What will heaven be like for us? Revelation 7:15-17 gives us the first of several pictures in this book which are meant to increase our hope and to encourage us to stay faithful to God. Heaven will be filled by the caring presence of God. And we shall be satisfied in a way we never could be on earth.

●Seven trumpets of warning blown (section 4)

Again a series of disasters is seen to ravage the earth, this time described in more fearsome picture-language. But now God's people are not involved. It is 'the rest of mankind' (9:20) who are being warned of the consequences of saying no to God. They are the people who will not listen, whatever God's witnesses may say (11:10).

The warnings, like the sufferings of the previous scene, will not go on indefinitely. By the time the last trumpet sounds this world will have come to an end (11:15), with a judgment which rewards some but punishes others. It will then be clear who is really in control (11:16-17).

This in itself is a warning: God's patience with sinful, evil people will run out one day. So we know that evil cannot dominate the world for ever. But meanwhile we also know that the church has the task of calling people back to God while there is still time. Tragedies and natural disasters are in a general sense a 'warning' that the time is short. They make people think. So we need to be ready to speak up.

●God's view of human history (section 5)

This time the curtain rises on something rather different. John's visions in this scene are not numbered (though it is possible to count seven of them, from 13:1 to 15:2). And there is, at any rate to start with, a story-line. It concerns a woman, a dragon, and the woman's son. Other parts of the Bible help us to identify the characters and what happens to them. In brief, it is the history of mankind, told in terms of the church, the devil, and the Lord Jesus.

The dragon is the serpent of Genesis 3, the devil of 1 John 3:8, the Satan of Mark 1:13, and the deceiver of John 8:44. His angels appear in Matthew 25:41, and his defeat on the 'heavenly' level (the level of spiritual reality) takes place in the time of Jesus' earthly life, Luke 10:18.

● Seven bowls of punishment poured out (section 6)

Another procession of angels now comes on the scene, emerging from the 'temple', that is, from the place where mankind is confronted by God. John sees not only God's glory and power, but also his anger and his indestructible life (15:7-8). He will outface and outlast all who oppose him. The trumpets warned his enemies, but the time for warning and repentance is now past, and from the angels' bowls punishment is poured out. If you compare this section with the trumpet warnings of section 4 you will see that they run parallel. But the first destruction was partial; this one is total.

So here is yet another picture of what is happening in history, this time from the point of view of how God finally deals with unrepentant wickedness. Bowl 6 brings the world to an end, with the last battle and the coming of Christ (16:15-16). With bowl 7, the divine punishment 'is done', and all is over.

● Babylon the prostitute (section 7)

This scene looks as though it ought to be easier to understand. Early on, John is shown a woman, a prostitute, and is told by an angel that she represents a city, Babylon. The angel tells him the meaning of several other items in the vision as well.

But these explanations are not so helpful as they may seem. The prostitute is sitting on a beast which has seven heads and ten horns , and the heads and horns stand for kings – but we are not told which kings. On the other hand, the prostitute herself stands for a city, and *we are* told which city. To think we need more information about the kings than about the city is to get things the wrong way round. As always, questions which other parts of the Bible shed light on are more important than questions which need explanations from outside the Bible. And it is about Babylon, not about the kings, that other parts of the Bible have a lot to say.

For Christians the term 'world' has a special meaning besides the ordinary one. It means everything in this life which is organized as if God didn't matter. This whole 'world system' is what Babylon the prostitute represents.

You cannot miss two things about it in these chapters. It is hugely wealthy, powerful, and glamorous. It is also rotten to the core, hateful to God, and doomed to destruction. The end of the world – the end of *this* 'world' – is by now looming very large in John's visions.

222

● The real conflict (section 8)

First in this section John is shown a spectacular battle scene, to help him understand the conflict between good and evil which goes on all through history. Other doom-laden pictures of conflict and judgment follow.

The rider in chapter 19 has three names. All of them can be found elsewhere, and those other passages make it plain that the rider is Jesus.

'The Word' (19:13) is what Jesus is called in the opening verses of both John's gospel and his first letter. 'Faithful and True' (19 :11) is a title of the one who dictates the letters to the churches in scene one of Revelation (3:14), and he must be Jesus, to go by the descriptions in 1:13, 18 and 2:18. 'King of kings and Lord of lords' (19:16) has already appeared in 17:14, where it describes the Lamb, and that in turn means Jesus (5:6-13; John 1:29).

But then comes a really difficult vision (20:1-3). It seems as though Satan's defeat is followed by a thousand-year period during which Satan is bound, and after that comes one last great rebellion before the day of judgment. What does chapter 20 mean?

Again, the Bible itself must be looked to for an explanation. Jesus came into the world to bring light and liberty to the nations (Luke 2:32; 4:18), and it was then, according to Mark 3:27, that Satan was bound. He still has power to attack God's people, but it is strictly limited. On this showing, 20:1-3 would be describing not what will happen after the great battle of chapter 19, but what did happen back at the time of Christ's first coming. The thousand years, a symbol for the whole of Christian history, would have begun then, and would end with what seems to be a brief upsurge of evil just before Christ's second coming.

214

●Jerusalem the bride (section 9)

The first scene of the book was set entirely in this world. This last one is set entirely in the next world. By the time it opens, 'the old order of things has passed away' (21:4). No-one has ever come back from heaven to describe it for us, but John's visions help us to understand it in picture form.

56

In Babylon there was nothing good, in Jerusalem there is nothing bad. The prostitute will perish for ever, the bride will live for ever. The whole system of things which tries to do without God, and everyone who belongs to it, is doomed; the church, the people of God, who belong to him through Christ, are destined for eternal glory.

We may still scratch our heads over the meanings, but it takes only a little imagination to find this scene overwhelmingly splendid.

●Conclusion (section 10)

The great book comes to an end, and with it the whole Bible, with one last picture of Jesus himself. He speaks to us, he promises to return, he gives us his grace – all his goodness and blessing.

Prostitute and bride in Revelation

The picture of 'Babylon' and 'Jerusalem' as two women, a prostitute and a bride, helps us to grasp what it really means for Christians to be God's people (chapters 17,21).

In the Bible the relationship between the Lord and his people is often described as a marriage. He is the husband, they are the wife. Isaiah 54, Jeremiah 3, Ezekiel 16, and Hosea 2, for example, all speak in this way, and so too does the New Testament (see Mark 2:19, John 3:29, and especially Ephesians 5:25-27).

The Old Testament prophets often show us the dark side of the picture, which is Israel's unfaithfulness to her husband. The prostitute here in Revelation represents the world of people who have no commitment at all to God, and habitually sell themselves to other 'lovers' – people or systems, forces or philosophies – which they think will give them what they want. The bride, the church, by contrast is totally and permanently committed to Christ and to living in his way, as he is committed to her.

PART 4 PUTTING IT ALL TOGETHER

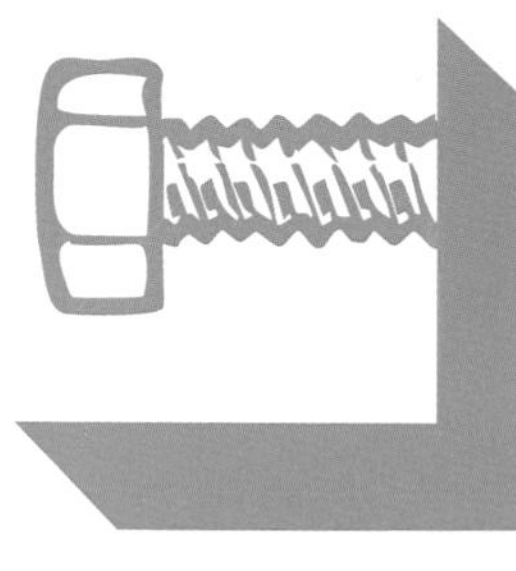

Investigating the Bible's claim to guide our way of life; defining the Bible's message and how to make moral choices.

The Good News
Bible
Guide

A VERY SPECIAL BOOK

by Peter Hicks

In many places the Bible claims itself to be a book different from all other books; not just better but in a class by itself, presenting the mind of God to the world. In this section we investigate those claims.

Best-seller

Nothing in life is as important as finding God and his will for us. Men and women through the ages have searched for God and his truth. Many have had rich experiences and gained deep insights. Some of these have been handed on in religious rituals or practices. Much has been preserved in writing: collections of the sayings of the wise and the holy, records of people's experiences of God and his ways, individuals' thoughts and ideas about God. Among them is much that is inspiring and good.

But it is the Christian's conviction that not even the finest of these writings reaches anywhere near the level of the Bible. Despite its age, and despite all the attacks that have been made on it, the Bible is still read more than any other book in the world. Well over 100 million new copies of the Bible or parts of the Bible are being produced every year; if we include selections of passages from the Bible the figure is probably in excess of 1,000 million.

Other books have been popular in their day. John Bunyan's *The Pilgrim's Progress*, for example, was for many years second only to the Bible in popularity in the English-speaking world. But it seems very dated and hardly relevant today. But the Bible remains relevant, and its effectiveness does not seem to diminish.

● One year's Bible production
The United Bible Societies are one of the largest producers and distributors of the Bible. Perhaps one third of the world's total Bible production comes from them. Their distribution figures for 1988 are listed below.

What is it that makes the Bible so special? Why should an apparently random collection of accounts of selected events in the Middle East thousands of years ago be so popular and meaningful today?

One answer is, of course, the simple fact that it is relevant. It is much more than a collection of ancient documents. It is a way to live and a way to find God. We read it and find

Bible distribution throughout the world (source, Bible Society, Swindon, with permission).

1988 World Scripture Distribution By The United Bible Societies

	Africa	Americas	Asia Pacific	Europe	Total
Bibles	2,774,753	5,050,073	3,894,851	2,371,762	14,091,439
New Testaments	1,581,098	3,642,454	6,538,278	1,147,607	12,909,437
Portions	4,514,022	8,418,745	21,940,097	2,651,887	37,524,751
New Reader Portions	1,629,204	3,320,665	10,477,424	120,398	15,547,771
Selections	6,498,933	321,428,255	235,912,625	5,945,876	569,785,689
New Reader Selections	589,837	20,076,272	22,110,959	118,770	42,895,838
Total	17,587,927	361,936,464	300,874,234	12,356,300	692,754,925

that what it says to us is true. It works. Its promises are fulfilled. It shows us God and we meet him. It tells us how to live and we find real life. It challenges, teaches, corrects and makes us the people we know we ought to be.

But we can still ask 'How does it do all these things?' And the answer to that is that this book, uniquely, is God's book. In it, in a very special way, God speaks to us.

The Bible is inspired

● God speaks to us

One of the great central claims of Christianity is that God takes the initiative. In his dealings with us he doesn't wait for us to take the first step, so that he can then respond. He moves first.

So, for example, he loved us before we started to love him (1 John 4:10). When we were lost and helpless, unable to do anything to save ourselves, he came in Christ to open up the way of forgiveness and salvation through the cross (Romans 5:8). Even though we may think that in the area of searching for and finding God we take the first steps, many have found that all the time we were searching for God, he, like the good shepherd, was searching for us.

The same principle applies when we are trying to discover truth about God and his will for our lives. Because God is so great and so holy, all our ideas and thoughts about him seem to be hopelessly inadequate. Our minds are limited to the familiar finite things around us. But God is infinite, far beyond our greatest thoughts and deepest understanding. If we were left to ourselves to discover God and his truth we would never make it. At best we could offer only some limited and tentative ideas, none of which could ever be sure enough to build our lives on. So, instead of leaving us groping, God has taken the initiative. He has spoken. He has revealed himself and his truth to us.

● Too great for words?

Some people find it hard to accept that God can reveal himself and communicate his truth to us in ways that we can understand. They feel that an infinite God is too great to limit himself to words or to any means of communication that human beings can grasp. But this is a wrong understanding of God's greatness. If he is so great, then he is able to do things that might seem impossible to us, including communicating in a way that we can grasp. I may not understand how he limited himself in order to reveal himself to us in Jesus Christ. Nor do I understand how he can express something of his eternal truth in human words. But I believe that his power and wisdom are great enough to enable him to do these things. And I also believe that his love for us is so strong that he has in fact done the 'impossible' and has come to us in Jesus and spoken to us in the Bible.

270-272

Of course it is quite impossible for our human finite minds to grasp all the truth of God. The full measure of his greatness, glory, holiness, beauty and love is far beyond anything we can comprehend. But the fact that we cannot know or understand everything about God does not mean that we can know or understand nothing. None of us, for example, will ever fully comprehend

the greatness of God's love. But we can all grasp something of the truth that he loves us. We do not need to understand all the technicalities of how a computer works in order to read off the correct answer to a calculation. Similarly, though there is much about God we cannot understand, that does not prevent him conveying some truth about himself to us. This we believe he has done.

● God revealed

God's greatest revelation of himself to us is in the life and ministry and teaching of Jesus Christ. But it is not his only one. He loves us so much and so wants us to know him that he gives us even more than his revelation two thousand years ago in Christ. He comes directly to us through the Holy Spirit. Down through the ages he has met with men and women personally: with Moses at the burning bush, or with others in different ways, warming their hearts with his love and challenging them with his holiness.

And a third way he has revealed himself and his truth to us is in the Bible.

I suppose that, if we were given the choice, most of us would opt for a 'burning bush' experience of God or, even better, we would choose to have lived in Palestine at the time of Jesus, rather than depending on a book for our revelation of God. The direct encounter with God or with God in Jesus seems so much more real and exciting.

But, on reflection, we may well come to feel that having the Bible is not too bad a bargain after all. It is packed with teaching about God and examples of his ways with men and women. It contains insights and truths that would have blown the mind of Moses and perhaps even of those whose knowledge and understanding of Jesus was limited to his earthly life and ministry. It gives not only descriptions of events and God's actions in history; it also supplies explanations of them in the form of theological reflection and interpretation. For example, the four gospels give us accounts of Jesus being crucified. As we read them we can in imagination share with the disciples the events of those dark hours. But the Bible does not stop with just the description. A few pages on, in Romans, we find a closely argued explanation of what the cross really means, and of how an event on a spring Friday in Palestine can transform our relationship with the living God.

We could add that having God's revelation to us in the Bible does not exclude 'burning bush' type experiences or the experience of meeting directly with Jesus in these days. God still can and does reveal himself directly to us. In fact the Bible has a special role to play in such revelations, as we shall see later.

96

The Bible

There are at least three ways in which we can think of the Bible as God revealing himself and his truth to us.

A record of revelation

It is, firstly, a record of revelation. It is a collection of accounts of God revealing himself and his word to people through the centuries. Supremely it records in detail his greatest revelation to us, that is in Jesus Christ.

A means of revelation

Secondly, the Bible is, very often, a means of revelation. God speaks to us today through his Holy Spirit. Sometimes this is direct, through the prompting of our thoughts or a message which we recognize is from the Spirit. But very often the Spirit uses the Scriptures to speak his message to us. As we read a Bible passage or hear it being taught during a sermon, the Holy Spirit takes hold of the written word and makes it the living word of God to our hearts. Instead of being God's revelation in a general sense it becomes specific to us; our hearts 'burn within us' (Luke 24:32); we know that God has used the words of the Bible as a means of his very special revelation to us.

A message of revelation

Thirdly, in addition to being a record of past revelations and a means God's Spirit uses to reveal God to us today, the Bible is itself a message of revelation. In its entirety it is a revelation from God to the world. In his wisdom and love God has chosen to give us this rich and complex collection of history and theology, of poetry and prophecy, of stories of Jesus and personal letters, as a message from him to all who will read or hear it. Though on occasion he may speak to us through other books, in this book supremely God is speaking. As Paul put it when he was writing about the Old Testament writings, 'all Scripture is God-breathed' or inspired by God in a unique way (2 Timothy 3:16).

● A God-inspired book

All the great Christian doctrines seem to be under fire from people outside and inside the church of Jesus Christ in these days. The doctrine of the inspiration of the Bible is no exception. There is no shortage of writers who deny that the Bible is inspired by God in any special sense; for them it is inspired only in the way that Shakespeare or Tolkien can be said to be inspired. But the Bible's claim for itself, on which the teaching of the Christian church has been based through the centuries, is much stronger.

Besides his statement that all the Old Testament Scriptures were God-breathed, Paul taught that they were in fact 'the very words of God' (Romans 3:2). In the same way the Christians of the early church were able to say that the words of one of the Psalms were actually God speaking by the Holy Spirit through the mouth of David (Acts 4:25).

136-140

● The authority of Jesus and the apostles

But we have an even greater authority than Paul or the early Christians for the claim that the Old Testament Scriptures are inspired by God, and that is the Lord Jesus himself. Though from time to time he had scathing comments to make about the way some of his contemporaries interpreted the Old Testament and managed to 'nullify the word of God' by the addition of their own traditions (Mark 7:13), his whole ministry was based on the highest regard for the Old Testament as God's revelation of his truth and purposes. Whether answering the temptations of the devil, or teaching his disciples, or engaged in controversy with the Jewish leaders, he continually referred to the Scriptures as the authoritative truth of God. (See, for example, Matthew 4:4; Luke 24:27, 45-47; and Matthew 22:43-46.) None of them was to be disregarded, not even 'the smallest letter' (Matthew 5:18); 'the Scripture cannot be broken' (John 10:35), it 'must be fulfilled' (Mark 14:49). All his life was lived under the conviction that the Old Testament was the word of God; and he taught that his followers should accept it as such too.

Besides teaching that the Old Testament Scriptures were inspired by God, Jesus claimed God's authority for his own words (John 14:24), and commissioned his disciples to continue his ministry and teaching (John 20:21-23; Matthew 28:18-20). Throughout the New Testament the apostles were aware that the message they proclaimed and the teaching they gave was not theirs, but God's. They could not be silent because they had to 'obey God' (Acts 5:29); the message had been 'revealed by the Spirit to God's holy apostles and prophets' (Ephesians 3:5); Paul received his message not from any man, but 'by revelation from Jesus Christ' (Galatians 1:12); the book of Revelation is explicitly called God-given (Revelation 1:1). Though there is only one place where the New Testament writings are placed specifically on the same level as the God-inspired Old Testament Scriptures (2 Peter 3:16), the New Testament writers clearly believed that what they were writing was God-given truth. And the generations of believers who collected and put together the twenty-seven books that make up the New Testament chose just those books because in them they recognized the authentic voice of God.

228

So the claim of the Bible itself, and the view of the church through the centuries, is that the Bible is in a very special sense a message of revelation inspired by God. He wanted the world to have such a message so that we should have access to the truth about himself. So he inspired the Bible writers to receive and pass on that message.

In itself this concept of God inspiring the writing of the Bible is not difficult to appreciate. God is a God who communicates. He has made mankind in his own image with the ability to receive communications from him. His greatest communication is in a person, Jesus Christ. But most human communication is in words. My wife can communicate with me by a squeeze of the hand or a look in her eye. But if she wishes to tell me that the car has a flat tyre or what sort of a day she has had she finds it easier to use words. So it is not surprising that God has chosen to communicate with us, not just in a person, but in spoken and written words.

●How did he do it?

We find it hard to understand how the infinite God came to this world in a human body and lived among us. In a similar way it is not easy to understand how God put his words into the minds of the Bible writers so that the God-breathed message was recorded accurately in the pages of the Bible.

Some Bible authors clearly did feel that the words they were speaking

were directly God-given.

But equally, in other parts of the Bible, the writers seem to have been a lot less conscious of being inspired. Those writing the narrative and history accounts in the Bible, in particular, may well not have been aware that God was directing their writing or speaking in any way through them, though that, of course, does not mean that he was not doing so!

One thing that recent scholarly study of the Bible has made clear is that, whatever means God used to inspire the writers, he did not bypass their minds or their personalities. John's gospel, for instance, is very different from Luke's; that is because he was a very different person from Luke. Each chose his material, arranged it, told the stories, outlined the teaching and added his comments in his own individual way.

Examples of God speaking directly to the authors

- At the giving of the Ten Commandments at Mount Sinai we are told 'God spoke all these words' (Exodus 20:1).
- When God called Ezekiel to be a prophet, he asked him to eat symbolically a scroll containing God's words. God then commanded him, 'Son of man, listen carefully and take to heart all the words I speak to you. Go now to your countrymen in exile and speak to them. Say to them, "This is what the Sovereign LORD says"' (see Ezekiel 2:1 - 3:11).
- Paul was conscious that the Holy Spirit at times spoke directly to him the message he had to pass on. 'We speak of God's secret wisdom ... not in words taught us by human wisdom but in words taught by the Spirit, expressing spiritual truths in spiritual words' (1 Corinthians 2:6-16).
- The last book in the Bible is specifically called a God-given 'revelation' (Revelation 1:1). Each of the letters to the seven churches starts with a phrase that claims that the messages are the very words of Jesus (Revelation 2:1, 8, 12, 18; 3:1, 7, 14).

97-98

160-162

178-179

228-232

It is the same with all the Bible writers. They collected their material, decided what to put in or leave out, chose how to tell their stories and so on. No doubt they were all godly people; being aware that they were writing about God's dealings with mankind they may well have prayed that God would direct them in their work. But they still had to do the work, and the mark of their personalities is stamped on the result.

The concept of inspiration, then, does not mean that God somehow

68-69

202-203

overwhelmed the human writers so that they had no effective part in the writing of the Bible. Doubtless he could have done this, but the evidence points the other way. It would seem that both the human writers and God played vital roles in the writing of the Scriptures. Paul's letters are Paul's letters; sometimes it cost him toil and tears to get on to paper what was in his heart. Jeremiah's prophecy is distinctively Jeremiah's. Matthew used and assembled his material in a way that flowed from his personality and particularly suited the mentality of the first-century Jews for whom he was writing.

But at the same time God was speaking through Paul, Jeremiah and Matthew. They were men he had specifically chosen to be his apostle or prophet or gospel writer. Whether they were aware of it or not, God was expressing his truth through their personalities, ideas and words. And God's truth is so rich that it can be expressed in many ways through different people and still be God's truth.

Those of us who preach put a lot of ourselves into our preaching; we spend hours in study and preparation; our presentation reflects our personalities; in many senses our sermons are *our* sermons. But at the same time it is our greatest desire that God should so direct and use our preaching that, despite our personal weaknesses, the voice of God will speak to our hearers. It doesn't always work out that way, but sometimes it does. Not all the words Jeremiah ever spoke or all the letters Paul ever wrote were inspired by God; but some were. And these are what have been collected into the Bible.

● The richness of the Bible

Another feature that recent study of the Bible has highlighted is that though, for convenience, we refer to the authors of the Bible as writers, large portions of it were not originally composed as written documents. In these cases there was no simple process of writing. The material was originally spoken. Collections of stories or sayings of the prophets or the teaching of Jesus would have been learnt by heart and handed on by word of mouth. This does not mean that they would have become distorted as they were passed on. In an age when few could read, people's ability to remember large sections of material learnt by heart was far more developed than ours is today. We depend on written records and memory banks; they had no such resources. Additionally, most of them would have been aware that they were dealing with important and holy things, and so they would have been especially careful not to let mistakes creep in.

After a time the material came to be written down. In many cases the writers doubtless had more material available to them than they could use. John, for instance, tells us that there would simply not be enough room for all the books if anyone were to try to record all the deeds of Jesus (John 21:25). But when the final writers came to select, arrange and put together the material others had passed on to them, they did it in such a way that God was able to speak his word and his truth through them.

It is not surprising, then, that we have such rich variety in the Bible. All the writers were different. They were individuals in their own right.

They were speaking or writing for different audiences. They used a wide variety of literary techniques. In many cases they selected from a rich store of handed-down material. And God, who made us all different and who loves individuality, gladly took them all and used them to communicate his message of revelation.

The rich mixture

God's willingness to use such a wide variety of Bible writers is similar to his willingness to use a wide variety of people in a local church. Every church is made up of a rich mixture of people, with different personalities and different gifts. But the Holy Spirit takes and binds us together in one fellowship and uses us all to achieve his purposes.

Just as the church is a very human collection of people, so the Bible is a very human book. But the humanness of the church or the Bible by no means excludes the power and purposes of God. The fact that the local church is made up of very diverse and very human people does not mean that God cannot work through it to bring about his purposes on earth. The church only fails to be God's agent if we refuse to hear God's voice and obey his directions. The Bible writers were godly people, willing to let God guide and direct their work so that others might have a true and reliable record of God's dealings with mankind. Thus they were open to being 'carried along by the Holy Spirit' (2 Peter 1:21). So God was able to use their work to express his truth.

What about the difficulties?

The Bible then is God speaking. It is his revelation in at least three ways: a record of his revelations in the past, a means by which he speaks to our hearts now, and an enduring message from God to the world. All this means that it is of incredible value and importance. But before we can go any further we must look at an issue that has kept many Bible scholars busy for a very long time.

We have seen that the Bible is both a human book and God's book. It is God-inspired, not just in a vague way but in a very specific way. God ensured that his words and his truth were conveyed by the Bible writers as they wrote their own thoughts and words. It would seem reasonable to assume that if God writes a book, even if he allows human writers to share in the task, he would write it well. In particular he would make sure it is entirely trustworthy, that it contains no untruths or mistakes.

'The local church is made up of very diverse and very human people.'

36

72

But, as we know only too well, it is not at all difficult to find passages in the Bible that seem to be untrue or mistaken. The story of the creation of the world in six days, for instance, seems to be contradicted by the findings of science. Even worse, there are some parts of the Bible which appear to contradict other parts. Matthew, Mark and Luke, for example, indicate that Jesus' last meal with his disciples on the day before Good Friday was a Passover meal; but John appears to say that the Passover meal was not until the next day. The conclusion seems to be that either he or they have made a mistake.

Is the latest view always right?

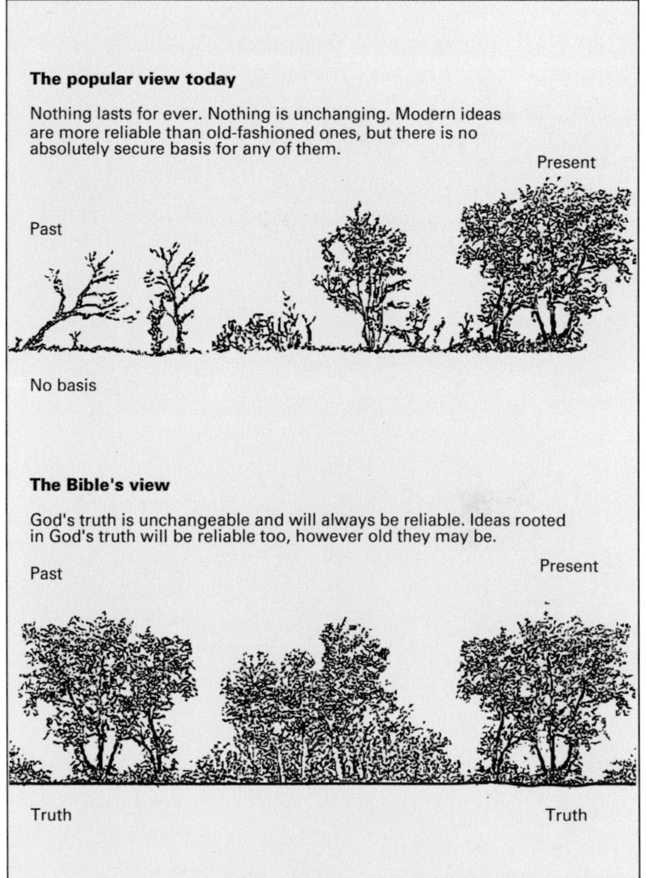

● Approach with care

What has gone wrong? Do we have to conclude, as some do, that the Bible is riddled with errors and therefore cannot be inspired? I don't think so. But the presence of problems and difficulties in the Bible means that we have to take a very careful look at the way we approach it.

● Not the *New Scientist*

We have to remember, for example, that the Bible was composed in a 'prescientific' age. This does not mean that the people were unintelligent or gullible. The earliest hearers of Genesis 1 would have spotted the 'discrepancy' between the 'six days' and the sun not being created until the fourth day just as easily as we do.

What it does mean is that we are not to press the language of the Bible for strict twentieth-century scientific precision as if it were part of the *New Scientist*. Genesis 1 is a glorious celebration of the fact that all things are made by God, not a 'scientific' description of how he did it.

There is a further point worth bearing in mind here. All too often we hear people dismissing the world view of the Bible writers as outdated and naive. An example commonly cited is their belief in a universe populated with spiritual forces, some good and some evil, which affect events in the world, a belief which modern science rejects. The assumption is, of course, that our contemporary view is advanced and correct; since it disagrees with the view of the Bible writers they must necessarily be wrong. But in fact it is highly unlikely that our 'advanced' world view is correct. Almost certainly, if the world lasts that long, in a hundred years or so people will

look back on the ideas of our generation and laugh at their naivety and mistakes. Though we may have made many wonderful discoveries and learnt a lot of things the Bible writers did not know, in no way can we claim to have found the final correct view of the world and everything that is in it, and thus to have established that their view was wrong. The most we can say is that the Bible writers viewed the world differently from the way most people at present view it. We cannot say that our present concepts prove that they were mistaken.

●A special approach to history

Another area where the minds of the Bible writers and their original readers functioned very differently from ours is that of history. It is tempting for us to approach the historical accounts in the Bible as though they were written according to the late twentieth-century rules of historical scholarship and accuracy. When we start to study them, however, we find this is not the case. The Bible writers are often very selective in the material they include. In the Old Testament, for example, a historically important king may be dismissed in a few words, while someone we might feel is unimportant gets lots of attention. The four gospels, by modern standards, are very poor histories or biographies of Jesus. Large sections of his life and even of his ministry are ignored; we have no description of his physical appearance; an incredibly disproportionate amount of space is devoted to the last week of his life; and so on. Further, the Bible writers felt quite at liberty to rearrange the order of their material if it helped to get across the points they wished to make.

In general, they were far more interested in providing instruction about God's ways with men and women than in writing a 'modern' history of Israel or even a life of Christ. John, for example, clearly states that his gospel, so far from being an academic historical record, is written so that we may be brought face to face with Christ and find faith and eternal life in him (John 20:31).

So we must be careful not to impose our contemporary rules for scientific or historical truth on the Bible. It was not written according to twentieth-century standards of scientific or historical precision. Rather we must seek to understand what it is saying according to its own standards. Sometimes this is hard; we are very conditioned by our own age and find it difficult to change gear in our thinking to follow the thought of another age. But if we are able to do so we will see our way through many of the difficulties we find in the Bible. We will appreciate, for instance, that strict chronological precision in the recording of events was not important or necessary to many of the Bible writers; so the gospel writers can record events in a different order or even telescope two or more events into one. None of this detracts from the truth of what they are saying.

31

340

Nor indeed need it worry us, for example, that Jesus is recorded as saying that mustard is the smallest of seeds (Mark 4.31), or that the New Testament writers often fail to quote the Hebrew Old Testament with strict accuracy, preferring to use the Greek version, or even a paraphrase of their own. Jesus' hearers and the gospel writers knew far more about the sizes of seeds than most of us do; they were able to accept the truth of what he was saying without being too fussy about seed sizes. In the same way, though all the New Testament writers firmly believed that every word of the Old Testament was God-given, they could happily use general or paraphrased quotations of Old Testament passages provided they conveyed the required truth.

●Facing the contradictions

Having said this, not all the difficulties in the Bible can be solved in this way. There still seem to be discrepancies and apparent errors of fact. For instance, we are all familiar with the story of David killing Goliath (1 Samuel 17). But 2 Samuel 21:19 seems to say that Goliath was killed by Elhanan. Scholars who accept the full inspiration and trustworthiness of the Bible have done much to solve many of these problems. Sometimes a mistake may have slipped into the text of the Bible as it was copied out by hand and passed on through the centuries. So, for example, the problem over Goliath may be solved by assuming that the person who was killed in 2 Samuel 21:19 was Goliath's brother; somehow the words 'brother of' have been lost; indeed, this explanation is borne out by 1 Chronicles 20:5 which states that the person killed by Elhanan was Lahmi the brother of Goliath.

181

In other cases further research casts light on the problem. So the issue of the date of the crucifixion in relationship to the Passover may be solved by evidence we have gained from the Dead Sea Scrolls that Pharisees and Sadducees followed different systems of fixing dates for feasts, with the result that both Thursday and Friday of that week were days when the Passover lamb was sacrificed. So the seeming contradiction between John and the other gospel writers disappears.

True, not all problems have been finally solved yet. But enough progress has been made to give us hope that, even if we are not yet able to find it, each problem does have a solution.

> **Still thriving despite everything**
>
> Beyond doubt one of the most remarkable things about the Bible is the way it has stood up to so much destructive criticism and still survives and thrives. No other book has been so criticized and dissected. No other book would have stood up to the treatment the Bible has been given.

●Why so many attacks on the Bible?

An important point to bear in mind is that most of the attacks against the trustworthiness of the Bible have come from those who are unable to believe in the supernatural, or who approach the Bible on the basis of the teaching of eighteenth- and nineteenth-century philosophers and theologians who specifically denied the possibility of God intervening in any way in human affairs. Starting with this assumption, such people necessarily reject the Bible's claim to be inspired by God. All accounts of miracles or acts of God in the world have to be explained away. Even fulfilled prophecy has to be rejected; if a prophecy turns out to be true, it has to be written off as a coincidence, or a later 'after the event' invention. God didn't meet Moses at the burning bush, nor did he make a way through the Red Sea, or speak through the prophets,

or come to us in Jesus. The Bible is just a human book full of mistakes and unreliable stories.

'Myth'

Since they assume that God cannot intervene in the world or in human affairs, some scholars conclude that we must treat as factually untrue stories of God speaking to men, bringing his people out of Egypt, raising Jesus from the dead, and so on. However, they say, we do not have to reject them totally; even if they are factually false we can still learn religious truths from them. So the exodus is a picture of the liberation we experience when we find God, and the 'myth' of the resurrection of Jesus expresses the wonder of our new life in God.

It is certainly true that a story can have a religious meaning even if it is not factually true itself. The stories of the Prodigal Son and the Good Samaritan are examples.

But in most cases the Bible writers claim factual truth as well as religious truth for their writings. For them the events they described are all the more meaningful in every sense because they really happened. God reached into people's lives in mercy and power. Jesus physically rose from the dead. The historical fact of the resurrection makes the religious truth of God's new life in us all the more sure and meaningful. The significance of Christianity is not something limited to the religious sphere; it is inseparably interwoven into every part of life – events, history, facts, experiences, the lot.

In fairness to the Bible writers we should be willing to lay aside any prejudice we may have against the idea that God can intervene in the world, and approach their claims and message with an open mind.

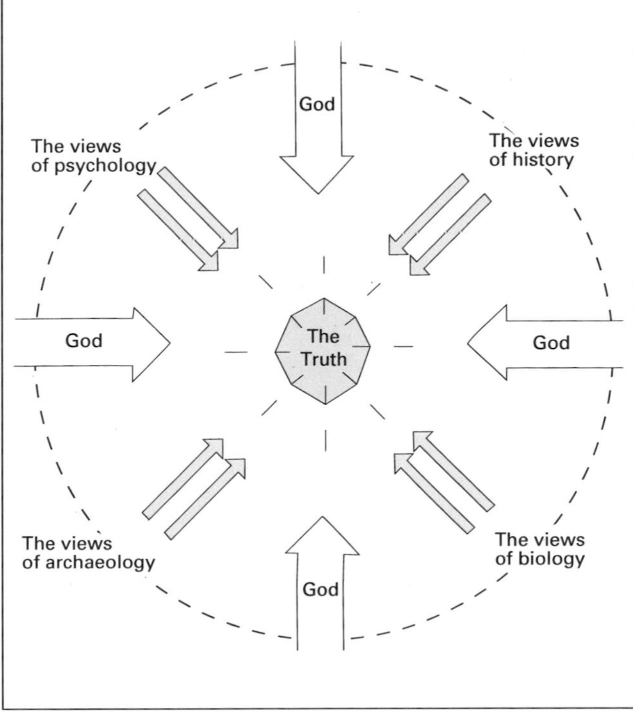

All truth is God's truth, but we can discover only a part of it. Only God has the complete view.

But we do not have to accept the basic beliefs of these critics of the Bible. Indeed, surely, if we are Christians at all, we must be committed to the belief that God does do things in the world and intervenes in human affairs, since we believe he has created us and we have experienced him coming to us in Jesus Christ. If this is so, then there is no limit to what he can do. Miracles and fulfilled prophecies in the Bible do not have to be 'explained away'. God is big enough for them. And difficulties that seem insurmountable for the sceptic can be seen in their true perspective. The old chestnut about whether or not it is possible for Jonah to have lived inside the 'whale' is really rather unimportant. The account tells us that the fish was a special provision by God to save Jonah (Jonah 1:17). The supply of a special fish is quite

272-273

170

within God's capabilities. We need spend no time speculating on how he did it; the Bible writer didn't think it important enough to tell us. We can go straight on to the real message of the book of Jonah: God's concern for the pagan city of Nineveh. The message *is* the vital thing but we do not need to deny the truth of the text in order to hear it!

We can accept the basic belief that God is able to intervene in human affairs and do supernatural things like giving us trustworthy revelations of himself in Jesus and the Bible without being in any way anti-intellectual. Indeed we might say that if we think of God at all we must think of him as able to do supernatural things. It is those who deny that God can do miracles or reveal his truth to us that are being intellectually dishonest in their use of the word 'God'.

●Don't leave your mind behind

So we are not being anti-intellectual or obscurantist in claiming that the Bible is trustworthy and true in all that it teaches us. It is God's book. It is God-inspired. It is stamped with God's dependability. And God has given us minds to use as we read and study it so that we can hear what he is truly saying to us in it. The study of the Bible is not something for the intellectually lazy or for those who come with minds closed to the possibilities of what God can or cannot say or do. Many a time it will challenge and stretch our minds, or humble our so-called wisdom. It is for us to learn to read it as it asks to be read, and to submit ourselves to its truth.

A 'march for Jesus' declares that Jesus is Lord.

The Bible carries authority

●The greatest thing of all

The Bible speaks to more of us than just our intellect. God has made us whole people with wills and hearts as well as minds. It is to every part of us that the Bible speaks.

So we come back to the greatest thing of all about the Bible. Though, on its own terms, it is dependable and trustworthy in all that it teaches, this book was not written to satisfy our curiosity about historical or scientific data. It was written so that we might hear the voice of God and let him change our lives. No approach to the Bible that stops short of this is adequate. We may debate the details and spend time puzzling over the problem passages. But if that is all we do we are no better than the Pharisees who 'diligently studied the Scriptures' but refused to accept Jesus (John 5: 39-40).

●Jesus is Lord

One of the great declarations of the New Testament era which has become prominent again in our days is 'Jesus is Lord'. It is a magnificent phrase, embracing the universal and the personal and much in between.

It declares the cosmic truth of Christ's victory over all powers of evil won on the cross and soon to be experienced by all creation. It also echoes the declaration of every believing individual: Jesus is my lord, lord of my life, my heart, my will, my mind, my ambitions, my possessions, my all. Jesus is Lord. He is the 'Mighty God', the Lord of all, 'Lord of lords and King of kings'. Whatever issues of authority arise in the Christian life or in the church, it

is at this point we must begin: 'all authority in heaven and on earth' is his (Matthew 28.18).

Christians declare that Jesus is Lord. The desire of every Christian must be to translate that declaration into action. He must be lord of each part of our lives. He must be lord of our churches and our Christian service in our communities. And it is our prayer that his lordship should be acknowledged and experienced throughout the earth, that his kingdom should come and his will be done.

●Hearing God's voice

For all this to happen we need to know and grasp clearly what is his will for our lives, our churches, our communities and our world. How are we to express his lordship? How does he want us to live? What is he saying to us, to the church and to the world in this generation?

To that question there is a bewildering range of answers. Some tell us that we hear God's voice by listening to the voices of the world. God speaks to us in the cry of the oppressed, the face of the hungry child, the lostness of today's city dwellers. But the voices of the world shout many different messages. The oppressed cry for violent revolution. Is that the voice of God?

We listen to learned theologians on our television screens or walk into a Christian bookshop and again we are confronted with a confusing range of views. There are those who deny that Jesus is God or that he rose from the dead. Others argue that a practising Christian can also be a practising homosexual. One denomination welcomes women into positions of leadership; another refuses to do so.

If we pick up a book of church history we find that controversy is nothing new. There have always been issues on which professing Christians disagree. All sorts of teachings and practices have been put forward at one time or another. Some have never gained much popularity. Others have been widely accepted and have become embedded in the traditions of parts of the church, only to be challenged in later generations by people with other traditions. How do we know the voice of God in all this?

The welcome rediscovery of the exercise of spiritual gifts and ministries in these days has brought its own problems. God still speaks through prophecies, words of wisdom, even dreams and visions, as he did in Bible days. But how are we to know that a 'word from the Lord' is truly the voice of God? How can we be sure that a vision is really from God and that we've got the right interpretation? After all, it is quite possible for two people to have 'messages from God' which contradict each other. How do we know which one to follow?

Again, we believe that God speaks directly to our hearts through the Holy Spirit. But recognizing the voice of the Spirit is itself not always easy. We are only too well aware that other voices can make themselves sound like the voice of the Spirit. John tells us to check out the spirits to make sure they are truly from God (1 John 4:1); but how do we do that?

Perhaps, faced with all the confusing voices clamouring at us, we take refuge in our own feelings. We like the thought of women ministers, so that settles the matter for us. Alternatively, we may feel the vital thing is to be rational; we like to think things through and decide

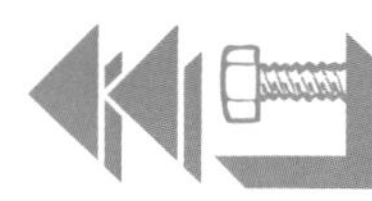

306

issues on the basis of whether or not our reason can accept them. But we are still left with the fact that different Christians feel and even reason differently. How are we to know whether or not our feelings and reasonings truly echo the voice of God?

I believe that God speaks to us in a wide variety of ways. His voice *can* be heard in the cry of the oppressed. He speaks to us through Christian leaders, books and church traditions – even those we disagree with! His Spirit uses prophecy and he speaks directly to our hearts. And he speaks through our feelings and our reason.

104

● The Bible: the final authority

But none of these ways of hearing God's voice is adequate on its own, or even in combination with the others. There is too great a risk of error. The world cries different things at us. Fashions among Christian thinkers and writers come and go. Even church traditions and official church teaching have from time to time been in error. We can mistake the voice of the Spirit. Our feelings and reasonings can lead us astray. And that is why God has given us the Bible. Only there do we have something that is fixed, something outside ourselves, that is not subject to the changing fashions and pressures of each generation. Written by a wide range of people over a long period of time, reflecting a rich complexity of situations, it forms as a whole God's authoritative revelation of his truth and his will to the world for all time.

80

As such it provides the basis from which we can assess all other ideas and teachings. God does speak to us in a wide variety of ways, quite apart from his revelation in the Bible. But he will never be inconsistent. He will not say something today in direct contradiction to what he has said in the past. So if we are challenged by the cry of the oppressed yet unsure about the demand for violent revolution, it is to the Bible we must turn to check where the authentic voice of God is on this issue. Current Christian teaching or long cherished traditions of the church are equally to be tested by the revelation of God in the Bible. And when John told us to test the spirits to see if they are from God, the foundational test is whether or not they tally with the voice of the Holy Spirit recorded in the Scriptures. God knows how easy it is for us to get things wrong, to be blinded by our feelings or thoughts, by the persuasive arguments of others or the pressures of the society around us. So he has given us his revelation in the Bible to be a lamp to our feet and a light for our path (Psalm 119:105).

● Using the Bible fairly

There is an important point to bear in mind here, as in all our dealings with the Bible. When we listen for the voice of God, and use the Bible to test what we feel God may be saying to us in all sorts of ways, it must be the whole Bible we use, and not just isolated bits. It is such a rich and varied book that we could, by being unfair to it as a whole and picking out odd verses here and there, find almost anything we want in it.

In particular we need to be careful over our use of the Old Testament. For us it must always be interpreted and applied in the light of the New Testament and supremely through Jesus. The complex issue of violent revolution, for example, must not be settled simply by arguing from some of the more warlike sections of the Old Testament. We need also to

take into account the teaching and example of Jesus and the New Testament writers who in fact lived in an occupied land and were well acquainted with the case for violent revolution against the Romans.

Even so, we may well have to acknowledge that our interpretation of the Bible's view on such a matter will differ from someone else's interpretation. It is the Bible which carries the authority not our individual view of it.

God has given us the Bible so that we may hear his voice clearly. But we must use the Bible rightly in discerning that voice. How best we can do this is the theme of part five of this book.

But before we end our consideration of the Bible's authority we must look briefly at two further issues. The first is the relative authority of the Christian church and the Bible. Is it not the church that gave us the Bible in the first place? Does not that therefore mean that the authority of the church is greater than that of the Bible? The second issue is raised by those who feel that to recognize that the authority of the Bible is greater than that of church traditions, theologians, words of prophecy or even our own feelings and ideas, is to put the Bible on a dangerously high level. We are in fact worshipping the Bible, and that is idolatry.

●The Bible and the church

It is true that in a sense the church gave us the Bible. God's people through the centuries have recorded God's deeds. Others have preserved the records and passed them on to us. It was the church in the generations following the writing of the New Testament that decided which books were to be included in the collection of Christian Scriptures. Without human authors and those in the church who passed on the Scriptures to us we would have no Bible today.

But of course the Bible is not just a human book. God is its author, as well as the human writers. Equally, the task of fixing the canon and ensuring that the Scriptures were handed down through the centuries was not solely the work of the church. God had a hand in it, too. Just as he used human writers to record his truth, so he directed those who, in a spirit of prayer and dependence on him, recognized which books expressed his authentic voice and so were to be included in our Bible, and passed on to us.

50

I suppose we could see this as a similar process to that of God's gift to us of salvation. It could be argued (and some have done so) that it is the church that gives us salvation, since most of us find salvation as a result of the work and witness of the church. But the fact that the church plays a key role in bringing us salvation does not mean that it is its

God, the church and the Bible.

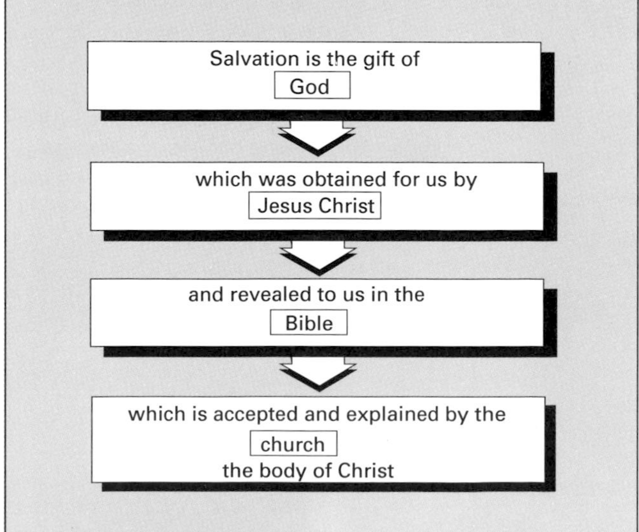

source. The only source of salvation is God. He may well choose to use the church to show us his salvation, but the church does not produce it.

So with the Bible. It is God's message to us. He has chosen to use the church to get it to us. But that does not make the church more important than the message. The message is the voice of God, and nothing can be more important.

●Bible worship?

And what of the suggestion that holding a high view of the Bible as God's revealed truth makes us guilty of idolatry, in that we become worshippers of a book? The answer here is straightforward. If ever we do become worshippers of a book, then we are idolaters. But to think highly of something is not necessarily to worship it. I have a very high opinion of my wife; but I would be guilty of idolatry only if I treated her as more important than God. Some religions do appear to worship their holy book. They treat it with the greatest reverence and even kiss it. Very few Christians treat their copies of the Bible like that!

14-16

It isn't the Bible we worship, but the God we find through the Bible. The Bible is a means to an end: a very important means to an even more important end. We value it highly, but not for itself. We study it carefully, but the focus of our interest is not in its pages. It is a gateway to God, and it is him alone we worship. He has spoken to us in the Scriptures, and it is his voice we desire to hear above all others. However highly we may regard it, we do not approach the Bible just to admire its beauty, to wonder at its inspiration, to rejoice in its wisdom or even to solve its difficulties. We approach it to find God. It is him we seek, his voice we hear, his face we see, his will we obey, his lordship we declare.

Your author speaking

I guess this chapter hasn't answered all your questions about the inspiration and authority of the Bible. But maybe it has said enough to show that there are answers. You can be sure that someone else has already found any problems you may find in the Bible. And you can be equally sure that someone has found a satisfactory answer. You may in time be able to work out all the answers for yourself. Or you may take a short cut and look up books on the Bible to find the answers there.

But meanwhile, besides thinking about and studying the Bible, don't miss out on reading it for yourself. You don't have to believe it all to find God in it. For years I had difficulty accepting some parts of the Old Testament. But as I read the sections of the Bible I could accept I found the reality of God becoming stronger, and my faith and understanding of God and his ways gradually developed until, almost to my surprise, I was able to accept all he says in the Bible.

So don't let the problem passages put you off the Bible. After all, they make up only a small part of the whole. Find out the answers to them where you can; but meanwhile try reading the parts you can accept. The best place to start, of course, is the gospels – Matthew, Mark, Luke and John. Here the focus is most clearly on Jesus. Work through the accounts of eyewitnesses and contemporaries of his life. Keep your ears open for God's word to you, and your heart open for his Spirit. I don't think you'll be disappointed.

DEFINING THE ESSENTIAL MESSAGE

by Donald A. Bridge

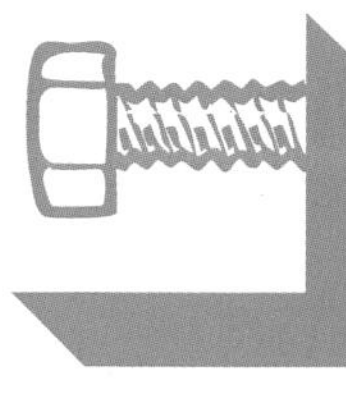

In this section we are standing back from the small print and looking at the whole Bible at once. What is it all about? What are the basic themes? What is the essential message that this book, these books, have to tell us?

PUTTING IT ALL TOGETHER

A multi-media show

333-362

As we have seen, the Bible is not just one long book. It is a collection, almost a library. It holds within its pages many different styles and it includes history, biography, poetry, laws, letters and drama.

Yet it *is* one book. It holds together as no mere collection of books could ever do. Its title simply means 'the Book'. It constantly claims to speak with the voice of God: it is not simply a compendium of ideas *about* God, but a message *from* God.

What does that message convey? It could be described as the announcement by God of who he is and what he has done to win back to himself a world that has lost him and its way.

249-250

Topol in the musical *Fiddler on the Roof* explains the value of tradition: 'It tells a man who he is and what God expects of him.' The Bible does rather more. It announces who God is and what he is like. It explains how he may be known. It also tells me who I am, where I fit into the scheme of things, what God expects of me and what my destiny is.

All of this is conveyed, not in a list of dry propositions and doctrines (with an alphabetical index to look them up) but in a colourful sweep of events in which the reader is caught up, seeing and hearing God at work.

We should not imagine Bible teaching as a kind of black-and-white still photograph of God framed and hung on a wall for our admiration. It is more like one of those multi-media shows in which twenty projectors throw coloured moving images on several screens, accompanied by sound and music, with occasional invitations to the audience to get up and get involved.

33

What God is like

We live in an age of communication. You can put a phone call across the Atlantic, take an air flight to Africa, or watch live Olympics from Asia.

The Bible exists because God is a communicating God. He wishes to be known and has gone to great lengths to be knowable. He makes himself known both in actions and in words. His actions included, for example, creating the world, rescuing Israel from slavery and sending Jesus to Bethlehem. His words give us his own explanation of the actions.

We are not left to guess the meaning, like someone watching a television play with the sound turned off. God has provided the sound as well as the vision.

For example, we might guess that God made the world because he needed to express himself, or because he needed his own creatures to give him energy (typically 'pagan' ideas). In fact the Bible tells us why – to house mankind, his highest creation, and through mankind to work out other great purposes for the universe. We might guess that God rescued Israel from Egypt because he dislikes Egyptians or because he favours freedom movements. In fact the Bible tells us why – because he is a compassionate God, and because he planned to make himself and his laws known through Israel's experience.

Then what does God tell us about himself:

● God is one

The *Sh'ma* is the ancient confession of Israel's faith. It has been chanted by worshippers, confessed

by martyrs, sung by concentration-camp victims. 'Hear, O Israel: The LORD our God, the LORD is one', (Deuteronomy 6:4). (*Sh'ma* is the Hebrew word 'Hear', with which the confession begins.) Jews were commanded to carry these words on their clothing, and to inscribe them on their doorposts (verses 4-9).

Because Israel persistently flirted with other religious systems that offered several gods and goddesses, the nation suffered repeated disasters until the lesson was learned.

A lot of practical consequences flow from God's one-ness.

There is one power in control of the universe

The whole concept of modern science sprang from this. If there are different powers competing for control, water might flow downwards on Mondays and upwards on Tuesdays. Gravity might work when *god A* is in control but go into reverse when *goddess B* takes a shift. But nature is predictable because one power prevails.

> He makes grass grow for the cattle, and plants for man to cultivate... The moon marks off the seasons, and the sun knows when to go down (Psalm 104: 14-19).

There is one standard morality

Today we live in an anything-goes culture. 'Right' and 'wrong' are defined by what 'everyone does', by the behaviour of characters in the latest soap operas, or by the neighbour with the loudest voice. But 'one God' means 'one morality'. He defines good and evil, saying 'This you must do, and this you must not do'.

● God is spirit

Although the Bible often uses picture language to 'describe' God, this is simply a kind of verbal visual aid to the reader's imagination. He does not in fact have hands or a beard, nor does he sit on a decorated chair with a footstool. His 'hands' represent his actions, his 'eyes' represent his knowledge, his 'ear' is his willingness to listen to prayer, and so on.

He is not restricted to one locality

A woman who met Jesus wanted to plunge into an argument about the right place to worship. In the Jerusalem temple, or on the Samaritan mountain? (In the parish church or the Salvation Army citadel?) His reply was that temples are out and mountains are off. 'Neither on this mountain nor in Jerusalem... God is spirit, and his worshippers must worship in spirit and in truth' (John 4:21-24).

36

We cannot catch God and put him into a box of our making.

He is everywhere

Yuri Gagarin, the first man to journey into space, commented when

he returned, 'I have been in the heavens, but I didn't see God.' But God says, 'Heaven is my throne and the earth is my footstool. Where is the house you will build for me?' (Isaiah 66:1). God was with Gagarin inside the space capsule, waiting in space to meet him, and waiting in Siberia for him to return. By a grim irony, God met him shortly afterwards, in a fatal road accident.

280

55

Nevertheless, God has personality

We must not imagine him as a kind of gas, filling everything. People often speak of the human spirit, or a spirit of adventure, or a mean spirit. They do not mean something vague and shapeless, but something very definite, expressed in human personalities and actions.

God's presence everywhere is both a warning and a reassurance. He can see the hidden actions and read the unspoken thought. He is also instantly available to respond to a cry for help or to listen to a prayer. The child who is lost, the motorist whose car goes into a skid, the patient slipping under the anaesthetic and the surgeon who operates ... all may know God's nearness at the same moment.

> He is present in every point of space, with his whole being. (Louis Berkhof – modern Dutch-American theologian)

God everywhere

Omnipresence is the technical word used for God's presence everywhere.

Where can I go from your Spirit? Where can I flee from your presence? If I go up to the heavens, you are there; if I make my bed in the depths, you are there (Psalm 139:7-8).

Of course God is not present *in the same manner* in every part of the universe. He holds the planet in space, imparts life to the plants, creates instinct in animals and speaks to the minds and consciences of people. To those who know and love him, his presence is even more distinct and vivid. But he does not need any of these people or things in order to have his own independent existence. It is we who need him.

God is in the leaf but he is also separate from it. We have no business worshipping trees!

● God is good

The ancient gods and goddesses of paganism were pictured with all kinds of human faults and vices – jealousy, cruelty, lust, prankishness, changeability. They were simply enlargements of mankind's own character, like huge shadows of themselves thrown on a screen.

The goodness of God means both that he has no faults of this own, and that he treats us in no way that is 'wrong'. It includes his truthfulness, his kindness, his love and forgiveness.

But it also implies that the very meaning of the word 'good' is found in God. A thing is good (or bad) right (or wrong) because he says so.

In today's society, standards of

God is ...

God is not a man, that he should lie (Numbers 23:19).

God is light; in him there is no darkness at all (1 John 1:5).

God is love (1 John 4:8).

God is kind to the ungrateful and wicked (Luke 6:35).

behaviour simply reflect changing opinion or convenience. Because God is absolutely good, his standards present an unchanging fixed point by which we can check good and evil. So both his 'one-ness' and his 'goodness' bear on our behaviour.

The mercy of God is one facet of his goodness. The original word is often translated in English Bibles as tender mercy, longsuffering, compassion and pity.

Mercy is the loving goodness of God shown to those who are in misery or distress, regardless of what they deserve or who is to blame.

The Old Testament makes constant reference to God's pity for the bereaved, his care for the poor, his indignation against social injustice that robs people of the good things of this world.

God loves

The LORD is good to all; he has compassion on all he has made (Psalm 145:9).

I know how many are your offences and how great your sins. You oppress the righteous and take bribes and you deprive the poor of justice in the courts (Amos 5:12).

Filled with compassion, Jesus reached out his hand and touched (the leper) (Mark 1:41).

In the life of Jesus this is vividly expressed in his 'having compassion' on the sick, the frightened, the aimless, the haunted and the suffering. When HMS Sheffield was sunk in the Falklands war, a leading churchman was asked, 'Where is your God now?' He replied, 'At the bottom of the Atlantic, weeping.'

Significantly, a complex theological issue in the early church had a simple suggestion added: 'All they asked was that we should continue to remember the poor' (Galatians 2:10).

The ancient gods and goddesses were merely enlargements of human characteristics.

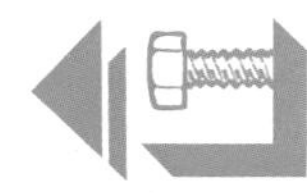

292-294

●God is holy

We often think of holiness as either another word for God's perfect purity, or a rather anaemic pious word for people who are 'too good to be true'.

In fact the root meaning is *differentness*. God is absolutely distinct from everything and everyone he has made. He is totally different in quality. There is no-one else and nothing else like him. Of course that includes his moral perfection, but many other things too.

Holiness is the thing about him that causes us to treat him with awe, to fear and revere him. Multiply by a million the kind of feeling you can imagine having if you met an alien from space, or if the earth began to shake for no apparent reason, or if you met someone face to face whom you have admired as a public figure:

Overpowering
Awesome
Majestic
Totally 'other'

Who among the gods is like you... majestic in holiness, awesome in glory, working wonders? (Exodus 15:11).

There is no-one holy like the LORD; there is no-one besides you; there is no Rock like our God (1 Samuel 2:2).

When I saw him, I fell at his feet as though dead (Revelation 1:17).

The modern resurgence of Christianity worldwide has inspired the composing of new worship-music. Much of it is simply this kind of Bible phrase put to contemporary music. Its use evokes (at least for some people!) a feeling of awe, gladness and 'littleness' all at once, and leads to quiet tears or silence. These are suitable reactions to God's holiness.

296-297

●God is love

This is the most misunderstood statement that the Bible ever makes about God. It does *not* imply that he is soft or sentimental, that he puts up with anything, or endlessly overlooks any insult and rebellion against him. God's love is his determination to do the best possible for us, consistent with who we are and what he is. The Christian recognizes love's most astonishing evidence in the fact that God has loved us in spite of all that has been done, and has sent his Son Jesus at terrible cost to rescue us. He has identified himself with our situation and welcomed us into his family (to which we had no right).

God so loved the world that he gave his one and only Son (John 3:16).

The Son of God ... loved me and gave himself for me (Galatians 2:20).

How great is the love the Father has lavished on us, that we should be called children of God! (1 John 3:1).

God is love (1 John 4:16).

●Summary

If someone asks what your favourite author or singer is 'like', you do not normally describe how they *look*. You describe how they write or sing, what effect they have on you, what message they are putting across.

So with God. The Bible does not (cannot) tell us 'what he looks like'. It tells us what kind of being he is, how he makes himself known, and what his aims are. In that sense the Bible gives us unique information about 'what God is like'.

Supremely, God is shown in Jesus. Here everything is expressed in actual human terms, worked out in what Jesus said and did, how he reacted and how he behaved.

Jesus answered, 'Anyone who has seen me has seen the Father' (John 14:9).

In the past God spoke to our forefathers through the prophets at many times and in various ways, but in these last days he has spoken to use by his Son.... The Son is the radiance of God's glory and the exact representation of his being (Hebrews 1:1-3).

Understanding God

●On and on and on ....?

'Who made God?' – is the question that every child asks. The simple answer is, 'No-one'. For the word *God* implies, 'someone who was always there'.

Of course that is difficult, if not impossible, to imagine. But so is the only logical alternative – a never-

ending series backwards (so to speak) of beings or blind accidents, each one caused by the one before. 'But what about the one before *that?*'... and so on.

The Bible begins bluntly (and without explanation) 'In the beginning God...' (Genesis 1:1). Before the universe began, he was simply 'there'. He is the eternal and everlasting God. But God has no ending, either.

God has no beginning

Lord, you have been our dwelling-place throughout all generations. Before the mountains were born or you brought forth the earth and the world, from everlasting to everlasting you are God. You turn men back to dust, saying, 'Return to dust, O sons of men'. For a thousand years in your sight are like a day that has just gone by, or like a watch in the night (Psalm 90:1-4).

The LORD reigns, he is robed in majesty; the LORD is robed in majesty and is armed with strength. The world is firmly established; it cannot be moved. Your throne was established long ago; you are from all eternity (Psalm 93:1-2).

In the beginning God created the heavens and the earth (Genesis 1:1).

Part of the problem is that we live within time, and God does not. We are walking along a line. It has the past behind us (which we cannot change) and the future in front of us (which we cannot see). Only at the point of 'now' do we touch the line – and that point changes every minute. This morning's 'present' is already 'past' by this afternoon.

Imagine now that God is in a circle around the whole of our straight line. He can 'see' the past and the future as clearly as the present.

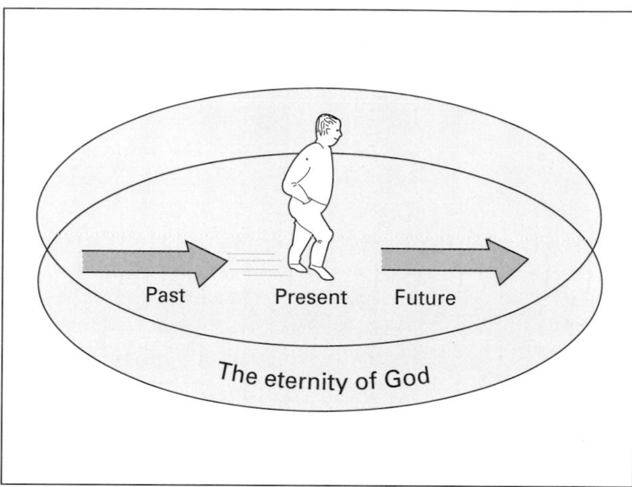

God includes present, past and future in his views.

Nothing comes as a surprise to him and nothing escapes his memory. He has all of eternity in which to consider and answer the split-second prayer of a driver whose car goes into a skid, a woman who finds herself attacked, a youth overwhelmed by a sudden temptation.

The special name by which God made himself known to Israel, YHWH (Yahweh, perhaps pronounced *Yar-way*) simply means 'I AM'. He is the unchanging being who lives in a constant 'present'.

God has no end

You will keep in perfect peace him whose mind is steadfast, because he trusts in you. Trust in the LORD for ever, for the LORD, the LORD, is the Rock eternal (Isaiah 26:3-4).

Your kingdom is an everlasting kingdom, and your dominion endures through all generations (Psalm 145:13).

They will perish, but you remain; they will all wear out like a garment. Like clothing you will change them and they will be discarded. But you remain the same, and your years will never end (Psalm 102:26-27).

Nothing takes him by surprise. He always takes the initiative.

●Who's afraid of the Old Testament God?

This provocative book-title underlines a genuine problem that many people have in matching the God of the Old and New Testaments. One schoolboy wrote, 'The Old Testament tells us what God was like before he became a Christian'.

108-112

Without putting it quite like that, people often suspect that the God portrayed in the first half of the Bible is angry, stern, vengeful and generally 'against us'. In contrast (they think) Jesus spoke of a fatherly, loving and welcoming God. In fact this is an exaggeration. Some of the sternest words about God's anger and judgment were uttered by Jesus. Some of the loveliest words about God's love were already in the Old Testament.

315-316

As always, the truth is found in a balance of the whole teaching of Scripture. God's anger is the inevitable reaction of his holiness against everything unclean, unholy and unjust. The Bible has to start there, because that is where its readers start – needing to face up to their guilt and danger. We will appreciate God's love only when we realize what little reason he has for loving us.

All decent people are angered by reported cases of child abuse or of adult rape. 'The monster must be punished and stopped', we all feel. However, we are selective – only certain things shock us. God sees *every* offence from a totally balanced and holy angle. *All* evil angers and grieves him.

'The wrath of God is being revealed from heaven against all... godlessness and wickedness' (Romans 1:18).

Yet from the very beginning God also spoke of his willingness to forgive and restore. The whole ancient system of sacrifices was designed to underline four balancing facts:

1 Everyone fails God.

2 There are painful consequences.

3 God has provided ways to say 'sorry' and to ask for his forgiveness.

4 The provision involves a 'sacrifice': suffering in place of the offender.

David describes his experience when he committed adultery. First he hid the fact and God relentlessly pursued him. Then he confessed it and found enormous relief in forgiveness.

'Wash away all my iniquity and cleanse me from my sin ... restore to me the joy of your salvation' (Psalm 51:2,12).

> People who do not actually read the Bible confidently assure us that when we move from the Old Testament to the New, the theme of divine judgment fades into the background.
>
> But if we examine the New Testament (it) is overshadowed by the certainty of a coming day of universal judgment, and by the problem thence arising: how may we sinners get right with God while there is yet time.
>
> (James Packer, *Knowing God*)

The New Testament does not destroy the picture, *but adds two extra details*:

1 Jesus taught that God invites us into a personal trusting relationship as Father.

2 As a result of the death and resur-

rection of Jesus, the problem of sin and punishment has been resolved. The sinless Son of God carried the judgment that we deserved. The old animal sacrifices were no longer needed. What they pictured is now reality.

Both details could, of course, only be added when Jesus had fulfilled the purposes of his coming and his dying. 'God was reconciling the world to himself in Christ, not counting men's sins against them ... God made him who had no sin to be sin for us' (2 Corinthians 5: 19-21).

Many people today find this teaching offensive and unacceptable. This is usually for one of two reasons:

1 Unlike earlier generations, modern man sees mankind as basically good and deserving. His problem is 'Why doesn't God treat us better?' Yet oddly enough it is this century that has clearly shown the horrors to which human badness can descend. Belsen, Cambodia and Hiroshima ... germ warfare, child abuse and drug peddling ... .

2 Crude popularization of the Christian message sometimes represents the Son of God lovingly persuading an angry Father to treat us better by 'taking the rap' for us. But the Bible teaches that Jesus' suffering declares God's love. God deeply hurt himself in offering Jesus up to the suffering that we deserved.

It is God who has settled the quarrel and made peace (2 Corinthians 5:19). It is the Father who showed his love by sending his Son (1 John 4:10). Jesus is God's love-gift to us (John 3:16).

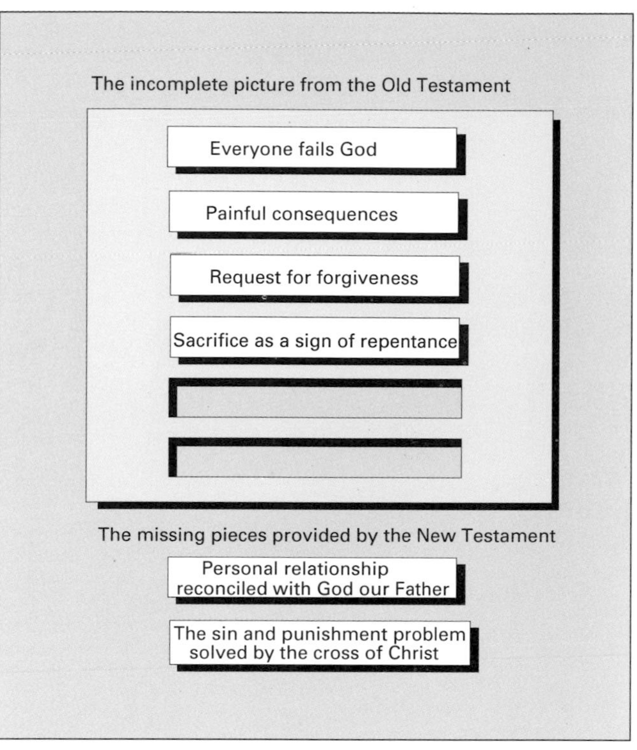

The New Testament fulfils the Old.

God in action against evil

'Judgment' is not malice but the reaction of perfect goodness to evil.

1 *God warns.* The threats and commands of the Old Testament are not outbursts of ill-temper but loving warnings. After all, he warns about hell in order to keep us away from it, not to push us into it. He cares enough to steer us clear.

2 *God acts.* Large-scale punishments like Noah's flood are also warning beacons. That particular event has found its way into the race-memory of many people-groups, as an object-lesson never forgotten.

3 *God guides.* The laws, rules, calendars and regulations which abound in the Old Testament go further than mere warning. They offer patterns and instructions to a better way. Rootless, insecure and self-destructive western society has learned the hard way, that 'permis-

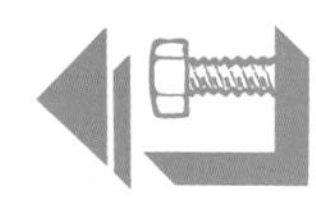
280

siveness' leads to new forms of bondage. God always said so.

4 *God sent Jesus.* 'The Word became flesh and made his dwelling among us' (John 1:14). By coming amongst us as Jesus, God deliberately involved himself in the world's self-created suffering. This identification with us came to a climax at his death on the cross.

5 *God sends his Spirit.* Through the Spirit's actions God is now at work in the world and in the church – changing society, combating ills and transforming people.

●Three in one

The word 'Trinity' never appears in the Bible. It is a kind of theological shorthand for a number of complex truths which the Bible teaches about God.

While insisting that he is 'one', it speaks of his activities in three different ways. Sometimes he is pictured as 'God-up-there', not literally up in the sky, but wholly different from us and wholly independent of the universe that he made. He gives us life, keeps us alive, controls the universe we live in and offers us a place in his family. The Old Testament speaks of him as The LORD (literally I AM – the one who always exists without past, present and future).

Jesus introduced the more intimate title of Father. This implies much more than the fact that we draw our life from him. It is an invitation to a personal relationship.

Sometimes he is described as 'God-down-here', uniquely active in the life of Jesus. We look at Jesus and see, more clearly than anywhere else, what God is like. 'No-one has ever seen God. The only Son, who is the same as God ... has made him known' (John 1:18 GNB).

Sometimes he is described as 'God-in-here', at work within the depths of the human personality, giving new instincts and fresh direction. This is the Holy Spirit of God.

Of course there is no hard and fast division between these activities. After all, the Spirit is also 'out there' (active in the world). The Son is also 'up there' (speaking up for us in heaven). And the Father is also 'down here' (showing his love and protection). It is all a reminder that God is simply too great to be encompassed in our words.

God in relationship

Much more is involved than a piece of arithmetic. It is easy enough to make fun of the difficulties of 'three-in-one'. But the three 'persons' who make up God are in a mysterious and marvellous *relationship* with one another. The Gospel of John specializes in this truth, described in Jesus' words.

The Father sent his Son to save mankind (John 3:16).

The Son only ever acts in harmony with his Father's wishes (John 5:19-20).

The Father and the Son agreed to send the Spirit (John 14:16).

The Son provides the only way to the Father (John 14:6).

> It is inconceivable that anyone sat down to think out any doctrine so improbable as the Trinity. It was forced upon them by experience. Convinced as they were of the unity and uniqueness of God, the disciples became confident that he was present in Jesus. After Pentecost they became assured that their experience of God's activity in their midst was nothing less than the continued work and presence of Jesus among them. (Michael Green)

The Father and the Son both make their home in the Christian (John 14:23).

The Spirit always draws attention to the Son (John 16: 13-14).

The Christian doctrine of 'the Holy Trinity' is an effort to put into words this complex of facts about God. Not surprisingly, it is really beyond definition. It invites faith rather than demanding understanding. The God who made the universe and fills it, and whose mind is vastly superior to ours, is hardly likely to fit satisfactorily into a human skull! It is said that Jews wear a small head-covering in order constantly to remind themselves 'God is bigger than my head'.

The Father – 'God up there' see 2 Chronicles 6:18; Nehemiah 9:6.

The Son – 'God down here' see Matthew 1:22-23; John 14:8-10.

The Holy Spirit – 'God in here' see Psalm 51:11; Romans 8:9.

Understanding people

Who am I? There are plenty of answers to that question. It depends where the observer is standing. To wild animals, mankind is a clever and powerful enemy. To the economist he is a statistic. A chemist might tell you that a human being is several litres of water and a few kilogrammes of assorted chemicals. To advertisers you are a consumer, and to business a customer.

One humorist defined a man as a *biped*. Then he remembered that birds also have two legs, so he amended it to a *featherless biped*. But monkeys have two legs and no feathers. So he added a third qualification: 'A man is a featherless biped who carries an umbrella.'

The philosopher Richard Niebuhr described mankind as 'a little animal living a precarious existence on a second-rate planet, attached to a second-rate sun'.

Perhaps the most striking fact about us is simply that we ask the question in the first place. If I am the result of accidental processes without any meaning, what leads me to ask who I am, and why I'm here?

● Human beings - nature's riddle

We are certainly a puzzling contradiction. Here is a being that can scale great heights of thought, perform great acts of compassion and plumb great depths of wickedness. How does the same animal produce Beethoven's fifth symphony *and* Belsen concentration camp? How is it that Asia contained Mother Teresa *and* Polh Pot? How does Africa produce Desmond Tutu *and* Idi Amin? What kind of mind discovers penicillin *and* invents bacterial warfare?

1 Straight from the hands of God

One of the Bible's song-writers asks 'What is man?' and then provides the basis for an answer – 'You (God) made him'.

> *Psalm 8:4-6*
>
> What is man that you are mindful of him?
>
> You made him a little lower than the heavenly beings and crowned him with glory and honour.
>
> You made him ruler over the works of your hands; you put everything under his feet.

The best-selling novel *Roots* stirred enormous interest because many people today, looking for a sense of identity ('Who am I?') feel that where we came from and how we got here are great clues to what we're doing here.

The writer of the Father Brown detective stories wrote, 'We have all read in books about the man who has forgotten his name. The man walks about the streets and can see and appreciate everything; only he cannot remember who he is. *Well, everyone is that man in the story'* (G.K. Chesterton).

By insisting that mankind was created by God, the Bible is not answering scientific questions about our biological make-up or our ancestry. It is telling us who we are and why we exist. God made us. We have a place in an immense plan. We were made for a purpose. We have a place in the world. We have a role in the play.

302

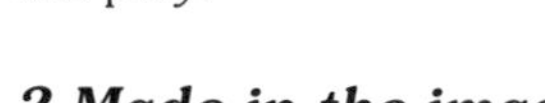

2 Made in the image of God

By using this phrase the Bible is *not* trying to say that we look like God, or he looks like us. Humanity reflects some of the facts about God.

According to the first page of the Bible, this 'image of God' is what distinguishes men and women from the animals:

Intelligence Humans, like God, think and reason, purpose and plan. In contrast, apparent planning in animals (like squirrels storing food for winter) seems to be simply instinctive.

Creation People, like God, invent and create, simply because they want to; not merely to meet some need. No-one actually 'needs' a musical score, a landscape painting, an ornamental garden or a poem. However far back we trace our ancestors we find them painting animals on cave walls. We would have to go a long way indeed to find animals painting our ancestors on cave walls!

Moral choice Phrases like 'It isn't fair', 'Give me my rights', 'You shouldn't do that' and 'I've a bad conscience' all reflect (without really thinking about it) a sense of right and wrong *outside of ourselves*, but striking a chord within us.

Relationship with God In spite of those pious and sentimental Christmas cards, the oxen and the sheep did *not* kneel and worship around the cradle in Bethlehem. Cattle don't say their prayers! Men and women have a capacity for worship, although it can become twisted and misdirected.

Relationship with others People cannot live in total separation from each other. They interweave, in relationships of love, friendship, hate, irritation, shared loyalties, shared needs, shared pleasure; all of which go far beyond a mere herd instinct. This too mankind derives from the Creator.

Ruling Both Genesis and the Psalm 8 readings refer to mankind in some way having authority over God's creation, as if trusted by him as a worker on his behalf. Today's envi-

ronmental and ecological problems illustrate two facts. Mankind can indeed control and manipulate his world. But its mishandling has drastic consequences.

●The fatal flaw

What went wrong?

'Man is now a horror to God and to himself and a creature ill-adapted to the universe, not because God made him so but because he has made himself so' (C. S. Lewis).

Have you noticed how often people are shocked by some human crime or cruelty or folly, and ask, 'Why did God allow it?' The real puzzle, of course, is why someone *did* it. The fact that we are 'allowed' to do things (good or bad) is part of our humanness. If we are not free we are not human. If we cannot make choices, we are not persons. God (in theory) might have chosen to make living puppets that only react to pulls on the string (or living computers that only work when they are programmed). But the result would not have been *people*.

Without the freedom to do right and wrong (and the ability to choose between them) it is hard to imagine how love and goodness and courage and joy would even be possible. But of course that also makes possible the opposites – hate and badness and cowardice and misery.

The Bible tells us that something has gone fundamentally wrong. Men and women not only often choose badly – they actually prefer to choose badly. They not only struggle between good and evil, but they find it easier to give in to evil. Children have to be taught to tell the truth, act kindly and be selfless. No-one needs to teach them to tell lies, act unkindly and be selfish. That is just 'doing what comes naturally'!

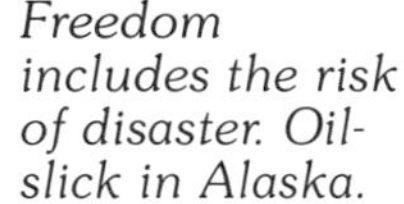

Freedom includes the risk of disaster. Oil-slick in Alaska.

In a dozen different ways – in picture language and in poetry, in theological phrase and in blunt literal terms, and with many examples, the Bible declares mankind to be fundamentally flawed. They are sinners.

The divine doctor's diagnosis:

> Psalm 51:5 Sinful from the time my mother conceived me.
>
> Romans 7:17 It is sin living in me.
>
> Romans 3:23 There is no difference, for all have sinned.

Sin is: Falling short of the mark (a term taken from archery) (Romans 3:23).

Flouting God's law (a picture taken from the law-courts) (1 John 3:4).

A condition of the inner motives (Jeremiah 17:9).

A settled state of hostility towards God (Romans 8:7).

An inward power 'reigning' over the human personality (Romans 5:21; 6:12).

309-310

204

> Dr D. R. Davies, an Anglican rector, stood on the smoking ruins of a bombed infant school where children had been killed. The local mayoress stood beside him. He grimly remarked 'another evidence of original sin'.
>
> The mayoress replied, 'I'm surprised that you believe in such a crude and horrid doctrine as original sin'.
>
> 'Madam', he replied, 'a fact as terrible as this requires a terrible doctrine to account for it.'

What happened in the garden? (Genesis chapter 3)

Almost at the start of the human story, something went radically wrong. The story of Adam and Eve, the fruit and the serpent, expresses deep and profound truths about the human situation. Jesus and his apostles treated it *both* as something that 'really happened' *and* as a picture of what keeps on happening.

Adam and Eve disobeyed a clear command of God.

They questioned his intentions.

They tried to make themselves equal with him.

188

They hid from him.

They were banished from his presence.

They fell out with each other.

The doctrine of 'original sin' (not a Bible term but another piece of theological shorthand) does not accuse everyone of being totally rotten, but of naturally tending towards the bad, like the 'biassed' ball in the game of bowls. We are not good people who sometimes slip, but bad people who quite often behave well.

Sinners are not basically fit people who sometimes have off-days, but chronically sick people who have good days. They need treatment.

We are not good citizens of heaven who now and again break a rule. We are criminals already serving a sentence. We sometimes behave ourselves in prison but we have no chance of earning remission.

First the bad news, then the good

So far the picture seems to be all gloom and doom. But in fact the Bible has more to say about God's answer than about the problem.

Unlike most religions (which think of human affairs moving in a circle and constantly repeating themselves) the Bible frequently insists that God is moving human life forward towards a goal.

The first great step towards that goal was to call one family into a special relationship with himself.

That in turn had a purpose, destined to lead to the coming of Jesus into the world, to rescue mankind. The next seven pages will examine what the Bible has to say about that unique person, and the purpose of his coming.

Jesus, the great enigma

No-one can ignore him for long. Calendars mark the time that has passed since his birth. America's president is constantly aware of the votes of his followers. Mr Gorbachev quoted him in support of *perestroika*. Every so often another famous sportsman or entertainer becomes a new disciple of the man of Nazareth. About one third of today's world population makes some claim to be enrolled under his banner. The one thing Jesus of Nazareth will not do is go away.

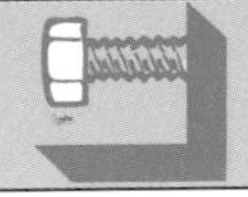

The global gospel (see also page 186).

Yet he lived over nineteen centuries ago, and never left the Mediterranean province of his birth. He wrote no books, but more books have been written about him than about any other human being. He launched no political party but has an estimated 1,600,000,000 followers. It took the authorities only one swift stroke to scatter his sect and put him to a horrible death. Yet his movement has outlived every empire and culture with which it ran parallel.

● Who is he?

There is no shortage of suggested answers. Artists and authors, politicians and pop-stars, philosophers and film-makers all jostle each other to explain Jesus.

He is portrayed as a revolutionary – and a pacifist. He is represented as religious rabbi – or radical reformer. He is hailed as a guru, a god, a spaceman or a hippy. His teaching (selected pieces) is quoted equally happily by capitalists and communists. TV programmes have presented him as a drug-using hypnotist or the architect of western civilization – Take your pick! People in every culture for twenty centuries have quoted him, puzzled over him, or argued with him.

Jesus Christ is the central fact and the key figure of Christianity.

Some opinions

I know men, and I tell you, Jesus was no mere man (Napoleon Bonaparte).

He is the divine Word from whom all truth comes (Clement – North Africa, 2nd century).

There is no other God but this man Christ Jesus (Martin Luther – 16th century German).

He was without blemish or defect ... he committed no sin (Peter – the Galilean fisherman).

We have always had a curious feeling that though we crucified Christ on a stick, he somehow managed to get hold of the right end of it, and that, if we were better men, we might try his plan (George Bernard Shaw – 19th-20th century Irish playwright).

After his death and resurrection, Jesus repeatedly explained how every detail of his life and work had been anticipated in the Old Testament. He saw himself as the key to its meaning. He chided his contemporaries for not facing the fact. 'You diligently study the Scriptures

86

because you think that by them you possess eternal life. These are the Scriptures that testify about me' (John 5:39-40).

● Will the real Jesus please stand up?

That is the title of at least two current books. One is British. It forcefully presents an all-round biblical view of Jesus. It assumes that the different facets in the Bible story can be reconciled to make a 'whole'. The other is American. It claims that Christians have distorted the picture of a Jewish Messiah and mystic.

Even within the main line of Christian church art, seemingly contradictory impressions of the Jesus-figure are represented.

In 1984 London Weekend Television screened a programme series entitled *Jesus – The Evidence*. The so-called evidence turned out to be an undigested assortment of contradictory theories. Self-styled experts went to elaborate lengths to 'prove' that Jesus was anything and everything except what he claimed to be.

What do we make of the many verbal portraits of Christ? All of them are at best half-truths; many are at worst gross distortions. Yet most of them appeal to some part of the Bible picture for support.

So how can there be so many facets of the same person?

How could Jesus be a revolutionary *and* a pacifist? How could he keep the religious law *and* favour the religious outcasts? How could he pray to God *and* claim to be God himself? Do the Bible accounts simply give us different people's personal interpretations of Jesus? And if they do, does that mean that we are all at liberty to have a stab at it ourselves, and produce our own interpretations?

Which one is Jesus?

The Bible does in fact give an all-round picture of Jesus in which the different facets balance and support each other. The gospel records (and later comments by the apostles) are in a sense 'interpretations' *but they are given by God*. Jesus promised the coming of a divine Interpreter (the Holy Spirit) after his departure. The result is a multi-faceted picture which is consistent and which comes from God through the writers, not from the writers through their private opinions.

> We did not follow cleverly invented stories when we told you about the power and coming of our Lord Jesus Christ, but we were eye-witnesses of his majesty... The voice came to him from the Majestic Glory, saying, 'This is my Son, whom I love (2 Peter 1:16-17).
>
> The writers were eyewitnesses. See John 21:24; Luke 1:1-4.
>
> They were promised God's guidance in their teaching and writing.
>
> See John 14:25-26; John 16:12-14.
>
> Jesus himself showed them how to interpret his life and work.
>
> See Luke 24:25-27; 44-49.

178-182

The gospel records do not give us a biography, in the modern sense. They are more like episodes in a TV series in which different contributors deal with different facets of a famous personality. A series about ex-Prime Minister Margaret Thatcher might include, 'Mrs Thatcher and the Falklands Factor', 'Margaret Thatcher, wife and mother', 'Thatcherism and the trade unions' and 'Margaret and the White House'. Some of the same facets will overlap separate episodes, but will be 'handled' differently. Each programme is selective; none is exhaustive.

So it is with the gospel records.

John does the selecting most obviously, and explains why:

> Jesus did many other miraculous signs in the presence of his disciples, which are not recorded in this book. But these are written that you may believe that Jesus is the Christ, the Son of God, and that by believing you may have life in his name (John 20:30-31).

● Who is this man?

Jesus gave numerous clues himself as to his own identity. He never actually said 'I am God' in so many words. Yet this is in fact what he was hinting.

> Jesus claimed to be equal with God (John 5:18).
>
> He forgave sins (which only God can do) (Matthew 9:5; Luke 5:20-21).
>
> He quoted the greater Old Testament description of God as fitting him (John 8:58).
>
> He claimed the ability to be present everywhere (Matthew 18:20; 28: 20).
>
> He said he was the source of all truth and life (John 14:6).

'There suddenly turns up a man who goes about talking as if he was God. He says he has always existed. He says he is coming to judge the world at the end of time... When you have grasped that, you will see that what this man said was, quite simply, the most shocking thing that has ever been uttered by human lips... Either he was a raving lunatic of an unusually abominable type, or else he was (and is) precisely what he said' (C. S. Lewis, *Mere Christianity*).

Philip said, 'Lord, show us the Father and that will be enough for us.' Jesus answered: 'Don't you know me, Philip, even after I have been among you such a long time? Anyone who has seen me has seen the Father' (John 14:8-9).

'I have had so many experiences of Christ's divinity, that I must say: either there is no God, or he is God' (Martin Luther).

Join all the glorious names

Reflecting on the amazing facts afterwards, those nearest Jesus had no hesitation in describing him as God. He was the key to all the puzzles of history and the answer to their deepest problems.

The prolific writer William Barclay collected in one book the titles of Christ. *Jesus As They Saw Him* lists 42 different descriptions given by New Testament writers. They include:

God
Son of God
Divine Physician
Saviour
Creator
Word of God
Image of God

These names all point in the same direction: that Jesus was, and is,

195

212

Putting the two facts together – God became a man

In the beginning was the Word, and the Word was with God, and the Word was God... The Word became flesh, and made his dwelling among us (John 1:1-14).

Being in very nature God he did not consider equality with God something to be grasped, but made himself nothing, taking the very nature of a servant, being made in human likeness (Philippians 2:6-7).

We do not have a high priest who is unable to sympathise with our weaknesses, but we have one who has been tempted in every way, just as we are (Hebrews 4:15).

There is one God and one mediator between God and men, the man Christ Jesus (1 Timothy 2:5).

God. The writer to the Hebrews underlines the point:

'The Son is the radiance of God's glory and the exact representation of his being' (Hebrews 1:3).

A man – the only real one!

Every strong statement about Jesus as God is matched with another that makes it clear that he was really human. He was born of a human mother (not arriving full-grown from space). He developed through childhood in the normal manner (Doctor Luke says, 'Jesus grew in wisdom and stature, and in favour with God and men' Luke 2:52... we might say, mentally, physically, spiritually and socially).

He knew the experiences of temptation, tiredness, hunger, thirst, pain. He knew how it felt to be angry, disappointed, happy, surprised, elated, despairing.

The statement that Jesus was really human is easier to understand but no less important than the statement that he was God. He could never be our example if he was never in our situation. He could not solve our problems by staying aloof from them. As God, he might feel sorry for our pain; as man, he felt the pain itself.

What a way to die! Crucifixion and resurrection

It is a very strange fact that a cross has become the symbol of Christianity. A puzzled tourist at the traditional site of the crucifixion said to this writer, 'I can understand you being impressed that Jesus was willing to die for his beliefs. But why treat his cross as a badge of honour? If someone lynched my grandmother I wouldn't carry a little gallows around. If a terrorist shot my friend, I wouldn't turn the bullet into a brooch.'

The comment showed that he had totally missed the point. Jesus was not a victim, a martyr or a casualty. He went deliberately to his own death, pointing to it as the focus and purpose of his whole life.

Of the four gospel records 50% is taken up with the death of Jesus and the events immediately leading up to it. A four-volume biography of Sir Winston Churchill will be completed in the next few years. What would we think if volumes 3 and 4 were totally taken up with the last week of his life and the day of his death?

●Why did Jesus have to die?

The apostles who followed Jesus explained the vital importance of his death in many different ways.

> He paid the price to ransom us (1 Timothy 2:6).

He carried our sins (1 Peter 2:24).

He experienced the curse that we deserve (Galatians 3:13).

He offered a sacrifice for the world's sin (Hebrews 10:12).

He died for our sins (1 Corinthians 15:3).

What all the word-pictures combine to make clear is that the death of one man nineteen centuries ago (by a method that was horribly familiar at the time) has a permanent effect throughout the centuries on our relationship with God. Without it there would be an immovable barrier between mankind and God.

How Jesus saw his own death

1 It was a 'must' to give people life (John 3:14-16).
2 It was the purpose he came for (Matthew 16:21).
3 It would make forgiveness of sin possible (Luke 24:45-47).
4 It would destroy the devil's power (John 12:31).
5 It would attract all types of people to himself (John 12:32-33).
6 It would set people free, as by the paying of a ransom (Matthew 20:28).

No Messiah that Jews could recognize could suffer such a death: for 'A hanged man is accursed by God' (Deuteronomy 21:23, RSV). 'An insult to God'; so says an ancient Jewish 'Targum' (a religious tract).

That in fact was exactly the problem that Saul of Tarsus, arch-persecutor of the early church, wrestled with before his conversion. He knew the grim Old Testament law which decreed that a criminal's body should be suspended from a tree or pole after execution. It demonstrated that sentence had been carried out. The law stated, 'Anyone who is hung on a tree is under God's curse' (this didn't mean that God curses someone *because* he was hanged, but that he was hanged because he had already been 'cursed' *i.e.* condemned and offered up for punishment).

The 'place of the skull', Golgotha, an ancient execution site outside the Damascus Gate of Jerusalem, thought by some to be the place of the crucifixion of Jesus.

Since Jesus' crucifixion was technically 'hanging from a tree', the very suggestion that he could be the promised deliverer from God would horrify any Jew. How can *he* be God's Son, when he seems to bear God's curse?

Paul shares the secret that eventually broke upon his own astonished understanding. Yes – Jesus was experiencing the curse. But it was not his – it was ours. He endured the awful sense of being condemned and banished from God – not for any misdeeds of his own (he had none) but for our misdeeds, for which he took the responsibility.

So Paul writes:

> All who rely on observing the law are under a curse, for it is written: 'Cursed is everyone who does not continue to do everything written in the Book of the Law'... Christ redeemed us from the curse of the law by becoming a curse for us, for it is written 'Cursed is every-

185

'The Lord is risen!'
'He is risen indeed!'

one who is hung on a tree (Galatians 3:10-13).

Some parallels

Dying for someone else is not unknown in human experience. Captain Oates walked into the blizzard to give his companions a chance to escape in Scott's expedition of 1912. A concentration camp inmate takes the place of the chosen victim.

Paying for someone else happens too: a parent pays a heavy fine for his child's crime, a research scientist drives himself to breakdown in order to perfect a cure.

All this and much more Jesus did on a cosmic scale at his crucifixion.

●Death's iron curtain smashed

Three days after his agonizing death Christ's tomb was empty. His enemies and friends alike were reeling under the impact of the news, 'Jesus is alive!'

The resurrection of Jesus was not an invented happy ending that spoils the realism of the story (as H.G. Wells suggested). It was God's 'seal of approval' stamped on everything that Jesus achieved by his life, suffering and death. It was a vital link in the great chain of Christ-made events that make it possible for men and women to know God.

Peter preaching the first fully Christian sermon on the foundation day of the church, said, 'This man (Jesus) was handed over to you by God's set purpose and foreknowledge; and you... put him to death by nailing him to the cross. But God raised him from the dead, freeing him from the agony of death, because it was impossible for death to keep its hold on him' (Acts 2:23-24).

Did it really happen?

The Bible is our own source of certain information about the resurrection. It speaks in strongly *physical terms* both of the death and the rising. There was a wooden cross, iron nails, a metal spear. The body was wrapped in linen and buried in a tomb with a rolling-stone door. By the third day the stone was moved, the tomb was empty, the linen cloths not unwrapped but unoccupied.

That day (and subsequently) people met Jesus, heard him, saw his scars, watched him eat, had his physical reality starkly pointed out.

'He said to them...Look at my hands and my feet. It is I myself! Touch me and see; a ghost does not have flesh and bones, as you see I have' (Luke 24:38-39).

Evidence 1 *The gospel writers give eyewitness accounts.*
Are they lies? Hallucinations? Symbolic stories not to be taken literally? Or do they bear the stamp of truthfulness?

Evidence 2 *There were both friendly and hostile comments.* If the gospels are to be believed the authorities offered an alternative explanation for the empty tomb. That indicates that there was an empty tomb to explain (Matthew 28:11-15).

Evidence 3 *Baptism*, practised by Christians from the beginning, symbolizes Christ dying and rising again. *Sunday* celebrates the resurrection each week. What started these customs, if not the event they celebrate?

Evidence 4 The early church made enormous gains in Jerusalem within weeks of the crucifixion – by preaching the resurrection. Any office-worker during a lunch-break could have torpedoed the Christian message by taking a ten-minute walk to point out the tomb and the body – unless the body wasn't there! The first disciples were transformed from trembling runaways to fearless witnesses. How and why?

The garden tomb still provides a striking visual aid to the Easter story, as it displays several of the physical elements. The staff often give lectures there to illustrate the strong arguments for the historical event.

Saul of Tarsus was both a qualified lawyer and a trained theologian. He was employed by the religious authorities to bring the first Christians to trial, imprisonment and sometimes execution. He interrogated many of them, probably under torture. What he heard from them (and what he already knew of the facts) pushed him ever further into a crisis of conscience. He feared that they were right about the resurrection and he was wrong. Eventually he met the risen Jesus himself, and turned around completely (see Acts chapter 9).

What the resurrection tells us

Jesus is who he claims to be – the Son of God (Romans 1:3-4).

The price he paid for our freedom has been accepted. 'Because of our sins he was handed over to die, and he was raised to life in order to put us right with God' (Romans 4:25, GNB).

A receipt for a payment in Britain is often stamped 'Received with thanks.' In America, the phrase is 'Paid in full.'

By raising him from death, God stamped his receipt on all that Jesus had paid on the cross.

We can be sure of life after death.

Since Jesus has risen, there is obviously a life to rise to, beyond the grave. So Paul calls him 'Christ...raised from the dead, the firstfruits of those who have fallen asleep' (1 Corinthians 15:20).

We can know Christ's presence with us. The Christian experiences the intimate presence, help and friendship of the living Jesus (Revelation 3:20).

Jesus is alive and at work today. Never has Jesus had so wide and so profound an effect upon humanity as in the past three or four generations (Kenneth Scott Latourette – 20th century historian).

The people of God

The Bible portrays many colourful characters: Abraham and his travels, Moses and his liberation movement, David and his battles, Esther and her beauty contest, Peter and his blunders, Mary Magdalene and her changed life. But it is not just a

PUTTING IT ALL TOGETHER

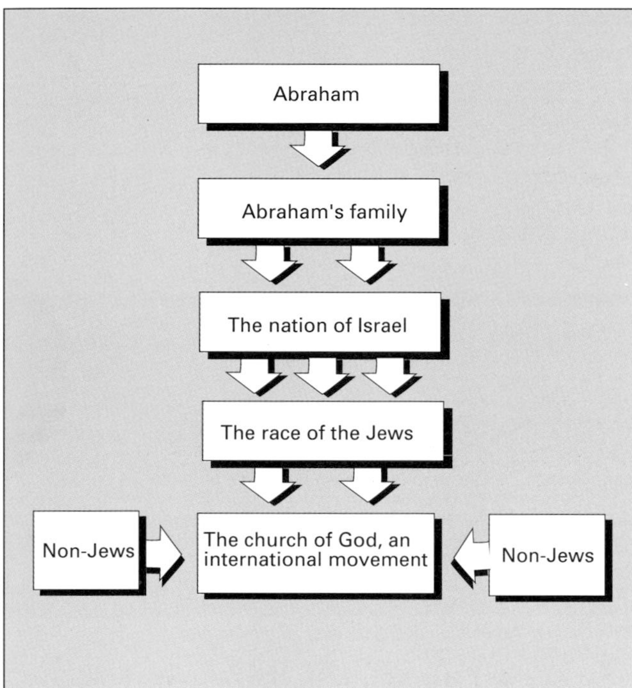

The growth of the people of God.

276-278

collection of individual adventurers. We miss a major biblical theme if we fail to notice a growing group: the people of God.

Abraham was promised a *family* who would bring enormous benefits to the whole world.

Moses turned a rabble of runaway slaves into a *nation*, to fulfil that promise. David forged the *nation's unity* under his kingship. Esther blocked anti-Semitic plans to exterminate their *race*.

In the New Testament Peter led a *church* that learned with him to become an international movement. Mary Magdalene was a symbol of the new status of womanhood within that *movement*.

●Walls come tumbling down

There were serious divisions in the ancient world, just as there are today.

Racially – Jews and non-Jews despised and disliked each other.

Socially – Free people and slaves lived in different worlds.

Sexually – Men despised, yet used, women.

Religiously – Enormous significance was attached to receiving or rejecting the religious rite of circumcision.

Politically – Much depended on whether you lived inside or outside the empire and were civilized or barbarian.

In two great statements the apostle Paul smashed down all of these walls of division.

> You are all sons of God through faith in Christ Jesus.... There is neither Jew nor Greek, slave nor free, male nor female, for you are all one in Christ Jesus (Galatians 3:26-28).
>
> Here there is no Greek or Jew, circumcised or uncircumcised, barbarian, Scythian, slave or free, but Christ is all and in all (Colossians 3:11).

The two simple ceremonies which Jesus gave to his church emphasize this. In baptism, people visibly join one body. In communion, they eat and drink together expressing their shared faith and experience. (Acts 2:37-47; 1 Corinthians 12:12-20; 10:17; 11:17-26).

●The people of Israel

Abraham's descendants were not picked out because of some special virtue. Jews don't have a unique religious genius or a natural flair for finding the truth. God chose them.

The annual Passover feast is still cel-

ebrated by Jews, about 3,500 years after its institution. Four cups of wine are shared, with each of which one of God's promises made to Moses is recited. '*I will* bring you out from under the yoke of the Egyptians... *I will* free you from being slaves... *I will* redeem you with an outstretched arm... *I will* take you as my own people and *I will* be your own God' (Exodus 6:6-7).

God's motive was not favouritism but demonstration. He chose a nation to be a living witness to the world, demonstrating in their national experience great truths about God and his plans. Their most precious possession was the written Law of God (and the rest of their Bible). This they held in trust for the benefit of the whole world.

> My brothers, those of my own race, the people of Israel. Theirs is the adoption as sons, theirs the divine glory, the covenants, the receiving of the law, the temple worship and the promises. Theirs are the patriarchs, and from them is traced the human ancestry of Christ (Paul writing about the Jews in Romans 9:3-5).

The people and land of Israel remain a puzzle to this day. Scattered throughout the world, they have never disappeared. Suffering many attempts to exterminate them, they have always survived.

● The kingdom of God

This theme is found in Old and New Testament alike. At times it runs parallel with the idea of a chosen race. For example, the promise was made to David, king of the new nation, that his succession would never cease (2 Samuel chapter 7).

Centuries later when Jews were enforced immigrants in Persia (today's Iran) Daniel was given a wider promise of a kingdom that would destroy and replace every earthly empire, and fill the world with the rule of God (Daniel chapter 7).

> *The angel to Mary, Jesus' mother*
> He will be great and will be called the Son of the Most High. The Lord God will give him the throne of his father David, and he will reign...for ever (Luke 1:32-33).
>
> *Jesus on trial before the religious authorities*
> The high priest said to him, 'I charge you under oath...tell us if you are the Christ, the Son of God.' 'Yes, it is as you say,' Jesus replied.... 'In the future you will see the Son of Man sitting at the right hand of the Mighty One and coming on the clouds of heaven' (Matthew 26:63-64).

The birth of Jesus was announced as the fulfilment of the ancient

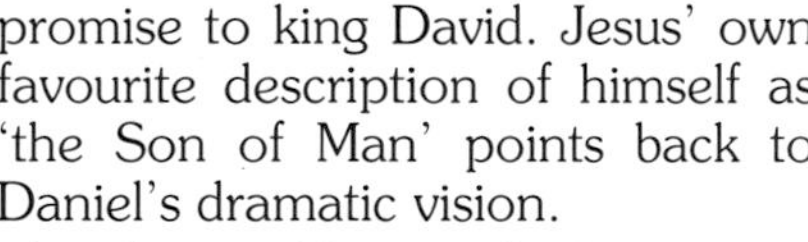

promise to king David. Jesus' own favourite description of himself as 'the Son of Man' points back to Daniel's dramatic vision.

214

The first public words Jesus ever said were an announcement that the kingdom of God had arrived – with him. People were called to 'repent' (change their ways) to be ready for it.

186

Kingdom of God – what does it mean?

The word is not geographical, describing a patch of ground (like the United Kingdom or Great Britain). It is a concept-word (like democracy, socialism or Africanization). But it is more than a vague ideal. The phrase means *the rule of God*. Where God has his way there his reign or kingdom is. So in the Lord's Prayer we are told to ask, 'Your kingdom come, your will be done on earth as it is in heaven.'

316-317

The kingdom of God – a composite picture

The prophets foretold it (Daniel 7:13-14).

The birth of Jesus inaugurated it (Luke 1:26-33).

The public actions of Jesus announced it (Matthew 4:17).

The life of Jesus demonstrated it. Here, at last, was a man in whose life God's will was perfectly seen, and his will perfectly done.

The teaching of Jesus described it. Much of his teaching and most of his parables were about the kingdom – his most-used expression.

The steps Jesus took to combat suffering, sickness and satanism demonstrated it (Matthew 10:5-8).

The death of Jesus, followed by his resurrection, opened the gates of the kingdom to all who repent and believe (Luke 23:39-43).

The preaching and sharing of the gospel announces its terms to all who will listen – and spreads its influence throughout the world (Acts 28:30-31).

The future return of Jesus will bring the kingdom to a visible and universal climax.

● The church

In the Bible, the word 'church' always means people never a place. It never describes a building, but always refers to believing people who may or may not meet in a building.

At the climax of his Galilee ministry Jesus invited his disciples to sum up (a) popular opinions about himself (b) their own conviction. When Peter boldly acclaimed him as promised Messiah and Son of God, Jesus replied, 'On this rock I will build my church, and the gates of Hades will not overcome it' (Matthew 16:13-20).

> Today's Banyas on the Israel-Lebanon border is the ancient Caesarea Philippi where Jesus spoke of building his church. It was known as the 'gate of Hades' for two reasons. A deep cave plunges semi-vertically into the ground, and was reputed to be the opening to hell. Carved idols in the nearby rock face were regarded a demonic. By using these words, Jesus may have been implying that the powers of darkness and evil would not destroy his plans for the church. In fact his death would bring the church into being. And none of the powers of paganism would be allowed to block its growth.

The Hebrew and Greek words translated 'church' have several

related meanings. They describe the 'congregation' of Israel that worshipped God during the desert journeys. They describe a selected 'council' committed to running town affairs.

The Christian church, then, is a called-out people with a distinct identity, eager to worship God and to express his rule.

Both the Greek and Hebrew words for 'church' or 'congregation' carry this vital meaning. The Israelites were 'called out' from paganism to worship God. A Greek town council was 'called out' from the population to rule and serve the town. The church is not a club anxiously canvassing for members, but a society which people are graciously invited to join. We don't do God a favour by signing up; he does us an amazing favour by letting us.

The church is described by the apostles as:

A living body (with every limb interrelated with the head) (1 Corinthians 12:12-27).

A beautiful bride (the object of Christ's love, destined for partnership with him) (Ephesians 5:25-30).

The city of God (a kind of spiritual Jerusalem, dedicated to God's worship) (Hebrews 12:22-24).

A new society in which the things that divide people become irrelevant (Ephesians 2:11-18).

A temple (not a building of stone and wood but a living shrine) in which all may come to God and worship him (Ephesians 2:19-22; 1 Peter 2:4-5).

In the Jerusalem temple of Jesus' time a 'dividing wall of hostility' separated the small watching area for foreigners, non-Jews, from the main worshipping centre for Jews only. Passing the barrier was punishable by death.

Paul (once a ferociously strict religious Jew) revels in the fact that the wall, so to speak, has been broken within the church.

'Remember that ... you who are Gentiles by birth...were separate from Christ, excluded from citizenship...without hope and without God... But now in Christ Jesus you who once were far away have been brought near through the blood of Christ. For he himself is our peace, who has made the two one and has destroyed the barrier, the dividing wall of hostility... His purpose was to create in himself one new man out of the two, thus making peace, and in this one body to reconcile both of them to God through the cross' (Ephesians 2:11-18).

> Paul, called to be an apostle of Christ.... To the church of God in Corinth, to those sanctified in Christ Jesus and called to be holy, together with all those everywhere who call on the name of our Lord Jesus Christ. I appeal to you, brothers... that all of you agree with one another so that there may be no divisions among you and that you may be perfectly united in mind and thought (1 Corinthians 1:1-2,10).
>
> Peter, an apostle of Jesus Christ... You are a chosen people, a royal priesthood, a holy nation, a people belonging to God, that you may declare the praises of him who called you out of darkness into his wonderful light (1 Peter 1:1; 2:9).

Letters to young churches

The second half of the New Testament is largely devoted to letters from church leaders (apostles) to the congregations scattered throughout the Mediterranean world. The letters were read aloud in

348-352

316-317

the churches, and were given the same authority as the Old Testament Scriptures.

The churches were like outposts of a heavenly empire, surrounded by an alien society, owing their allegiance to God. 'Our citizenship is in heaven' (Philippians 3:20).

Living to please God

Much of the Bible is devoted to example and instruction in Christian living. This is more than mere morality; it is a matter of relationship with God.

●Becoming a Christian

Enthusiastic converts can give the impression that there is only one pattern of entry into Christian living. It has to be sudden, unexpected, dramatic and emotional.

The Bible never insists on that. But it does insist that no-one is either born a Christian or drifts unaware into becoming one. Every conversion involves a work of God and a deliberate human response.

Although it may or may not be outwardly dramatic, the change from unbelief to belief is described in radical terms.

Peter calls it 'new birth into a living hope.' Paul speaks of 'dead' people coming to life with Christ.

'Born-again' is not a recently coined American religious slogan. It is the Bible description of the Christian's life-changing encounter with the power of Jesus. (John 3:1-8; 1 Peter 1:3; Ephesians 2:1-7; James 1:16-18).

God calls for two great responses to his offer of new life in Jesus. We must repent and believe, *i.e.* show faith.

Repent

Repentance means literally a change of mind and attitude. We need to have second thoughts about our own lives and about God.

We have to agree with God's analysis and accept his verdict.

Unpacking the word further, it proves to be:

a call to conversion – we must own up to God and apologize;

a call to correction – we should put right anything that is within our scope of putting right. Apologies should be made, lies abandoned, stolen goods returned. During a time of religious revival in Ulster during the 1930s a warehouse had to be put aside to hold all of the returned property stolen from shipyards. In Jesus' time Zacchaeus the crooked tax collector repaid everyone whom he had defrauded. In the early church new converts burned their occult literature (Luke 19:1-9; Acts 19:17-20). When John the baptizer was pressed to explain what he meant by repentance, he told the greedy to share their goods, the dishonest to correct their accounts, and soldiers to stop bullying and complaining about their pay (Luke 3:7-14).

Faith

The second starter in Christian living is *faith*. This too is a word that needs to be unpacked. It isn't good enough to say, 'Well, I believe in God – I suppose someone must be up there.'

Faith involves accepting the facts

God has given plenty of information about himself and his plans. The ordered world of nature, the nagging voice of conscience and the observed experience of other peo-

ple all offer evidence. The Bible offers even more, and the life and teaching of Jesus most of all. The Bible nowhere demands 'blind faith', based on sloppy prejudices and unexamined assumptions.

Faith involves admitting a need

'Nothing in my hand I bring,' says the old hymn-writer. Even when we begin to think seriously about God we instinctively want to give him something and put him in our debt. It won't do and it can't be done. He needs nothing; we need everything.

Grace is the word used to describe God's attitude to the undeserving. He does not love us because we are lovable, but because it is his nature to love.

He does not give us his friendship and pardon because we deserve it, but simply because he chooses to. 'For it is by grace you have been saved, through faith – and this not from yourselves, it is the gift of God – not by works, so that no-one can boast' (Ephesians 2:8-9).

Faith involves depending totally on Jesus – for pardon and a new direction. By dying and rising again, Jesus has dealt with the dark problem of our guilt and the judgment we deserve. We are told to 'believe in Jesus' (Acts 16:29-34; Romans 10:9). That means depending on what he has done, turning from old ways of living, surrendering one's life to his control and trusting him for the power to live a new life. 'What does Jesus want me to do?' becomes the paramount question in every area of life – work, leisure, attitudes, standards, choices and relationships.

Repentance and faith are our side of the coin; not that they earn or deserve God's favour, but rather that they open the door to all that God freely gives. But what is God's part in the transaction?

He brings the repentant believer into a new relationship with himself. Once the judge from whose condemnation we were hiding, he is now the Father into whose family we have entered.

He creates a new spiritual dimension within the believer. The Holy Spirit 'makes his home' in the human heart. New appetites and new attitudes are discovered. There is a new sense of direction and a new desire to live a life that pleases God.

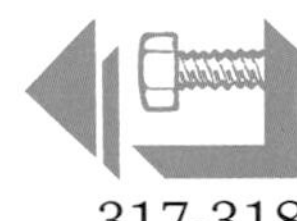

317-318

New Testament pictures of the Holy Spirit.

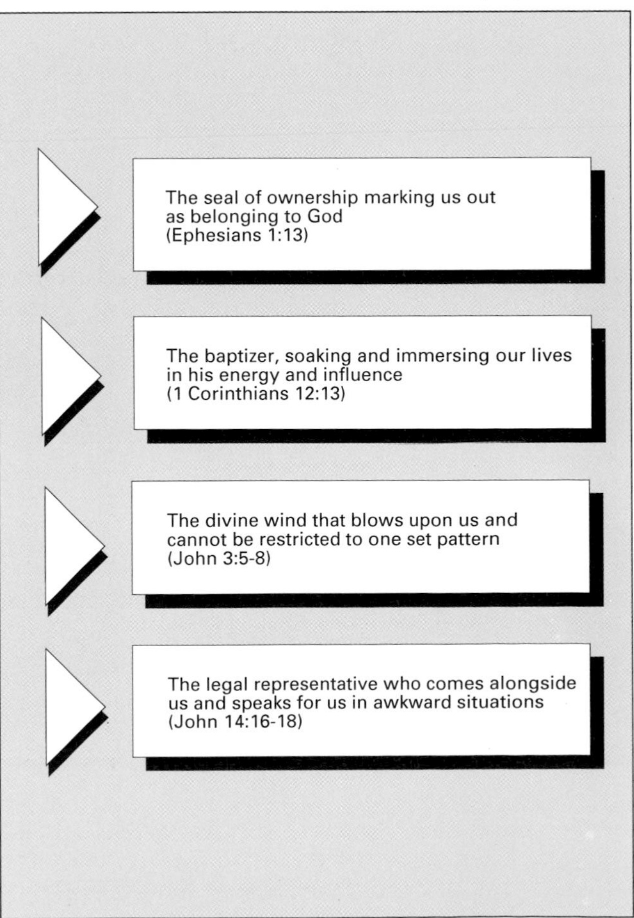

260-261

256

●Holy Spirit, giver of life

A person, not just a power

Although some of the symbols of the Spirit might suggest a mere 'force' (wind, oil, fire, *etc.*) he is in fact a powerful divine and holy 'person'. The secret of Christian living is to 'keep in step with the Spirit' as Paul says.

'Live by the Spirit and you will not gratify the desires of the sinful nature... They are in conflict with each other... You are led by the Spirit... The fruit of the Spirit is love, joy, peace, patience, kindness, goodness, faithfulness, gentleness and self-control... Since we live by the Spirit, let us keep in step with the Spirit' (Galatians 5:16-25).

What is described here is a living partnership between the Christian and the Spirit.

One of his tasks is to integrate us into the life of the church and supernaturally to equip us to fulfil our function there. The enthusiasm and ability to bear witness to our faith in a hostile world comes from the Spirit.

204

The gifts of the Spirit are abilities stirred up and encouraged by God's Spirit, to make the church function more effectively. They don't all have to be colourful, melodramatic or mysterious. Their purpose is not to promote personal ego-trips but to 'build up' our fellow Christians.

Where in the world are we going?

The Bible has much to say about future prospects for the human race. Major themes are God's plans to rescue the human race, the struggle between good and evil and what happens beyond the grave.

●God to the rescue

'Judgment'

Much of the Bible is occupied with God's response to the mess that mankind is in. His 'judgments' upon nations are warnings to them to mend their ways and to turn from greed, injustice and cruelty. Through the prophets he condemns:

The national breaking of promises (Ezekiel 17:11-19),

Expansion of borders by atrocities (Amos 1:13-15),

Lack of pity for fallen nations (Obadiah 10-14),

Intrigue and corruption (Nahum 3:4),

Exploitation of the poor (Amos 5:11-14).

'Hear this, you who trample the needy and do away with the poor of the land...skimping the measure, boosting the price and cheating with dishonest scales, buying the poor with silver and the needy for a pair of sandals... The Lord has sworn... "I will never forget anything they have done."' (Amos 8:4-7).

God called Israel to be a model society

'This is what a nation ruled by God would behave like.' The laws given through Moses are laws for a healthy society.

They condemn violence.

They distinguish between justice and private vengeance.

They urge neighbours to settle disputes peacefully.

They protect property.

They enforce social responsibility.

They make people more important than things.

They set life within a framework of gratitude to God.

(See Exodus 21-23 for a lengthy 'code of practice' that covers all of this.)

The Christian church

In the New Testament, the formation of a worldwide church takes the story further. Although the church is bound for a destiny beyond time and space, it also has a transforming influence here and now. Christians are to act as lights in a dark world and salt in a corrupt society.

Of course the church has often failed to live up to this. Yet many of the uplifting and healing influences in successive societies and empires have in fact been directly Christian. The nurturing of family life, promotion of just laws, protection of the weak, healing of the sick, abolition of slavery, spread of political freedom, promotion of learning, all of these are due to Christian influence and action.

Paul wrote a letter to the empire's capital. Its advice on moral, social and political behaviour is stunningly superior to the accepted attitudes of the day. Unwanted babies were killed at birth, women treated as chattels, slaves regarded as subhuman, fights to the death supported as a spectator sport, gross sexual depravity encouraged. Paul wrote:

> Hate what is evil; cling to what is good. Be joyful in hope, patient in affliction. Share with God's people who are in need. Bless those who persecute you. Live in harmony. Submit to governing authorities. Pay taxes, for the authorities are God's servants. Do not commit adultery, do not murder, do not steal and do not covet. Behave decently, not in orgies and drunkenness.
>
> (Extracts from Romans chapters 12-13).

● The struggle between good and evil

Where is the world actually heading? Towards a nuclear holocaust? Or universal famine? Or ecological disaster? Or is there a brighter future? A kind of Utopia in which people will learn to live in harmony and harness the planet's resources to provide for all? Marxists believe in an inevitable progress towards a just society, but seventy years of failure to produce one on their own terms does not suggest much likelihood of success. In fact the opening of the last decade of the twentieth century saw a widespread revolution against the communist world-view. 'Free societies' base their hopes on mankind's essential goodness and good sense combined with enlightened self-interest – 'what's good for me is probably good for everyone.' The results so far are hardly encouraging. Yawning trade deficits, super-luxury for some and increasing poverty and starvation for many of

78-79

Student unrest in Moscow.

the world's population, suggest that all is not as it should be. Neither system takes sufficiently seriously the built-in twistedness of man's nature. The Bible recognizes that, but matches it with God's purposes to rescue and redeem the race. So it leads us to expect a continuing conflict between good and evil, between the church and the world, between God and Satan.

On the dark side – wars, disorders, persecution and natural disasters will continue.

'When you hear of wars and rumours of wars, do not be alarmed. Such things must happen... Nation will rise against nation, and kingdom against kingdom. There will be earthquakes ... and famines... You will be handed over to local councils and flogged in the synagogues... All men will hate you because of me' (Mark 13:7-9,13).

214

On the bright side Jesus promised the ever-increasing spread of the Christian gospel. This has happened in ways unimaginable at the time, and to countries whose existence was then undreamed of. In a succession of waves with troughs between, the message of Jesus has in fact advanced, meeting both opposition and acceptance. The biggest wave so far experienced has come in the second half of this century, especially in Africa, Asia and South America.

229-230

> The gospel must first be preached to all nations... Whenever you are arrested... say whatever is given you at the time, for it is not you speaking, but the Holy Spirit (Mark 13:10-11).
>
> All over the world this gospel is producing fruit and growing (Colossians 1:6).

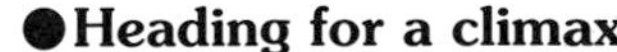

●Heading for a climax

Is the world actually getting better or worse? The Bible anticipates both at once: a polarizing of good and evil coming to a final crashing climax.

Much of the Bible's picture of the future is in pictorial and symbolic language. There are warnings about a malign person or power demanding total political and religious obedience – the 'man of sin', the 'beast' and the 'antichrist'. There are lurid pictures of natural disaster and colossal loss of life. Some of the word-pictures in the last book of the Bible look disconcertingly like ecological disaster and economic collapse. Christians differ in their interpretation of the details, the order of events and so on, but all tend to agree that the Bible points clearly to a 'winding up' of the world order.

Finally, there is the promise of the personal, visible return of Jesus Christ, and of a new age of peace and harmony.

> Collapse and disorder...Revelation 18
>
> The return of Jesus...
> 1 Thessalonians 4:13-18.
>
> Universal peace and justice... Isaiah 2:1-4.
>
> The day of judgment... Revelation 20:11-15.
>
> Followed by the perfect new community...Revelation 21:1-5.

●Beyond the grave

Is death the end? The question has always fascinated people. The ancient Egyptians raised sky-scraper pyramids because they thought not. When the Romans first came to Britain, they found natives who were willing to lend money on a promise of repayment in the after-life.

The subject is more than a coffee-table debate. If life offers no more than the short stretch from cradle to grave, there is little hope of a square deal. Florence Nightingale and Adolf Hitler share the same fate. A murdered child and her killer finish up the same. Most of us shrink from that conclusion. But is there any way to be sure of something better?

Daffodils, doctors and ouija-boards

Judging by the opinion polls, most people believe in life after death. Hopeful conclusions are drawn from the fact that spring flowers reappear after every winter's 'death'. Modern medical science provides intriguing examples of near-death or after-death experiences. Some people experiment with dubious attempts to pick up a message 'from the other side' (something which the Bible in fact forbids – Deuteronomy 18:9-13).

Quality not quantity

The Bible approaches it differently. It is more concerned with a quality of life than with mere 'survival'. People whose lives are linked with God in personal friendship and trust share something of God's eternal dimension.

Jesus argued that God *is* (not was) the master and friend of those who died long ago. 'He is not the God of the dead but of the living' (Matthew 22:32). So what the Bible calls 'eternal life' means much more than simply living for ever (wouldn't I get *bored*? you sometimes wonder). Jesus offers fulness of life through knowing God (John 17:3). Once we can say,

> O God, in you I take refuge...
> you are my Lord,

We can go on to say,

> You will fill me with joy in your presence,
> with eternal pleasures at your right hand (Psalm 16:1,11).

Truth from the empty tomb

People often say, 'If only someone were to come back and tell us...' In fact someone did. The resurrection of Jesus is one of history's most certain facts.

Paul, who was eventually convinced by the evidence, saw Christ's resurrection as proof positive of life beyond the grave: '...the guarantee that those who sleep in death will also be raised' (1 Corinthians 15:20, GNB).

For the Christian, conscious already of a living link with the risen Son of God, it is sufficient to know that the conditions of that after-life, however hard to imagine now, will be marvellously better than anything here. I will be recognizably myself, yet stunningly changed. Jesus' resurrection-body was the same yet different from the flesh that suffered pain and death. My 'new body' will include an on-going link with my previous life, yet will be something new – what the apostle calls a spiritual body. The connection between the new and the old will be something like the link between a seed planted in the ground and the plant that grows from it.

272-273

> Someone may ask, 'How are the dead raised?
> With what kind of body will they come?...'
> When you sow, you do not plant the body that will be, but just a seed.... So ... it is sown a natural body, it is raised a spiritual body (1 Corinthians 15:35, 37, 42, 44).

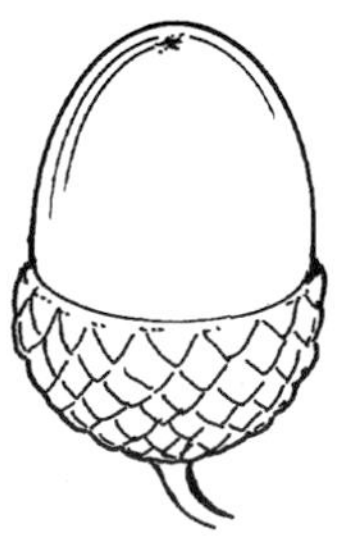

The splendour of that future day is so unimaginable that the Bible tends to tell us what will be absent, rather than what it will be like.

> They will be his people, and God himself will be with them... He will wipe every tear from their eyes. There will be no more death or mourning or crying or pain, for the old order of things has passed away (Revelation 21:3-4).

We can supplement the list: no more war, no more hunger, no more sickness, unemployment, child abuse, AIDS...

Will everyone be the same?
The Bible says firmly not. The logic is clear. Heaven and eternal life are matters of quality (the life shared and sustained by God, found in Jesus). If the sharing has not taken place and the trust not been expressed in this life, then there is nothing to take into that life. For those who have given to God the crowning insult of turning down his offer of life (obtained at enormous cost) there is nothing else to offer...

> How... severely do you think a man deserves to be punished who has trampled the Son of God underfoot? (Hebrews 10:29).

So the Bible speaks of a hell as well as a heaven. C.S.Lewis, the great twentieth-century writer and converted atheist puts it starkly:

> In the long run the answer to all those who object to the doctrine of hell is itself a question: 'What are you asking God to do?' To wipe out their past sins and, at all costs, to give them a fresh start? But he has done so, on Calvary. To forgive them? They will not be forgiven. To leave them alone? Alas, I am afraid that is what he does.

The Bible often uses highly picturesque and symbolic language to describe 'hell' and 'judgment'. It clearly involves conscious shame and a dreadful experience of receiving just deserts for wrongs done. If the language of symbol is needed, this is not because the real thing is less severe, but because it is dreadful beyond description (see Luke 16:19-31 for hell; Revelation 2:11-15 for judgment; Romans 2:1-11 for punishment and reward).

The essential message in a nutshell

The famous English poet, Milton, wrote two great poems called *Paradise Lost* and *Paradise Regained*. These titles could well sum up the whole sweep of the Bible's message. It begins with guilty mankind banished from the tree of life (Genesis 3:23-24) and ends with the healing of the nations as they return to that tree (Revelation 22:1-2). It begins with a curse on fallen mankind (Genesis 3:17) and ends with the curse lifted (Revelation 22:3-5). The central point is a very different tree where the Son of God 'redeemed us from the curse...by becoming a curse for us' as he 'hung on a tree' (Galatians 3:13). The world's religions often picture mankind as going round in circles: the Bible sees world history heading in a straight line towards a clear terminus and a new beginning. The Bible traces that line and shows every reader how to find a place on it.

4.3

GOD'S WORD FOR TODAY'S CHOICES

by David H. Field

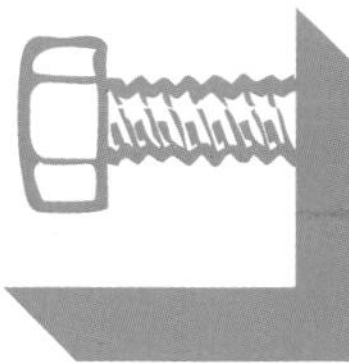

Even in the complexity of the 'tomorrow's world' that we live in we can find guidelines in the Bible to help us to make the difficult moral choices we all face. This section unpacks the principles.

Page

248-250

The book that empowers the choices

The Bible is an amazing book. With God's full authority, it sets out his design for the world. It spells out the way human beings spoiled that design. It describes how God himself mounted his rescue act in history, to liberate people from the results of their own wrong-headed lifestyles. And it predicts, more accurately than any human long-range forecaster, how everything is going to turn out in the end.

That alone would be enough to mark out the Bible as the book everyone needs to read. But even that is not quite all.

As well as unscrambling the mystery of life, the Bible tells us how we should be living it here and now. Again it speaks with the full authority of God's Word. It draws the line between right and wrong, so we can find God's way through the maze of our personal moral choices. And it sets up signposts to direct whole communities and nations, so people can live with one another in harmony.

●The book that changes lives

There are other books which set out to tell us how to behave, but the Bible caps its advice and instructions with an extraordinary claim. Instead of simply acting as a signpost, pointing its readers in the right direction, it insists that it can actually change those who follow its directions. That does not mean it has some kind of magic in its pages. It is the practical way God uses his written Word to channel his power into the lives of his people.

Here is how the New Testament makes this claim itself:

> The word of God is living and active. Sharper than any double-edged sword, it penetrates even to dividing soul and spirit, joints and marrow; it judges the thoughts and attitudes of the heart (Hebrews 4:12).

The Bible uses many metaphors to describe the impact God's Word can make on a person's life. Here are a few of them:

It is – a fire that burns and a hammer that breaks (Jeremiah 23:29).

- milk and solid food to build up strength (Hebrews 5:12-14).
- light to guide (Psalm 119:105).
- a sword to win battles (Ephesians 6:17).
- a mirror to reveal the 'real me' (James 1:23-25).

●Use with care!

The more powerful the tool, the greater the care needed in using it. And the Bible is no exception to this rule. Its power to guide and its strength to change character are immense. But it can also cause devastating damage if it is used wrongly.

It is worth pausing to identify a few of the pitfalls that may trap an unwary reader who turns to Scripture for instant guidance.

1 Using verses as props

Most of us have strong, set opinions about many things. And it is very tempting to use the Bible, not as a check on our ideas, but as a source of useful ammunition to reinforce them. We all know how easy it is to find an isolated verse in Scripture to support any theory or practice which we are determined to hang on to.

Often the results are more curious than serious. In the earlier days of film-making, one well-known preacher tried to deter members of his congregation from going to the cinema by quoting a verse from Paul's letter to the Ephesians. It reads (in the Authorized Version), 'Have no fellowship with the unfruitful works of darkness, but rather reprove them' (5:11). Whatever the rights and wrongs of cinema-going, Paul would surely have been astonished to hear his words used in that particular way.

Occasionally, the consequences of proof-texting (as it is called) are crucial. Take the debate about homosexuality, for example. Where does the Bible stand on same-sex relationships?

For a quick answer, many people would go straight to the story of Sodom (making the mental link between Sodom and sodomy). If God's judgment fell on Sodom, they conclude, it must follow that all homosexual behaviour is wrong today.

The conclusion may well be true (we shall be thinking more about it later). But it is quite wrong to prop it up by appealing to this particular passage of Scripture alone. If you read the story through (in Genesis 19), you quickly discover that it is all about attempted rape. No-one today pretends that rape is right. The arguments in the media are usually about the morality of loving homosexual unions where there is full consent on each side. Certainly the Bible nowhere sanctions such relationships, but my point here is that it is an issue on which the Sodom story has nothing directly to say.

2 Ignoring the time-gap

We forget at our peril that most of the Bible was written to people who lived a long time ago. Their living conditions, problems and opportunities were often quite different from ours. To discover what God is saying to us, we first need to find out the reasons behind the instructions he gave to them.

Large families were considered a great blessing in Old Testament times.

The Old Testament's teaching on the family is a good case in point. Married couples were encouraged to have as many children as they could. 'Sons are a heritage from the LORD, children a reward from him,' sings the Psalmist. 'Like arrows in the hands of a warrior are sons born in one's youth. Blessed is the man whose quiver is full of them' (Psalm 127:3-5). Childlessness, on the other hand, was considered a disaster. 'God has taken away my disgrace,' Rachel gasped in gratitude when, at last, she had a baby boy (Genesis 30:22-23).

306

This approach to parenting sounds strange to us, tuned in – as we are –to times when an explosion in the world's population threatens food supplies and highlights the need for birth control. The reason why the Old Testament urges its married

60-62

readers to pray for large families does not stimulate our prayers in quite the same way today. They needed to boost a thin population to fill a land where the conditions demanded plenty of workers and warriors. We need to plan the size of our families to conserve precious resources and avoid the hazards of over-population.

There is no inconsistency or clash. We, like they, seek God's guidance in planning our parenting. But our changed conditions make us extra careful in carrying over into our modern world the details of biblical teaching which was originally meant for them. There is a time-gap to jump.

77

> ***The time-gap***
> Ignoring the time-gap between Bible times and our own can lead us to apply biblical teaching wrongly. Deuteronomy 21:18-21 illustrates this danger well. There, the order is given for rebellious children to be executed by stoning.
>
> To understand the instruction, we need to grasp the reason behind it. In days when there was no probation service and no developed prison system, a gang of powerful young men could threaten the life of a whole community. Lethal measures were needed to combat a deadly threat.
>
> Today, when society can be protected effectively by less extreme methods, the letter of this Old Testament law has become obsolete – though not the principle on which it rests.

3 Facing new issues

Perhaps the greatest difficulty facing the Bible user today is the lack of any direct biblical guidance on many crucial modern topics.

A glance at the headlines in any newspaper makes the problem obvious. How do we make decisions about abortion and euthanasia? What attitude should we take towards genetic engineering? The Bible has plenty to tell us about war, but which side should we take on the nuclear issue? It would be very easy to add to the list. Where guidance is most needed, the Bible is apparently silent.

●Look for the principles

To avoid the pitfalls, there is one essential rule to keep in mind when using the Bible to unravel moral dilemmas. It is vital to *hunt out the main principles* behind the Bible's teaching, and then apply those principles to the matters under consideration.

There is a 'principle-shaped' solution to all three of the problems we have just identified.

1 Finding the principles under the rules

This is the sure way to avoid the first two traps we have spotted – making the Bible say what it does not mean (even when we sometimes wish it did); and failing to notice the time-gap which separates Bible times from our own.

Often the process is very easy. For instance, when the Ten Commandments say, 'You shall not commit adultery' (Exodus 20:14), the principle at stake is obvious. The Bible makes it plain that the marriage relationship is intended to be exclusive and permanent (see Genesis 2:24). Any act of adultery, therefore, breaks the marriage principle.

In clear-cut cases like this, the problem (if there is one) lies in obeying the Bible's rule, not in understanding what it means or how it applies.

Sometimes, though, a little more spadework is needed to dig out the

principle. Take Jesus' instruction about glances which lead to thoughts (if not acts) of adultery. 'If your right eye causes you to sin,' he told his followers, 'gouge it out and throw it away' (Matthew 5:29).

Did Jesus mean his words to be obeyed to the letter? If so, the churches would be full of one-eyed Christians. But he did not. He was simply taking a leaf out of the rabbis' books. To drive a serious point home, they would deliberately exaggerate it. Here Jesus does the same. His Jewish hearers would immediately understand what he was doing, and make the necessary adjustments. And we need to put ourselves in their shoes, grasping the principle he was illustrating (that it is morally dangerous to let our eyes wander), before we apply this important aspect of his teaching to our own lives.

2 Finding the principles which relate to the problems

This is the way out of the third difficulty we noted earlier – that is, finding help with modern problems on which the Bible has nothing directly to say.

> **The Jews had a word for it**
>
> In Jesus' day, the rabbis used two main teaching methods. There was *halakah*, which consisted of strict rules that were meant to be obeyed in every detail. And there was *haggadah*, the name given to vivid teaching which often included deliberate exaggerations, to get the main points across more strongly. *Haggadah* 'rules' were not meant to be observed to the letter.
>
> Jesus used both devices. If we are to understand his teaching rightly, we must consult commentaries to discover which teaching method he was using in any particular passage.

There are two stages to this exercise. First we need to dig underneath the problem itself to see what it is all about. And then we must find the biblical principles which relate to the issues we have unearthed.

That may sound horribly complicated, but it is usually not so hard as it seems. Take the debate about the rights and wrongs of abortion, for example.

If you look up the word 'abortion' in a Bible concordance, you will draw a complete blank. Scripture simply does not deal with the business of ending pregnancies artificially. But what is our modern debate really about? Ask that question, and biblical guidance is only just round the corner.

From the pregnant woman's point of view, a request for abortion often masks distress. She may be hurting physically, if the pregnancy threatens her health; or psychologically, if she has been raped or if the child's father does not want to know.

Immediately, the biblical principle of compassion comes to the fore. Jesus' attitude to suffering people was stamped all over with compassion (see Matthew 15:32; Luke 7:13). He did not wait to find out if they were to blame for their predicament. He could never face human need without himself hurting in response to it. (The word the gospel writers use to describe his feelings means, literally, 'to ache in the guts'). And he instructed his followers to respond to people in need with the same loving generosity (see Luke 10:29-37).

Applying this New Testament principle, modern Christians will not wish to identify themselves with any anti-abortion pressure group which ignores the needs of women who

305

want their pregnancies terminated.

From the foetus's angle, of course, the situation looks entirely different. Its life is threatened, whether because a scan has revealed abnormalities or simply because it is unwanted by the woman who carries it. And immediately other important biblical principles come into play. The Bible has plenty to say about the treatment of disabled people. The stress is always on special care, not extermination (see, for example, Leviticus 19:14; Matthew 15:30-31). And there are strict biblical rules protecting innocent life (see Genesis 9:6).

Such principles convince many Christians that abortion must be resisted as something thoroughly wrong. Faced with the objection that a foetus is only a potential person, without a baby's full human rights, they would point to passages in the Bible which assume that human personhood begins before birth (*e.g.*, Psalm 139:13-16; Ecclesiastes 11:5).

So although there is no Bible regulation which bans abortion specifically, several relevant biblical principles emerge once the main points at issue have been uncovered. And the same applies to other topics in today's headlines which did not exist in their modern form in Bible times.

Sex outside marriage

Some old moral problems have taken on new shapes. Having sex outside marriage is just one example.

The New Testament bans it (see 1 Corinthians 6:18; 1 Thessalonians 4:3). But some commentators suggest that this biblical veto no longer applies because times have changed.

Modern contraceptive technology, they say, means that unwanted pregnancies need not happen; and the discovery of antibiotics is the answer to sexually-transmitted diseases (except AIDS!).

The principles on which the Bible's teaching about sex rest expose the error of this suggestion. Extramarital intercourse is not only wrong because it brings risks of disease and pregnancy. Over and above those considerations (which the Bible does not even mention) it is a bad practice because it tears up God's design for human relationships (see 1 Corinthians 6:13-15).

Putting God at the centre

How can you tell the difference between right and wrong?

Moral philosophers have tussled with that question for centuries. Some suggest that human beings have a kind of moral 'sixth sense'. Just as we recognize certain things as beautiful (even though we cannot say why), so we label other things as good (although we cannot explain our reasons).

Others have a more rational explanation. Brain-power is the answer, they tell us. We work everything out in our minds. If murderers were allowed to go unpunished, it does not take us very long to reason out what the consequences would be. No-one would dare to walk down the road unprotected and social life would collapse. So we label murder as wrong and make a law against it.

The Bible has a totally different explanation. 'Right', it tells us, is everything which matches the character and will of God. And 'wrong' is everything else.

● God defines goodness

Jesus taught this basic principle of

Christian morality with startling simplicity. One day he met a wealthy young Jewish leader who began their conversation by calling him 'Good teacher'. At once Jesus took him up on his use of the word 'good'. 'Why do you call me good?' he countered, 'No-one is good – *except God alone*' (Mark 10:17-18).

Some years later, Paul echoed these words of Jesus in his letter to the Christians at Rome. You work out what is best, he told them, by detecting God's will. And you discover *that* by consulting his law in your Bibles (see Romans 2:18).

The mention of 'law' reminds us that most of the Bible's moral teaching is presented in the form of rules and regulations. It is not at all like a modern text-book on morality which sets out theories and arguments and then leaves the reader to work out his own conclusions. The Bible's conclusions are pre-set, either 'Do!' or 'Don't!'.

This grates on modern ears. If someone tells us to behave (or not behave) in a certain way, our immediate reaction is to ask indignantly, 'Why?' or 'Why not?'. The Bible rarely stops to give explanations for its commands. And the reason is plain enough. If God's will fixes the boundary between right and wrong, and if the Bible is his Word, explanations are unnecessary. God does not have to justify himself to anybody.

The big difference between a Christian approach to morality and any other is that the Bible's standard of goodness is *personal*. If a Christian is questioned about a moral issue, he will not rush off to the library for a text-book. He will direct the enquirer to the character of the living God.

Moses learned this lesson in a way he could never forget. During one of their meetings in the desert, God promised him, 'I will cause all my goodness to pass before you.' And when the promise was honoured, Moses was not presented with a special book – or even a set of stone tablets. Instead of that he was confronted by an awesome revelation of God's character: 'The LORD, the LORD, the compassionate and gracious God, slow to anger, abounding in love and faithfulness, maintaining love to thousands, and forgiving wickedness, rebellion and sin' (Exodus 33:19; 34:6-7).

351-354

● Copying God

Being good is being like God. It is as straightforward as that. So it comes as no surprise when God's people are told again and again in the Bible to copy him.

Sometimes the instruction is so sweeping that it is terrifying. The Old Testament's command, 'Be holy, because I am holy' (Leviticus 11:44-45; 19:2) is matched by Jesus' astonishing requirement of his followers, 'Be perfect, therefore, as your heavenly Father is perfect'

(Matthew 5:48). If that goal cannot be reached in this life, it does at any rate fix the Christian's eyes on the only moral standard that ultimately matters.

At other times, the call to copy God is very specific. 'Be merciful,' said Jesus, 'just as your Father is merciful'. And in case that did not strike home with full force, he pointed out in the same breath that God's standards of mercy make heavy, practical demands on those who attempt to reflect them. 'Love your enemies, do good to them, and lend to them without expecting to get anything back. Then your reward will be great, and you will be sons of the Most High, because he is kind to the ungrateful and wicked' (Luke 6:35-36).

257

Paul sums up this aspect of the Bible's moral teaching by linking the duty to imitate God with a call to copy Jesus, who reflects his Father's character perfectly. 'Be imitators of God, therefore, as dearly loved children and live a life of love, just as Christ loved us and gave himself up for us as a fragrant offering and sacrifice to God' (Ephesians 5:1-2).

What is God like?

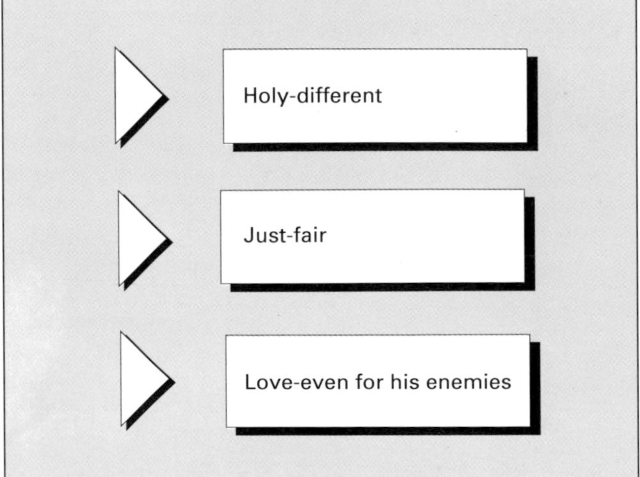

● So what is God like?

If God wants us to copy him, the most important thing we can do in shaping the way we live is to find out more about him. And that opens up exciting new ways of using the Bible. We have already sketched in some aspects of God's character in the last few paragraphs. Without attempting to paint a full word portrait (that would take a library of books!), here are the main characteristics of God that the Bible encourages us to imitate.

1 God is holy

Holiness is not really just one of God's qualities. It is the shorthand term the Bible uses to describe all of them put together. 'Holy' means 'different'. God is utterly different from anyone and everyone else. As Hannah exclaimed, in a flash of insight, 'There is no-one holy like the LORD' (1 Samuel 2:2).

Holiness is like a jewel. It has many facets. But if we blindfold ourselves and concentrate on morality alone, God's holiness stands for his moral perfection. He is so pure that he cannot even bear to look at evil, the prophet Habakkuk explains (1:13).

Hiding from God's holiness. Faced with such awesome purity, people's first reaction is to run away and hide. Isaiah spoke vividly for the rest of us when he reacted in panic to a vision of God in his holiness. His eyes burning and his ears still ringing with the voices of angels calling 'Holy, holy, holy! The LORD Almighty is holy!', he could only whisper, 'There is no hope for me! I am doomed because every word that passes my lips is sinful, and I live among a people whose every word is sinful' (Isaiah 6:1-5, GNB).

Peter had exactly the same experi-

ence when he glimpsed Jesus' holiness from the security of his boat. A miracle had happened. And Peter's reaction was not to clap his hands and shout for joy. He just wanted to put as much distance between himself and Jesus as he possibly could. 'Go away from me, Lord,' he pleaded, 'I am a sinful man!' (Luke 5:4-10).

Jesus himself explained the reason for this apparently strange response. 'Everyone who does evil hates the light, and will not come into the light for fear that his deeds will be exposed' (John 3:20). We are all less than perfect. When the light of God's holiness shines into the murky corners of our lives, we recoil by retreating into the shadows.

Sharing God's holiness. Nevertheless, God's challenge to his people is absolutely clear. They must share his holiness (Hebrews 12:10). 'Therefore be holy, because I am holy,' the Lord tells Israel (Leviticus 11:45). 'Just as he who called you is holy, so be holy in all you do,' echoes Peter – the man who had done his best to escape from Jesus' purity a few years earlier (1 Peter 1:15).

In practical terms, this means that Christian conduct should always be distinctive. ('Holy', remember, means 'different'.) That is why the Old Testament law is so full of rules and regulations which were designed to keep God's people separate from their Canaanite neighbours. And this is the reason behind the New Testament's insistence that 'religion that is pure and undefiled before God' is 'to keep oneself unstained from the world' (James 1:27, RSV).

Being holy in the world. But this is also a point where Bible users may find themselves pulled two ways. God made the world, we are told, and he loved it enough to send his Son into it at the first Christmas (John 1:10; 3:16). Yet the Bible tells us that 'the whole world is under the control of the evil one' and 'anyone who chooses to be a friend of the world becomes an enemy of God' (1 John 5:19; James 4:4). It all seems rather confusing.

The key to the puzzle is to understand how the word 'world' is used in Scripture. Sometimes it means 'the world of people', and in that sense it remains the firm object of God's love. But in other places it means 'the spirit of the age' – the sinister influence of a world order which is in open rebellion against God.

The spirit of the age infiltrates our lives through the advertisement hoardings we pass along the road, through the programmes we watch on television, and even through the way the news is presented in our favourite newspapers. In that sense of 'world', Christians who take seriously God's call to be holy must be constantly on the alert against the risk of contamination.

69-72

127

Jesus fitted the two halves of this biblical teaching together when he prayed for his followers, 'My prayer is not that you take them out of the world but that you protect them from the evil one' (John 17:15).

The Bible's call to holiness is a call to separation from everything in the world that is hostile to God. But the holy Christian is not the Christian who retreats to a desert island in an attempt to escape from the world's hostile influences. He or she is a person who gets immersed in the world of people as deeply as Jesus did, exposing evil with God's light and preserving goodness as his salt (see Matthew 5:13-16).

2 God is just

The New Testament uses a vivid expression to describe the even-handed way in which God deals with people. It is actually two words rolled into one – the word 'taking' added to the word 'face'. 'Face-taking' means treating some people in a special way because they are rich, influential, powerful or popular.

God has no favourites. This is something that God does not do. He never takes people at their face value. 'I now realise how true it is that God does not show favouritism,' Peter exclaimed when his own racist brand of 'face-taking' lay exposed (Acts 10:34).

Jesus' enemies accused him of many things, but this was a fault even they could not find in him (see Luke 20:21). And this is a characteristic which has no place in the Christian's lifestyle either, warns James. He sketches a vividly humorous cartoon of snobbery in church life under the very serious caption, 'My brothers, as believers in our glorious Lord Jesus Christ, don't show favouritism' (James 2:1-13).

Mixed marriages

One of the ways the Old Testament Law told God's people to live distinctive lives was by banning mixed marriages. Speaking of the other nations who inhabited the promised land, the Law said 'Do not intermarry with them. Do not give your daughters to their sons or take their daughters for your sons' (Deuteronomy 7:3).

That sounds dangerously like racial discrimination. But the same law goes on to make it clear that the reason for the ban was religious, not racial. Such marriages were vetoed because foreign wives and husbands would inevitably threaten the holiness of God's people by introducing their own gods and the immoral practices associated with their worship (see verse 4).

The New Testament makes the same point, without any racial overtones, when it instructs Christians not to be 'mismated with unbelievers' – though marriage is only part of what Paul had in mind when he wrote those words (see 2 Corinthians 6:14, RSV).

The Old Testament's law-code is securely based on this principle of even-handedness. 'Do not pervert justice,' the law insists. 'Do not show partiality to the poor or favouritism to the great, but judge your neighbour fairly.' And the tail-piece to this regulation reminds the people where this standard of fairness comes from: 'I am the LORD' (Leviticus 19:15-16).

Ensuring justice for the poor. Sometimes, though, God does not seem to be scrupulously fair. Quite often he is described as deliberately favouring the poor and oppressed. Mary's passionate song of praise when she shared the happiness of her pregnancy with Elizabeth almost makes God sound like a modern

revolutionary.

'He has performed mighty deeds with his arm,' she sang, 'He has scattered those who are proud in their inmost thoughts. He has brought down rulers from their thrones but has lifted up the humble. He has filled the hungry with good things but has sent the rich away empty' (Luke 1:51-53).

So does the Lord have a bias after all?

The different pictures the Bible paints of a God who treats everyone with absolute fairness, and a God who champions the poor, are in fact entirely consistent.

The image we should keep in mind is of a pair of scales. In ordinary life, the scales of justice are out of balance. Poor people are powerless people. Inevitably, they receive less than their fair shares. More often than not they suffer oppression at the hands of those who have more money and more power than they do. When God acts as their champion, he is not expressing a personal bias in their favour. He is simply adding his weight on their side to make sure the scales balance.

The Old Testament prophets were well aware of this when they lashed out in God's name against the wealthy and powerful. The God of justice will have no mercy, they warn, on those who buy the needy for a pair of sandals (Amos 8:6). No-one can divert the Lord's attention from injustice by hiding behind a religious facade. 'When you spread out your hands in prayer, I will hide my eyes from you,' God warns his people through Isaiah. 'Even if you offer many prayers, I will not listen. Your hands are full of blood; wash and make yourselves clean. Take your evil deeds out of my sight! Stop doing wrong, learn to do right! Seek justice, encourage the oppressed. Defend the cause of the fatherless, plead the case of the widow' (Isaiah 1:15-17).

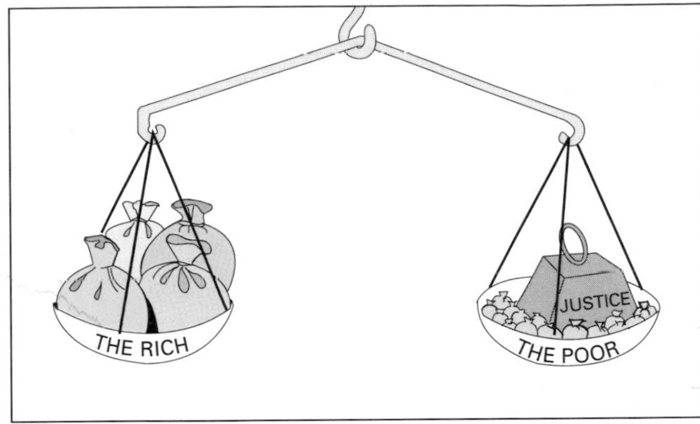

Bias to the poor.

The just wage

In the power structures of the biblical world, the boss held all the cards. Not surprisingly, the Bible is sharp in condemning employers who abuse their power by exploiting their work force. 'Woe to him who builds his palace by unrighteousness, his upper rooms by injustice,' thunders Jeremiah, 'making his countrymen work for nothing, not paying them for their labour' (Jeremiah 22:13).

Over in the New Testament James, too, sounds very much like a militant shop steward. 'Look! The wages you failed to pay the workmen who mowed your fields are crying out against you. The cries of the harvesters have reached the ears of the Lord Almighty' (James 5:4).

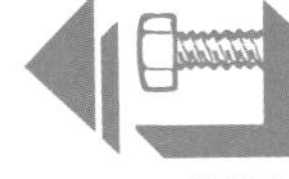

307

Fair structures. Apart from these strong warnings against injustice, which he put in the prophets' mouths, God commanded that the structures of society be adjusted to ensure that the rich did not become richer at the poor's expense. Each year, poor people were to be given special privileges at harvest time. They were to help themselves to the left-overs after the crops had been gathered – and the farmers were instructed to make sure that there was always something worth collecting (see Leviticus 19:9-10).

There were longer-term arrangements, too. At the end of every three years, a tenth of the land's produce must be given away to the poor for nothing (Deuteronomy 14:28-29). In each seventh year, the fields themselves were to lie fallow, and the poor allowed to gather anything that grew of its own accord (Exodus 23:10-11). And at the end of every period of forty-nine years the great Year of Jubilee was to be celebrated. Then land and property that had been sold had to be restored to its original owners free of all charge, and any poor people who had been forced to sell themselves as a last desperate resort must be set free (Leviticus 25:8-17).

It all added up to an impressive social programme which accurately reflected the just character of Israel's God.

3 God is love

The change in grammar is worth noticing. 'Holy' and 'just' are adjectives. They describe what God is like. 'Love' is a noun. It tells us what God actually *is*. As John puts it, 'Whoever does not love does not know God, because God is love' (1 John 4:8).

But what sort of love does the Bible have in mind when it talks about God in this way? It is a question worth asking, because 'love' is an umbrella word which, in our experience, can be used to cover anything from liking a holiday resort to having sexual intercourse.

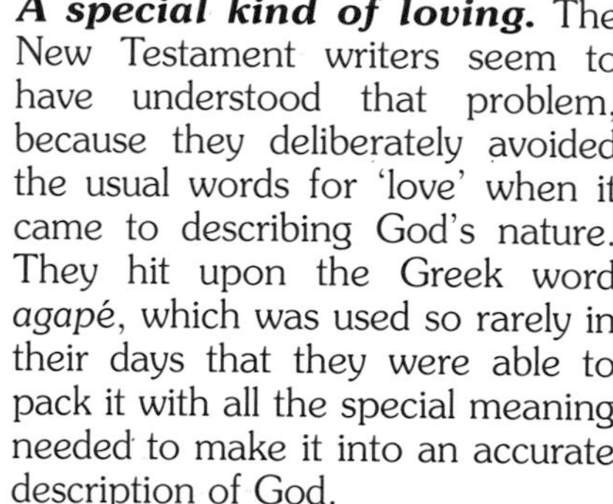

A special kind of loving. The New Testament writers seem to have understood that problem, because they deliberately avoided the usual words for 'love' when it came to describing God's nature. They hit upon the Greek word *agapé*, which was used so rarely in their days that they were able to pack it with all the special meaning needed to make it into an accurate description of God.

Used in this way, *agapé* is a love of the will. That distinguishes it from the emotional kind of loving which is expressed by a kiss and a hug. Loving someone in this *agapé* sense is not the same as liking them (though the two may, of course, go together). As John explains, 'This is love: not that we loved God, but that he loved us and sent his Son as an atoning sacrifice for our sins' (1 John 4:10). If we had been made to wait until God found us likeable, Christmas and Good Friday would never have happened.

Agapé is bigger than friendship, too. It takes two to be friends, but *agapé* love goes on working when it is kicked in the teeth. Paul reminds us that Jesus went to the cross when we were God's enemies, not his friends (Romans 5:10). That is what God's love is all about.

Agapé is also stronger than the love-ties which bond families and nations together. These exclude everyone outside the group to which the loved ones belong. *Agapé* love includes everyone who needs loving, whether they are in the family or not. Jesus told his famous story of the Good Samaritan to make exactly that point, when he was challenged about the meaning of 'loving your neighbour' (see Luke 10:25-37).

This is the kind of love that God is.

326

He meets the needs of the unattractive and undeserving, at great cost to himself. And he calls his people to copy him in their own love lives. John, again, puts it very clearly: 'Dear friends, since God so loved us, we also ought to love one another' (1 John 4:11).

> ***Love without strings***
> Closely linked with *agapé* love is the idea of grace. This is a difficult concept for modern Bible users to grasp, because the word has changed its meaning so completely. Grace in the Bible does not mean gracefulness of movement, but an act or attitude of love which is totally undeserved by those at the receiving end.
>
> Grace is a characteristic of God's. He showed it most obviously and generously in choosing and redeeming his people, in both Old and New Testament times (see Deuteronomy 7:6-8; – Galatians 1:15-16).
>
> As with God's other characteristics, Christians are told to build the grace factor into their own lives. Jesus told his followers, 'If you love those who love you, what credit is that to you?.... Even 'sinners' do that .... But love your enemies, do good to them, and lend to them without expecting to get anything back' (Luke 6:32-36).

God of the covenant. You sometimes hear it suggested that the Old Testament describes a severe God who rules his people harshly by law, while the New Testament pictures a God of love who dispenses with rules and regulations altogether. Neither idea is true.

There are certainly plenty of rules and regulations in the Old Testament, but they are all set in a framework of love. That is because the Old Testament Law is *covenant* law. To the Old Testament believer the covenant stood for the love relationship God had established with his people. Keeping God's rules reinforced that relationship, so obedience to the Law was not a cold, grudging duty but a response of joy to the divine Lover. 'The precepts of the LORD are right, giving joy to the heart,' sings the Psalmist. 'They are more precious than gold, than much pure gold; they are sweeter than honey, than honey from the comb' (Psalm 19:8-10).

God's love provided the people of Israel with the stimulus they needed to keep his commandments. Only rarely does the Old Testament back a call to obedience with a threat (for one example, see Exodus 22:22-24). Far more often, the motive for law-keeping is sheer gratitude to the Lord for his loving acts (see, for instance, Deuteronomy 15:12-15).

Love is the greatest. When Jesus was asked to pin-point the greatest commandment in the Old Testament Law, he replied with his two famous rules of love. 'Love the Lord your God with all your heart and with all your soul and with all your mind and with all your strength.' And 'Love your neighbour as yourself' (Mark 12:28-31).

The New Testament writers certainly got the message. As Paul puts it, 'Let no debt remain outstanding, except the continuing debt to love one another, for he who loves his fellow man has fulfilled the law. The commandments ... are summed up in this one rule: "Love your neighbour as yourself"' (Romans 13:8-9).

34

It would be quite wrong, however, to conclude that the New Testament *replaces* rule-keeping with loving, as the key to Christian behaviour. On the contrary, the two belong together, like different sides of the same coin. Jesus showed the way

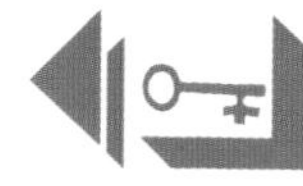
359

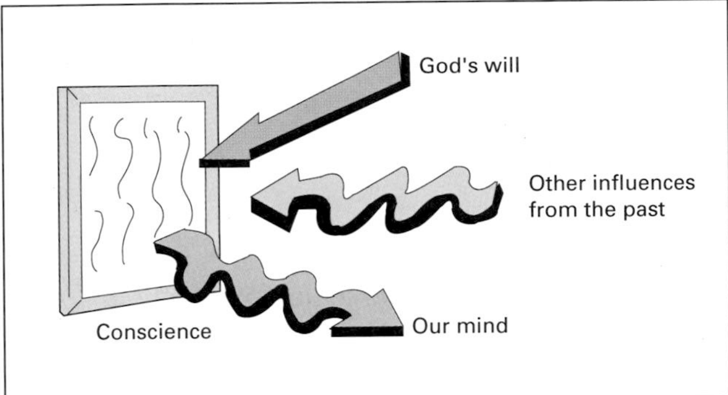

Conscience, a distorted reflector.

himself: 'If you obey my commands, you will remain in my love,' he encouraged his disciples, 'just as I have obeyed my Father's commands and remain in his love' (John 15:10).

There is no clash between the Old Testament and the New in their teaching about love and law. Both parts of the Bible insist that our desire to keep God's law is a sure sign that our love-relationship with him is in a healthy state.

● A divine reminder

So 'right' is everything which matches God's character. And we discover what God is like by becoming familiar with his self-revelation in the Bible. From there we learn three particularly important truths about him. He is holy. He is just. And he is love.

But the Bible is not our only source of knowledge about God's character and standards. What about people who have never read a page of the Scriptures? Are they totally ignorant about the difference between right and wrong, just because they have not read about God in the Bible?

In his letter to the Romans Paul answers that last question firmly in the negative. Even those who are totally unfamiliar with the Bible know something, however dimly, about God's character, he insists, because they are made in his image.

He draws a distinction between those who know their Bibles (Jews) and those who do not (Gentiles). People without any biblical knowledge are still aware of the dividing line between right and wrong. Even Gentiles have their moral standards. That is because 'they show that the requirements of the law are written on their hearts, their consciences also bearing witness, and their

Conscience

Our consciences are like trick mirrors in a fairground. They reflect God's image, but often in a distorted way, because that image has been spoiled by sin, even in the best of us. They also echo other less desirable influences in our lives – from childhood, perhaps, or from our past and present social environments.

That is why the Bible never says that the conscience is always the voice of God. The two must be kept distinct. In Paul's words, 'My conscience is clear, but that does not make me innocent. It is the Lord who judges me' (1 Corinthians 4:4).

Conscience does often speak with God's voice, but it can mislead us in either of two contrasting ways. It may challenge us over things which should not make us feel at all guilty. In those cases we need to hang on to John's reassurance : 'If our conscience condemns us, we know that God is greater than our conscience and that he knows everything' (1 John 3:20, GNB).

Or, far more often, the conscience may not prick us when it should. Paul writes about liars whose consciences have been anaesthetized. They have told so may lies that the voice of conscience has fallen silent when it should be screaming (see 1 Timothy 4:2).

thoughts now accusing, now even defending them' (Roman 2:15).

In other words, even the most determined non-reader of the Bible has an instinctive awareness of God's demands, because he or she has a conscience. The conscience acts as a reflector, beaming back moral information about God's character from the divine image in which every individual is created. That is a fact of human life. No atheist or agnostic can escape it. God's law is written indelibly on the human heart. No man or woman can plead complete ignorance of God's values and standards, because no-one can undo the way he or she has been made.

Paul's main aim here is not to excuse the non-Christian by suggesting that people can lead good lives without God's help. He rejects that brand of human optimism completely (see, for example, Romans 3:23). He is simply blocking off an escape route the non-Christian may try to take. Because everyone has the requirements of God's law written on his heart, no-one can say 'I don't know what God expects of me, so he can't blame me for the way I live.'

Putting people next

As Bible users, we must put God first in finding our moral bearings. He shows us the difference between right and wrong by revealing his own nature to us.

Even those who do not find out what he is like by reading the Bible have a vision of his goodness, blurred though it may be, because they are made in his image. His law is written in their hearts.

And this fact points us, as Bible users, to a further resource in fine-tuning our ideas about morality.

The Bible not only tells us that God created human beings. It also makes known many of his intentions for man and woman as their maker. And that, in turn, reveals some vital truths about the way human life is meant to be lived.

●Made in his image

The most vital truth of all is tucked away at the very beginning of the Bible's account of mankind's creation. 'So God created man in his own image, in the image of God he created him; male and female he created them' (Genesis 1:27).

Here is the key factor which makes people entirely different from animals and the rest of creation. This is not the place to think of all that it means to display God's likeness; but the Bible encourages us to make the connection between the unique way we are made and the way we should behave.

1 People are valuable

If my life is indelibly marked by God's image, I am incredibly precious. And the same is true of everyone else.

This is why murder is such an outrageous offence. Someone has described it as 'killing God in effigy'. The Bible puts it equally strongly: 'Whoever sheds the blood of man, by man shall his blood be shed; for in the image of God has God made man' (Genesis 9:6).

We have already seen the bearing this verse has on the abortion debate. It also provides Bible users with a signpost to guide them through modern discussions about euthanasia.

Looking down at an accident victim in a hospital bed who has no hope of recovering consciousness, it is tempting to say, 'He is just a cabbage. The merciful thing to do is to put him out of his misery. We would do it for a pet. It is cruel not to do it for him.'

Those are understandable sentiments, but they ignore the fact that the man in the bed is made in God's image. His life is still immensely valuable. He can still relate to God (that is part of what bearing God's image is all about), even if he cannot respond to visitors. And it is entirely wrong to put his existence on the same level as a dog's or cat's.

The Bible has a very high view of animals. Jesus compared himself to a good shepherd who is willing to put his personal safety at risk when his sheep are attacked. But he also taught very clearly that animal life cannot be compared with human life for value. 'How much more valuable is a man than a sheep!', he exclaimed. 'Don't be afraid; you are worth more than many sparrows' (Matthew 12:12; Luke 12:6,7). Putting a pet to sleep at the vet's is entirely different from offering euthanasia to a desperately sick man or woman in a hospital.

2 People are equal

Pondering the Old Testament's teaching on creation, one Jewish rabbi wisely remarked, 'No-one can say, "I am descended from a more distinguished Adam than you".' Human divisions of sex, class and race begin to look ridiculous in this biblical light (see Acts 17:26). The dignity and equality which creation in God's image gives to every human being brands all discrimination as wrong.

> There is an important difference between killing a person deliberately and allowing someone to die naturally.
>
> When a sick man is terminally ill, and death is approaching fast, the doctor attending him may withhold a drug, or refuse an operation, which would cause him more suffering, though prolonging his life for a little while longer.
>
> This is sometimes called 'passive' euthanasia, but there is a world of difference ethically between refusing to 'strive officiously to keep alive' and euthanasia proper. The Bible condemns the taking of innocent life, but it also recognizes the inevitability of death (see Ecclesiastes 3:2).

Translated into modern terms, the denial of any person's equal worth is a slap in God's face. 'He who oppresses the poor,' says the book of Proverbs in typically blunt fashion, 'shows contempt for their Maker' (Proverbs 14:31).

Here is the biblical way in to modern discussions about racism. Colour prejudice was apparently not a feature of life in Bible times. The only representatives of the black races we meet in Scripture are the Ethiopians, and they seem to have been accepted on exactly the same terms as everyone else (compare, for example, Jeremiah 13:23 with 38:7-13; and see Acts 8:26-38). But racism was still alive and well. And it found an especially sharp focus in the bitter conflict between Jews and Gentiles.

Is God a racist? Some have suggested that God himself was responsible for this division. After all, it was he who made the Jews his 'chosen people'. And the Old Testament law clearly discriminated between the

way Israelites and foreigners were to be treated. A foreigner could be charged interest on a loan, but not a fellow-Jew. And the regulation about compulsory cancellation of debts every seven years applied to Jews only – foreigners were not allowed any such concession (see Deuteronomy 15:1-3; 23:19-20). Is this not the ugly face of racism?

It is certainly not. Racism is selfish, and the Old Testament makes it absolutely clear that Israel was not to exploit her great privileges selfishly. God's special favours were not intended to make her despise other nations, but to serve them.

That note is struck as early as Genesis 12:2-3, where God's pledge to make Abraham's descendants into a great nation is capped by the promise, 'And all peoples on earth will be blessed through you.' Centuries later, Solomon's prayer at the dedication of the temple shows that this crucial point had not been lost with the passing of the years (see 1 Kings 8:41-43). Israel received God's special treatment only in order that she might become the channel through which he would treat other nations specially too.

In ordinary life we see nothing strange in giving special privileges to those who give us special services. We do not grudge a doctor special parking rights, and we willingly give way to a fire engine we meet with its siren blaring on the road. It should not seem odd to find God dealing in a special way with a nation he had chosen to serve the rest of the world in a unique fashion.

The laws which discriminate between Israelites and foreigners ought not to surprise us either. The foreigners who lived in Israel were tradesmen. So the distinction the Old Testament draws is similar to the difference we accept today between doing business with a client and helping out a member of the family.

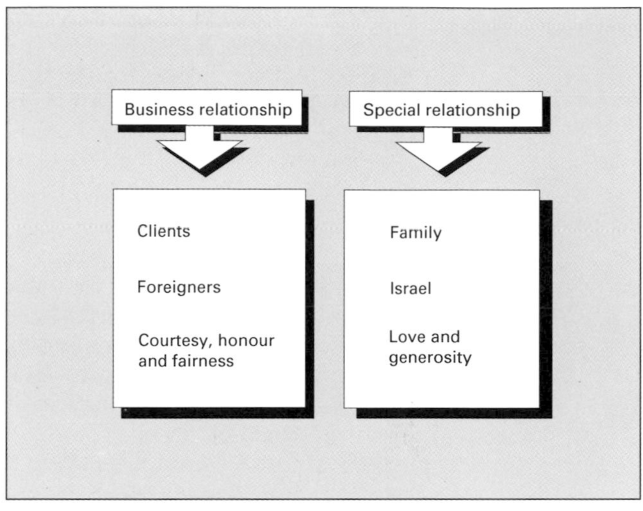

Ancient Israel's relationship with foreigners is like ours with business clients.

When a Christian businessman lends money on a commercial basis, he naturally expects to make a profit. But when he makes a private loan to his son or daughter, no-one dreams of accusing him of discriminating unjustly if he waives all interest payments. In the same way, letting a relation off a long-standing debt is a gesture of family love, not a show of prejudice. This is the light in which we should view the Old Testament's laws about interest and loans. Not charging interest or demanding repayment from a fellow-Israelite was, as one commentator describes it, a 'brotherly bonus', not an act of racism.

The Old Testament Law does, in fact, come down very strongly against all racial prejudice. 'Do not illtreat foreigners who are living in your land,' warns the law-code of Leviticus. 'Treat them as you would a fellow-Israelite, and love them as you love yourselves.' The book of

97

Numbers is equally sweeping: 'For all time to come, the same rules are binding on you and on the foreigners who live among you. You and they are alike in the LORD'S sight' (Leviticus 19:33-34; Numbers 15:15, GNB).

> ***Slavery***
> One of the most obvious threats to human equality in Bible times was the institution of slavery. Scripture does not attack the system directly, but it does require that slaves are treated humanely.
>
> The Old Testament contrasts sharply with other ancient Near Eastern law-codes in this respect. Hebrew slaves were guaranteed their freedom after six years (though some decided to stay in service – see Exodus 21:1-6); while foreigners shared in the celebration of festivals and were allowed a day off on the sabbath along with everyone else. And legal penalties deterred harsh masters (see Exodus 21:20, 26-27).
>
> In the Greco–Roman world of New Testament times, slaves were sometimes treated as disposable property. Paul, however, insists on good relationships between Christian masters and servants, with respect on both sides (Colossians 3:22 - 4:1; 1 Timothy 6:1-2).
>
> Finally, there is more than a hint in the New Testament that the Christian gospel makes the institution of slavery itself redundant, along with other artificial human divisions and distinctions. 'There is neither Jew nor Greek,' Paul declares, 'slave nor free, male nor female, for you are all one in Christ Jesus' (Galatians 3:28).

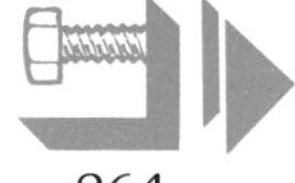

264

●Made for relationship

When God prepared to create human beings, he said, 'Let *us* make man in *our* image,' (Genesis 1:26). The use of the plural was not accidental. It reflects the doctrine of the Trinity, with its reminder that there is relationship in the Godhead. So when man and woman were created in God's image, they were not made as isolated individuals, but as beings-in-relationship.

The second chapter of Genesis enlarges very helpfully on this theme. It tells us that God made woman to relieve man's aloneness (see Genesis 2:18). Each needed the other. And when man saw what God had done, he responded with words that weave their way through the rest of the Bible. He said, 'This is now bone of my bones and flesh of my flesh' (verse 23).

Bone of bone and flesh of flesh

That phrase is a beautiful description of the close intimacy a husband enjoys with his wife. But it is applied far more widely than that in Scripture. It is the foundation stone on which all the Bible's teaching about human relationships rests.

We find the same words used to describe the blood-ties of an extended family ('Remember also that I am your bone and your flesh,' Abimelech reminded his uncles and aunts in Judges 9:1-2, RSV). And they appear again when all the tribes of Israel express their national solidarity ('Behold, we are your bone and flesh,' they assured king David in 2 Samuel 5:1, RSV).

Over in the New Testament, Paul picks up the same phrase in his letter to the Romans. Writing about his ministry as an evangelist, he tells his Gentile readers (if the words are translated literally) that he is bringing them the gospel 'to make my flesh jealous' (Romans 11:14). He means, of course, his fellow-Jews (and that is how his words appear in some modern translations). Even as

a Christian, Paul still yearned for the Jewish kinsmen who persecuted him, because they were 'bone of his bone and flesh of his flesh.'

The conclusion is unmistakable. Close relationships are a mark of human life, as God intends it to be.

Marriage

This is the context in which the Bible sets its teaching on marriage. Both Jesus and Paul describe the marriage relationship in words drawn straight from the account of creation in Genesis: 'For this reason a man will leave his father and mother and be united to his wife, and they will become one flesh' (Genesis 2:24; see Matthew 19:5; Ephesians 5:31).

That sentence stands marriage on three legs, like a stool or a tripod.

In the first place, there is an important *social change* when two people get married. Leaving father and mother was a major social event in Bible times. The ceremony was an elaborate affair. All the couple's relations were involved, and the festivities often lasted for a week or longer.

Today, the involvement of society in a couple's wedding is expressed by the presence of a legal registrar, the formal signing of a marriage register, and the attendance of witnesses. The details may be different, but the principle is the same. Marriage, according to God's plan as well as the law of the land, is not a totally private affair which the couple can keep to themselves and which the rest of the world need never know about. It marks the breaking up of one vital social unit ('a man leaves his father and mother') and the creation of a new one ('united to his wife').

Secondly, there is an *exclusively loyal, trusting relationship.* That is expressed briefly but clearly in the expression 'be united'. The word used in Hebrew means 'stick tight', and it appears elsewhere in the Old Testament to describe the affection Ruth felt for her mother-in-law (she would never desert her), and the loyalty the men of Judah felt for David (they would rather die than abandon him).

And thirdly, there is the *seal of sexual intercourse.* 'Becoming one flesh' means more than going to bed together. It covers the sharing of all the material things the couple possess. But physical intercourse lies at its heart.

According to Scripture, these are the three conditions which must be met if there is to be a true marriage. Anything less is just cohabitation.

Sex

The reference to sexual intercourse in the context of marriage helps to explain both the joy and the caution that Scripture expresses in its attitude to physical love-making.

48

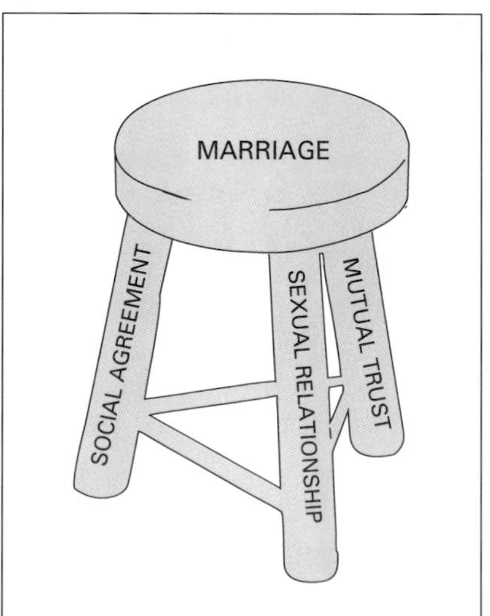

49

Secure marriage (Genesis 2:24).

The joy is there for all Bible users to see. It contrasts strongly with the anti-sex image the church seems to have gained for itself in modern society.

The goodness of sex. Sex was, after all, one of the features of God's creation which he pronounced 'very good' (Genesis 1:31). It was certainly not the cause or effect of man and woman's fall into sin.

205-206

The whole of the Old Testament endorses sexual intercourse as a particularly precious gift from God to a married couple. The book of Proverbs is particularly direct. 'May you rejoice in the wife of your youth,' it tells the young husband. 'May her breasts satisfy you always, may you ever be captivated by her love' (Proverbs 5:18-19).

147-148

The Song of Songs is a book which unashamedly celebrates the pure delight of sexual attraction. It is a mistake to interpret it simply in spiritual terms as a glamorous picture of the believer's relationship with Christ. Here are one or two typical excerpts:

'Your eyes,' whispers the man, 'are doves behind your veil ... Your lips are like a scarlet thread, and your mouth is lovely ... You are all fair, my love; there is no flaw in you ... you have ravished my heart with a glance of your eyes.'

She is equally ecstatic about him : 'My beloved is all radiant ... his head is the finest gold ... I am my beloved's, and his desire is for me ... My beloved is mine and I am his ... I am sick with love.'

In the New Testament, Paul is often branded as a woman-hater. That is an unfair caricature. He certainly draws attention to the advantages of staying single and celibate, but the words at the beginning of 1 Corinthians 7 which are often used to prove that he was against all sexual contact ('It is good for a man not to marry') ought to appear in quotation marks. They are not Paul's, but his correspondents'. In this part of his letter he is responding to points made to him earlier by members of the congregation at Corinth. This is simply one of them.

It does in fact tell us more about the situation at Corinth than it does about Paul's attitude to sex. The city of Corinth was proverbial for the sexual vice that riddled its society. Many church members had themselves been deeply involved in those corrupt practices before they became Christians (see 1 Corinthians 6:9-11). Now they were so ashamed of their past lives that they wanted nothing more to do with sex at all. Even some of those who were married had apparently decided to opt out of physical love-making (see 1 Corinthians 7:5).

It was a natural reaction, but an unbiblical one. So Paul resists it. Husbands and wives should reinforce their relationships by having intercourse, he insists. Any break in their pattern of love-making must be only a temporary arrangement, and should leave neither partner feeling cheated (see verses 3-5).

Across the sea, similar problems

were creating splits in the church at Ephesus. Again, Paul puts his foot down. He tells Timothy (who had gone to Ephesus as his delegate) that people who put Christians off marriage are being heretical, not holy.

Such anti-sex attitudes are quite wrong, he argues, because 'everything God created is good, and nothing is to be rejected if it is received with thanksgiving' (1Timothy 4:1-4).

A sex life that honours Christ

A negative approach to sex coloured the history of the Christian church until the Reformation (in the sixteenth century). If was rooted in an idea called dualism, which elevated the life of the mind and soul at the expense of the body. Sex, therefore, was spurned as something sub-spiritual if not thoroughly dirty.

The Bible has no room for dualistic theories of this kind. It treats the body with respect and honour. When Jesus was born, the human body took centre stage in the drama of redemption, as it did at his death (when Jesus 'bore our sins in his body on the tree,' 1 Peter 2:24).

Paul draws a direct line between the value of the body and the need to live a sex-life that honours Christ. 'The body is ... meant ... for the Lord, and the Lord for the body,' he tells the Christians at Corinth. 'Do you not know that your bodies are members of Christ himself? ... Do you not know that your body is a temple of the Holy Spirit?' (1 Corinthians 6:13,15,19).

Sex outside marriage

The Bible's veto on sexual intercourse outside marriage is set within this very positive framework.

There is no doubt that Scripture does ban extramarital intercourse of any and every kind. Jesus extended the Ten Commandments' clear condemnation of physical adultery to cover deliberately contrived sexual phantasies in the mind (Exodus 20:14; Matthew 5:27-28). Paul repeats the Old Testament's prohibition of same-sex intercourse (Leviticus 18:22; Romans 1:26-27). And the New Testament has a blanket word, *porneia*, from which we get the word pornography, covering all sex outside marriage, which forbids single people from expressing their emotional drives or close friendships in genital acts (1 Corinthians 6:18; 1 Thessalonians 4:3).

The reason behind the ban (see especially 1 Corinthians 6:12-13) reaches back to God's creation plan for human beings and his purpose for sex within it. People are different from animals. Animals copulate merely to satisfy a physical appetite and to have offspring. But that 'merely' does not sum up God's whole purpose for human sexuality.

As we have already seen, the Bible teaches that man and woman were created as sexual beings to reinforce human relationships. And sexual intercourse is meant to be the seal on that special relationship which reaches its climax in 'becoming one flesh'. To treat it as anything less is a tragic shrinking of God's intention.

A kiss and a cuddle can mean 'I like you very much.' But intercourse is a deeper kind of body language altogether. It says, on each side of the relationship, 'Whatever the future holds, I am giving myself to you for the rest of my life, and the oneness we share will always be ours alone.' That kind of commitment is what the Bible understands by marriage.

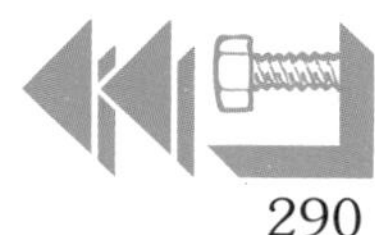

290

Homosexual unions

Are permanent, loving homosexual unions right in God's sight? Pressure groups inside as well as outside the church insist that they are. But it is hard to see how the Bible can be used to support this conclusion.

The New Testament in particular is clear that same-sex intercourse is wrong. In Romans 1 Paul describes it as 'exchanging natural relations for unnatural ones' (verses 26-27). In 1 Corinthians 6 he includes it in a list of actions and attitudes which are incompatible with the lifestyle of God's kingdom (verses 9-10). And in 1 Timothy 1 he specifies it as something which God's law forbids (verses 8-11).

●Made for management

Back in the creation story, God gave the newly-made man and woman a blessing and a command. These set human beings (who were already uniquely created in his image) still further apart from the rest of nature.

God told them, 'Be fruitful and increase in number; fill the earth and subdue it. Rule over... every living creature' (Genesis 1:28).

From this starting-point we can trace the Bible's approach to the environmental issues in today's headlines. And we can also detect here a positive biblical contribution to modern discussions about the value of work.

Man, woman and the environment

God put man and woman in charge of their environment. But that did not give them the right to exploit and abuse it selfishly.

The Bible expresses this warning most clearly in its constant reminders that people are themselves part of their God-given habitat. They cannot simply detach themselves from it and manage it arrogantly from a safe distance. Its destiny is too closely bound up with their own for that.

This note is struck very early on in the biblical story. In the third chapter of Genesis, man and woman's disobedience to God drew from him the jolting comment, 'Dust you are, and to dust you will return' (Genesis 3:19). Their sin would affect not only their own future but even the ground they walked on: 'cursed is the ground because of you,' he told them (verse 17).

Then, after the flood, we are shown the other side of the coin. God's promise to Noah specifically takes in the rest of creation as well as mankind: 'the covenant I am making between me and you and every living creature with you' (Genesis 9:12).

After Israel's escape from Egypt, the Law reminded God's people that care for their environment was one of the covenant responsibilities. Their animals were to have a share in the household's sabbath rest each week (Exodus 20:10). And when, at last, they were able to leave the desert and cross the Jordan, God gave them instructions for the agricultural care and conservation of the promised land, alongside laws designed for the welfare of men and women (see Leviticus 25).

The New Testament echoes the same theme. When Jesus wanted to illustrate how much God cares for individuals, he hit upon the word picture of a good shepherd hunting high and low for a lost animal (Matthew 18:10-14). The main purpose of the illustration was, of course, to highlight the love of God for people, but the fact that God's

love could be described in these terms at all tells us a great deal about the care Jesus believed people should take of animals.

Mankind's relationship with his environment should therefore be marked by respect and humility – an attitude which is rooted in the fact that our technological ability to manage our surroundings today is a God-given responsibility dating back to the time of creation.

The writer of Psalm 8 saw this very clearly. Looking up at the night sky, he was overwhelmed by a sense of human insignificance:

'When I consider your heavens, the work of your fingers, the moon and the stars, which you have set in place, what is man that you are mindful of him, the son of man that you care for him?' (verses 3-4).

But then he lowered his eyes, and was immediately impressed by the awesome role people have to play in God's management plan for his world:

'You made him a little lower than the heavenly beings and crowned him with glory and honour. You made him ruler over the works of your hands; you put everything under his feet' (verses 5-6).

Man, woman and their work

God's commands to man and woman to 'be fruitful and increase in number' and to 'fill the earth and subdue it' gave them a twin vocation in life. It was also a joint vocation.

Work and the family. Today, we still live with the vestiges of an artificial distinction between work and parenting. Looking after the home and children, some assume, is primarily the wife's responsibility. Having a lifetime's career is primarily the husband's.

In this respect, the Bible is firmly on the side of the feminists. There is, however, an implied criticism here of the extreme feminist reaction which downgrades parenting and home-making as second-rate activities. God's creation plan puts doing a job and bringing up a family on the same level. Both are essential parts of mankind's role in managing the world. The fact that one is usually paid while the other is not may add fuel to the fires of discrimination. But, biblically, payment is irrelevant.

This very basic creation teaching also explains why most unemployed people today feel frustrated, degraded – and even sometimes suicidal. To be deprived of the opportunity to work is to be robbed of a vital aspect of one's humanity. Working is as natural to mankind as sunset is to day (see Psalm 104:19,23). And in a society where working and wage-earning are assumed to be the same thing, it is inevitable that people who cannot get paid jobs feel they have been thrown on society's scrap-heap and treated as less than human.

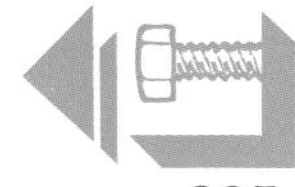

295

311

Blue collars and white collars. The second part of the Bible's creation story asks important questions about another ingrained set of attitudes about work in modern life. God put Adam and Eve in the garden of Eden 'to work it and take care of it' (Genesis 2:15). The two expressions describe different working activities. 'Work' refers to manual labour, while 'take care of' is a management term. So the roles we tend to distinguish so sharply today (management and labour) were harmoniously integrated in God's creation plan. In modern language, Adam was given the twin responsibilities of being an agricultural labourer and an estate manager.

> ***God the worker***
> The Bible paints for us a very daring portrait of a working God. He labours with his hands (Psalm 19:1; compare Isaiah 45:9). And he works executively (Psalm 33:6; 148:5).
>
> He even experiences job satisfaction (Genesis 1:31) and has a rest day (Exodus 31:17).
>
> In all these ways the Lord models the approach to work and rest which the Bible encourages men and women to share, as beings created in his image.

50

Leisure time. God made man and woman as workers. But he did not make them to work all the time. In the Ten Commandments, the order to work for six days in each week is balanced by the equally firm instruction to rest for one.

Here is a neglected corner of biblical teaching for the modern Bible user to explore. Many Christians today puzzle about their leisure time and the way God wants them to spend it. Scripture's teaching about the sabbath (which is far too rich to be linked only to the way we spend Sundays) provides clear principles to guide us.

The biggest signpost has just one word on it – *change!* God has so made people that they need periodic change from their regular occupations. This is the main point the Ten Commandments make in their instructions about sabbath-keeping. All men and women need to keep a balance in their lives between work and rest.

'Work', as we have seen, means far more than a paid job. It stands for the major component in any person's life. Similarly 'rest' means more than inactivity. It represents a minor component in life which will balance the major one suitably. If my full-time paid job has me sitting behind a desk, the 'rest' God means me to build into my life may well include vigorous exercise.

> ***The different day***
> The dominant idea of 'change' can be traced right through the Old Testament's sabbath teaching.
>
> Out in the desert, the Israelites were told to stay in their tents on the sabbath day, because that was the only change possible in their weekly routine at that time (Exodus 16:29). But in more settled days the details of the regulations naturally changed.
>
> The farmer was told to stop ploughing, even in the middle of the season (Exodus 34:21). The housewife must not light the fire, as she would on other days of the week (Exodus 35:3). And the travelling salesman had to put his samples down (Jeremiah 17:27).
>
> Everyone needed the kind of change on the sabbath day which was appropriate to his or her occupation.

The mix between major and minor which the Bible advises is a ratio of 6:1. But the New Testament warns us not to be slavish in keeping to that pattern legalistically (see Colossians 2:16-17). The balance may vary from person to person (dictated, perhaps, by the demands of shift work), and from time to time at different stages of life. But the principle itself stands firm. Man and woman have been made in such a way by their Creator that regular change needs to feature in the way work and leisure time are planned.

Society spoiled and restored

God models goodness. He reveals his nature clearly in Scripture, so as Bible users we are left in no doubt as to what our personal moral goals should be.

God has also revealed his plans for the way he means us to relate to one another and to the world in which he has set us. By following through the principles of our Creator's scheme in the Bible's pages, we can discern the signposts which will guide us along right paths through the dilemmas of modern life.

But that is by no means all. The Bible is a realistic book. Holding up a model for us to copy and a set of signposts for us to follow is not enough. We need more.

● Spoiled people

The reason we need more help is vividly described in the third chapter of the Bible, and uncomfortably reflected in our human experience. The first man and woman disobeyed God. And we, their descendants, are rebels too.

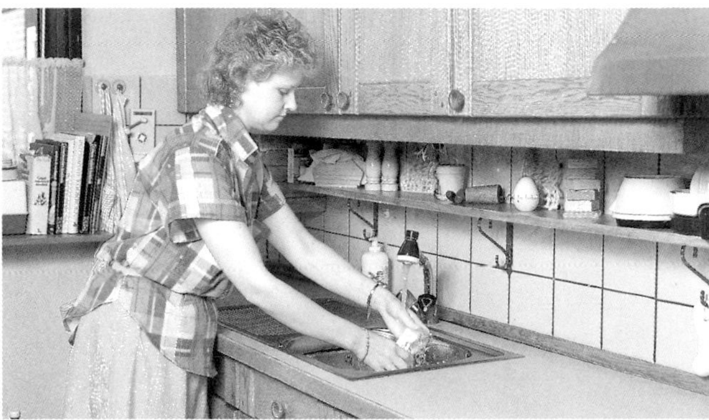

People need change from their regular occupation.

193

The technical term the Bible uses to describe human disobedience is 'sin'.

And sin deals two hefty blows to our moral capabilities. It blurs our vision of what is right and wrong; and it blunts our will power to do the right thing once we discover what it is.

God is good, and we are all created in his image. But that image has been fatally spoiled by sin. So our perception of goodness is hopelessly distorted. We are like drivers trying to find our way in a thick fog. The signposts are there to guide us, but we cannot see the lettering clearly. Often we go wrong.

The fog is patchy. Sometimes we do know the right way to go. But even then we prefer not to follow the guidance we get. We are bigheaded and pigheaded. We think we always know best.

The Bible recognizes these human failings and compensates for them. God's voice in our consciences is often muffled or distorted, so he has given us detailed rules and regulations to make his demands absolutely clear (see 1 John 4:19-21). And our obstinacy in resisting his will (see Romans 7:15-23) is held in check by clear statements and examples of the penalties that will follow if we disobey him.

265-266

351-354

The structures of the Law, with its penal code, take us into some of the most difficult parts of Scripture. They are often not easy to understand or use. But we need the guidance of their principles because we are sinners. So the time and attention we give to this aspect of the Bible's teaching will be well rewarded.

The lesser of two evils

Sometimes, in this sin-soaked world, the best that can be done is to choose the lesser of two evils. The Bible's divorce regulations illustrate this principle well.

God's ideal for marriage leaves no room for divorce at all. He hates it, says Malachi (Malachi 2:16). But sin's influence means that marriages do break down. So the Old Testament provided for estranged couples to divorce, as a damage limitation exercise (see Deuteronomy 24:1-4).

Jesus and Paul both recognized that in some situations divorce could be justified as the lesser evil. The grounds they pin-pointed were sexual unfaithfulness and desertion by the non-Christian partner in a spiritually mixed marriage (see Matthew 19:9; 1 Corinthians 7:12-15).

● Sin's dimensions

The Old Testament's account of mankind's first act of rebellion against God illustrates the way sin stains the whole of human experience, and prepares the way for some of the more detailed legislation that follows. It also provides a convincing biblical analysis of many social evils which confront us in modern life.

303-305

1 Sexual relationships

Apart from destroying their relationship with God, man and woman's fall into sin ruined their relationship with one another.

When God challenged Adam about his act of disobedience, Adam's first reaction was to blame his wife (Genesis 3:12). Then God turned to Eve and set out the one fact of fallen human experience which accounts for all sexual discrimination and for most broken marriages ever since: 'Your desire will be for your husband, and he will rule over you' (verse 16). The Hebrew word for 'rule over' carries the idea of arrogant compulsion, not protective strength.

Submission

Some see Paul's instruction that wives should submit to their husbands (Ephesians 5:22) – echoed by Peter (1 Peter 3:1) – as an unfortunate sexist hangover in the New Testament. But the context shows that this is not so.

Paul prefaces his command with a directive that Christian relationships like marriage should be marked by mutual submission (verse 21); and he follows up his instruction to wives by requiring that husbands imitate Christ's self-giving love in their attitude to their wives (verse 25).

The keynotes of the New Testament's teaching on marriage are sacrifice and responsibility, not selfishness and domination.

Even before this interchange, the seeds of sexism had already been sown. Before their rebellion against God, 'the man and his wife were both naked, and they felt no shame' (Genesis 2:25). But now their desire to hide from God was matched by embarrassment about their physical differences (see Genesis 3:7). For the first time, they became aware of each other as sex objects, not as

persons. So they covered their genitals, because that was where their gaze now rested when they looked at each other.

It is a small jump from these beginnings of relational breakdown to our modern experience of the broken marriage and the pornographic magazine. The scene is also set for the Old Testament Law's provision for divorce (see Deuteronomy 24:1-4), and for its condemnation of all sexual behaviour where the aim is selfish gratification without a self-giving relationship (see Leviticus 18:23; 19:29).

2 Working relationships. The intrusion of sin had serious repercussions on man and woman's experience of work as well. The end result was that 'the LORD God banished him (Adam) from the Garden of Eden to work the ground from which he had been taken' (Genesis 3:23).

Either side of the garden fence the ground belonged to man's Creator, of course, but the symbolism of exclusion marked the beginning of conflict. Instead of work being a positive, fulfilling seal on mankind's relationship with the Creator, as it was meant to be, it became a battleground where man and his working environment found themselves on a painful collision course.

'Cursed is the ground because of you,' God told Adam, 'through painful toil you will eat of it all the days of your life. It will produce thorns and thistles for you...By the sweat of your brow you will eat your food' (Genesis 3:17-19).

Conflict between working people was not far behind, as selfishness, envy and greed took the place of harmony and cooperation. At the heart of the murderous row between

MAN	WOMAN	
		Before the fall Mutual love and equality (Genesis 2:23-25)
Arrogant domination	Servility and rebellion	**After the fall** Mutual antagonism 'sexism' (Genesis 3:16)
Self-giving love	Humble devotion	**After the cross** Mutual submission (Ephesians 5:21)

Relationship between the sexes, spoiled and restored.

Cain and Abel recorded in Genesis 4 lay human jealousy, when God accepted the fruits of one man's work but rejected the other's. Ecclesiastes' commentary on the world of work centuries later is only a step away from this situation: 'I saw that all labour and all achievement spring from man's envy of his neighbour' (Ecclesiastes 4:4).

The Old Testament Law curbs this kind of envy and greed in two ways. First, it protects the employee against the ruthless employer (long before trade unions were invented to fill a similar role). Hard on the heels of a general warning not to defraud or rob comes the specific rule, 'Do not hold back the wages of a hired man overnight' (Leviticus 19:13).

Deuteronomy 24 explains the principle at stake: 'Do not take advantage of a hired man who is poor and needy...Pay him his wages each day before sunset, because he is poor and is counting on it' (verses 14-15). When you are paying a person who lives from hand to mouth, delay is fraud. Modern applications are not hard to find. Large firms that delib-

144-147

307-308

erately pay their small suppliers six months or more in arrears to suit their own profit or convenience may not be taken to court, but they are clearly breaking the spirit of this biblical regulation.

Secondly, the law safeguards the interests of the customer against the sharp practice of the unscrupulous tradesman. 'You must have accurate and honest weights and measures,' warns Deuteronomy 25. 'For the LORD your God detests anyone who...deals dishonestly' (verses 15-16).

Here we have the forerunner of modern legal measures to counter commercial cheats who deal in such things as useless guarantees, false delivery dates and misleading advertisements.

Laziness

The way sin spoils people's experience of work leads naturally and inevitably to laziness.

Both Old and New Testaments are scathing in their criticisms of the lazy individual. 'How long will you lie there, you sluggard?', asks the book of Proverbs angrily (6:9). Paul had the straightforward answer. 'If a man will not work, he shall not eat,' he told any work-shy members of the church at Thessalonica (2 Thessalonians 3:10).

Laziness is not, of course, the same as enforced unemployment.

● Government and order

Writing to Christians at Rome, Paul makes a sweeping and controversial statement about God and government. 'Everyone must submit himself to the governing authorities,' he insists, 'for there is no authority except that which God has established.' And he goes on, driving the point home, 'The authorities that exist have been established by God. Consequently, he who rebels against the authority is rebelling against what God has instituted' (Romans 13:1-2).

A perfect community would need some structures of government to oil the wheels of social life, but Paul has a more sombre role in mind for the authorities of the state. In a community of sinners, some recognized means of stimulating the conscience and deterring antisocial behaviour is essential. That, Paul

Christian duties to the state

Paul does not hesitate to spell out the responsibilities of the individual citizen.

First, the authorities have the right to levy taxes, and Christian citizens have a duty to pay them (Romans 13:6-7). Here he could have quoted Jesus' famous reply when he was asked whether it was right to pay taxes to an occupying power (see Mark 12:13-17). Those who use Caesar's services are under obligation to make some payment to Caesar in return.

A second Christian duty (even harder, perhaps, to fulfil) is to treat the official with respect and honour (Romans 13:7). A man or a woman in a position of responsibility may not command any respect at all as a person. But as an office-holder of the state, he or she carries the formidable authority of God's own servant.

Thirdly, all officials have a legitimate claim on the Christian's prayer time (see 1 Timothy 2:1-4). Prayers like these are really evangelistic requests, Paul points out, because when the authorities are doing their job well, by maintaining law and order, the evangelist can get on with his work in peace.

says, is the role of the person invested with authority. 'He is God's servant to do good' because he is 'an agent of wrath to bring punishment on the wrongdoer' (verses 4-5).

Paul is not making the naive claim that all who find (or fight or bribe) their ways into seats of power are men and women of integrity. His own experience of officialdom gave the lie to that. So did his reading of the Old Testament, where king after king of Israel and Judah turned out to be a rogue. His main points are much more basic and important.

They are, firstly, that God retains his sovereign power over the mightiest human rulers; and secondly that he desires people throughout the world to live together under conditions which encourage order and make the promotion of justice possible.

Confronting injustice. When those in authority abuse their power and act unjustly, two courses of action are open to God's people, according to Scripture.

They have a duty to *protest*. The Old Testament prophets spoke out particularly bravely against unjust rulers. Elijah, for example, confronted Ahab with great courage after the king had contrived the death of a man whose vineyard he wanted for a royal vegetable garden (see 1 Kings 21). And Nathan was no less bold in exposing king David's adultery with Bathsheba (2 Samuel 12:1-14).

In New Testament times, John the Baptist continued the prophetic tradition with his blunt words for Herod (see Matthew 14:1-5). And Jesus, of course, as well as identifying himself openly with the oppressed, was outspoken in his criticism of the political and religious leaders who were responsible for their predicament (see, for example, Matthew 23).

If words fail, there are circumstances when *civil disobedience* is the right course of action. So we find Paul staging the first recorded Christian sit-in when he refused to budge from jail after the authorities had realized

God in overall command

The Old Testament insists that God still rules the world. Even the mightiest king is as putty in his hands.

In Jeremiah's time, thousands of knees trembled at the name of Nebuchadnezzar, king of Babylon. His armies threatened Jerusalem. But God was still in control of events. The great king would continue his conquests, but only with the Lord's permission.

Through Jeremiah's words, God proclaimed his sovereignty: 'With my great power and outstretched arm I made the earth and its people and the animals that are on it, and I give it to anyone I please. Now I will hand all your countries over to my servant Nebuchadnezzar, king of Babylon' (Jeremiah 27:5-6).

Is civil authority always to be obeyed?

Peaceful protest against the law of the land.

106

that they had punished a Roman citizen unfairly (see Acts 16:16-40).

God's people have a special duty to dig their toes in when those with political authority make demands which cut across his commandments. Disobedience was the only possible response when Nebuchadnezzar ordered Shadrach, Meshach and Abednego to worship his giant idol (see Daniel 3:1-18). And the apostles could react in only one way to the Sanhedrin's instruction that they should give up speaking to others about Jesus. Their words ('We must obey God rather than men!') have been repeated by many Christians since when civil authorities have demanded that they fall into line by disobeying God (see Acts 5:27-29).

The Bible is silent about a third option – *armed rebellion*. Before Jesus was born, Mary sang with joy about God's revolutionary activity in bringing down rulers from their thrones (Luke 1:52); and at least one of the apostles was a freedom fighter. But Jesus consistently refused to accept the role of a political revolutionary (see, for example, John 6:15).

He rode into the arms of his enemies on an animal of peace, and submitted to unjust execution when (as he said himself at the time of his arrest) battalions of angels were on call to rescue him (see John 12:14-15; Matthew 26:51-54).

●Punishment and war

Justice can be upheld only if injustice is punished. It should not surprise us, therefore, to find a developed penal code in the Old Testament and broad hints in the New Testament that the civil authorities have a God-given right to punish offenders (see John 19:10-11; Romans 13:4).

The death penalty. The aspect of the Old Testament's legal system which causes most problems to modern Bible users is its generous provision for capital punishment.

Murder is the offence for which the death penalty is most often prescribed (see, for example, Exodus 21:12; Leviticus 24:17). The reason for that is plain enough: 'Whoever sheds the blood of man, by man shall his blood be shed; for in the image of God has God made man' (Genesis 9:6). Exceptions are made for unintentional homicide (see Exodus 21:13;Numbers 35:9-15).

Whatever our views about the rights and wrongs of capital punishment today, the plain justice of the biblical case can hardly be questioned. If one human being deliberately takes the life of another, he cannot complain if the state takes his in return.

What is far more disturbing is to find that a person could also be put to death in Old Testament times for certain sexual offences (see Deuteronomy 22:20-25; Leviticus

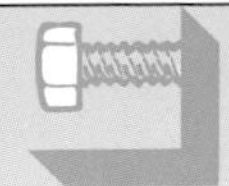

20:10-16), for kidnapping (Deuteronomy 24:7), for defiance of parental authority (21:18-21) and for blasphemy (Leviticus 24:16). What are we to make of that?

First, we must take a step back. Times have changed. Old Testament Israel was a theocracy, a nation specially chosen by God to model his divine standards. None of us breathes that kind of social and political air today. Our aim, therefore, in using the Old Testament's penal code is not to campaign for its re-introduction but to appreciate the principles on which it was founded.

Those principles are clear enough. A model society was seriously threatened by individuals who defied the standards and values on which it was based. All the offences which attracted the death penalty were direct or indirect acts of rebellion against the Ten Commandments. In other words, they endangered the foundations on which the theocracy rested. That is why the requirement of the death penalty was constantly followed by the words, 'You must purge the evil from among you' (see, for example, Deuteronomy 13:5; 17:7, 12; 19:13, 19; 21:21; 22:21; 24:7).

War. God's provision for the exercise of justice extended into the international scene. Once more, difficulties await the modern Bible user in deciding how to handle some of the relevant Old Testament passages, especially those that deal with warfare. And again, our main aim must be to appreciate the principles on which wars were fought, not to encourage our own governments to deal with other nations in a similar way. In Old Testament times God's people fought holy

Restitution

One significant aspect of the Old Testament's penal code which is often neglected today is its provision for restitution. If one man injured another, or stole some of his animals, part of the offender's punishment was to pay for the victim's medical expenses or for replacement oxen and sheep – plus interest (see Exodus 21:18-19; 22:1-4).

The purpose behind this provision was to mend broken relationships by forcing the offender to face up to the personal injuries he had caused – something which is much harder to achieve when the culprit is shut away in jail.

60-63

wars at his command. Today we may fight just wars, but never crusades.

It is the nature of God's commands to his people that raises our eyebrows. His instructions for the conquest of Canaan are typical: 'In the cities of the nations the LORD your God is giving you as an inheritance, do not leave alive anything that breathes. Completely destroy them...' (Deuteronomy 20:16-17).

108-112

The battles that Israel fought to gain control of the promised land sound very much like the aggressive acts of a warlike tribe, intent on expanding its territory with a callous disregard for the innocent people it was displacing. But that is a complete misreading of the situation.

The Canaanites' fate was, in fact, deserved punishment for centuries of the most awful atrocities. Israel was God's instrument of judgment. 'It is not because of your righteousness or your integrity that you are going in to take possession of their land,' he assured the nation bluntly 'but on account of the wickedness of these nations, the LORD your God will drive them out before you' (Deuteronomy 9:5).

There is very little teaching about the after-life in the Old Testament. If people in those times were to see the Lord as the just God, they had to see his judgments in the here and now. If the wicked were not punished in this life, it was not at all clear that justice would catch up with them after death.

186

God as judge

It is sometimes said that because God is love, he could never have commanded the extermination of the Canaanites. But that is to ignore the fact that the first two acts of mass destruction in the Bible are said to have been carried out by God himself – the flood and the destruction of Sodom (Genesis 6:7; 19:1-29).

The New Testament does not draw a veil over these stories of God's past judgments. It uses them to teach about his judgment to come. Jesus compares the terrible events that will be triggered off by his second coming with the fate of Sodom and of Noah's contemporaries (see Luke 17:26-30).

The note of mercy is never missing (Noah was saved from the flood and Lot from Sodom), but the whole Bible is utterly consistent in portraying the Lord as a God who judges sin severely. In Paul's terse words, 'God cannot be mocked. A man reaps what he sows' (Galatians 6:7).

● Restored people

So the Bible is a realistic book. It does not deal with tough-skinned sinners as though they are tender innocents. It recognizes the spoiling effects of human selfishness and greed, and it proclaims God's judgment on injustice in terms so strong that we are sometimes left feeling awed and uncomfortable.

But the Bible is also an optimistic book. Above everything else it is a record of God's love and salvation. And the life, death, resurrection and ascension of Jesus had a transforming effect on men and women's potential to live the quality of life that God always intended for his people.

God's kingdom

The kingdom of God (or of heaven) is a major New Testament theme. But at the heart of it, 'God's kingdom' is the gospel writers' way of describing 'God's activity as king'. And it is this royal activity of God which adds new dimensions to Christian living.

For one thing, it intensifies the challenge of living a life that pleases God. The demand to 'repent' (made by both John the Baptist and Jesus as they announced the kingdom's coming) expresses this very vividly. Repentance means far more than saying sorry. It means turning your back completely on your former way of life. The wealthy must part with their money to feed and clothe the poor, John told those who came to him for baptism. And the powerful must stop exploiting the weak (see Luke 3:10-14). Without that complete, decisive about-turn, there is no way into God's kingdom (see Matthew 21:28-32).

Secondly, the coming of God's ruling authority in the person of Jesus provides Christians with a fresh stimulus to live life at a higher ethical level. The Christian slave's attitude to work will be transformed, writes Paul, if he does what he is told to please his royal Master. And love in marriage will receive fresh impetus

when it is modelled on the self-giving love of Christ (see Colossians 3:22-24; Ephesians 5:25-27).

Thirdly, and most crucially, God's reign in the believer's life releases new power for living. An intensified challenge and a fresh stimulus can lead only to despair if they are not matched by new resources. But those resources are available, the New Testament promises, when Christ's royal power penetrates every corner of the Christian's lifestyle.

Negatively, God's rule means liberation from sin's grasp. The grip of sin on our lives is so powerful, Paul insists, that nothing less than the death of our old selves will loosen it. Jesus died to make such a clean break possible. As we repent of our failures and put our faith in him, we share in his royal victory. So sin's mastery of our lives is smashed (see Romans 6:6).

Positively, as sin's stains are wiped away, the Christian receives the right 'to put on the new self, created to be like God in true righteousness and holiness' (Ephesians 4:24). We have seen how God made man and woman to be like himself, and how that fact colours the Bible's teaching about the values of life, work and sexuality. We saw also how human sin spoiled all that, blurring the image in which man and woman were created. Now comes the great reversal!

Those who put themselves under God's rule share his power. This is why Jesus was able to ease his followers' dismay when the rich man walked off sadly, rather than obey his instruction to sell all his belongings.

The disciples showed their amazement when Jesus summed up what had happened by saying, 'How hard it is for the rich to enter the kingdom of God!' He responded to their surprise by reminding them of God's resources. 'With man this is impossible, but not with God; all things are possible with God' (Mark 10:23-27). The rich man's problem was not that he was wealthy, but that he was unwilling to submit his whole life to God's rule.

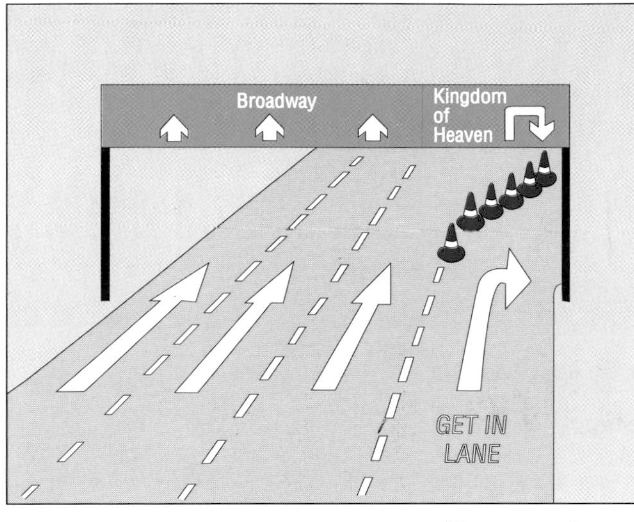

U-turn to the kingdom of heaven. God's kingdom is not straight ahead. It requires the U-turn of repentance to enter it.

Power to change

The gospel has power to change lives. Paul did not just teach this as a matter of theory. He knew from his personal experience that it was true.

Writing to the church at Corinth, he catalogued the sins he knew were represented in the lives of the congregation. They included sexual perversion, swindling and theft.

But he could end his list on a note of triumph. 'That is what some of you *were*,' he wrote. In Christ's power they were changed people (see 1 Corinthians 6:9-11).

The Spirit's work

It is the Holy Spirit who aligns the Christian's attitudes and behaviour with God's will. 'I will put my Spirit in you,' promised the Lord through Ezekiel, 'and move you to follow my decrees and be careful to keep my laws' (Ezekiel 36:27).

The New Testament lists five ways in which the Spirit brings his power to bear on the believer's lifestyle.

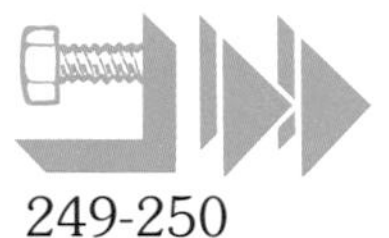

249-250

He guides. Daily life produces problems that genuinely puzzle us. We want to do God's will, but we are not sure what it is. At these times, especially, we need the Holy Spirit's prompting. 'Since we live by the Spirit,' writes Paul, 'let us keep in step with the Spirit' (Galatians 5:25).

He exposes. From his vantage-point within the believer's life, the Holy Spirit unmasks anything we do, say or think which displeases God. How can a Christian possibly go to bed with a prostitute, asks Paul, when the body he is abusing is the Holy Spirit's home (1 Corinthians 6:15,19)?

He controls. There are times in every Christian's life when temptation strikes and the 'old self' threatens to take over. At those moments the Holy Spirit provides the strength we need to resist. The New Testament reassures us that the Spirit will give us the necessary will power to live victorious lives, 'for it is God who works in you to will and to act according to his good purpose' (Philippians 2:13).

296

He motivates. The chief motive for Christian behaviour is *agapé* love. But (as we have seen) this kind of love is very special and supremely demanding. Where can we find the resources to live and love in this unique way? Only from the Holy Spirit. But we can feel encouraged, because 'God has poured out his love into our hearts by the Holy Spirit, whom he has given us' (Romans 5:5).

He unites. Sin disrupts relationships. The Holy Spirit mends them. So the Bible instructs Christians to 'make every effort to keep the unity of the Spirit through the bond of peace' (Ephesians 4:3). It is when local churches submit humbly to the Spirit that they find harmony and coordinate their activities in a way that honours God (compare 1 Corinthians 12:12-27).

Christ the bridge

The gospel does not only unite sinners to God. It builds bridges across the widest gaps between warring groups of people.

In Bible times no conflict was sharper than that between Jew and Gentile. But the death of Jesus brought the two together. Christ's purpose, writes Paul, was 'to reconcile both of them to God through the cross, by which he put to death their hostility' (Ephesians 2:14-22).

The Bible never pretends that victories over temptation and sin come easily. Indeed Jesus taught that the battles would actually intensify when people put themselves under his rule. Some of his followers, he predicted, would suffer terribly if they remained true to him and his standards (see Matthew 5:10-12).

But optimism meets with realism in the pages of Scripture. Whatever the pressures, God's staggering resources are available and adequate. So the optimistic note is the dominant one. 'May the God of hope fill you with all joy and peace as you trust in him,' Paul concludes, 'so that you may overflow with hope by the power of the Holy Spirit' (Romans 15:13).

PART 5

KEY TO PROGRESS

by John F. Balchin

The nuts and bolts of Bible study and how to get on with it.

The Bible: chapters and verses.

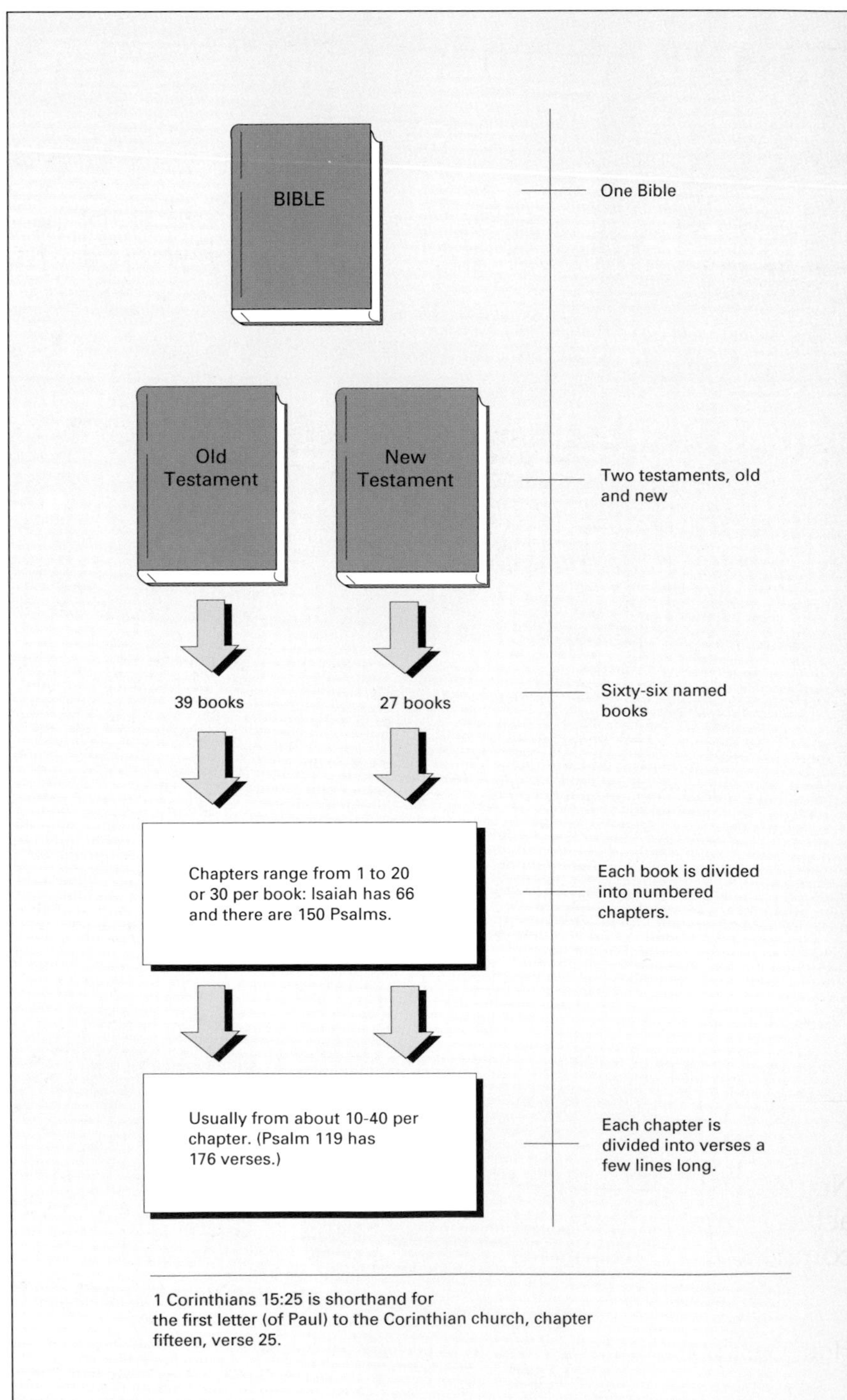

5.1 READING PLANS

No amount of learning about the Bible will ever do much for us if we do not actually read it. So here are some straightforward hints on how to simplify a complex task. Where do I begin? Read on.

How to approach the job

Imagine that you are sitting down with your Bible for the first time. You have been told that, as a Christian, you ought to read it, and yet you are finding it difficult to know how to start. Do you begin at the beginning with the first book, Genesis? But then, the person who told you about the Christian faith seemed to concentrate much more on later parts like the Gospel of John or Paul's letters. Should you begin there?

Opening the Bible for the first few times can be very confusing. It's rather like walking into a library. Until you know where the novels are and where the non-fiction is to be found you can be a bit lost. When you have been there frequently you know by experience which shelves to go to. It's much easier, however, if there is a plan of the library available. Then you can take in where everything is at a glance.

Our aim in this book has been to give you something of an overview of God's 'library', the sixty-six books of the Bible. Now it's your turn to walk around, take down some books and read them. So, how do we best go about it?

●Right the way through

That is certainly one approach. Begin with the book of Genesis and work your way right through to the book of Revelation. This will give you a comprehensive idea of what is

Chapters and verses

The story of how the Old and New Testaments came to be split up into chapters and verses is long and complicated. The original writings had no divisions. The Jews divided up the Hebrew text of the Old Testament on roughly the same lines as ours, but the numbering of some of the psalms is different, and sometimes the chapters break at a different point from our modern versions. So, for instance, we find that their Isaiah chapter 9 begins with our chapter 9 verse 2, and their Joel chapter 3 begins with our chapter 2 verse 28.

The chapter divisions which we have were not finalized until 1228, and the verses not until 1551, and we have to live with the results.

On the one hand they are a great advantage in that they give us a simple way of finding our way around the Bible. We know that Psalm 96:4 is the fourth verse of Psalm 96 (even when it's shortened to Ps.96:4), and that 1 Timothy 4:1-16 is a whole chapter in Paul's first letter to his young apprentice. It is an easy system to learn, and useful when it comes to memorizing verses of Scripture.

However, there are drawbacks. There are places where the sense runs on beyond the natural breaks in the writing. For example, the argument of 1 Corinthians chapter 10 really ends with chapter 11 verse 2, while 2 Corinthians chapter 6 verse 14 to chapter 7 verse 1 is obviously one section.

Sometimes chapter divisions break up longer sections in an unhelpful way too. How many people get to know 1 Corinthians chapter 13 without realizing that it is a very important part of Paul's teaching about spiritual gifts contained in chapters 12 to 14? We face a similar problem when we learn verses. The danger is that we see them as isolated units of Bible truth without realizing that they are part of whole passages which in turn give them their fullest meaning.

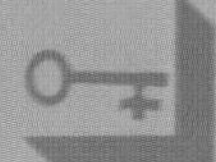

in the Bible. You will not be tempted to ignore some books and spend all your time with others, and that should have an influence on what you believe. Imbalanced beliefs can result from a partial reading of the Scriptures.

What is more, it will begin where Jesus and the apostles began. We sometimes forget that the only Bible they had - and the one which they heard read to them every sabbath - was the Old Testament. That is why there are so many references to the Old Testament in the New Testament, and also why there are many more allusions to it which the person who has never read the Old Testament will miss altogether.

The big problem with coming to the task this way is that some of the earlier books in the Bible are not at all easy to understand, especially if you happen to be a new Christian. The apostle Paul wrote about giving his new converts 'milk, not solid food' (1 Corinthians 3: 1-2), and what he meant by that was that he established them in the simple, basic truths of the faith before he went on to the more complicated ones. So it might not be the best policy to begin at the beginning and work your way through. You might not get very far before you begin to ask, 'What *is* this all about?', and then be tempted to give up, despairing of ever coming to understand it.

This might, therefore, be a very good method for those many older, more mature Christians who have never actually read the Bible right through. If they persevere from Genesis to Revelation, they will make a whole number of surprising and delightful discoveries which will help them in their Bible study ever after (it is particularly useful if they make brief notes of what they have found as they go along).

A variation on this theme, which has been used in the past, is to read the Old and New Testaments side by side, taking a chapter or two from each every day. This would certainly give you a more varied diet. But whichever way you do it, unless you are prepared to tackle large chunks of the Bible each day, it will take you a very long time to get from cover to cover. There must be easier ways!

●A bite at a book

86

We must not forget that, although individual Bible texts can mean a great deal to us, the original authors wrote whole books which usually had a theme running through them. Exceptions to this might be some of the collections of material, for example, the books of Proverbs and Psalms, or some of the longer prophets.

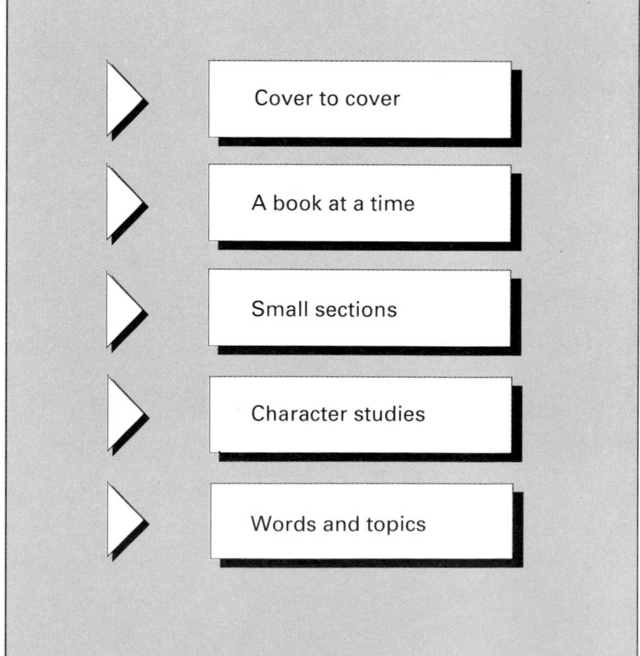

Varieties of approach to Bible study.

This means that the logical place to start is by reading a Bible book by itself right through at one sitting. This is not as difficult a job as it might seem at first. It's possible, for example, to read through Mark's gospel at a steady pace in about three quarters of an hour. After all this is the way we would read books normally, even though the longer ones, like Genesis, may take two or three sittings.

The real value of this approach is that we see how the author has developed the theme. We get a far better idea of where he wanted his readers to go. We see isolated verses, not to say events, in the settings he intended.

Once again, it is extremely useful for future or further study to make notes as you go along, and to try to get an idea of the sequence of events or argument. It's rather like using an x-ray machine to see the skeleton on which the author has hung all the flesh of his book.

364-368

It is not only a useful method, it is indispensable if we are going to go on to look at shorter passages and verses. If we have not first stood back, as it were, and taken in the whole book, we might be tempted to understand the detail in ways that the original author never intended.

With this in mind, it's good to read through a book more than once. If we are attentive, we will pick up different things each time, and so get a clearer idea of the whole. *Remember, the parts really only have their full meaning when you set them in the whole.*

●Under the microscope

Whereas reading long sections of the Bible is a very useful exercise, the point comes when we want to get down to its detail and ask what the words and sentences actually meant and mean for us. This necessarily means reading much shorter portions than whole books (unless you stick to books like Obadiah and Jude!), and for this you will need some sort of plan.

Of course, you can make your plan as you go along by reading to the next natural break in the story or the argument. In some translations of the Bible the job has already been done for you. The text is divided into sections, frequently shorter than a chapter, usually with headings which tell you what is in each division.

Daily Bible reading notes usually follow this plan too. Although some are based on readings from all over the Bible, many take you by short steps through a book.

Because you are only dealing with short sections in this way, it gives you time to begin to ask detailed questions about the meaning of the passage. It's at this point that your study notes, commentaries, Bible dictionary, atlas and other aids come into play as you ask yourself the exact meaning of a Bible word, or puzzle out why they did things as they did all those years ago.

Make your own notes as you go along, or you will lose a great deal of your hard-won truth. This is particularly important if you have a job in the church which requires you to teach the Bible to others, like Sunday School teaching. It means that you can go back to what you have discovered for yourself in the past when you are preparing a lesson or a Bible study.

●The people in the book

For a change – and it's sometimes good to have a change in Bible study method – why not set out to discov-

er all you can about a particular character in the Bible? The people described for us there are pictured 'warts and all', and we may learn almost as much from their mistakes as from what God did with them.

The first step is to collect together all the information you can find, every reference there is to that particular person in the Bible. Sometimes their stories will be quite compact, like those in Judges. At other times they will be spread across several chapters, like David, Elijah or Paul. Sometimes you will have to root out references to them as, like Peter or Barnabas, they appear on different occasions.

If you are having difficulty in finding every reference to a particular person in the Bible, you should be able to find most of them listed for you in a concordance or Bible dictionary under that name.

Try to build up your own picture of what they were like. Be prepared to recognize that they were as human as you are, and as open to temptation and error. At the same time, look for the possibilities involved when people are taken up, gifted and used by God.

Some Old Testament characters are used in this way in the New Testament. If you are studying them see what the New Testament authors had to say about them.

●Words and topics

Another very fruitful approach to Bible study is to follow a word like 'righteousness', 'truth' or 'love' through all the books of the Bible to see how it was used. Once again, a Bible dictionary can be very useful here, sometimes more useful than a concordance which lists all the occurrences of the particular term.

> It is very important, when looking at the people of the Bible, to remember to put them in their own setting and culture. It would be very unfair to expect Abraham or David to act like Christians, for example. They lived at much earlier stages of God's dealings with us. The remarkable thing about them is not that they seem to make monumental mistakes, but rather that, working with so little, they often exercised far greater faith than we do.

This is because words change in their meanings as time goes by, and are used in different ways by different authors – and sometimes by the same author.

How do we determine what a word means in the particular place where it has been used? The answer is to look at its setting, the words around it, because this will give you a clue as to how the author is using it.

What we want to avoid is giving every word the same meaning wherever it is found – language simply does not work like that – or pouring every meaning a word ever had into it every time we read it.

Akin to single words are Bible topics. Do we want to know, for example, what Jesus meant when he spoke about 'the kingdom of God'? If we do, we will have to trace that theme through the Old Testament and into the gospels, collecting together the references and building up the picture for ourselves. Do we want to know what the Bible teaches about the Holy Spirit? Similarly we have to get out our concordances, and look up every reference if we are not to come to an unbalanced conclusion.

If we want to concentrate our study somewhat, we can follow a theme

316-317

317-318

Shades of meaning	
A good example of different shades of meaning is the word 'love'. Quoting only from the *New International Version* we find for instance:	Most of these come from the pen of one author, John, and all translate the same word (*phileō* in Greek). In Greek there are other words for love too, just to complicate matters!
Luke 20:46, 'They love to be greeted in the market-places.'	It gives them a smug feeling of satisfaction.
John 12:25, 'The man who loves his life will lose it.'	He puts his own safety and comfort first.
John 11:36, 'See how he loved him!'	Jesus was so fond of Lazarus that he wept at his death.
John 15:19, 'If you belonged to the world, it would love you as its own.'	The world looks after those who go its way.
John 21:17, 'Simon, son of John, do you love me?'	Are you devoted to me and will you follow me?'
John 5:20, 'The Father loves the Son.'	There is total unity of being between two persons of the Trinity.

through the writings of a particular author like Isaiah, John or Paul. In this way we can discover that they had to teach about great subjects like salvation and judgment, faith and love.

The possibilities are wide and varied. This is the stuff of which Bible dictionaries are made, and the raw material for what we call 'biblical theology' which is, more or less, what the Bible has to say on topics like these.

● Studying with others

Although it's good to read the Bible for yourself, it is often useful to come to it with other Christians, sharing your findings. There are those, of course, who have the gift of teaching, and who are able to make the Bible clear and plain, sometimes to large numbers of people at once. Ideally this is what should be happening in our churches, as week by week we explore God's Word together. This is what we should expect and pray for as we come. That is why it is a good habit to take a Bible to church, not just to follow the reading, but to look up the references for yourself.

Another popular and frequently helpful way to look at the Bible is in small groups. The value of this approach is that, although the group leader will have prepared the study, it gives an opportunity for each person to share their particular insight with the others. It also gives the leader the opportunity to see and put right any obvious misunderstandings which crop up during the study.

If you go to a small group study, take time to have a look at the passage and the notes (if they are provided) before you get there. Take your

Bible along, and be prepared to share what you feel God has been teaching you through the passage in question. If you are a young Christian, listen to the others, especially to older and more mature believers who will have acquired a wide knowledge of the Bible, often over many years. Do not be afraid to ask questions.

One of the most helpful things about small group study is that it is often most practical. You can hardly leave a study without someone saying, 'But what do we have to do about it?' or 'How is this going to work out in my life?', and this is where all Bible study should be leading.

●Read widely, read slowly

All this talk about study might be somewhat daunting to the person who finds it hard to read, let alone get down to the hard graft of notes, dictionaries, concordances and the like. But it is not as terrifying as it seems.

When we become Christians, by his Holy Spirit God gives us a new appetite for spiritual things which we never had before. It is this new instinct which gets us into studying the Bible. We discover that the hard work of taking the Bible apart to see what we should believe and how we should be living can be real pleasure. Often we will come across a truth which we have never realized before, a promise, some aspect of God's goodness, or something else which makes our heart leap as the Holy Spirit shows us God's truth.

And there is another way of enjoying Scripture too. Sometimes it is good to put away the detailed study, to sit down comfortably, take up your Bible, and just read! Read it for pleasure as well as for instruction. Relax into the fascinating world of Scripture, and let it speak to you as it will.

Some old saints had the habit of reading the Bible slowly and prayerfully until it spoke to them in their current situation. For whether it is a matter of detailed study or wide reading, whether we do it on our own or with others, if we come to Scripture with the right attitude, that is always the thrilling possibility.

●Meditation

Meditation is an old-fashioned word, and until recently, a lost art. The Old Testament psalmist knew all about it. 'Oh, how I love your law!' he wrote, 'I meditate on it all day long' (Psalm 119:97). So it must be something that we can do at any time of the day, and not just in those special times we set apart.

> The aim of Bible study is not just to learn parts of the Bible, or even to understand it. The goal we have in mind is nothing less than getting to the point of thinking biblically about everything we do. As we have seen, if the Bible is the Word of God, it must contain God's thoughts and introduce us to God's perspective on the world, life and everything. That means that if we can soak our minds in God's Word for long enough, we will begin to think his thoughts after him. We will begin to see the world from his point of view. This, in turn, will condition how we act and react. God's purpose for the Christian is the renewing of our minds (Romans 12:2), and one of the most important means he uses in this is our study of the Bible.

If Bible study is like preparing and then sitting down to a meal meditation is like digesting it. If we have spent time studying it, trying to

understand and apply it, committing it to memory, then through the day, when our minds would otherwise be idle, it has a chance of coming back to us. Sometimes we have the thrilling experience of seeing how the very passages we have been looking at apply to particular situations at work or at home.

But meditation is something more than just casually remembering what we have read. It is taking time to chew it over and think it through. It may be just a word or a phrase from our reading. We have worked hard to understand what it means in its setting, now we let it run through our minds. As we do so we begin to push out the edges of our thinking, using our imagination as well as our reason to explore the further reaches of the truth under review.

Sometimes it's good to sit down quietly and close your eyes, shutting out the world. Some people find it helpful to jot down their thoughts as they come to them, something like this:

'God is faithful ...' (1 Corinthians 10:13)

– that means he doesn't change, that you can rely on him absolutely.

It must have been dreadful – and probably still is – to have a god you can't depend on – you would never know where you stood with him ...

But it isn't like that with the Lord ...

He doesn't lie – all his promises are true, you can take him at his Word, he is absolutely trustworthy.

That means he's going to stand by me in my weakness; when I'm tempted (that's what the passage was all about) – and even when I sin' ... at least didn't John say that?

'If we confess our sins, he is faithful and just and will forgive us our sins' ... (1 John 1:9).

I wish all my friends were like that.

But then, am I like that? After all, I'm supposed to be getting more like him

– how faithful, reliable, am I?

– can people trust me?

– do I keep my word?

What am I like at work?

– in my marriage?

– with my friends ...?

You don't have to be very clever to meditate. You just need a Scripture to start you off, and then a bit of mental discipline so that your mind doesn't wander off (God is faithful ... people aren't always reliable ... I wonder why the postman didn't call today? ... I really must remember to send that parcel to Jim next time I'm in town ... Oh, and we need some more coffee too ...)

Take a little time and try it; you will find that it will get easier the more you do it. After all, as Christians in the past have often pointed out, it is an art.

5.2 BIBLE STUDY DO-IT-YOURSELF

This section is short but crucial. The general guidelines sum up much of what is important in the rest of the book. The Scripture Union method and the relationship between prayer and Bible study lead us into the devotional core of Bible reading: our relationship with the God who stands behind the words.

Page

Some general guidelines

Before we start looking in detail at how to understand different sorts of passages from the Bible, here are some general rules:

1 Get hold of a good translation, one which does not take too many liberties with the text of Scripture. You can't go far wrong with the *New International Version*.

2 Read the portion slowly, trying to take in what it is trying to say – and then read it again to reinforce that, and you will find that you notice things you missed first time through.

333-362

3 Decide which sort of writing you are dealing with. Is it a Bible story, or poetry, or teaching? As we will see, we need to approach different types of passage in different ways.

4 Put the text or passage into its setting. Why was the book written and where does this particular section come? What do you know about the time and circumstances when it was written? If you are concentrating on one Bible text, make sure you relate it to what comes before and after.

5 Work out how the writer has put the passage together. See how he has built up the story, or worked out his argument.

364-368

6 Try to decide the exact meaning of the words. Is the author using picture language? How? What are the words actually saying? Are there Hebrew or Greek ways of putting things which we would not use nowadays?

7 Use your imagination and try to put yourself into the picture. What would it have been like to have been there? How would the first readers have heard those words?

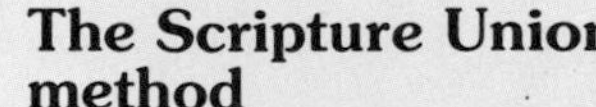

The Scripture Union method

Over the years countless readers of Scripture Union Bible notes have found it useful to come to their daily Bible reading in the following way:

PRAY

that God will speak to you as you read his Word

READ

carefully, listening for what God is saying to you

THINK

* What is the main point of this passage?

* What does it teach you about God – the Father, his Son Jesus Christ, or the Holy Spirit?

* Is there a special command, promise, warning or example that you should note?

* What fresh insight does the passage give into yourself, your situation and your relationships?

DO

What practical action should you take?

PRAY

* Use the reading as a basis for praise, confession and prayer for yourself and others.

8 If you come across a difficulty, compare that passage with easier passages on the same subject. Sometimes the references in the margin, if you have them, will help you here.

9 Go for help. Look up your notes, or Bible commentary if you have one. Check out the words in the concordance or Bible dictionary (we will be explaining these later). Ask your minister or someone who has had more experience in studying the Bible than you have. Make up your

own mind. If you can't solve the problem there and then, don't worry; you may understand it later.

10 Ask yourself what God is saying to you through the passage, either directly or indirectly. What practical lessons can you learn from it? If God spoke in that way in those circumstances, what would he be saying to us in ours today?

Prayer and Bible study

Because the Bible is not just another book, but rather the way in which God frequently speaks to us, our approach to it is obviously very important.

Of course God can and does use it regularly to speak to people who have very little time for him, and who are even critical and sceptical in their approach. But as Christian believers we should come to it with faith, with expectancy and, most important, being willing to submit our wills to God's will as he reveals it through our study.

That is why it is most natural to come prayerfully, asking God for his help as we read it, deliberately putting ourselves 'under the Word of God' as the Reformers described it. This principle applies whether we study it privately, or whether we listen to it being expounded in public. Come asking and God will give you what you need; so Jesus himself promised.

Over the years many have used the simple 'Scripture Union prayer' which is itself part of Scripture: 'Open my eyes that I may see wonderful things in your law' (Psalm 119:18), and found that it has helped them to come with the right attitude.

What is God saying to you?

Not only may we move into our Bible study with prayer, we may move from it in the same way too. We may turn the thoughts, themes, promises and commands which we have read into praise, confession, petition and intercession for others. Have we been reading about God's faithfulness? Praise him for it, and ask that our own trust in him and in his supply may be deeper. Have we been studying his righteousness? Then ask him to forgive our unrighteousness; pray that our lives may reflect his holy character, and that we may work to see the wrongs in society about us righted.

This is nothing new. Read Daniel chapter 9, and see where his Bible study led him!

Memorizing Scripture

One well-tried method for retaining what you have read is to commit it to memory. That great psalm about the value of Scripture, Psalm 119, tells us that hiding God's Word in our hearts is one way of preventing us from sinning (Psalm 119:11).

This psalm was composed in sections, each verse of a section beginning with the same letter of the Hebrew alphabet, probably making it easier to memorize.

From the way the New Testament authors quote the Old Testament, it is apparent that they also had their minds filled with Scripture. Perhaps they deliberately set out to learn it, as many Jews did in those days. Perhaps they had become familiar with it through repeated sabbath readings in their synagogues. Sometimes when quoting from memory, they get the sense rather than the actual words of the original.

With our convenient chapter and verse divisions, it is fairly easy for us to memorize verses from the Bible, and we can learn the references too.

The Navigators' *Topical Memory System* has allowed many to commit a large number of significant verses to memory. Their method is to print important verses with their references, on small cards which can easily be carried in the pocket and referred to at odd moments during the day. By continually reviewing a verse it gets lodged in the mind and easier to recall.

The problem of single verses, of course, is that it is all too easy to take them out of their setting and make them mean less than they should.

This means that it is often more helpful to learn chapters or passages.

For example, we have some wonderful descriptions of Jesus Christ like Philippians chapter 2, verses 5 to 11, or Colossians chapter 1 verses 15 to 20. Similarly there are some powerful passages in the Old Testament like Isaiah chapter 40, while many of the psalms make great material for committing to memory.

In your studies you will come across sections which mean a great deal to you. Note these; read them through several times; try writing them out, and you will find that learning a passage is not such a hard task.

All this assumes, of course, that whether verses or passages, you have thoroughly tried to understand them and to apply them to your own life first. Repeating Bible passages parrot-fashion, like rattling through the Lord's Prayer, will do nothing to bring the great truths of God's Word to bear upon your life.

5.3 DIFFERENT KINDS OF BIBLE WRITINGS AND HOW TO RECOGNIZE THEM

On page 330 the third general rule concerning understanding the Bible says, 'Decide which sort of writing you are dealing with.' How can you do that? The following section gives a run-down of the different kinds of Bible writings that you will meet and tells you how to recognize them. There are also worked examples of how to get the best out of them.

Stories and histories

Many of us were introduced to the Bible through its stories, those great and gripping tales of Moses in the bulrushes or David and Goliath. And great tales they are. The Bible authors knew how to tell a story, how to introduce their characters, how to build the tension, and how to leave you with a sense of relief at the end.

But they were not interested merely in telling tales. They are different from the usual story-tellers in at least two respects. First of all, the events they portrayed actually happened, and although they were sometimes written up long afterwards, the descriptions in the Old and New Testaments go back to eyewitnesses who were there.

Again, they were not just retailing interesting information about people and their affairs. They were profoundly aware that, whatever people did, God was at work in the background – and sometimes in the foreground too. At times this is spelled out clearly; on other occasions we have to perceive it for ourselves. For example, God is not named at all in the book of Esther, and yet the story is all about God's providence and overruling.

129-130

Stories, or narratives as we call them, make up a good proportion of the Bible. Around 40% of the Old Testament is narrative, while in the New it is the foundation of the gospels and the substance of the book of Acts. Because of this it is a good point to begin as we ask ourselves how we should get down to the actual work of understanding the Bible.

To do this, it is important that we recognize what Bible narratives are and, perhaps just as important, what they are not. They are not what we would usually describe as 'teaching', although they may contain teaching (the four gospels, for example, are as much Jesus' teaching as an account of what he did and where he went). What we mean by a Bible narrative is generally an account of something that happened. It describes certain events that took place at a certain time in a certain place. Although we may derive lessons from what happened, if we want straight teaching about Christian living we need to go, for example, to the New Testament letters, rather than stories in the book of Acts.

The Bible stories frequently underline and illustrate what we learn about God, and his ways with us, from other clear statements of the truth elsewhere in Scripture. In fact, we can sometimes get hold of a truth far more easily this way. To say 'You can trust in God to protect you' is hardly as appealing to our imaginations as the story of David and Goliath; to state that sin doesn't pay is not nearly as forceful as the story of David and Bathsheba and its consequences. God knew that many of those who would read the Bible would be like those who originally wrote it: ordinary people who needed their hearts stirred as well as their minds informed.

●Written with a purpose

It is equally clear that those who put the stories together had that in mind too. Sometimes they state their purpose quite clearly. 'Jesus did many other miraculous signs in the presence of his disciples, which are not recorded in this book,' wrote John when summing up his gospel, 'But

these are written that you may believe that Jesus is the Christ, the Son of God, and that by believing you may have life in his name' (John 20:30-31). Similarly Mark begins his work, 'The beginning of the *gospel* about Jesus Christ, the Son of God' (Mark 1:1). In other words, what follows is not just a collection of stories about an interesting man; it is a message, the Good News no less, to which we must respond personally. But it comes to us in narrative form.

Sometimes the writer's purpose lies not so much on the surface but in his obvious interests which emerge as he goes along. We see this when the author of Chronicles rewrote Kings, and put in a great deal of information about the priests and their duties, or in Matthew's gospel with its frequent references to the Old Testament. He was clearly writing it to convince a Jewish readership about the claims of Jesus.

Sometimes we have to take on board the total impact of the book to see why the author wrote as he did. When, after a succession of miserable failures on the part of God's people, God had to step in and save them, the author of Judges comments, 'In those days Israel had no king; everyone did as he saw fit' (Judges 21:25). This sorry condition prepares us for the next book where God gives Israel a king, even though things did not work out quite as they should have done. But that's another story!

One thing about Bible stories which we have to appreciate is that they do not always have a happy ending. But then, that's how life really is, and the authors saw their job as telling us how things were, not how they, or we, would have liked them to be. So the Bible characters come across with all the imperfections of human nature as we know it. That's why Bible narratives have their fair share of errors to avoid as well as examples to follow. Sometimes we're not told what we ought to do in response to what happened. Then we have to understand the actions of the people in the light of the clear teaching that we find in the rest of the Bible, and come to our own conclusion.

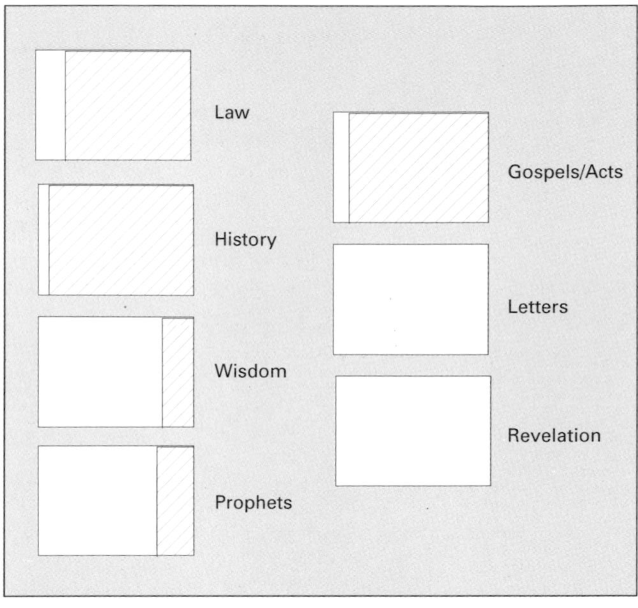

Where are the Bible's stories?

Think of Jephthah, a man God had greatly used to lead God's people to victory, slaying his only daughter as a human sacrifice because he had rashly vowed to give to God the first living thing he met on his return (Judges 11:1-40). We are not told whether he was right or wrong, but we should know from what the Bible teaches elsewhere. Or take the election of Matthias to replace Judas Iscariot (Acts 1:12-26). Were they right or wrong to use the casting of lots? Should they have waited for Pentecost? We are not told. Luke simply tells us what happened.

● Use your imagination

One of our problems in understanding narrative is that we look back at Bible events from the twentieth century and with Christian eyes. If we are going to understand what went on, we have to make a real effort and use our imaginations to 'get inside' the situations described. We need to ask questions like, 'What must it have been like to be the character in question?' 'How much can we reasonably expect them to know when it comes to God's will?' 'How would we have reacted to what happened to them?' and so on. Try to put yourself back into the times of Abraham, Elijah, Nehemiah or the apostles.

Don't expect too much of Bible characters. Think how little average Christians know about their faith in spite of having Bibles in their own language, and of being exposed to regular Christian preaching. Remember that God revealed some truths slowly and over the years.

So how do we actually extract lessons for ourselves from Bible narratives? After all, we do not read them just for entertainment or general interest. We do so for help in our Christian living. Events in history, in spite of what they say, are unrepeatable. We are not called upon to lead Israel into battle. We do not have the privilege of witnessing Jesus healing the sick. We were not there at Pentecost. All these occasions were 'one-off', just as every event in our lives is unique and unrepeatable.

And yet, when we think of our own lives, we can see how we learned lessons along the way. If things have gone particularly badly for us, we

Bible stories – in practice

Here is a short and very familiar story from the life of Jesus as told in Mark 4:35-41. What sort of questions ought we to be asking when we study it for ourselves?

1 Where does this come in the gospel? Is it part of something Mark is trying to get over to us?

2 Is there anything we need to know about boating in Galilee which will help us to understand what happened?

3 Try to put yourself in the disciples' shoes; how would they have felt before and after the miracle?

4 What does it tell us about Jesus?

5 What lessons are there here for us?

6 Do we learn anything else from this passage?

That day when evening came, Jesus said to his disciples, 'Let us go over to the other side.' Leaving the crowds behind, they took him along, just as he was, in the boat. There were also other boats with him. A furious squall came up, and the waves broke over the boat, so that it was nearly swamped. Jesus was in the stern, sleeping on a cushion. The disciples woke him and said to him, 'Teacher, don't you care if we drown?'

He got up, rebuked the wind and said to the waves, 'Quiet! Be still!' Then the wind died down and it was completely calm.

He said to his disciples, 'Why are you so afraid? Do you still have no faith?'

They were terrified and asked each other, 'Who is this? Even the wind and the waves obey him!'

Now let's answer the questions:

1 If we have read right through Mark's gospel we may have seen that, for about the first eight chapters, almost everything that happens poses the sort of question the disciples asked after the miracle. It is all leading towards Peter's confession of Jesus as the Christ, the Messiah (8:27-30). After that the road leads downwards to Jerusalem and the cross and resurrection because, although Jesus was the Messiah, he was a different sort of Messiah from the one they were expecting.

2 From your Bible dictionary or commentary you might have learned that sudden squalls are a feature of Galilee. Even so, it must have been severe for experienced sailors like these to be so frightened (or was the boat overloaded?). We also need to remember that they were entirely dependent on either sails or oars.

3 Their fear of drowning before the miracle was replaced by a different sort of fear – the awe which comes from knowing that you are in the presence of the supernatural. Have you ever experienced that?

4 The story tells us how completely human Jesus was. He could not always be on demand; there were times when he had to leave the crowds behind, however needy they may have been. It tells us that he could get very tired, but it also shows us how much he trusted in his Father to look after him and his disciples. It also illustrates his amazing authority, something which Mark has been underlining as he has described what Jesus did (he addresses the storm in the same way that he had spoken to a demon-possessed man in 1:25). We are dealing with someone here who is obviously no ordinary man. But who alone has authority over wind and sea?

5 We can, no doubt, think of many parallel situations in our own lives when our reaction to difficulties and threats of various kinds has been fear and panic, and when we need to hear Jesus' words addressed to us, or rather, to the things which threaten us. What we need is what the disciples lacked, confidence in a heavenly Father and in his Son.

6 Note the clues in the story that we are dealing with eyewitness evidence here: they took Jesus just as he was; there were other boats involved too; Jesus was asleep on the boat cushion in the stern. Whoever first told this story had been there with him in the boat.

resolve not to get into that sort of situation again. If things have gone well we try to put the same principles into operation in future. We extract lessons or principles from what has happened to us and we can do the same when we look at other people's lives too. We don't have to learn the same lessons over and over again (unless we are particularly stupid), and we don't have to learn the hard way.

When we come to Bible stories about situations, events and, more particularly, the people involved in them, we can adopt the same method. What lessons did they learn or should they have learned? What promises did they claim? How did God lead them? How did they respond? Or where did they go wrong? Is their lack of faith and disobedience, and what it led to, something from which we can learn?

It is also quite legitimate to suggest parallels between their situations and our own. Did they have difficulties and problems? So do we. Did they put their trust in God? So must we. How did they do it? How must we? What we must avoid, of course, is turning the stories into allegories

59-60

giving every detail a spiritual meaning. There are allegories in the Bible, but the Bible stories were never intended to be read that way.

● Eyewitness evidence

On a number of occasions in the Bible we are reminded that what we are reading goes back to people who were actually there at the time. Sometimes there is a clear claim to be an eyewitness. For example, Peter tells us this categorically when describing the transfiguration (2 Peter 1:16-18), and Paul insists upon the resurrection of Jesus for the same reason (1 Corinthians 15:3-7). In fact the words 'witness' and 'testimony', used frequently in the New Testament, originally carried the idea of 'eyewitness' (often to the historical event of Jesus' resurrection).

The personal source behind the fourth gospel – probably John the apostle – is described like this (John 21:24), and he makes a very strong claim to have personal knowledge of Jesus when he writes his first letter (1 John 1:1-3). Even a later generation was aware that the gospel that they preached went back to those who had been there, who had seen and heard Jesus (Hebrews 2:3).

Eyewitnesses.

At one point the book of Acts appears to have been almost Luke's travel diaries (from 16:11 he begins to write 'we'), and although there is less of this in the stories of the Old Testament, most of Nehemiah, for example, is a personal account too.

Added to this, there are often little give-away details in the accounts which no-one would have thought of putting in had they simply been making the stories up. For example, who else would have said that 'the other disciple' outran Peter and hesitated at the tomb entrance, only to have Peter barge past him (John 20:3-6), except that very disciple who was remembering the details as he dictated them? And who would have thought to describe the grass as green at the feeding of the 5,000 (Mark 6:39 – an important pointer to the time of year because the grass in Palestine is not always green), unless he had been there, and because he had seen it, it had stuck in his mind?

The charge that the Bible stories were concocted, even for the best reasons, merely to teach moral lessons, falls down on at least two points. First of all, the authors of both Old and New Testaments shared a faith which put a high value on the truth and telling the truth. To write lies, even pious lies, would be for them a contradiction in terms. Then we need to remember that, most certainly for Christian authors, there was nothing to gain by it and everything to lose.

To claim, for example, that you

believed that Jesus was raised from the dead because you had seen him alive after the crucifixion, did not enhance your position in society! It made you a marked man, liable to receive similar treatment from the same authorities who had connived at Jesus' death. And yet they persisted in doing so, because they could not do otherwise. As Peter put it to the Jewish council, 'We cannot help speaking about what we have seen and heard' (Acts 4:20).

●God used editors

Although some of the Bible books were written directly by the people involved – Jeremiah dictating his prophecies, and Paul his letters – many were put together by editors who used information which they got from others. For example, although Luke included some of his own memoirs in Acts, he was dependent on others to tell him what went on both during Jesus' ministry and during the early days of the church. He himself tells us that he took great pains to make his record accurate (Luke 1:3-4), and this must have meant interviewing many of those who were directly involved.

But, like many other Bible authors, he was prepared to use documents written by others. We are fairly sure that along with Matthew, he used both Mark's gospel and another written source containing a good deal of Jesus' teaching (it also seems to have been used by Matthew). This is not surprising, because he himself tells us that others before him had attempted to draw up an account of what had happened during Jesus' lifetime, although he makes it clear that he is not concerned with mere hearsay. He wanted eyewitness evidence (Luke 1:1-2).

So it is obvious that his prime concern was to tell Christians who had not been there what had happened and how it had happened. There must have been enormous interest in the life and teaching of Jesus, and when those directly involved were not available for questions or, more particularly, when they began to die off, it was absolutely necessary to get their testimony written down if it was going to be preserved accurately.

We must not underestimate the demand to know about what Jesus said and did. However, like all authors and editors, Luke would have had particular people in mind when he wrote, and a particular message to get across to them.

We see this when we compare his gospel with the others. Mark, who in all probability wrote down Peter's memoirs, tells us about his clear purpose in writing (1:1). However, he actually includes very little of Jesus' teaching. Luke fills out the picture, using his other source together with the results of his own research. Matthew starts at the same point, but rearranges the material into orderly blocks. What is more, as he has Jews in mind, he demonstrates how Jesus fulfils a succession of Old Testament predictions.

195-197

182

John gives us his own personal recollections, but he is highly selective in what he describes. There are only seven miracles recorded in John's gospel (and not one is an exorcism), but we do have extended blocks of Jesus' teaching calculated to bring us to faith in him. Because he generally describes the Jews in a hostile sense, and on occasion explains their customs, he seems to be writing with Gentiles in mind.

We can see the process going on in

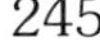

245

When did it happen?

The Jews did not think about dates and the ordering of events in the same way that we do. Our idea of history is that of a succession of happenings, recorded in strict date order. There *were* times when they 'put a date' on what they recorded, as with the reigns of the Old Testament kings (some prophecies are dated this way), or as Luke carefully dates Jesus' birth (Luke 2:1-2), but it isn't always as clear as that. They obviously worked within a broad framework of beginnings, endings and the developments in between, but they were not always so concerned about which particular event came after which. This can be seen in the gospels.

This is probably because the authors were more interested in what the events meant rather than in the order in which they happened. This may offend our twentieth-century western ways of thinking, but historians have also come to realize that any meaningful account must select what it records, and give prominence to the important happenings.

This is exactly what we find happening in the Old Testament and in the book of Acts. Sometimes the authors of the Bible stories will telescope long periods of time into a couple of verses, while elsewhere they will write several chapters about events that took place in a few days. This means that their treatment of Bible 'history' will seem very uneven to us.

Remember that Bible study is not merely learning about the Bible. It has to do with grasping its message. Sometimes, with our modern, western ways of thinking, we become over-concerned with the incidental packaging of Scripture, and in the process miss out on its significance, that is, what God is trying to say to us through it.

31

the gospels as well as in parallel books like Kings and Chronicles, but it must have been happening whenever authors put together their collected materials. Part of the miracle of Scripture is that God could overrule their efforts and intentions to produce what he wanted in the books that resulted. This is just as true when they left things out as when they included them. It is the resultant book which is important, and not just the various sources which they drew upon. How they did it may lead scholars into all sorts of fascinating detective work, but when all is said and done, it is the books as they are which God intended us to regard as Scripture, and to study as we find them.

Poetry and song

Many of us will remember learning poetry at school. For some it opened a door to a wonderful new world full of colour and power. For others it was hard work (perhaps we were made to learn it too early, before we could appreciate it). However it was, poetry is a very important part of life, and something which we use extensively in Christian worship. Our choruses, hymns and songs are poetry put to music, and history has shown that, whenever there has been a fresh moving of the Spirit of God on his people, it has risen to the surface in song.

What is poetry? It's the use of words and phrases in a particular way, a way which either expresses, or which calls up in us, feelings in a manner which other writing cannot. Poetry is usually about something (unless it is nonsense poetry, which

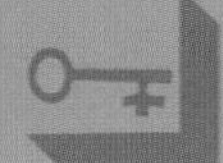

is usually just for fun). The secular poet tries to express what he or she feels about themselves, other people, the world in which they live, and so on. The poets in the Bible had far more to get lyrical about. They spoke about God, and the wonders of his ways with the world and with men and women, about his salvation and the grand plans he has for the world – in fact, the whole scope of their faith. But they were not just making theological statements; they were expressing their feelings and responses in ways which conjure up the same sort of feelings in those who were to read what they wrote.

The way that poetry does this is to make much of word pictures, symbols and images drawn from a variety of sources and applied in different ways. Take the opening of that best known psalm, 'The LORD is my shepherd.' God is not a literal shepherd any more than we are literal sheep, but by taking up a picture which in those days spoke loudly of provision and direction, it brings home the truths about God providing and leading in a powerful way.

This introduces us to a basic principle when it comes to understanding the poetry of the Bible. Poetic pictures and symbols are not to be taken literally. In fact, what is important to the poet is not the symbol, but his feeling about the truth that it expresses. Our faith is not merely a matter of knowing the right theological answers; it is not even being able to recite a creed correctly. It is a matter of being personally involved with the truth. It will involve knowing the facts with our minds, but if we do not *feel* about them they have not really become ours. Bible poetry attempts to express that feeling, and to draw the readers into it as well.

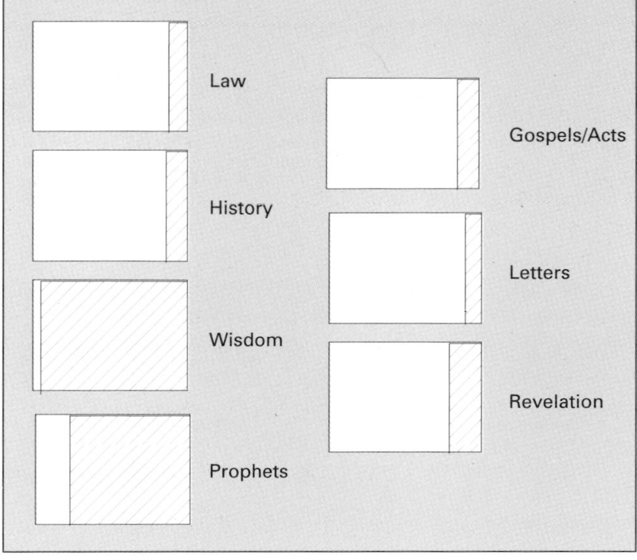

Where is the poetry in the Bible? (see page 132 for details).

138

● Hebrew poetry

Hebrew poetry was rather different from our own which, over the years, has extensively used words that rhyme. The Israelites were more interested in statements that balanced. For example, when Zophar indignantly says of Job,

> 'Are all these words to go
> unanswered?
> Is this talker to be vindicated?'
> (Job 11:2)

he is really saying the same thing twice, in two different ways (though the second statement usually carries on the thought of the first a little further).

Sometimes the poet makes his point with a contrast, where the second statement is the opposite of the first:

> 'The lions may grow weak and
> hungry,
> but those who seek the LORD lack
> no good thing' (Psalm 34:10).

Sometimes it gets much more complicated, one thought building on another. Take the statement which begins:

'The Spirit of the Sovereign LORD is
on me,
because the LORD has anointed me
to preach good news to the poor.
He has sent me to bind up the
broken-hearted,
to proclaim freedom for the
captives
and release for the prisoners,
to proclaim the year of the LORD's
favour and the day of vengeance
of our God... (Isaiah 61:1-2).

It's the sort of statement which is not only full of parallels, it grows on itself to produce a bigger and bigger picture of what the Servant of the Lord will bring about.

Where do we find this poetry in the Bible? 'Almost everywhere' is the answer, because even in 'non-poetic' sections of Scripture, the themes are sometimes so profound that the writers put down their words with a poetic lilt to them. More specifically, the book of Psalms is an obvious starting place. The hymnbook of the Israelite faith, it expresses the widest range of feelings and thoughts, both individual and corporate, that God's

136-141

Let's sing a hymn – with David!

Many of us will have recognized something special about the Psalms, whether or not we have consciously thought of them as poetry. We have read them and heard them read; sung them (sometimes in rhyming form as hymns) and heard them sung. Let's have a closer look at one to see if we can understand it better, and let it do its work in us.

Psalm 23

A psalm of David

The LORD is my shepherd, I shall not
be in want.
He makes me lie down in green
pastures,
he leads me beside quiet waters,
he restores my soul.
He guides me in paths of
righteousness
for his name's sake.
Even though I walk through the
valley of the shadow of death,
I will fear no evil,
for you are with me;
your rod and your staff,
they comfort me.
You prepare a table before me
in the presence of my enemies.
You anoint my head with oil;
my cup overflows.
Surely goodness and love will follow
me
all the days of may life,
And I will dwell in the house of
the LORD
for ever.

1 Do we know when and how it was written?

2 How do I know that this is poetry?

3 What are the main pictures being used?

4 Are there customs and practices which I need to understand?

5 What does it tell me about God and his dealings with a believer?

6 How do I feel when I read it through with understanding?

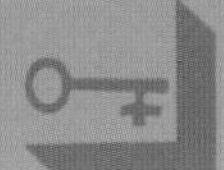

How did you get on?

1 This psalm is traditionally credited to David (see Psalms in the Bible),and there is no reason why it should not come from the shepherd-boy poet who became the king. There is no indication as to when he wrote it. It simply seems to be a meditation about God's goodness based on his own experience.

2 We know that it's poetry because of the way in which the statements balance one another. In most modern Bibles it will be set out as poetry.

3 Actually there are two pictures: the shepherd looking after his sheep, and the host entertaining his guest (otherwise you have the rather quaint picture of sheep sitting up to a table!). The psalmists often did move from one picture to another, just as it suited them. Note that Jesus Christ used both these pictures of himself (John 10:11-16; Matthew 22:1-14). In the Near East of David's day, kings were often referred to as shepherds.

4 We will need to know how the eastern shepherd cared for his flock, leading it out to pasture and protecting it from danger. The rod and staff are counterparts of a shepherd's crook and club. We will also need to know about eastern hospitality, and about the way in which the host anointed his guests with fragrant oil. We also need to know that to eat at the same table expressed close fellowship.

5 It tells me that God cares, that he provides, restores, guides and protects his people. 'Paths of righteousness' speak of a life which pleases him; 'for his name's sake' reminds me that it is not because I deserve it, but because of what and who he is (summed up by his 'name'). It also tells me that he vindicates those who put their trust in him, whatever other people might think of them (remember that David's enemies were a real threat to him and his kingdom). It also shows me that God's goodness is not only for this life but for ever. To live in the house of the Lord is a picture of open access to and fellowship with God.

6 Read it through quietly, slowly and prayerfully – and see for yourself!

people experienced, and all in poetry.

But it doesn't end there, and in this respect we are far better off than in the old days. Early translations of the Bible tended to put everything in solid blocks. There was no indication whether it was poetry or not, which could be very misleading. Modern translations attempt to set out poetry to look like poetry, from some of the earliest, like the song of Moses (Exodus 15:1-18), through many Old Testament expressions of prayer, praise and lament. It includes books like Job, Proverbs, Ecclesiastes and the Song of Songs, and also most of the prophetic writings.

In the New Testament we have some wonderful examples in the songs of Mary and Zechariah (Luke 1:46-55, 68-79), while a good deal of Jesus' teaching has a poetic ring about it – for example, the Beatitudes (Matthew 5:3-10). Paul frequently becomes lyrical when writing in his letters about the glories of Christian living. There may even be early Christian hymns embedded in his work (see Philippians 2:6-11). By the time we get to Revelation we are plunged back into the world of symbols and

132

images in a big way.

So whatever we might think about poetry, we will need to come to terms with it if we are not going to miss out on large tracts of Scripture. When we do, however, we will find that it adds a whole new dimension to our understanding, and to our expression of the Christian faith.

Parables

180

One of the ways in which Jesus is remembered best is that he told stories, and that the crowds who followed him about loved to hear them. These stories are called 'parables' in the gospels, a word which can mean anything from something compared with something else, to a riddle where you have to guess the meaning. It may be because of this that parables have suffered so much through the history of the church. After all, with a good bit of imagination, you could make them mean all kinds of things, just as it suited you.

Where are the parables in the Bible?

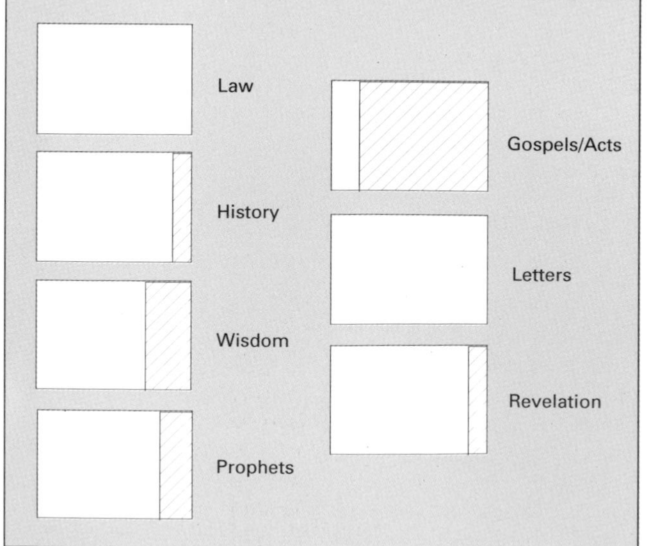

This was particularly so when people regarded them as allegories, that is, stories where every little detail must mean something special. There is a famous interpretation of the parable of the Good Samaritan which makes the Samaritan a picture of Jesus, while the man robbed symbolizes a sinner. It ends up with the inn being the church, and the 'two pence' which the Samaritan gave to the innkeeper being baptism and the Lord's supper! You don't have to be very clever to see that this was not what Jesus meant by it at all.

We also need to think about the way in which Jesus used parables. There are times when he seems to be simply illustrating a point. His story about the men who built their houses on rock and sand is fairly obvious in its meaning (Matthew 7:24-27). If you refuse to act upon what Jesus is saying, you are inviting disaster. Many of his shorter, 'mini-parables', are really only illustrations. The disciples are described as 'the salt of the earth' and 'the light of the world' (Matthew 5:13-16); they are warned about false prophets who are like wolves in sheep's clothing (Matthew 7:15); they are asked if they would give their children unwholesome things to eat like stones or snakes (Matthew 7:9-10). Maybe these are not strictly parables in the fullest sense, but they show how Jesus used picture language to get his point across.

● Involving the hearers

The reason he used picture language at all is that he could take up something which his hearers knew all about, and move from that to spiritual truths which would otherwise be harder to grasp. Sometimes it is a matter of contrast as well as

comparison. That is why some of his parables are followed by a 'How much more will your heavenly Father...' do this or that. There is some truth in the old definition of a parable as 'an earthly story with a heavenly meaning'. It was that, and at times, a great deal more.

The skill in telling a story lies in the ability to build a world of words and to take your hearers into it, so that they almost become part of the story. That way they get so involved that they begin to feel along with the characters in the story, to take sides, to decide how it should work out – and then to feel genuine relief or surprise when you get to the punch line. Jesus was a master when it came to telling stories like that. He did it so well that we sometimes have the involuntary reactions of his hearers thrown in along with Jesus' words.

This was particularly so when Jesus' parables worked out in ways which the audience did not expect. The parable of the Pharisee and the tax collector praying in the temple (Luke 18:9-14) would have shocked his first hearers. For them, the Pharisees were good men who took their religion seriously. How was it then, that God accepted the miserable tax collector, a collaborator and a crook, rather than this good man? Again, the Good Samaritan was a contradiction in terms. For the Jews of that time there were no good Samaritans! And the parable of the wicked tenants (Matthew 21:33-41) carried a horrific message for the Jewish authorities who, we're told, knew that it described them (verse 45). To suggest that God might deal with them in a similar way was unthinkable and unacceptable.

One of our problems when it comes to understanding the parables is that we often miss their impact because we are not living in Jesus' day and aware of everything that was happening then. We know, for example, that many Pharisees were hypocritical because Jesus said it in very straightforward language elsewhere (see Matthew 23). We also know about loving one's neighbour, and about what ultimately happened to the Jews in Palestine. In fact, we're usually so familiar with the stories themselves that we have to use a good deal of imagination to get back and stand in the crowd alongside those who first heard them.

Although Jesus did teach new truths with his parables, the important point was how people reacted to them, how they touched their lives, even by upsetting them at times. One of the ways in which we can recreate that first reaction is to see what the parable was all about originally, and then write a modern version of it. Instead of Jews and Good Samaritans you might have Protestants and Catholics in Northern Ireland, or Jews and Arabs in Israel.

●Just one meaning

Another of our problems in understanding the parables is that, with a number of them, we seem to have lost their original settings. Although in some cases we are told what sparked the parable off – like the lawyer's question about neighbourliness and the Good Samaritan (Luke 10:25-37), elsewhere they just begin with no setting at all. Some come as part of a collection (see Matthew 13). In situations like this, we have to do even more background work than usual, asking ourselves what might have been the sort of circumstances in which Jesus first told his tale.

59-60

It is now generally agreed by the scholars who have studied parables in depth that there is usually one main message per parable. As with every good story, the story-teller sketches in the background, the details of which are really only scenery. The mistake that early interpreters made was to look for meaning in every brush-stroke, and that distorted what Jesus was trying to say.

When we get hold of this point, it will help us to understand some of the harder parables. Take, for example, the parable of the unjust judge who had to be besieged by the widow before she could get her case heard (Luke 18:1-8). Jesus is not suggesting that we have to besiege God, or that he is unjust. The point is that she was so concerned about her case that she persisted until she got satisfaction. It's a matter of 'How much more...'

Or what about the story of the dishonest estate manager (Luke 16:1-9)? We have no need to spiritualize the details as has been done in years past (the manager has been under-

Let's look at a parable

Here is an example of one of Jesus' parables with many of the features which we have mentioned.

1 Where does this parable come in the gospel?

2 Should we know something about local customs?

3 What is the main point of the story – and what is just scenery?

4 Is there any background to these ideas?

5 How did the hearers respond?

6 Did Jesus himself give us any explanation?

7 How can we feel the force of this parable in our own situation?

Matthew 21:33-41

There was a landowner who planted a vineyard. He put a wall around it, dug a winepress in it and built a watchtower. Then he rented the vineyard to some farmers and went away on a journey. When the harvest time approached, he sent his servants to the tenants to collect his fruit. The tenants seized his servants; they beat one, killed another, and stoned a third. Then he sent other servants to them, more than the first time, and the tenants treated them the same way. Last of all, he sent his son to them. 'They will respect my son,' he said.

But when the tenants saw the son, they said to each other, 'This is the heir. Come, let's kill him and take his inheritance.' So they took him and threw him out of the vineyard and killed him.

Therefore when the owner of the vineyard comes, what will he do to those tenants?

'He will bring those wretches to a wretched end,' they replied, 'and he will rent the vineyard to other tenants who will give him his share of the crop at harvest time.'

Now for an explanation:

1 It comes, in Matthew's gospel, as part of Jesus' teaching during his last week in Jerusalem. The Jewish authorities were looking for some way to trap him and get rid of him, and there was great hostility in the air.

2 We need to know that one of the ways of renting out land in those days was to take a proportion of the produce as rent. This was a fair system in that whereas in years of bumper harvests the landlord did well, he got less when the harvest was poor. The landlord's action here was quite right and legitimate.

3 The main point has to do with the shocking behaviour of the tenants. The rest is scenery.

4 The whole idea of a vineyard would speak to a Jewish audience, as Israel had been likened to one more than once in the Old Testament, though there it was usually one which did not yield the fruit it ought to have done.

5 The hearers are obviously so caught up in the story that they pass judgment on the tenants and incidentally on themselves.

6 Jesus went on from this parable to drive the point home, 'Have you never read the Scriptures: "The stone the builders rejected has become the capstone; the Lord has done this, and it is marvellous in our eyes"? Therefore I tell you that the kingdom of God will be taken away from you and given to a people who will produce its fruit. He who falls on this stone will be broken to pieces, but he on whom it falls will be crushed' (Matthew 21:42-44). It also goes on to tell us that the Pharisees knew that Jesus was talking about them (Matthew 21:45). We will need to look up the verses Jesus quotes (Psalm 118:22-23), and we might also note the way in which they are used elsewhere in the New Testament.

This ought to lead us to the central message of the parable, which has to do with the way in which the Jews would treat Jesus (and had treated the prophets before him), and the judgment which would follow.

7 Think of a modern situation where we have enormous privileges for which we are ungrateful, and which we assume are untouchable – and then think of the shock we would feel if they were taken from us.

stood as everything from Christ to Satan!). The point is that if a dishonest man could do a bad thing well, how much more should God's people do good things well?

● Concealing the truth!

There is another angle on parables, however, which is perhaps hardest for us to understand. We find it in Jesus' own explanation of why he always spoke to the crowds in parables while explaining them privately to his disciples (and we still have some of those explanations). He tells us, in effect, that he uses parables not as we might immediately think to make the truth plainer, but to conceal it (Mark 4:10-12)! He supports what he says by referring to the prophet Isaiah (6:9) where we are introduced to a very profound if unpalatable truth.

In Biblical terms, receiving the truth is not merely a matter for mind or intellect. It has to do with heart and will. Present the truth to people whose attitude to God is basically disobedient and rebellious, and they will not only reject it, they will become harder in the process. Share the truth with someone who is seeking, and they will recognize it and embrace it. The people who heard Jesus' stories would hear them in two different ways depending how or where they were, spiritually. For some they would be just interesting tales; for others they would be life itself. Parables are a watershed. For behind the whole process is an even deeper idea, and that is that you only see what God has for you as God himself opens your eyes.

So we find Jesus leaving the crowds with his stories to think over, but patiently teaching his disciples what they meant in private. They were the ones who were privileged to see things from the inside, and our aim in studying the parables is to share that privilege. If we are going to do that, it will not only mean coming to them with thinking minds, but with believing hearts and obedient wills.

196

●Parables in John's gospel

Most of Jesus' parables are to be found in the first three gospels, but when we come to John's gospel we find a rather different approach. Jesus still uses picture language, and there are parables, but they are not the miniature stories which we find elsewhere. They are more like extended illustrations.

The description of Jesus as the good shepherd (John 10) is a well-known and very beautiful picture of Jesus' self-giving love but it is not really a story. It tells us in an extended way what a shepherd does for his sheep, and at one point is overlaid with the idea of Jesus being the gate to the sheepfold as well (10:7-9). Jesus is very clear in his application of the picture, but it lacks the sort of involvement of the hearers that we find in the other gospels.

202-203

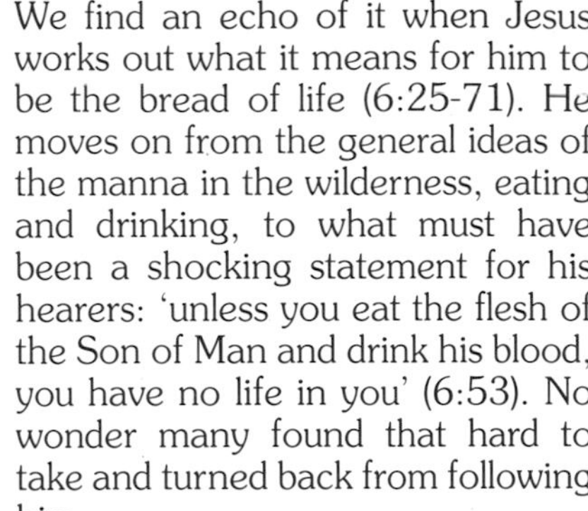

We find an echo of it when Jesus works out what it means for him to be the bread of life (6:25-71). He moves on from the general ideas of the manna in the wilderness, eating and drinking, to what must have been a shocking statement for his hearers: 'unless you eat the flesh of the Son of Man and drink his blood, you have no life in you' (6:53). No wonder many found that hard to take and turned back from following him.

Of course, it may be that he had his own disciples primarily in mind when he spoke like this. This would certainly be true of his picture of the vine and its branches (15:1-17). We find it in the setting of his final upper-room teaching about the future and the Holy Spirit. In fact, instead of being a self-contained story, it is rather an illustration which runs off into teaching.

There are those who have argued that John used the very incidents of Jesus' life and ministry as parables, and there may be something in that. Did the miracle of turning water into wine signify the differences between the old and new covenants (2:1-11)? Was the healing of the man born blind a symbol of spiritual blindness and Christ-given sight (9:1-41)? It's an interesting line of thinking, but one which needs great care lest we fall into the old trap of spiritualizing incidents, and reading into them all kinds of things provided by our own imaginations.

Letters

Outside the gospels and Acts, the bulk of the New Testament is taken up with letters, although they are certainly different from the sort of

letters with which we are familiar today. Written to individuals and churches, they give us a first-hand insight into what was going on in those days, and contain a good deal of important teaching on a variety of subjects.

On the surface, it might appear that we have here the easiest sort of Bible book to understand, and there is something in that. However, everything that has already been said about putting a Bible book in its setting applies to the letters as well. They too need to be read right through to get an overview of where the author is going.

If you do this, you will find that each author had his own distinctly personal style of writing. You have John, who seems to take you for a wandering tour around his subject, moving from topic to topic. Again you have James, a man who deals with different topics a paragraph at a time, abruptly moving on to the next. Peter and Paul like to develop their argument in quite lengthy passages, although Paul is just as likely to diverge and deal with a side issue on the way. The general pattern of Paul's letters begins with teaching about Christ or the gospel, and then moves on to practical application (although there are exceptions to this rule). Perhaps Hebrews is the most strictly controlled and thoroughly developed letter in the New Testament, moving steadily from one point to the next and building on what has gone before. Instead of waiting until halfway through, like Paul, to apply what he has been saying, the author regularly sums up his message and rams it home for the readers.

Although we have much about the Christian faith worked out for us in the letters, it is wise to remember

Letter-writing styles.

that none of them was written as a sort of 'What Christians Believe' manual. They were all put together to meet particular needs in particular situations – what we call a collection of 'occasional' writings – and this is why some points seem to be overstated at times. After all, if the problem vexing a church had to do with the reputation of Jesus, you would expect to find a vigorous defence of him, whereas if it were some moral problem where Christians were finding it difficult to apply their faith to life, you would expect emphasis on practical things. Because of this, it is important to compare what a letter might be teaching with lessons from other letters and the gospels, and to aim for a balanced understanding of the truth.

Getting at the background

One of our first jobs when studying a New Testament letter is to read between the lines and decide what were the actual problems and circumstances which made the author write as he did. Sometimes these are fairly obvious; over others even

326

the experts will disagree. For some of the letters we are able to draw upon the background history of the book of Acts, which tells us how some of the churches were founded, and introduces us to some of the characters. Beyond that we have to go to sources of information outside the New Testament which we will find in commentaries and Bible dictionaries.

77

We then need to break the letter down into chunks that we can handle comfortably. Usually a chapter is just too long for this. It might be better to take a paragraph at a time. Having done that, we need to attempt to follow through the argument. Try to get hold of the main subject, and then break down the argument into steps, following the author's thinking. In this way you will see how he gets where he wants to go, and how he digresses away from his main point, or adds afterthoughts along the way.

One of the ways in which Paul in particular develops his arguments is to take on an objector in an imaginary audience, and to answer his questions. Perhaps it was because he was used to handling crowds in public, but it makes for a lively debate (there are a series of questions like this in Romans). On other occasions he deals with questions which have been asked him (see 1 Corinthians 7:1), or situations which he has heard about and which demand treatment (for example, Galatians 1:6-7).

Then a close examination of the words used can be very profitable. What did they actually mean, or perhaps more important, how were they being used? Remember that the meaning of the word is determined by the words around it, and that sometimes the same word can mean different things, certainly when used by different authors and sometimes even by the same author. Even common terms like 'faith' and 'life' can have different meanings, while Paul can use the word often translated as 'law' in several different ways in the same passage! The important thing to ask is, 'How is this word being used here?'

● Application

When it comes to applying what is said, there is much which speaks to us directly from that time into our own. However, there is also a fair amount of material which related to what was a very different situation from ours. When this happens we need to get behind the particular teaching and discover the principles underlying it. We must ask ourselves, 'Granted that their culture was very different from ours, what made Peter, Paul, James or the others write as they did?' For example, James' description of poor behaviour in church would not happen that way today (James 2:1-7). The stewards would hardly tell you to stand for the service or sit at someone's feet! But the passage does have a great deal to say about snobbishness and favouritism. In this way, even first-century references to the length of people's hair or to parties where idol-sacrifice meat was eaten can be translated into sound advice for today.

There are, of course, some passages where we simply cannot be dogmatic, usually because we do not know what the author is referring to. However, the drift of the passage is usually enough to tell us the point that he is trying to make. Take that strange reference to 'baptism for the dead' which Paul slips into his argument for resurrection (1

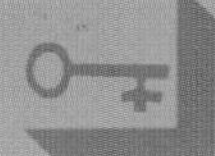

Corinthians 15:29). There must be more than a dozen possibilities of what it might mean, some more plausible than others. The Corinthians doubtless saw Paul's point immediately. They knew what he was referring to, but the plain fact of the matter is that we do not know what it means. Conceivably archaeologists or historians might turn up something which will throw light on the subject, as they have for other difficult Bible passages, but right now we do not have enough information to be absolutely sure. But we see what Paul was saying in general. It is only one part of a very much larger, longer argument for the resurrection of the dead.

Law

One of the reasons why we do not recommend people who are just beginning to study the Bible to read it straight through is that, after the first book and a half, they will run straight into a mass of rules and regulations which will be hard going to say the least. Buried among them you will also find some very interesting accounts of what happened to God's people on the way to the promised land. But much of the time you will be reading through lists of laws which seem to have little or nothing to do with life today.

The first five books to the Bible were

92

'Dear Friends....'

As we have already seen, it is possible to break down a letter into sections which deal with different topics. Let's take a fairly straightforward section from a letter to see how it, in turn, may be broken down into its basic argument.

1 Thessalonians 4:13-18

Brothers, we do not want you to be ignorant about those who fall asleep, or to grieve like the rest of men, who have no hope. We believe that Jesus died and rose again and so we believe that God will bring with Jesus those who have fallen asleep in him. According to the Lord's own word, we tell you that we who are still alive, who are left till the coming of the Lord, will certainly not precede those who have fallen asleep. For the Lord himself will come down from heaven, with a loud command, with the voice of the archangel and with the trumpet call of God, and the dead in Christ will rise first. After that, we who are still alive and are left will be caught up with them in the clouds to meet the Lord in the air. And so we will be with the Lord for ever. Therefore encourage each other with these words.

1 Where do we find this section in the letter?

2 Are there words or phrases which I need to look up in order to understand?

3 What is the problem?

4 How does Paul deal with it?

5 What do I learn about the subject under discussion?

6 How can I apply these truths in my situation today?

What has Paul to say to us?

1 After reminding the Thessalonians of how his visit to them went, Paul begins to deal with some practical issues which seem to be vexing them, from 4:1. There is a fairly abrupt break between verses 12 and 13, so it looks as though he is dealing with a new topic here. The same subject however, the return of the Lord Jesus Christ, is carried over into chapter 5.

2 If we have never come across teaching like this before, there will be a number of things about Jesus' second coming which may be new and startling. But the language here is generally clear. We will need to know that 'falling asleep' is a gentle way of speaking about death, and perhaps that an archangel is a chief angel. If we look up the word 'hope' in a Bible dictionary, we will discover that it is a much stronger word in the New Testament than our vague wishes about the future. It is forward-looking faith which reaches out to what has been secured for us and promised to us. We also need to be aware of the fact that when Paul speaks about people being 'in Christ' or 'in the Lord', it is his shorthand for being a Christian.

If we consult a commentary we may discover that the whole picture of going out to meet the returning Lord Jesus was very much like what happened when a city got an official or state visit (the technical term for that in Greek was '*parousia*', which is the word translated 'coming' here).

3 Reading between the lines, the problem seems to have been this: the new Christians at Thessalonica had been taught to expect Jesus' return, but some of them had already died (we don't know why – it was probably from natural causes; it was not necessarily as the result of persecution). So won't they miss out on the Lord's second coming in that they won't be around when he comes back?

4 Now we can lay out Paul's argument step by step.

1. Be reassured:
We need not grieve as unbelievers do – they have nothing to look forward to and we do.

2. Why?
a. Jesus died and rose again – so death has been dealt with – which is why he can bring with him those who have died.
b. We have his word – those left alive will have no advantages.

3. How so?
a. The Lord is coming in glory.
b. At that time – those who have died will rise – those left alive will join him and them.
c. Everyone will be with Christ for ever.

4. So then:
Use this truth to encourage one another (especially those who are grieving the loss of a friend or loved one).

5 From a passage like this we get an insight into some of the details of Jesus' second coming. But it isn't the whole picture. The point that Paul is dealing with is how to regard Christians who have died. He is not concerned to give a comprehensive account of what will happen when Jesus comes back. We may, however, fill out the picture from other New Testament passages which deal with the same subject.

6 People may not be concerned nowadays that their dead friends may have missed out on the second coming of Christ. This is because many, many Christians have died since that time, and it looks as though there might be more dead Christians raised at the end than live ones waiting for their Lord. The fact of Christ's death, resurrection and promised return, however, is the basis for our hope. We can live in the light of what Christ has done and will do for us when he returns. So we may face death unafraid, and we also have a good reason why, although we will naturally grieve in our bereavements, it doesn't need to be a hopeless grief.

a section all on their own in the Hebrew Old Testament. The Jews called them 'The Law (or *Torah*)', and when we look at them more closely we can see why. There seem to be rules here about everything: in fact, there are over 600 in total. They tell us how worship was to be regulated, including which sacrifices had to be offered, or which clothes the priests had to wear, which festivals had to be observed and so on. But there are also regulations about most other aspects of life too.

Some are broad rules like 'You shall not murder'; others deal with particular situations like what to do if you come up in a rash, or if your neighbour moves your landmark. There are rules about relationships, rules about eating, rules about what to do and not to do on the sabbath day, rules about how to build your house, rules about how much you should give back to God.

●Do they apply to us?

The inevitable question, of course, is 'Do they apply to us?' After all, they are in the Bible which we regard as the Word of God. How can we possibly apply them to our lives today?

In order to understand Old Testament laws, we need to grasp what God did for his people, the Israelites. When they were little more than a rabble of slaves in Egypt, he fulfilled the promises he had made to their ancestors and, using Moses, he led them out to freedom. They were to become a nation in their own right, and they were to have a land of their own. Most important, they were to have a special relationship with God.

There was to be a two-way agreement between them and God himself. He would be their God, providing for them, leading them, prospering and protecting them and, in return, they were to be his people. They were to be marked out from every other nation by what they did and did not do. It was what was known as a *covenant* in those days, the sort of arrangement which was made by a powerful emperor with his subject kings. Keeping his laws represented their side of the bargain. They marked them out as his own people.

Some of the laws were aimed at detaching them from pagan practices like the way they consulted spiritualistic mediums or even cooked their food. There were sinister overtones in a number of accepted local customs, and the Israelites could not afford to be involved in them.

55

Whereas some of the rules stipulated distinctive ways of doing things in order to make them different from the rest, we can see now that many of them were also for the physical and moral health of the nation. For example, some of the laws contain basic principles of hygiene and safety. Others regulate demands for revenge by what was just. Others encapsulate sound moral sense (and as such they are a great improvement on other law codes from those days).

It was all part of God's great educational programme for his people. His laws told them both symbolically and directly that they were dealing with a holy God who wanted a holy people. They taught them that moral failure mattered and had to be dealt with both in a legal way, and in the ritual of sacrifice. In that respect they revealed the uncomfortable fact that human nature by itself is prone to sin. Try as they would (and frequently they didn't try very hard),

God's people found it impossible to keep his laws by themselves.

34

●The new agreement

This is where the new covenant comes in. God would make a new arrangement with his people, unlike the old one. This time he would provide the motive power, the inner desire and ability to live a life which pleased him (Jeremiah 31:31-34). But the way into this new agreement would only be by means of the sin-dealing death of his Son and the work of the Holy Spirit, and it is in these that the New Testament authors glory. Christ himself claimed to fulfil the Old Testament law, not merely by what he said, but by who he was and what he did.

That is why the apostles can insist that rule-keeping is not the way to gain God's favour. In fact, the demands of God's laws are such that they only reveal our inability to live the sort of life that God requires. It is because of what God does in a believer's heart and life that, by the Spirit, he begins to fulfil God's requirements for the first time in his experience.

This is why many of the old requirements no longer operate.

> So do we abandon the old rules and forget them altogether? No, because they are part of God's Word to us. We need to deal with them as we deal with stories from the Old Testament, going behind their statements to discover the underlying principles. If we do this we will find that they speak to us today about God's holiness, justice and mercy.

They had to do with the old covenant and being a citizen in Israel. But this is also why the great moral imperatives of the Old Testament are carried over into the New. Laws like the Ten Commandments, and God's requirement that we love him and our neighbours, still stand. In fact, if we love him, by the Holy Spirit indwelling us, we will gladly put them into practice in our daily lives.

Wisdom

In the Old Testament, along with the priests and the prophets, we sometimes find mention of 'wise men'. We often overlook this group, even though they are responsible for some of the most daring books in the Bible. Every nation has its wise men. They act as counsellors, advisors or policy makers. They are people who have a big view of life, a good memory and a subtlety of mind which makes them ask awkward or non-obvious questions. The advice they give is based on experience, either their own or that of others. Not all wise men saw the truth as the others did however. We have a classic contest between two who gave differing advice to David's rebel son, Absalom (see 2 Samuel 17).

In course of time their highly valued statements on a variety of subjects came to be collected and circulated, and not only within Israel. There were wise men in Egypt and Mesopotamia too, and often their general conclusions are remarkably similar. This is especially true when it comes to conduct at court, where people had to learn how to tread carefully when dealing with all-too-human monarchs. But there was also a great deal of common ground when it came to lessons learned

from life. In this way, wisdom became an international affair in the world of the Old Testament.

The book of Proverbs is a collection of such wisdom, compiled from several different sources, and full of wit and common sense. That is why some of it is specifically directed at young people starting out in life. 'You don't have to learn the hard way', is the message that comes through. 'You can learn from the hard-won experience of others.' This is one of the reasons why wisdom comes to us in simple catchy statements and contrasts, penny packets of truth if you like. They were obviously meant to be memorized and then called to mind as the occasion demanded.

Because they are short and memorable they are not meant to be exhaustive statements about the subject in hand. They take up one particular aspect of a truth and hammer it home. Because of this they are not always true in every situation. But then this is how our proverbs work. 'Look before you leap' is very good advice at times, but its opposite, 'He who hesitates is lost' is equally true in another set of circumstances. Old Testament proverbs are no different. Added to this is the Jewish practice of making a point by exaggerating it (it's known as *hyperbole* and we find it elsewhere in the Bible, including the teaching of Jesus). This has the effect of further overstressing one side of the truth.

●Wisdom as a person

To get across the point that the life of wisdom is the best life and the most prosperous, the wise men took an interesting step. They started to picture wisdom as a person. For the young men wisdom is

described as a beautiful woman. 'Fall for her', they are advised, 'Avoid the self-destruction of loose living offered by the adulteress'. And so we find wisdom speaking for herself, calling to them, offering to entertain them, prosper them and care for them. The fact that the Hebrew word for wisdom was feminine and could be spoken about as 'she' helped in all this.

141-144

This combined with another thought, however. All true wisdom comes from God. It is God's wisdom, for God alone is all-wise. But God was there before the creation of the world. Hence wisdom was there too. After all, we see enough of his wise way of doing things, his own particular brand of intelligence and cleverness, in the created world around us. It was in this way that they could speak about wisdom in personal terms, working alongside God in creating the world (Proverbs 8:22-31). There is no doubt that at this point it is all poetry, but it was something which future Jewish philosophers speculated about, and something which the early Christians seized upon to explain who Christ was.

One of the crucial differences

between Jewish wisdom and that of other neighbouring countries is the setting in which we find it. The Israelites were people aware that they had a special covenant relationship with the Lord. So for them 'the fear of the Lord', a living recognition of who he is and what he does, had to be 'the beginning of wisdom' (Proverbs 9:10). There are many, many lessons which we can draw from the common pool of human experience which are sound practical and moral sense, but there is an added dimension for the believer. He relates everything he learns to God, and therein lies the problem which is addressed in the other two wisdom books, Job and Ecclesiastes.

136

141-144

144-147

●Health and wealth?

A surface reading of Proverbs might give the impression that, if one kept all the good advice there, prosperity, health and the good life must follow automatically. The fact that they don't raises questions and sometimes doubts in the honest, enquiring mind. When the godly and innocent suffer instead of doing well, it seems that God isn't being fair. If the Israelites had not believed in a just God, there would have been no problem. But they did and there was! Job is a good example of this. He did all that was required of him with God and man, and yet he lost everything and suffered from a dreadful disease into the bargain.

132-136

It is here that we are introduced to another method of handling wisdom which we must grasp if we are not going to make some far-reaching mistakes in understanding these books. The wisdom authors were prepared to take up and pursue false thinking as well as true. So you find Job's friends pounding him with a superficial prosperity teaching. 'God prospers those who obey him,' they maintained. 'You are suffering, therefore, you must have sinned. Repent and ask forgiveness, and God will prosper you once again.'

Of course, there is a good half truth here. If we put ourselves and our affairs in God's hands, he can do things with us that we could never do for ourselves, but prosperity is not guaranteed. So if we take the statements made by Job's friends out of their setting in the book they could be very misleading. We need to see them as part of the total argument. So when we study Job, although it is a very long book, it is very important that we get an overview to see where the author is going.

Ecclesiastes is even more subtle, so subtle in fact, that many have wondered how it got into the Bible. The author, on the surface of things, seems to be a pessimistic materialist who lives for the things of time and sense. 'Get the best out of life while you may,' he seems to be saying, 'There's no telling when it will end.' But that's not the total picture, for here and there throughout the book we have references to God and statements of faith.

Some have suggested that several people had a hand in writing the book, contributing several views without making it clear who wrote what. Certainly more than one person was responsible for its final form, and it may be that its message is, 'Here is an error to avoid' rather than, 'Here is an example to follow'.

But it might be much more clever than that, a book written not so much for believers as for unbeliev-

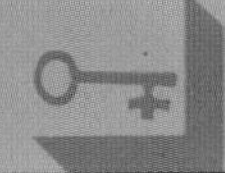

ers. It says to the many who exist just for pleasures and possessions, 'Live that way if you will, but what have you got at the end of it? It doesn't lead anywhere. But then, don't complain about the emptiness and the lack of purpose in your life. If *things* are all there are, what more do you expect?' The almost casual references to God seem to indicate what is afoot – and incidentally betray what he really believes.

Either way, in this respect, Ecclesiastes is a book well suited to our own day because it drives the reader back to ask ultimate questions about himself, and life, and meaning – and God.

> The wisdom books were written by clever, intelligent people, and because of this they need some hard thinking if we are to understand them. They are the nearest we get in Scripture to philosophizing about life and its meaning, the asking of deep and basic questions. In the Bible, however, we have not only the questions of honest men who were prepared to face life as it was; we have the answer supplied by a faith in a God who made us and who has everything under his control.

Prophecy

Collections of prophecies take up over a quarter of the Old Testament. Some are very memorable and speak powerfully to us today with little explanation. Others are quite remote from us and our situations, to the point where we wonder what they are going on about. That is always dangerous territory, because it easily becomes the happy hunting ground of the crank who professes to find all kinds of plausible meanings. That is why, over the years, prophecy has probably suffered more abuse than most other types of biblical writing.

One of our unfortunate drawbacks is that, for many, prophecy has to do with foretelling the future. And as most of us are curious about what is going to happen, because it is knowledge usually withheld from us, anything which appears to let us in on the secret is extremely attractive. However, although biblical prophets were, at times, given an insight into the future, that was not their prime function. Their job was to speak on God's behalf to his people in a particular situation, warning them about his judgments and promising them his blessing on certain conditions. So when it comes to understanding the message of the prophets we need to remember that much of it was aimed at the people who were alive at the same time as the prophet. In that sense they are similar to the New Testament letters which, although containing universal truths, were addressed to particular church situations.

360

● Reconstruct the scene

This means that in order to find out what they were saying we must first reconstruct the scene when they were preaching. The historical setting of a prophecy is all-important. For this we can go to the narrative sections of the Old Testament which supply us with a good deal of information about what went on in Judah and Israel while the prophets were in operation. We can also go to Bible dictionaries and commentaries for further information. This is because, as a result of the painstaking work of archaeologists, we have a mass of information about Bible

61-63

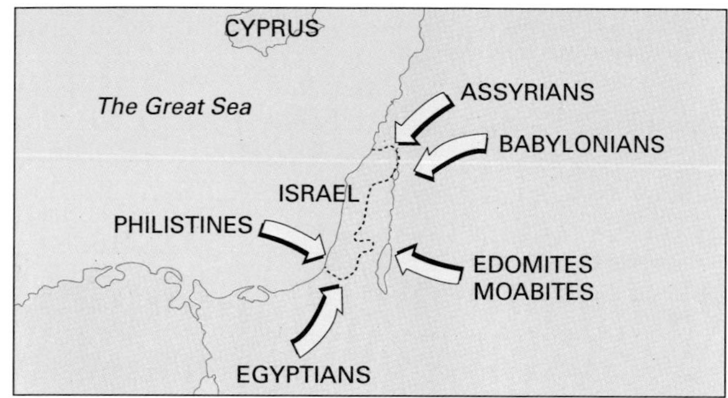

The holy land: the buffer.

times from places like Egypt and Mesopotamia.

Throughout the prophetic period, Israel was more or less a buffer between the great empires in these areas. That is why independent records of their fortunes, their kings and their influence often ties in with what the Bible says. Their campaigns into Palestine are particularly interesting, because when an army marched through or by the country the Jews were inevitably affected. It's against the background of these great earthly powers that the prophets maintained that Israel's God was all-powerful and sovereign in the affairs of men.

If we can match the particular prophetic message (or oracle as it is called) with a set of events in Israel's history, it will mean much more to us. In some cases this is fairly easy in that the prophecies are frequently dated by a year in a king's reign, or by an outside event. We can then apply the rule we learned when dealing with narrative and ask, 'If God dealt with his people in that way in those circumstances, how would he deal with us in ours?'

There are some prophecies , however, which are extremely difficult to date accurately. It does not help when we discover that the collections themselves were not put together in date order. For once our general rule about reading a Bible book right through does not apply. It would not help us very much if we did. When we come across a prophecy like this which we find hard to place, we must look up a commentary to see the sort of educated suggestions that have been made about its setting. Even the experts can be unsure. This does not mean that the prophecy is valueless. God can speak to us through his Word even though we might not know the original setting.

● Reinforcing the old covenant

Much of the predictive prophecy in the Old Testament has to do with the situation as it was then, that is, the prophets told Israel what would happen in the immediate future. This would either be fearful, in that God would use the outside situation as a judgment on them, or it could be a relief as the Lord eased the pressure or freed them from oppression. Some of these predicted happenings are conditional. If Israel did not repent of her evil ways and turn back to God, he would judge them, but it all depended on the 'if'. Should they really return to the Lord, then the judgment would not take place.

More than once the prophets make much of the fact that Israel has a God who speaks and acts in contrast to the idols of the nations. In that sense prophecy is a sign, a pointer to the fact that God takes his part of the covenant bargain seriously even if they frequently did not. For, in terms of general truth about God, the prophets were really saying nothing new. They were merely underlining and reinforcing the agreement which God had made with his people years before.

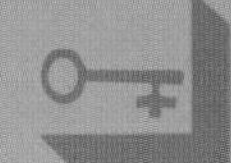

●Looking forward to a new covenant

Why is it, then, that the New Testament writers make so much of Old Testament prediction? The answer is, quite simply , that whereas many of their predictions have now been fulfilled in Israel's history, God also gave them glimpses of the distant future as well. In a way, the failure of God's people and the disillusionment which came with it forms a fitting background to this future message. Although so many ideals had been shattered both in the nation of Israel and in its kings, the days would come when things would be what they ought to be. There would be a new covenant, for it had become painfully obvious that they could not keep the old one unaided. There would be an ideal, Spirit-filled king who would reign over the world in righteousness and peace.

And there were other, darker predictions about suffering and rejection being the way to this new and wonderful arrangement which the apostles only discovered after the death and resurrection of Christ. Jesus himself had gone through the Old Testament with them after that amazing reversal, showing them which Scriptures pointed to him (Luke 24: 27, 45-47). That is why we find their preaching and their letters studded with Old Testament references, particularly from the prophets (although we need to remember that other Old Testament writings could be 'prophetic' in this sense).

Sometimes these predictions are difficult to disentangle because the prophets tended to superimpose the immediate future on the distant future. It was as though they looked out on a series of hill ranges which, from far away, all appeared to be at the same distance. What they did not see were the deep valleys in between. So it is possible to have a prophecy relating to their own time superimposed on one to be fulfilled several hundred years later. It is like looking at history through bifocals!

34

153

●Prophecy fulfilled more than once

The other form of fulfilment has to do with the curious double meanings or secondary meanings of Old Testament prophecy. There is some truth in the idea that history has a habit of repeating itself. Or it may be that future events or personalities are foreshadowed by a sort of trial run in the past. Or it could be that the universal spiritual principles which will come to the surface at the end, express themselves partially in people or circumstances in history as we know it. However it comes about, it was possible for a prophetic word to apply to the prophet's own time and to the future. A run through of Old Testament prophecies finding their fulfilment in the New Testament will reveal both these things happening.

> The Jews themselves were quite aware that their Bibles predicted future events. That is why, when Jesus came on the scene, there was expectation in the air. A sobering truth, however, is that they got most of it wrong! For example, the popular idea of a Messiah was of a worldly deliverer, and they had no idea that he must suffer, die and rise again. All this ought to make us pause before we rush into Old Testament prophecy to dig up all kinds of 'predictions' yet to be fulfilled.

184

Beware!

We must ask ourselves, first of all, if the prediction we are looking at was not fulfilled in or shortly after the prophet's own time. Or, if it is conditional prophecy, whether it needed to be fulfilled at all. We then need to go to the New Testament to see what Jesus and the apostles made of it. After all, they were continually on the look out for Old Testament evidence to support their claims. If they missed what appears to us to be a clear prediction, it must make us ask if we are on the right track. We also need to consider whether the statements we are looking at are meant to be taken literally, or if they are poetic (most prophecy is written in poetic form).

85

If, after we have run all these tests, we still feel that we have an unfulfilled statement about the future, we should handle it cautiously, knowing that far better people than we have been dreadfully wrong when it comes to predictive prophecy. It must be true that some things will only become apparent to us as they happen, just as some aspects of biblical truth become more important to us as our circumstances change. Then, like the early Christians, we will be able to draw strength from the fact that God has had everything worked out from the beginning. In the meantime, the purpose of Bible study, and that includes its prophecies, is not that we might build up a comprehensive 'history of the future', but that we might get on with living for the Lord in the present. Predictive prophecy can becomes so fascinating that we can actually be led away from the truth – which was written to be lived – into useless speculation.

Types of prophecy (see also page 153).

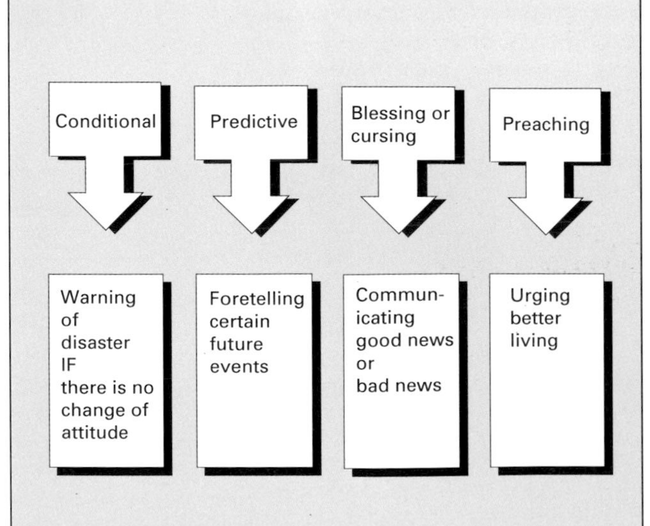

The language of pictures

One of the problems confronting anyone who wants to write about spiritual things is that he or she is confined by earth's language. This is the language of concrete, tangible things, the language of the senses. But an experience of God happens on another plane and in another dimension. How can you put it into this-worldly language? It's a problem that mystics have wrestled with for years.

But the converse is equally true. How is God going to reveal himself to earth-bound, body-limited human beings? In the final analysis, of course, he had to do this for us by coming himself in human form.

There is a language which spans the gulf, and we find it whenever religious subjects are broached. It is picture language, the language of analogy. That is, we think of something in this world with which we are familiar, and we say that God is

somewhat like this or that, 'somewhat' because God is really only like himself. Even a word like 'father', which Jesus taught us to use of God, has serious limitations. Our understanding of fatherhood is a very pale reflection of his.

Picture langauge, when pictures 'stand for' something about God or his ways – the word we use is 'symbolize' – is found all through Scripture. God is a 'shield' or a 'rock'. Jesus is the 'good shepherd'. We know that God is not a literal shield or rock, or Jesus a keeper of sheep in the literal sense. We are using language in a special way, in a non-literal way.

This sort of picture language lends itself to poetry, and that is why you will find plenty of images and symbols in a book like Psalms. As prophecy was generally written in poetry, it's not surprising that you find it there too, and it's in the world of prophecy that we also find a striking development. We find it first in the Old Testament, in books like Isaiah and Ezekiel, and more especially in Daniel. We find it in full voice in the New Testament in the book of Revelation.

● Dreams and visions

It isn't just that the authors have used picture language to illustrate the points they are trying to make. It's all picture language from beginning to end, vast and often nightmarish scenes, painted for us in lurid colours. Step out of, say, the New Testament letters into the book of Revelation, and you step into another world, a world of beasts and candles and bowls and plagues. And yet it is not an entirely different world, because under it all you can see that the author is really talking about the same things.

This sort of writing is a style on its own. It's called *apocalyptic* after the type of writings where it is found, for we have not only the biblical books we have cited; the Jews between the Old and New Testaments wrote many similar works in the same style. They mostly follow the same pattern. They are usually connected with the name of some Old Testament character like Moses or Enoch. They claim to be what these people saw in dreams or visions, and they are generally all about the end of the world and the run up to it. Because they claim that God revealed what they wrote, their books are called 'apocalypses' from the Greek word for 'revelation'. The word literally means 'an unveiling' or 'taking the cover off' something. The writers claimed that God had taken the lid off the future for them.

228-232

The language which they used, and which is also used in the book of Revelation, is drawn largely from the Old Testament. Events, situations, happenings are picked up and given symbolical value. We do the same thing at times. If we say, 'He's met his Waterloo', we mean that he has met his match and has been finally defeated, just as Napoleon was defeated by the Duke of Wellington at the battle of Waterloo. We are using the language in a non-literal way. We in no way mean to imply that he has somehow met something relating to a village in Belgium!

In the same way, apocalyptic language takes up images from the Old Testament, often combines them with others, and builds them into grotesque scenes like something from surrealist art. The question arises, 'Why ever did they do it?' Part of the answer was that they were trying to speak about the other, spiritual world in the language of this one. Perhaps another aspect may have to do with the difficult times in which they wrote, when God's people were being persecuted for their faith. Using Old Testament pictures like this would encourage those who knew their Old Testament, while confusing their enemies, should the book fall into their hands.

85

Problem passages

What do I do if I come across a passage in the Bible which I simply cannot understand? It may be that it doesn't seem to make sense by itself, or it could be that it appears to contradict something else which I am perfectly sure is biblical. How can I handle a passage like that? Try this check list:

1 Have I taken pains to read the whole book, so that I can see how the author is using this particular section? Or am I taking it out of its setting, and making it mean something he never intended?

2 Have I understood the background to the passage sufficiently? Have I remembered that when the Bible books were written, they were addressed to some situations rather different from our own. Have I understood things like the geography, the customs and culture, the way that people lived then?

3 Have I come to terms with the type of writing with which I am dealing? Have I been treating narrative as narrative and poetry as poetry? Or have I been understanding symbols and pictures in a literal way, or spiritualizing what is really a straightforward story into something it was never meant to mean?

4 Have I understood what is being said? Have I really done my homework and asked what the words themselves mean, or how the author is using them at this point? Have I made the mistake of making them mean what they don't, even putting my own meaning upon them?

5 Am I still wearing my twentieth-century spectacles? Haven't I realized that the people in Bible times actually thought differently from me? Am I in danger of emptying the passage of what it really means because I am so conditioned by my western way of thinking? Am I really coming with an open mind, or have I pre-judged the issues (which is prejudice!)?

6 Have I taken all the biblical evidence into account? Have I looked at other passages on the same subject which may well throw light on this one?

7 Have I consulted others who have a wider background knowledge than I have? Have I taken pains to go to a commentary, a Bible dictionary or my minister or Christian teacher? Am I humble enough to ask?

8 Have I come prayerfully enough? Hearing God speaking to me through his Word is not just an academic exercise. It is the Holy Spirit who makes his truth true to us. Have I asked him to do that?

9 Have I simply got to admit my ignorance at present? Is this an issue where I have to admit, humbly and reverently, that I do not know – yet? Is it something I must put in my 'suspense account' until something comes along which will shed more light on it than I have at present?

10 Am I using this passage with its problems as an excuse for not facing up to the clear teaching of Scripture? However much I may not understand, there is more than enough that is perfectly plain and obvious. Is my questioning honest searching, or just another form of rebellion? Have I submitted my will as well as my mind to God?

5.4 USING THE RESOURCES

As well as notes and devotional material you will need reference books to help you to deeper understanding of the Bible.

Commentaries

A commentary on a Bible book is simply someone's attempt to understand and interpret it. The same can be said about Bible reading notes, or a sermon, or a lecture about the Bible. There is nothing inspired or infallible about a commentary or study notes. The people who write them are more or less gifted to do so, and although they will have worked hard to give us their considered opinion as to what a passage of Scripture might mean, they can get it wrong! This means that, when using any kind of commentary, we have to be prepared to do some hard thinking ourselves. They are no short cuts to all the answers. They are aids to our own studies, and no replacement for the prayerful thought we need to give to understanding and applying the Scriptures ourselves.

Nowadays there are generally two kinds of commentary which really correspond to the two basic questions we have to ask when we come to the Bible: 'What *did* it say?' and 'What *is it* saying?'. Many modern commentaries stop with the first question. They concern themselves with things like the historical background to the passage, the meaning of the words and the force of the argument, what we call matters of *exegesis*. They are of help when it comes to applying the Bible to life only if they lead us to ask the question, 'What is it saying to me now in my situation?'

73-77

Perhaps today's authors are reluctant to do what preachers have to do ever Sunday, and what many writers of the older commentaries did automatically. When they wrote a commentary in the old days, authors had no hesitation in saying how it ought to work out in practice. Some of those older commentaries, although dated in their language and approach, are often good value for money. A number have been reprinted, while you can still find bargains in second-hand bookshops, or on the lists of those booksellers who specialize in second-hand theological books. Perhaps the best known is Matthew Henry's commentary.

There are still good 'devotional' or 'homiletical' commentaries (as they are called) around today, but they are fewer than formerly. A good devotional writer will also have done his homework with the text of Scripture, will have worked hard at the background and meaning of the passage, and will then go on to tell us what it should mean for us. Bible reading notes usually try to answer both questions, but being necessarily brief, they cannot delve into the problems in the text in the same way that a book can.

Perhaps the worst of all worlds is the writer who sets out to write a devotional commentary and who simply hasn't done the basic work of understanding what the Bible book was saying when it was first written. That sort of author will end up giving us a string of blessed thoughts which may or may not have any adequate biblical foundation.

● Points to look out for

So what should we be looking for in a good commentary? First of all we need to be told as much as possible about the historical setting of the book. We need to know about what was happening in the world at that period. We should expect to have the customs of those days explained for us. Perhaps most important, we

will be looking to gain an insight into how the people thought and expressed themselves in those far-off times.

This means that our commentator will be up on his biblical archaeology, and will also have drawn upon those writings outside the Bible which illustrate the subject in hand. For example, if I am a commentator writing on the New Testament, I will need to know about what was going on in the first-century Roman empire. I should have researched the history of the Jews between the Old and New Testaments, in that the situation to which I am introduced in the gospels is the product of political and religious movements of those times. So I will spend time studying the writings of the Apocrypha, the Dead Sea Scrolls, the Rabbis and the other literature of that period, all of which throw light on what was going on in Palestine when Jesus came on the scene. If I do not do this spadework I am in real danger of seriously distorting what the New Testament has to say.

How much of this will actually be put into the commentary will depend on whom the commentary is written for. Those written for

Examples of commentaries on 1 Corinthians, chapter 3.

Called to be God's Own People

FRI 22 APR

BE CAREFUL HOW YOU BUILD

The picture changes in today's passage. Paul leaves the farm labourers sowing and watering, and his mind goes to another familiar situation which can help us to understand more about what it means to be God's own people – this time working on a building site.

READ: 1 CORINTHIANS 3:9b-23

'You are also God's building' (9b). Paul lays down some firm principles to help us to do a good job. Our foundation must be the best possible – Jesus himself (11). We, as builders, need to be qualified and skilled but not looking for a strarring role (10): here is a hint of the discussion later in the letter about spiritual gifts. We need to use the best materials (12, 13). Paul may have been thinking of the strange jumble of decorated classical buildings and shanty-town slums which made up the city of Corinth. Our Christian service is often a pretty odd mixture too, that couldn't be described as gold and silver.

It's vital to build with the right materials because the building will be tested (13). Corinth experienced earthquakes and fires. The equivalents in church life are the daily pressures and the sudden crises. And one day the Head of the church will put her through a final test. What then? In v 15 we find two truths which we need to hold together in tension: our salvation is certain and secure; our lives and our work will be examined by God. He cares about their quality because we belong to him (23) – and his Spirit lives in us to help us build well (16).

PRAYER: Lord, I long to build for you with beautiful and long-lasting materials. Help me to work alongside others. Thank you that we all belong to you.

Daily Bread daily devotional Bible readings from Scripture Union.

Paul likens himself to *a skilled master builder*, one who brings all his experience and knowledge to the work and assigns tasks to individual workmen. The Greek word gives us the English 'architect' and it is obvious, most of all to the architect himself, that he cannot do everything and that he depends on the skill, the craftsmanship, the sheer hard labour of many other fellow-workers. Paul has done his particular job: he has laid the foundation, by clearly proclaiming Jesus Christ and him crucified (2:2). His reason for doing that was to ensure that the faith of the Christians at Corinth rested securely in the power of God on Jesus himself, the only sure foundation (*cf.* 2:5 and 3:11).

Some in Corinth were talking as though Paul himself was the foundation-stone of their church life: but no human being can sustain the life of any church or any Christian. Pastors and preachers move on and die: only a church built on Jesus Christ survives. There may even be an oblique reference here to the Peter-party who could have been relying on Peter, the rock, as the foundation of the church.3

Once the foundation has been securely laid, the building must go up. Paul laid the foundation, *and another man is building upon it* (10). Indeed, several people are involved in building the church at Corinth and Paul is concerned all the way through this letter that the church should be built up in faith and love. That is the explicit thrust of chapters 8, 10 and 14; but it is the heartbeat of the whole letter.

It is common to interpret verses 12–15 in terms of a Christian's quality of life as revealed on *the Da*... context Paul is, in fact, describing the qu... those contributing to building ... *take care how he builds* (10) ... and indeed an...

The Message of Corinthians modern devotional commentary by David Prior (IVP, 1985).

9. Three times in this verse the word *God* comes first: 'God's fellow-workers are we; God's husbandry, God's building are you.' The effect is to emphasize strongly the fact that the human instruments do not matter. All is of God, and all belong to God. It is not quite certain that *we are labourers together with God* is the right translation of *Theou gar esmen sunergoi*. It could mean 'fellow-workers with one another in God's service'and this would suit the context very well. Despite the attractiveness of this rendering, however, the translation of AV is probably to be preferred, for it is the more naturalway to understand the Greek (cf. Mk. xvi. 20). It is a startling expression, which sets forth in striking fashion the dignity of Christian service. The word *georgion*, translated *husbandry*, occurs only here in the New Testament. The word can mean 'field', or the process of cultivation. There is a similar ambiguity about *oikodome-*, *building*,whichmay signify the edifice or the process of erection,. Thus Paul may mean that the Corinthians are the field, the building, in which God is at work. Or he may mean that they are God's work in cultivation and building. Incidentally the metaphor of building is a favourite one with Paul, but it is not found often in the New Testament outside his writings.

The First Epistle to the Corinthians a shorter exegetical commentary by Leon Morris (Tyndale Press, IVP, 1958)

ministers, theological students and scholars will have lengthy discussions of the original Greek, Hebrew and Aramaic terms. They will try to include a summary of the discussion of the issues through the history of the church. They will quote from other commentaries and theological works. They will also spend a great deal of time discussing how the Bible book was put together.

Much of this goes right over the head of the average reader who understandably finds it plain boring. That is why he needs to look for a commentary by someone he can trust to have done the background work – or by publishers who get that sort of person to write for them – but who can summarize it all in language which is understandable. There aren't many of these around, but there are more than there were.

One of the problems the ordinary reader has to face when reading a commentary is one that he has to deal with when listening to some sermons. If authors – or preachers, come to that – approach Scripture without a clear awareness that it is the Word of God, or without a sympathy with its supernatural message, they are hardly likely to interpret it aright. They may be able to give us a good deal of information about the historical background, but if they are out of step with its basic thrust, we cannot expect them to be of much further help. For example, if commentators are not prepared to take Scripture at its face value as being what it claims to be, we will find it hard to trust their findings. Or if they spend their time explaining away clearly factual statements, especially in the realm of the supernatural, we will wonder if they are qualified to tell us what it is saying.

●Applying the principles of Scripture

When it comes to the text of Scripture, we will want to know, as far as we can, what the original author intended to write. This will mean a hard look at the words he used, and why he used them. It will also mean grappling with the problem passages. In the more 'academic' commentaries these problem areas are often discussed in great detail, and all the possible answers given. This would prove to be somewhat tedious for an ordinary reader, but we do want to know where there is a problem, and even if we are not introduced to all the possible permutations, we want our commentators to tell us when they are giving us their considered opinion and why.

All this will take time and space, and that means that we will be looking for commentaries which tackle one or two Bible books at a time. The 'one-volume' Bible commentaries, where all the books of the Bible are covered in one fat tome, are good general introductions, but they simply do not have the space to deal with all the issues properly. If we have the time and the money, it is good in invest in more than one commentary per book. In this way we can consult both opinions before coming to our own conclusions.

For the real value of a commentary is not in supplying us with ready-made answers, but rather in stimulating us to think more deeply about the passage we are studying. That means we have to be asking our own questions when we come to a passage of Scripture. It means that, when we read a commentary, we must feel free to disagree with the author if what he is saying doesn't seem to add up. But we should make up our own minds.

A good devotional commentary will take us from the text into the everyday situations which we all face. It will take the principles of Scripture and apply them to home, school, college and workplace. It will do more than inform our minds; it will feed our souls. It will get us thinking about the deep issues of life. It will challenge and reassure, encourage and take us to task. For this to happen, we need an author who is not just in touch with his books, but in touch with people and the real-life problems and opportunities they face every day. Above all, we need someone who has a teaching gift, who is able to make the truth clear and memorable for us.

Concordances

A concordance is a summary of all the places in the Bible where I can find a particular word. For example, if in my Bible study I came across words like 'salvation' or 'sin', and I wanted to know where else they occurred, I could simply turn to my concordance, look them up (they are printed in alphabetical order), and I would find a string of references of verses in Old and New Testaments, usually with a few words from each verse to indicate how and where the words were used. With common Bible terms, I might find that I had dozens of references; with those used less, maybe only two or three. A concordance is an additional help when you want to find a verse you half remember. Look up the words that do come to mind, and the chances are that you will find your verse somewhere in the list.

For all their use, concordances have several limitations. The first is that they are inevitably tied to a particular English translation. Some of the great concordances of the past were, understandably, based on the Authorized Version, particularly those that list all the occurrences of a particular word. Most concordances, because of limited space, only offer a selection of what their compilers consider to be the most important words.

Another difficulty arises out of translation. A Greek or Hebrew word might be translated by more than one English word, but we have no means of knowing that. In the same way, one English word may translate more than one word in the original languages. Young's massive *Analytical Concordance* does this most helpfully providing an English transliteration of each word, but smaller concordances do not give this kind of detail.

Perhaps the greatest weakness with concordances is that we might be tempted to make a word mean the same thing every time it happens. As we have seen, a word must be understood in its setting. That is how the author uses it, and in fact, he may use it with a different sense in a different setting.

> When using a commentary or commentaries, as with all our Bible study, it is good to keep notes. In this way, over the years, we will be able to make up our own commentaries on Scripture. Our studies will not be lost (memory alone is so often unreliable!), and we will be able to add to them on some future occasion when we work through that particular book again. If we add in the lessons which the Lord has been teaching us along the way, they will become a diary of our spiritual pilgrimage through God's Word.

326

Bible dictionaries and atlases

In this respect, Bible dictionaries are of greater help even though they do not record every occasion a word might occur as a concordance often does. What they do is to take up Bible words, subjects, topics, characters, customs and places and collect together what Scripture has to say about them. So, if I look up 'sin' or 'salvation' in a Bible dictionary, I will not only get a list of Bible references where the words are found, I will also get a discussion on what they mean and how they are used.

Bible dictionaries are of great help when it comes to understanding the background to Bible study. If, for example, I am studying a letter like 1 Corinthians, and I want to know the sort of place to which it was addressed, I look up 'Corinth'. I should be given a map of where to find the city, and a mini-history of the place, including how it fits into the Bible story. I will be supplied with references to look up for myself, cross-references to other relevant topics in the dictionary, and a list of titles for further reading should I want to know more.

Remember that though the authors of Bible dictionaries attempt to remain as factual as they can, there will be an element of interpretation in what they write. This means that we should treat Bible dictionaries in the same way that we deal with commentaries. Wisely used, they can be of great help.

Theological dictionaries are similar, though usually written for students and ministers. They concentrate on Bible words which have particular theological importance, collecting together the references, and commenting on how the words were used at different times and by different authors. One valuable development is that nowadays they usually group together words with similar meanings, so that you end up with an overview of the subject in hand and not just a knowledge of a particular word.

Bible atlases do for the geography of the Bible what concordances do for its words. They are particularly useful when we want to find out where something in a Bible story was happening. We can then look the place up in the index and find it with cross-references. Remember that some of the sites of biblical towns and places are still a matter of scholarly opinion, for whereas a number have been dug up and identified, many have not. Another problem arises from the fact that different places were lived in at different times. The best sort of Bible atlas will take you through different periods in Israel's history to show you when some locations came into prominence and when others were either obscure or non-existent.

A Bible atlas is not really a substitute for a visit to the holy land. It is very difficult to get an idea of the shape and size of the country until you have seen it, but from a Bible atlas you can work out things like distances between places, heights and depths, the rivers and the mountains. These should give you a feel for the land, especially if you add in a study of its climate (which you will find in a Bible dictionary). As long as you remember that roads and communications were very primitive in Bible times, a Bible atlas can do a great deal to fill in the background to Bible events.

PART 6

INDEXES

Note: in the Scripture index 'f.' means, 'and the next verse'; 'ff.' means, 'and the following verses'. In the general index 'f.' and 'ff.' refer similarly to pages in the Manual.

Technical terms

A list of some of the commonest terms used in the Bible but not in everyday life.

Most of these words appear in the general index which indicates page references in the Manual.

Altar
Special structure, usually flat-topped, built of metal, wood or stones, for making offerings and sacrifices to God (Exodus 20:24-25; 38:1-7; 1 Kings 9:25).

Apocalyptic
Type of Jewish/Christian literature generally about the end of the world and the run up to it and full of rich picture language, for example Daniel 7-12 and Revelation.

Apocrypha
Jewish writings from the period between the end of the Old Testament and about 100 AD, not considered worthy of inclusion in the Bible but nevertheless valuable for private reading.

Apostle
Title meaning, 'one who is sent', given to those entrusted with a special mission in the early church but usually reserved for the twelve disciples and other leaders (Acts 1:23-26).

Ark of the Covenant
Wooden box originally containing the stone tablets on which the Ten Commandments were written and later the scrolls of the law. It represented God's guiding presence with his people (2 Samuel 6).

Ark (Noah's)
Wooden boat in which Noah, his family and the animals escaped the flood sent by God (Genesis 6:14ff.).

Ascension
The bodily return of Jesus to heaven ending his appearances after the resurrection (Acts 1:4-11).

Atonement
The reconciling of God and sinners achieved by Christ's death on the cross (1 John 2:2).

Baal
Canaanite nature-god whose cult challenged the worship of the Lord throughout Israelite history (1 Kings 18:18).

Blessing
Either material or spiritual good things, given to a person by God (Ephesians 1:3).

Canon
The authoritative collection of books belonging to the Old and New Testaments.

Christ *see* Messiah

Christian
Title (originally a nickname) already in use in the New Testament period to describe a follower of Jesus Christ (Acts 11:26).

Church
The community of believers in Jesus Christ in a particular place and throughout the world.

Confession
The admitting of sin and guilt to God, or the public declaration of loyalty to him (1 John 1:9; Luke 12:8).

Conscience
Ability of a person to decide between right and wrong both in their actions and in their relationship with God (Hebrews 13:18).

Conversion
The once and for all turning from sin to God (repentance) and committing of oneself to Christ as Lord and Saviour (Acts 3:19).

Covenant
Agreement, especially between God and his people, setting out the special relationship between the parties.

Devil *see* Satan

Disciple
Any person committed to following and obeying Jesus but especially the Twelve and those others who accompanied him during his ministry (Luke 14:26-33).

Dispersion (Diaspora)
Term describing the scattering of the Jewish people throughout the non-Jewish world (John 7:35).

Eternal Life
The fulness of life through knowing Jesus Christ that starts now and continues after death (John 17:3).

Evangelist
Person gifted to make known the good news of salvation through Jesus Christ (Ephesians 4:11).

Faith
The attitude which believes and trusts in God and sees things from his point of view (Acts 16:30f.).

Fall
Mankind's original decision to go their own way rather than submit to God's authority (Genesis 3).

Father
Jesus' most common way of describing God, emphasizing his tender and loving relationship with mankind, and especially with believers (Matthew 6:9).

Glory
The revelation of God's being, nature and presence to mankind especially through Jesus Christ (Hebrews 1:3).

Gospel
The good news that God has opened up the way of salvation for all who put their trust in Jesus Christ (Luke 4:16-21).

Grace
God's generous giving of undeserved forgiveness, love and salvation (Ephesians 2:8-10).

Heaven
The place where God's children will enjoy his presence and love after death and where sin will no longer have any power over them (1 Peter 1:4).

Hell
The place of punishment and destruction for sinners and exclusion from the presence of God (Luke 16:19-31).

Holy
Word used to describe God's 'otherness' and in particular his moral perfection, which can also be used of people or things set apart for him and his service (John 17:17-19).

Hope
Expectation of future blessings, based not on present circumstances but on faith in God's limitless goodness and mercy (Romans 5:5).

Idolatry
The offering of loyalty and worship which rightly belongs to God to another being or object (Isaiah 42:8).

Incarnation
The coming of God to earth in Jesus Christ as a fully human being (Colossians 2:9).

Inspiration
God's influencing or prompting men and women with his message or will, especially where the writing of Scripture is concerned (2 Timothy 3:16).

Kingdom of God
God's coming to rule in the world to free and save his people, seen most clearly in the person and life of Jesus (Matthew 12:28).

Love
The Bible's one-word description of God (1 John 4:16); also the inner power which moves a person to self-sacrifice for the good of the loved one (1 Corinthians 13:1-13).

Messiah (Christ)
Hebrew (Greek) title for the promised anointed deliverer of the Jews, popularly understood then in terms of political freedom (John 1:41).

New birth
Work of the Holy Spirit within a person as a result of meeting Jesus Christ, which leads to a new beginning for their life and a complete change in outlook (John 3:3).

Passover
Jewish spring festival commemorating the rescue by God of the Israelites from slavery in Egypt (Exodus 12).

Promised land
The land of Canaan, promised by God to Abraham as a home for his descendants (Genesis 12:7).

Prophecy
The revelation of God's present and future will through a human being.

Redemption
Rescue of sinners from slavery to sin through Jesus' death on the cross (Ephesians 1:7).

Repentance *see* Conversion

Resurrection
Jesus' bodily rising from the dead and the future rising of all believers to eternal life (John 11:25).

Revelation
God's showing of his nature, will and purposes to mankind, especially through Jesus Christ, who is the image of God.

Righteousness
The result of living one's life in line with God's will, impossible by human effort but achieved through faith in Christ (Romans 3:21-26).

Salvation
Term describing not only the redemption of the sinner by Jesus but also the new life of spiritual wholeness and blessing that results from it and which will come to completion at Christ's return (Romans 5:9).

Satan (Devil)
Name of the supremely evil being, opposed to God and his people, defeated by the death and resurrection of Christ and to be utterly destroyed at the end of time (1 Peter 5:8).

Saviour
Title of Jesus used to describe his role as God's agent of redemption and restoration.

Second coming
The return to earth of Jesus Christ in glory to judge mankind and establish God's kingdom (1 Corinthians 15:24-26).

Sin
Rebellion against God and falling short of the perfection his will requires (Romans 8:7).

Son of God
Title used of Jesus which points to the unique relationship he has with his heavenly Father who sent him into the world (Matthew 11:27).

Son of Man
Title Jesus often used of himself (*e.g.* Mark 8:31), perhaps to draw attention to his humanity, but perhaps also with reference to the figure of authority spoken of by Daniel (Daniel 7:13-14).

Spirit, Holy
One of the three Persons of the Trinity (see below). God in his power working in the world through Jesus Christ and given to believers to strengthen and guide them (John 16:5-15).

Temple
National Jewish holy place of worship and sacrifice in Jerusalem. The third and final temple was destroyed in 70 AD.

Trinity
Way of describing the relationship in the Godhead between the Father, the Son and the Holy Spirit.

Truth
Quality of being reliable and authentic (as opposed to false). Jesus claimed both to reveal the truth (John 1:17) and to be its personification (John 14:6).

Wisdom
The ability to make right judgments based on a knowledge of God's ways and to apply them to daily life (Luke 21:15).

Word of God
God's message revealed in the Bible and through the person and teaching of Jesus and taken up by his followers.

General index

Scripture index

Not all references to the Bible text are indexed here, but the following are the most significant:

Maps index

On the maps in the Manual:

Towns are shown in ordinary roman type:

Jerusalem

Countries and tribes are shown in capitals:

SYRIA

Modern names are shown in brackets:

(Black Sea)

Natural features are shown in italic type:

Euphrates R

R = river : L = lake :

Mt = mountain(s) : I = island